SEXUAL *Revolution* IN BOLSHEVIK RUSSIA

Pitt Series in Russian and East European Studies

Jonathan Harris, *Editor*

SEXUAL *Revolution* IN BOLSHEVIK RUSSIA

Gregory Carleton

UNIVERSITY OF PITTSBURGH PRESS

Published by the University of Pittsburgh Press, Pittsburgh, PA 15260
Copyright © 2005, University of Pittsburgh Press
Manufactured in the United States of America
Printed on acid-free paper
10 9 8 7 6 5 4 3 2 1

Library of Congress Cataloging-in-Publication Data
Carleton, Gregory.
  Sexual revolution in Bolshevik Russia / Gregory Carleton.
      p. cm. — (Pitt series in Russian and East European studies)
  Includes bibliographical references and index.
  ISBN 0-8229-4238-0 (cloth : alk. paper)
    1. Sex customs—Soviet Union—History. 2. Communism and sex—
Soviet Union. 3. Soviet Union—Social life and customs. 4. Soviet Union—
History—1917–1936. I. Title. II. Series.
  HQ18.S65C37 2004
  306.7'0947—dc22
                                                        2004015827

"I say to her: 'dear, every healthy man is a demon, and every healthy woman a demoness. Sex mandates it. Sex is the supreme commander. Just as in all other aspects of life, the revolution should be a revolution of sex, a revolution of love.'"

—from Boris Chetverikov's *Aftergrowth*, 1924

Contents

Acknowledgments

This book emerged from no plan or specific orientation. It is rather the fruit of one too many afternoons spent leafing through journals and newspapers of the early Soviet Union in search of entirely different quarry: Mikhail Zoshchenko. He was one of the most widely read authors of the period, yet in tracking down reviews of his stories, I found that popularity and published interest are not one and the same thing. In countless places, no matter the politics involved, I continually ran into other articles and pieces, of which the contents were often more interesting (and amusing) than my original topic. Their sheer number opened up an entirely different face of Soviet culture, one that had precious little to do with what I had assumed constituted the real issues of the 1920s. The material was simply too intriguing and engaging to pass up, and so a new file went into the cabinet, which rapidly became a drawer and then, Leviathan-like, almost took over the whole thing. Yet only with the completion of the first project could this one graduate from the back burner to the front.

If this book's inception was somewhat accidental, the form it now takes certainly is not. For this I am indebted to many, the first of whom is Ronald LeBlanc. After supplying me with pointers, tips, and material for years, he patiently read and critiqued an earlier (and much longer) variant of the manuscript. Without his generosity and insight, this book would be a far inferior product. The same must be said about Herbert Eagle and the anonymous second reader who pored over the version initially offered to the University of Pittsburgh Press. Their comments provided the necessary balance for a literary scholar who sometimes wades into history. I also extend my hand to Nathan MacBrien and Jonathan Harris at Pitt who labored extensively over the manuscript in its various forms. Not only were their suggestions and observations essential but the professionalism and integrity they demonstrated throughout made the project a much more enriching experience. Anne Gorsuch and Charles Nelson read parts as well and provided useful commentary. I sincerely thank all of these comrade-colleagues for their time, effort, and support on my behalf while recognizing that any errors, gaffes, or biases are mine alone.

My gratitude also extends to the Davis Center for Russian and Eurasian Studies at Harvard University, which twice gave me the opportunity to present talks based on this material and thus to receive necessary feedback. The Mellon Foundation generously provided Tufts University with funds to support this research. The staff at the Komsomol archives in Moscow (then known as Tsentr khraneniia dokumentov molodezhnykh organizatsii) was both patient in receiving and generous in answering my research needs; indispensable too were the services provided by the Lenin State Library and Harvard's Widener Library.

I dedicate this book to my wife, Gina, though this token in no way can match what she has meant in my life.

SEXUAL *Revolution* IN BOLSHEVIK RUSSIA

★ CHAPTER I

Introduction

S **TUDIES** of sexuality in Russian culture, particularly of the Soviet period, are relatively recent, for obvious reasons. Sex was not originally seen as a substantive topic for those studying the Soviet Union, since it was assumed that it had never really been an issue there; Bolsheviks, ran the stock impression, were more interested in factories and tractors than in each other. That some even questioned whether Lenin consummated his marriage to Nadezhda Krupskaia was enough to suggest that Marxist revolution and sex were on opposite sides of the room. And if anything slightly risqué, such as a work by Boris Pilnyak, emerged, it was an anomaly that Stalin eventually quashed. In 1969 Eric Hobsbawm likely had this legacy in mind when he dismissed the idea that revolution on both the social and sexual fronts could be linked. Marxism's record with regard to sex, sexual enlightenment, and sexual liberation was abysmal, leading him to declare in *New Society* that they were mutually exclusive. No conservative himself, he saw this incompatibility as irrefutable and unfortunate. "There *is*, I am bound to note with a little regret, a persistent affinity between revolution and puritanism."[1]

Such dismay can easily be understood, given the widespread impression in the West that the October Revolution had bequeathed to the world nothing but cultural and emotional blight. At the height of Stalinism, almost twenty years before Hobsbawm's comments, it seemed that "sexcrime" might not merely be a phenomenon of Orwellian society. To call the Soviet government puritanical was a gross misstatement; it was afflicted by a paralyzing fear of love and eroticism. In "Sex and the Soviet Union" (1951)—a study whose title may have sounded like an oxymoron—Vera Sandomirsky advanced *1984* as a potential key to Soviet mores, recalling O'Brien's taunt to the broken Winston, "Orgasm will be abolished." After surveying the "ludicrous" attempts to express intimacy in contemporary Soviet literature, Sandomirsky questioned whether Orwell's grim prophecy was coming true.[2] Even earlier observers had wondered if public chastity was no mere by-product of revolution but an almost necessary condition of it. In 1926, Walter Benjamin registered the complaint that sparked Sandomirsky's contempt and Hobsbawm's dismay. "As is well known," Benjamin noted in his Moscow diary, "the 'bagatellization' of love and sex life is part and parcel of the communist credo."[3]

Yet Benjamin was wrong. Early Soviet culture did not produce a novel on a par with the eighteenth-century best-seller, John Cleland's *Fanny Hill,* with its bare-all subtitle, *Memoirs of a Woman of Pleasure,* or, a century later, the anonymous *My Secret Life: An Erotic Diary of Victorian London,* with its bare-all text. But Bolsheviks did not treat sex as a trivial distraction, a bagatelle. Both Benjamin and Hobsbawm would have been startled by the triumphant assertion in 1927 that sexual behavior in the Soviet Union was "a mirror of the times," that "this is why we [Bolsheviks] have decided to probe into it, not fearing if [the mirror] turns out crooked."[4] Probe they did, leaving behind a treasury of writings on sex that is daunting in its sheer volume. Commentary on sexual behavior found expression in the most diverse media: party platforms, sociological studies, surveys, health brochures, journals, newspapers, special handbooks, published diaries, and letters to editors. The topic was manifest in nearly all of the decade's literary currents: proletarian, modernist, fellow-traveler, experimental, and "independent." Benjamin was not ignorant of the Soviet artistic world, yet ironically he made the above observation during a visit to Moscow in the year when debate over sexuality in culture was at its height. This debate crossed generational lines, spurring conflict between the party's old guard and its newest members, as well as provoking a decisive split in the Komsomol (Communist Youth League), the official youth organization. It was a central occupation for doctors, sociologists, writers, and critics. For young workers and students, emboldened by the promise of a new communist future, perhaps no other issue captivated their attention as much as sex after the revolution. This obsession made them write letters to journals, surreptitiously share literature in class, and wait in lines at libraries. Youth's predictable interest in sex led to unpredictable results, as it forced party leaders to leave their ideological ivory towers and try to find a common tongue. While most Soviet Marxists, young and old, did not practice the free lifestyle Hobsbawm may have had in mind, many had something to say about it.

People could not remain silent in the midst of a revolution that was the most audacious effort in history to give men and women freedom to live and love as they chose, to release them from the prejudices and restrictions of the past. Construction of this romantic paradise required the demolition of bourgeois laws and religious traditions that imprisoned people in degradation and misery, where money poisoned relationships; where couples were locked into failed marriages; where unions could be denied because of racial, religious, or class differences; where a woman was a husband's property and his economic dependent, unable to travel or change residence without his permission; where the biological nature of sexuality, contraception, and the danger of disease were shrouded in ignorance; where women risked their lives to have abortions; where illegitimate children starved.

Deliverance from this hell was of immediate importance to the revolution. Only weeks after seizing power, with the country slipping into civil war, the Bolsheviks began to institute new laws and codes that reshaped the meaning and function of the family.[5] Church weddings were no longer recognized. Divorce could be quickly granted to one party without explanation. Entering into or ending a marriage meant simply a reshuffling of paper. Doctors could perform legal abortions. Because illegitimacy was no longer a social category, a man was legally responsible for all his children, not merely those fathered in marriage. Later, cohabitation or de facto marriages were recognized as legal unions. The goal was to give women equal status in marriage and to protect them if a union dissolved; to ensure that no one was trapped in a union that had gone wrong; to allow women to terminate a pregnancy if they could not support a child (at this time the state could not always assume charge); and to safeguard all children, regardless of the condition of their birth. Sex was to be recognized in terms of both procreation and pleasure, and it was to be treated openly. A campaign of sexual education would focus on contraception, hygiene, and preventing venereal disease.

The Bolsheviks were not the first Russian revolutionaries to foreground such issues in their dreams of emancipation. In the nineteenth century, central objectives of the radical left were gender equity and sexual freedom (variously defined against society's insistence on monogamy and conjugal sex used only for procreation).[6] As enshrined in Nikolai Chernyshevsky's novel, *What Is to Be Done?* (1863), only the reformation of intimate life, whether manifested in a woman's right to choose a mate or in complete asceticism could precede society's full liberation. Nor did sex become a dominant feature of public discourse only after the Bolsheviks' rise to power. Laura Engelstein has chronicled how prerevolutionary Russia was saturated with sexual images—legal, medical, commercial, journalistic, and artistic.[7] In the upheavals after 1905, sexuality provided a primary metaphor through which to express anxieties arising from class and ethnic conflict.

Yet despite conservatives' attempts to link social disorder with sexual license, an emerging consumer culture could not forgo the power of sex in advertising. Doctors, too, used sexuality as a basis for defining and treating newly discovered pathologies, while philosophers like Vasily Rozanov saw in sexual health the key to revitalizing Russia's collective soul. Sexual desire and the consequences of its expression (or denial) had already become a central concern of Russia's literary elite, reflected most famously in Tolstoy's *The Kreutzer Sonata* (1891), a novella championing continence that at first had to circulate clandestinely because of its daring content.[8] With the relaxation of censorship a decade and a half later and modernism's tendency to challenge taboos, the subject exploded in literature. It again seized the reading public's attention in two works that took the opposite tack: Mikhail Artsybashev's *Sanin* (1907), which suggested that hedonism, particularly of a sexual kind, was the proper response to the crisis following the failed 1905 revolution. Anastasia Verbitskaya's *The Keys to Happiness* (1908–1913), a sensational six-volume tour of a young woman's attempt at self-discovery and self-fulfillment, because of its copious sex and multiple suicides came to exemplify for critics a new phenomenon known as "boulevard literature."[9]

The October Revolution did not resolve the contradictions of this problematic legacy. The same rhetoric, metaphors, fears, and beliefs (particularly in medicine and biology) returned in the debates of the 1920s. Yet the Bolsheviks believed that their policies regarding sexual behavior would deliver them from the hypocrisies that had defined bourgeois society. The unintended result, however, was to add yet another layer of questions, often extremely practical ones. With the bourgeois moral order discredited, should monogamy still be a goal? If not, what kinds of personal relationships were ideal? The problem lay in the very freedom that was promised. We should remember that in the 1920s there was no single voice of authority, standard of enforcement, or model for social relations; uncertain times gave free rein to conflicting interpretations. Did sexual liberation mean the triumph of common sense over convention, or would it open the gates to widespread promiscuity? Would the lifting of legal constraints and the assault on bourgeois traditions cheapen sexual love? Could youth, especially, be trusted to exercise self-discipline if emotional concerns were brushed away? The result would be catastrophic if people fell into unchecked profligacy. Yet some could argue that decoupling romance from sex might increase workers' effectiveness by rechanneling the energy typically wasted in courtship into greater productivity. As seen in the dream of Sergei Strezhnev, a character in Aleksandr Yakovlev's novella "No Land in Sight" (1924), temporarily yielding to Dionysus in an "animal act" could guarantee stunning efficiency in the factory:

> Once a year, in the spring, all men and women should run out of the cities into the woods and mountains or to the seashore and dance, giving themselves to unbridled love until they are fully exhausted. Then, res-

olute and temperate like monks return to the cities and, not knowing sexual distraction, work all year building a beautiful life, a life of freedom and the spirit. All one's strength will then be devoted to labor.[10]

Neither good worker nor good lover (if that is the proper word), Sergei never puts his experiment to the test, yet the logic behind his compartmentalized utopia reflects the same question facing Soviet policy: how to balance social duty with physical needs? Could society define the two through a common frame of reference and achieve success on both fronts? More to the point, would a strictly rational approach to sexuality guarantee emotional satisfaction? Many believed so. The triumphalism that struck Eve Grady, wife of an American engineer working in the Soviet Union during the twenties, reflected something substantive, not just surface patriotism: "We have the most glorious system of marriage in the world," her tour guide declared, one proof being her own "free" (that is, unregistered) marriage. Her question to the startled Grady, representative of all victims of capitalism, made it clear that her own reward was not just "spiritual love": "You have not free marriage in America? How strange. Yet—I have heard—you are what they call sex starved, is it so?"[11]

How the revolution was first seen from abroad was colored by the new openness toward sexual behavior in Soviet Russia. To sympathetic observers, the sexual revolution proved that the Bolsheviks' goal in 1917 was not tyranny but "complete liberty."[12] For V. F. Calverton, founder of *Modern Quarterly*, its ideals were marked by "astounding intelligence" that had finally rescued women from an endless cycle of oppression: "In Soviet Russia, for the first time in the history of the modern world, this inequality [between the sexes] has been ended. Indeed, we may say that while morality in the past has been made for men, *morality in Soviet Russia is made for women*."[13] In the widely read *Humanity Uprooted* (1929), Maurice Hindus argued that equality was meant in the fullest sense. He cited a female psychologist who proudly declared that "love in its physical aspect will no longer remain primarily an erotic right and enjoyment of the male."[14] Yet men also benefited, Calverton assured his audience, since the new laws put an end to the bourgeois double standard and the obsession with property that had long distorted emotional expression.

Love and the sex life have been freed of the superstitions and silences which had clouded, confused, and bound them; marriage has been liberated from the religious and ceremonial rites in which it had once been bound; divorce has been converted into an intelligent device, disenslaved from duplicity and deceit and accessible to all. As a result, morality has

been emancipated from the stereotyped stupidities of an enforced convention and an inelastic code.[15]

Moreover, one could choose a partner without bowing to prejudice or calculating material gain. As Ella Winter suggested after her visit at the end of the
decade, perhaps only in the Soviet Union could true love flourish: "Differences of race, religion, nationality, social grouping, rarely bar a marriage. No
loveless marriages are entered into for the sake of a title or prestige. . . . Since
property, racial, religious, and other of the traditional qualifications for the
marriage partner have been abolished, there is practically freedom of sexual
selection."[16]

The cornerstone of appeal, in Winter's words, was the Bolsheviks' "rational, common sense approach," captured in her memorable title, *Red
Virtue*. Enthusiastic observers disagreed only in identifying what constituted
the most salient achievement in the Soviets' social policy. For Fanina Halle
and Calverton, it was legalized abortion, marking, in the latter's words, "the
most remarkable and intelligent advance in modern morality."[17] In turn,
Hindus regarded the availability of divorce as "one of the greatest revolutions
of the ages."[18] All were impressed by the quality of sex education available to
the young. Pamphlets, books, lectures, and films openly and honestly addressed pregnancy, birth control, venereal disease, and prenatal care—in stark
contrast to the prudery and silence that reigned elsewhere in the West, especially in America.

The same praise extended to fiction, the traditional source of recreation
and edification for Russians. Hindus, one of the few observers who knew
Russian, did not share Benjamin's dismay. "In the new literature," he proclaimed, "no subject outside of the Revolution itself commands as stirring attention as does sex."[19] For him, Soviet writers treated sexuality with the social
conscience of a doctor or teacher. The subject was omnipresent, but only in
the sense of what was good or necessary. Whatever the Soviet Union's weakness as an economic power, morally it had outstripped the West in only a few
years. "The air," Halle noted, "is agreeably wholesome, really pure."[20] And if
there were any filters or screens, then in Hindus's eyes they cleansed society of
what truly cheapened sex:

> They have closed the old houses of prostitution, which in days of
> czardom were as distinctive a feature of every Russian community out-
> side of the village as vodka shops or bazaars, and they have been waging
> a relentless war against underground harlotry. . . .
>   The injection of sex lure in any form into commercial life they have
> likewise banned. There is nowhere a hint of sex in the displays in shop

windows or in the amusement places. There is scarcely a trace of sex sug-
gestiveness in Russian motion pictures. . . . The Russian newspapers and
magazines are singularly free from sex scandals or sex tales. . . . Nowhere
in restaurants or theatres are there displays of pictures of voluptuous
maidens in a variety of semi-nude poses, such as greet the eyes of the vis-
itor at every step on certain streets in Berlin. The revolutionaries regard
the exploitation of a woman's body for commercial gain as a vicious in-
sult to womanhood. Nowhere in Russia are pornographic pictures peddled around openly or secretly—they are not to be had. The Russian
public does not crave and does not demand vicarious forms of sex excitement.[21]

Most like Hindus could only commend the Soviets on this account. If sex was
publicly recognized and to a degree legitimized in the West only in its most
decadent form, here was the correct path. The new Russians, as they were also
known, would not shun sex or drive it into a corner; and in so doing, some
believed, they were better suited to set an example for the world.

In selling Soviet society to their audience, Hindus and others stressed that
Russians had always retained something of the noble savage, a healthy pagan
core, not suppressed by the ideals of occidental chivalry and Christianity. In
consequence, there was "a casualness in their attitude toward sex which is
hard for the Anglo-Saxon mind to grasp."[22] Once liberated from unnatural
barriers, they were not ashamed of their bodies and not afraid to speak of
them. The typical woman, Hindus observed, "talks of sex with no more re-
serve than of music, the theatre, the weather."[23] From this impression came
the argument that the family code, particularly after the recognition of de
facto marriages in 1927, had returned Russians to their natural state.[24] Astonished that this change had been debated for nearly a year and was voted on by
committee instead of being issued by edict, Calverton exclaimed, "Here is a
morality, then, that actually expresses the voluntary desire and choice of a
people." The straightforward, common-sense Bolshevik approach was not
"the device of one group . . . to foist a morality upon another."[25] As Winter
explained, now Russians were free to be honest with themselves and each
other.

Russia has been called a dour gray country in matters of love and romance, a country of "love locked out." It is said there is no time for love-
making, that flattery and coquetry are too frivolous, as fox-trotting is too
bourgeois.
   Visitors to the Soviet Union, however, find that Russians are natural
about their sex lives; they admit and take into account the biological and

physiological basis of sex. The Western poetic ideal of romantic love, the tortures and delights, "sighs and tears and pale wanderings," have little appeal for the Bolshevik. If two comrades are in love, they go to the home of one of them. If there is no child and either finds the association unsatisfactory, they part. It is really a nation-wide system of companionate marriage.[26]

Ever ready to defend his roots, Klaus Mehnert, a Russian-born German citizen, even declared: "The young Russian, indeed, is no prig, and has no intention of becoming one."[27] The Bolsheviks, soon to be stereotyped as cold fish, had discovered the key to a healthy sex life and rewarding emotional relationships. The way to satisfy the heart was to use the head.

So it seemed to the left. Western conservatives, on the other hand, met Bolshevik attempts to reform the family with rage and alarm. The hyperbole now sounds comical, yet one can sense in the right's broadsides against Soviet policy in the 1920s a genuine fear. The threat was not that of military conquest, of troops storming through Europe and across the Atlantic, but that Soviet ideas of home and family might surreptitiously come in through the back door. For the right, much as for the left, the rallying point was the status of women. Both, ironically, argued in similar terms: to protect women from being treated as property. If for the left this meant deliverance from a patriarchal system, for the right it meant defense against women becoming a "nationalized" resource of the state, that is, possessions for men's pleasure. As Royal Baker wrote in *The Menace Bolshevism* (1919), "Woman, the mainstay, the encourager of mankind, is dragged from her lofty position and placed without protection, for the lusts of the vicious—the evil-minded. They are at the mercy of the brute."[28] The family code of 1918, issued in the name of emancipation, was nothing but a cover for making women "public property for all Bolsheviki Government citizens." It made "free love" official doctrine, institutionalizing what Americans had seen as a menace to public morality since the ascendancy of Victoria Woodhull. It was irrelevant that most Soviet officials also denounced free love. Open divorce could have only one result: "What has free love done for Russia?" Baker asked. "Every woman can be a legalized prostitute. Homes are wrecked, the joys of the fireside with the children's mirth when at play are gone. Everybody does as he or she likes. The woman, who is your wife today, may be another man's wife tomorrow."[29]

In *Red War on the Family* (1922), Samuel Saloman warned that the Bolsheviks were "political tricksters" who spread "unholy propaganda." Their "satanic majesties," Lenin and Trotsky, had succeeded in duping an entire population by promising an earthly paradise while creating an earthly hell. Now they were again at the same game. Lenin's real motives in emancipating women were prurient. He had unleashed the dogs of revolution only to secure the delights of lust: "Freeing woman from the 'slavery' of the kitchen and the nursery and the tasks allotted to the sex by the unemancipated civilization of the past is supposed to have one definite and glorious result, and that is with more time at her disposal she will be free, entirely so, to devote herself to free and unrestrained love—in the newer and emancipated sense."[30] While Bolsheviks claimed to be the most progressive thinkers, Baker could only see them as the most primitive: "This free love idea is undoubtedly the greatest attack against the female sex that has ever been devised. Even the lowest form of savages who indulge in the wildest spirit of cannibalism is far superior to such barbarism as this indecent, hellish, state license. Never before has any portion of the world made such a retrograding step in civilization as Russia in her reign of Bolshevism."[31]

Bolsheviks being lower than the lowest of savages, they had no need for pornography, since they were the living incarnation of it. Salomon's accusation of a "wholesale ravishing of females of all ages in Russia," was hollow, its primary source being Isabel Hapgood, a translator of Tolstoy who had refused to touch *The Kreutzer Sonata* thirty years earlier because of its "indecent" content. She reported that a friend in Petrograd had told her that "at a fixed date all women between the ages of 16 and 45 (I think) were to be mated, regardless of their own will in the matter."[32] The mass spectacle, of course, never materialized, but its absence would not dissuade Saloman or others. Since the Bolsheviks had eliminated the laws protecting the sanctity of the monogamous family, Russia could only descend, he believed, into a grisly "saturnalia of the reds," a "free-love mill."[33]

The image of Bolsheviks as sexual decadents was not just the stuff of broadsides but also informed more serious works like Rene Fulop-Miller's *The Mind and Face of Bolshevism* (1928), which absurdly sought to connect the Bolsheviks with the Khlysty sect (Christian self-flagellants) because both were prone to orgiastic outbursts, so-called "African nights." Indeed, Fulop-Miller even suspected that Komsomol youth harbored "a sort of erotic cult in which wild unrestraint often prevails."[34] To be sure, "African nights" were a staple of literature, not life, but it is clear that as much as Winter and other supporters saw the "natural" sexual character of Russians as sane and sober, anti-Soviet writers were quick to paint it as decadent, exotic, and unbridled. No matter if one called it African, Oriental, Russian, or Slavic, it certainly was not a product of civilized Europe or America.

Tenacious polarization had long been a defining feature of Western interpretations of Russia, with or without its modifier "Soviet." It was fueled by careless, often sensationalist reporting, as Charles Merz and Walter Lippmann made clear in their 1920 roasting of the *New York Times* coverage of the revolution and civil war. "In the large," they commented, "the news about Russia is a case of seeing not what was, but what men wished to see."[35] Tunnel vision was nowhere more obvious than in the hysteria surrounding Bolshevik plans to "nationalize" women. The canard had begun with the alleged discovery of a poster in war-torn Saratov announcing the mobilization of women ages seventeen to thirty-two to be distributed "amongst [men] who require them." Local anarchists were first suspected, but they logically protested that they were against state appropriation of any property, human or otherwise. Accusation then fell on proto-fascists out to discredit the left, and finally the Bolsheviks. Although no poster was ever produced, the rumor quickly spread and similar reports sprung up in Samara, Smolensk, Vladimir, and Khvolinsk.[36] Lenin reportedly laughed at the story, and early in 1919 the U.S. Senate officially debunked the myth.[37]

Western ignorance, fear, and idealism rang so loudly in the 1920s because almost no one could remain neutral when looking upon a country undergoing total revolution. The Soviet Union had become fertile ground for both the right and the left to project their particular anxieties and desires, yet first impressions were governed by another factor of which few seemed conscious: the Soviet environment, despite propaganda to the contrary, was in utter disarray. The October Revolution threw up such a large cast of characters—embittered emigrés, impassioned workers, confused peasants, committed party activists, and upstart youth—that from this motley collection foreign observers could select one to paint the country in any color. The same was true of daily experience, as recognized by Jessica Smith, one of the more judicious eyewitnesses from the West. Despite the dictates of Soviet laws or codes, she noted that with regard to actual sexual behavior "no mould has yet been set." Given her work in famine relief, her visits to factories, schools, and families, and with her knowledge of the language, she realized that no single view represented the whole population: clearly sexual behavior was a contentious issue among Soviet citizens themselves. Young people growing up in unprecedented conditions were "trying desperately hard to find a solution." The question, of course, was how they should live, what made one a good citizen, and what kinds of relationships were conducive to this goal. Understanding why interpretations of the sexual revolution in the USSR could be so self-assured and yet so diametrically opposed, Smith concluded:

> By a careful choice of the facts that came out of the discussions [with youth] you could prove that communists had introduced polygamy, that they killed their babies, that immorality was flourishing as nowhere in the world before, that the family had been abolished, that a regime of

complete asceticism had been inaugurated, that communist women were refusing to have babies, that all women were being forced to have a great many babies or almost anything else you wanted to prove.[38]

Sexuality and the Revolution

What Smith intuitively recognized is the point of departure for this book. Revolutions are of particular, almost unique value for any study of culture. A revolutionary context is one in which relations of power and the discourses that enable them are inchoate and immature; old paradigms have been dethroned, yet sufficient time has not elapsed for new ones to stabilize and gain the authority of a naturalized veneer. Moreover, revolutions are never of one valency or direction. The iconoclasm that marks sociopolitical upheaval unleashes many voices and a spirit of inquiry that may be at odds with or may supersede the "official" revolution's intentions.

In the 1920s, sexuality was a domain of just such a conflict of interests, reflected in nearly all segments of the population. Indeed, some authorities complained that sex often seemed to be the only part of the revolution that young people cared about. Whether in deed or solely in word, their fervor, which could spill into questionable and colorful extremes, could not be denied. As the generation that would lead the world to communism after 1917, many transferred their iconoclastic enthusiasm to an issue closer to themselves. As the idea of revolution descended to their level, sexuality and its social manifestations took on meanings and values that outstripped the more straightforward intentions of the Bolshevik old guard. The clash of hopes and dire predictions was not just something heard in the distant West but a fact of the revolution on its native soil.

In studying sexuality in the early Soviet Union, I sought to cast as wide a net as possible. The result was a cacophony of voices that defy cataloguing in the usual frames of reference. This verbal chaos was itself an important discovery, revealing aspects of the party and Bolshevik culture to which we are not accustomed. It introduced new names, new literature, and new issues to an already complex and dynamic environment. To make sense of it all required streamlining and categorizing, yet to focus on one group, approach, or event would betray the true spirit of the period and belie the confusion that prevailed at the university, on the factory floor, or even in the Kremlin.

This book is about how the sexual revolution was written and received in Bolshevik culture, with a focus on the mainstream press and the proletarian, Komsomol, and party voices that dominated the field. The contributions of futurism and the avant-garde enjoyed only limited exposure at this time and, as with film, were generally ignored in subsequent debates. This book's title, therefore, does not embrace the totality of the sexual revolution in the Soviet Union, but rather its most salient and contentious points.

Chapter 2 establishes the parameters of public interest and concern about sexual behavior, as well as the many lenses through which sex was understood in the revolutionary environment. Chapter 3 explores ideological and medical attempts to formulate models and come to terms with the diffusion of new attitudes and behavior, while chapter 4 highlights the confusion and backlash resulting from the failure of those models to present a unified message. Chapter 5 examines the scandals that erupted in 1926 when this confrontation became dominant in literature and seized the attention of readers, writers, critics, and party authorities. Chapter 6 analyzes how the representation of sex subsequently became the flash point in critical debates over literature's purpose and its assumed impact on real life, and chapter 7 demonstrates how controversies raised by a number of deliberately ambiguous works informed the debate. Finally, chapter 8 discusses why by the early 1930s the problem of sex was essentially expunged from "real" Soviet literature as a viable topic.

To give primacy to the voices of Bolshevik culture necessitated reserving for the conclusion theoretical commentary and discussion. By now the sexual revolution in the Soviet Union has become a viable topic of scholarly analysis, open to dissection through cultural theory and newer ideological concerns, and thus shorn of its polarizing effect.[39] Early commentators were almost compelled by weight of politics to view Soviet family policy as threat or dream come true. Today, however, the attempt to revolutionize family life no longer stands before us as monster or myth. Its image has been streamlined; gone are the idealism and hysterical excess of before. Dispute, nevertheless, continues.

In *The Women's Liberation Movement in Russia* (1978), Richard Stites provided a brief yet essential overview of the prominent voices and relevant attitudes. It stood out for its sympathetic portrait of Alexandra Kollontai, champion of women's liberation and head of the women's section of the party (Zhenotdel) from 1920 to 1922.[40] His study overturned the standard Western view that she was a primary instigator of the alleged debauchery of 1920s Russia.

Yet the popular image of early Soviets as ethically bankrupt and sexually corrupt returned in Mikhail Stern's *Sex in the USSR* (1979) and Mark Popovsky's *The Superfluous Third* (1985), both of which held Kremlin leaders responsible for implanting in the population "the desire to live without any moral standards whatsoever."[41] Popovsky ignored Lenin's decidedly unspicy personal life, while Stern branded him a "sexual pigmy." Instead, blame for the corruption of Russian culture was shouldered back onto the "ravings" of

Kollontai and the peccadilloes of certain fellow travelers. Symptomatic of Stern's and Popovsky's resurrection of the traditional view is the double damnation that marks both works: official attempts to curb the perceived libertinism in society are roundly condemned as an intrusion into people's private lives. Either way, censure of Soviet actions, whether seen as encouraging debauchery or totalitarian control, remained the centerpiece of argument.

The same condemnation has continued in Igor Kon's *The Sexual Revolution in Russia* (1995), the first comprehensive study of the subject published in both post-Soviet Russia and the West. Self-described as one of the country's first "sexologists," Kon surveys Soviet policies from the revolution to glasnost and blames the government for failing to acknowledge sexuality as vital to human life. In his stinging indictment, official silence nurtured ignorance, which led to tragedy: rampant sexism, sexual abuse, rape, and abortion used as a primary form of birth control. When authorities did open their mouths, Kon is no less forgiving: "Bolshevik philosophy on gender and sexuality was as primitive as that of a caveman's club."[42] The details he provides establish a nightmare of failed policies that are distinguishable from each other only by the degree of malice and mistake. Indeed, the resulting disdain and ridicule only confirm the traditional view of "red love" that has prevailed since the beginning of the Cold War.

By contrast, Eric Naiman's *Sex in Public: The Incarnation of Early Soviet Ideology* (1997) has put to rest the perception that sex was a taboo subject for Soviet culture. Following the lead of Michel Foucault's *History of Sexuality,* this work makes a fundamental contribution to the field not only in its theoretical approach but also in the material accessed. Drawing on little-known medical, legal, literary, and journalistic sources, he astutely observes that in 1920s Russia "talk about sex became a metaphor—and symptom—for thoughts about something else: politics and ideology."[43] The profound anxiety created by the tension between Bolshevik ideals and an imperfect reality was reflected, most dramatically, in public discourses of the body and sexuality. As utopians, Bolsheviks were obsessed with the idea of purity, both ideological and corporeal, which manifested itself in a "particular dread of erotic urges." Yet the result was not silence on the subject of sexuality but its opposite. The party, in effect, suffered from a grand return of the repressed: sex erupted into the public sphere and generated a panoply of concerns over menstruation, anorexia, and castration—all of which embodied deep ideological and political concerns.

For Naiman, however, this is only half the picture. If heightened attention to sexuality was an unintended product of the Bolshevik mentality, it was deployed with a specific purpose, particularly in popular literature and its reception. While Kon, Stern, and Popovsky attack party officials for their ignorance or for encouraging profligacy, with Naiman they are guilty of something more ominous: a concerted strategy to "investigate," "infiltrate," and "colonize" personal life by "seducing [young people] into a public discussion" of sexuality. The lure was sex itself. Salacious works gave rise to controversy; journals fed debate, and critics feigned anger in order to whip up hysteria. Readers and participants in public meetings were encouraged to make themselves heard, yet in truth this was a trap set by the party "to keep alive the notion that there was a debate." The Komsomol and media organs drew attention to atrocious behavior not for self-criticism, as was officially claimed, but to keep sexuality in the limelight so as to justify the need for social control. As Naiman writes, "By publishing pictures of abject sexual depravity," the Komsomol "score[d] its greatest successes—and its most significant conquests of personal life."[44]

Such a strategy, if true, was not necessarily the product of, in Naiman's words, "conscious manipulation." Like Foucault, he recognizes that "discourse acquires power over all speaking it, gaining a momentum of its own." The proviso is necessary in order to avoid the impression of a master puppeteer directing society. Thus, for example, even someone like Lenin in his famous interview with Clara Zetkin could not avoid repeating certain inconsistencies in the Bolshevik rhetoric on sex.[45] However, while leaders were sometimes victims of their own discourses, never did this translate into loss of control or authority in the broader domain of cultural interaction. In the scenario laid out above, what circulated in public reflected the designs and wishes of those in power. As Naiman argues, Lenin, and after his death the Central Committee, held literature under their collective fist, exerting a "powerful influence" on the composition and reception of texts. Cultural interaction thus became almost an artificial phenomenon that offered a semblance of dialogue, but in truth all public speech acts, even if motivated by contrary intentions, played directly into the state's hands. The resulting discursive prison, as Naiman describes, preserved agency solely for the institutions of power.

> The following pattern was established. An author would publish a work
> of fiction that aroused prurient interest and purported to discuss "the
> problem of sex." An outburst of critical letters or articles would follow
> close on the heels of publication, provoking in turn published "disputes"
> and editorial comments. Virtually all the participants in the debate
> would focus on sexual "excesses." The writers would first depict degener-
> ate behavior within the Komsomol; critics would then charge them with
> slander or else would bemoan the depravity they had unmasked. Komso-
> mol writers made virtually no attempt to discuss in positive terms how

sexual life *should* be structured, and very little attention was paid to the broader issue of sex roles in society. Rather both "sides" attacked "depravity" using almost exactly the same terms. The real object of the debate, the destruction of the autonomy of "personal life," was achieved phatically—that is, by the very fact that sex was the "topic" of repetitive discussion for such a sustained period of time.[46]

The choreography is impressive. The proliferation of skeptical quotation marks suggests that little of a spontaneous or authentic nature actually happened. Discursive acts were essentially scripted, nearly every voice co-opted by an overarching plan. The rhetoric is repeatedly determinist: power created "a vortex that drew the reader/listener into its center as it sought to destroy his autonomy." Little, as a result, was what it seemed. Anger was not anger; dispute not dispute; both were tools, in Naiman's projection, of a grand bait and switch:

> Fiction and apparently hostile criticism were cut from the same cloth. Fiction, journalistic outrage, and public meetings functioned to excite and then control debate along lines that brought sex increasingly within the purview of a national polemic concerned with eliminating differences—not sexual differences but the difference between public and private life.[47]

The recent studies critical of Soviet policies and actions come from different theoretical schools and are shaped by different political motivations. Popovsky and Stern resurrect earlier moral outrage at Bolshevik license; Kon underscores the failure to confront sexuality in an enlightened way. All three subscribe to an Orwellian conception of language and power: official falsification of abject conditions, bolstered by incessant propaganda, enforced conformity; in short, language covering reality. Naiman embraces a postmodern stance where subjects are seamlessly co-opted and entrapped, unable to conceive of themselves outside the constraining discourses deployed by governing institutions. His approach diverges radically from the others, yet paradoxically at the same time it reasserts and relies upon an image of the party as the formative agent of Soviet culture with society its hostage. The difference between the two approaches lies in which strategy of subjugation is employed. Yet both see the party as not only a vociferous machine devoted to a single purpose—control of the population—but also one highly successful in its efforts. Whether through police action and censorship, or through the more unconscious force of discursive constraints, the party succeeded in regulating and suppressing the individual. In fact, the image of Bolshevik Russia informed by Foucault's work is arguably more frightening and depressing than that of the traditional totalitarian school. Even Naiman suspects that some might find his view of early Soviet society "unnecessarily bleak."[48]

The objection can immediately be made that this comparison is a gross simplification, confusing two diametrically opposed views of how power manifests itself and operates in society: power as constriction versus power as production. I would be the first to admit guilt for this if the discussion were to remain in the realm of theory. However, what interests me more than differences in enabling theories is the application of theory to historical conditions. Regarding sexuality, both the traditional and postmodern arguments seek to explicate the mechanisms and consequences of Bolshevik control of the population. That the two should overlap is not surprising. While postmodern approaches generally deride "the desire to discover a past reality and reconstruct it scientifically," in actual practice they nevertheless construct—and assume the validity of—models for understanding the reality of historical experience.[49] Information about the past now may come from different sources and may be analyzed through different lenses, yet this does not stop us from assigning motive, determining effects, and judging outcomes. Whatever the theoretical ramifications of the "linguistic turn" in history and cultural studies, and its concomitant suspicion of empirical analysis, we tend to assume of our works what has traditionally been the case. In short, we are still concerned with the artifacts and voices of historical reality, no matter how discursively mediated.[50]

With its rejection of the repressive hypothesis and its goal of grounding discourse analysis in an empirical historical context, Naiman's paradigm breaks new ground and raises fresh questions.[51] In concrete terms, what precisely were the successes "scored" by the Komsomol in the 1920s? How do we move from analyzing discourse per se to describing historical conditions? While Naiman emphasizes Bolshevik discourse, his argument makes specific claims on how Soviet reality was consequently affected, and he expects that his paradigm should be judged by "traditional historigraphic authenticity."[52] His invitation opens a door for assessing the claims made by this latest theoretical shift. If Soviet literature on sexuality is described as a tool of the party, then we should consider the entire range of literature published then. To compress readers into a single group, assuming homogeneity of taste and reading habits, invites attention to individual responses. If Soviet institutions of power are assumed to have unity of voice and intention, as with the assertion that journals and other media sources were working in concert to entrap readers, we should substantiate that assertion with empirical proof.

If for the foreseeable future we are to understand Soviet culture through the concept of power, whether in old or new redaction, then we should seek more resolutely to examine its true effects and engage the real experience of writers, readers, and critics. I say this not out of inherent rejection of the discourse-power vector but from the natural hesitation that arises in the face of any theory that has become for all intents and purposes a canon of interpretation. Much of the primary material I encountered did not fit received theoretical paradigms and sometimes challenged their validity as explanations of early Soviet culture, whether at the micro or macro level. Not only do revolutions constitute some of the most exciting—and awful—periods of history, they are invaluable to us because the clash of interests that erupts in their wake can disturb the clean models used to map and interpret cultural dynamics.

My intention is not to delegitimize previous work, as I trust my debt to it is evident. Instead, my goal is to reconstruct a fuller picture of what circulated in literary culture and why. In so doing, I hope to bring out its anomalies and paradoxes, particularly with regard to its reception by critics and average readers who accepted this literature as a vital part of both their ideological and personal lives. What emerges is a conflict between official objectives and actual practice, but the clash goes beyond standard polarities of state against citizen, party against writer, or government against youth. A focus on ambiguities, which are for me the defining characteristics of literature about the sexual revolution, may seem to deflect attention from top party leaders as the central agents of Soviet culture. Yet perhaps, as others have demonstrated, this is necessary. It enables us to concentrate on how such literature was experienced by youth and literary critics, for whom the party was not necessarily a monolith or monster but instead an institution beset with conflicts and contradictions, most of which came into full, public display.[53]

Showing the breadth of voice both inside and outside the party apropos of sexuality allows for a more concerted historicization of today's leading ideological and theoretical paradigms. Despite new models, an unstated but continuing goal of critical analysis has been to indict Soviet policies of the 1920s.[54] The condemnatory language sometimes employed is understandable, and few, including myself, would seek to defend or justify practices then. At the same time, however, our tendency to rely on extremes, as if early Soviet society could only be a dungeon, reflects the field's own ingrained prejudices. The majority of studies on the sexual revolution in Bolshevik Russia offer roles that are generally fixed and certainly unenviable: party members as intolerant, prudish, machiavellian, and power hungry, while all others are their victims. To move beyond this image, my motivating questions focus both on the quantitative and qualitative dimensions of the discourses of sexuality:

what was written and why, how it was received, how youth understood themselves within this rhetoric, the nature of attempted official control of private life, and whether such attempts backfired.

The objective is not simply to analyze the tension between popular response and official intention, or to highlight the bizarre, intriguing ways in which sexuality was represented in an environment of utopian desire and belief, but to question ingrained conceptions of discourses of sexuality, literary culture, and the party. The controversy surrounding the sexual revolution puts in relief critical facets of early Bolshevik culture that might permit a more nuanced understanding of it in its totality. Those who have concentrated on party intentions are all correct to a degree; I would not deny that the latter were marked by an impulse to control society. Nevertheless, more is at stake; much more happened outside of and despite this fact. Cold War or not, we are still in the grip of an image of the party as the end all of Bolshevik culture and often continue to marshal evidence to prove how villainous, megalomaniac, or hypocritical it was. Yet we should question how central the party actually might have been, and how strong and unified was its approach.[55] While acknowledgment is often made of these internal divisions and of the complexity of the early Soviet environment, little is generally made of this fact. Party members did not agree about the nature of perceived problems or how to solve them, and this confusion "above" was not ignored by those "below." It is arguably the primary reason why sexuality became the subject of real, open debate. Discussion certainly ended in the 1930s when, in an old-fashioned exercise of power, the spigots were essentially shut off. Yet we should not read history backwards. Just as the October Revolution inaugurated a series of further revolutions, just as it was the catalyst for multiple questions and iconoclasms, the party, the ostensible executor of revolution, had many voices. So too did the country.

★ CHAPTER 2

A Revolution Comes of Age

Scandal as Prologue

IN the spring of 1906, Maksim Gorky set aside the manuscript of *Mother*, the opus of worker rebellion whose hero, Pavel Vlasov, potential martyr and model ascetic, became an inspiration for many. Pavel was an icon closer to life than his literary godfather, Chernyshevsky's Rakhmetov, a detached, desexed, sleep-on-nails hermit who flits through *What Is to Be Done?* as a distant dream of the future. Gorky interrupted work on *Mother* to write a small sketch of New York City after an inhospitable reception. He had come to the United States to raise money for the Bolshevik party, but when American generosity fell short, Gorky exacted revenge. "City of the Yellow Devil" is a dirge for an urban cadaver imprisoned in fog, strewn with garbage, its inhabitants crushed under iron and concrete. Only a nameless young thief resists spiritual and physical enslavement in a city bled dry by capitalist gold. Willing to violate law and scorn custom, he alone earns the epithet "alive."[1]

Though dwarfed in size, "City of the Yellow Devil" complements Gorky's *Mother* (1907). A micro picture of despotism and oppression, it substitutes the abuses of Western capitalism for those of tsarism. The protagonists of both works embody resistance. Of the thief we know little other than his contempt for the world. He is one in a long procession of Gorky's heroes defined by opposition and struggle. The writer's applause for the outlaw stance—if the state is by definition unjust and criminal, then any action taken against it is automatically sanctified—had recently become radicalized after Bloody Sunday in January 1905. A personal witness to the slaughter of peaceful demonstrators in St. Petersburg, he wrote to Leonid Andreev: "Life has been built on cruelty and force. For its reconstruction, it demands cold, calculated cruelty—that is all! They kill? It is necessary to do so!"[2] Overnight he graduated to true revolutionary, collecting arms and turning his apartment over to

19

making bombs. The literary embodiment of this shift is Vlasov, in whom political conviction tames the rebel. Discipline and self-control mark his character. Women and marriage he has forsworn; he lives by the credo expressed by his comrade, Nikolai: "Family life reduces a revolutionary's energy, it always does!"[3] What is not reduced, however, is the pride, as with the thief in "City of the Yellow Devil," that fuels defiance. Political maturity cannot do this and, as Gorky seems to suggest, should not. Revolution needs the strength, daring, and ego of the individual, whereas the latter might welcome, consciously or not, the opportunity to elevate personal protest to a political stage.

Gorky came to America, appropriately enough, to escape arrest in Russia, and he flaunted his status as political criminal. As much as his rough-cut Bolshevik sympathies, "City of the Yellow Devil" seamlessly combines an anticapitalist tract with his youthful mantra: "I entered this world to fight it."[4] Gorky did not begrudge his notoriety. When American readers objected to this Russian upstart, he proudly wrote back: "More than 1,200 objections! I'm terribly fascinated by the tempest whipped up here. It's wild! People say I'm here to make revolution; that, of course, is nonsense, but I have succeeded in making a lot of noise."[5]

The tempest, however, had little to do with his radical politics or literary ability; instead, the cause was sexual indiscretion. Gorky arrived with a translator, Maria Andreeva, identified as his "charming wife," and they were initially welcomed by a liberty-loving audience. With the memory of the Bloody Sunday massacre still fresh, Bolshevism could be accepted in the West as a crusade against tsarist despotism. Then it was revealed that Andreeva, all charm aside, was the mistress of this ambassador of the left—information strategically released by the Russian embassy after it had failed to convince U.S. immigration officials to keep him out. (Gorky's estranged wife, Katerina Pavlovna, had remained in Russia.) When the *New York World* published this scoop, the two were expelled from their hotel, and all meetings and receptions were canceled. One of their defenders, H. G. Wells, exclaimed: "It was like a summer thunderstorm. At one moment Gorky was in an immense sunshine, a plenipotentiary from oppression to liberty, at the next he was being almost literally pelted through the streets." A few papers ineptly claimed that Andreeva was Gorky's wife, but details of his private life could not be disclosed "without placing in deadly danger the lives of scores, and perhaps thousands of his fellow-countrymen." More shrewd observers were appalled by this "social lynching" by Victorian Americans, "anxious to aid and abet murder" but unable to "countenance matrimonial irregularities." For Wells, this ridiculous affair proved that America was "no more than the luminous hive of multitudes of base and busy, greedy and childish little men."[6]

Gorky tried to recast the controversy as about politics, not sex, but the tradition of associating Bolshevism with sexual impropriety had already begun. Gorky was not upset, however. Unable to arrange meetings with the likes of Mark Twain, Jane Addams, or William Dean Howells, he relished the storm of scandal. Perhaps only the revolutionary embraces the title of persona non grata, exemplifying the narcissism inherent in any revolutionary stance regardless of whether, as with Marxism, the individual is theoretically downplayed. The tension is self-perpetuation. Revolution may aim to save the world but the revolutionary often gravitates to the position of one against the world.

This was a role Gorky had long embraced. His famous "Song of the Storm Petrel" (1901), published in the Marxist journal *Life,* inspired Emelian Yaroslavsky, a member of the party's old guard, to declare it the "fight song of the revolution" that had as much impact on the "masses" as any party proclamation.[7] As the harbinger of revolution, the storm petrel flies by itself, over the cowering seagulls, loons, and penguins, to challenge the darkening clouds above. This "proud demon" is by necessity alone; a flock would kill the majesty, the grandeur of solitary opposition to the world. The image ran a deliberately close course with events in Gorky's life. The intoxicating mix of notoriety and fame, precipiated by his own social indiscretions, only fueled his vanity. The tempest was testament to his own importance, to his success in bucking the establishment, and, like the thief in his story, to being "alive" in the real world of politics and power.

The first scandal involving Bolsheviks and sex had something of a perverse quality to it. Occurring a decade before the revolution and on foreign soil, it helped to shepherd in a literary character—an ascetic—who would become socialist realism's first acclaimed hero. It also confirmed America's reputation as a bulwark of puritanism, but also suggested that worries about Bolshevik profligacy, which would erupt in fifteen years, might have weight. The scandal was a portent of a possible grave threat to early Soviet society, particularly its youth: the image of the rebel as professionally committed to revolution yet marked by a personal code of defiance and transgressive behavior. On "enemy" soil, this potentially combustible mix could be tolerated. Yet what might happen once the tables were turned, after victorious revolution? Here was a nearly intractable paradox within the revolutionary paradigm. As Gorky's fiction and personal experience demonstrated, the discourse of revolution amplifies the individual subject, no matter if theoretically conducted for the collective good.[8] It promotes the social objective while inviting the ego-inflating impression that anyone, from the anonymous worker or peasant to the forgotten student, can make history. As with the flight of storm petrel, revolution can propel one above the mundane or, just as easily, it can turn the mundane into the momentous. It romanticizes defiance, whether political, as with Gorky's Vlasov; personal, as with the thief; or both, as embodied in Gorky himself. In such an environment roles for asserting one's autonomy and identity, whether malcontent, experimenter, iconoclast, or even ascetic, can find immediate validation. Which role should dominate after 1917, when moorings for social norms collapsed, would become a central question not only for many young people but for the party and Komsomol as well. Its most dramatic forum would be discourse about sexuality.

Rebels with Too Much Cause

When real revolution came, it made power tangible and seemingly available to many—not just Bolsheviks. This sense of empowerment found its greatest audience perhaps not in a class but in a whole generation.[9] As David Khanin reminisced in 1930, the revolutionary years were a heady time for upstart and impatient youth. The downfall of tsarist rule meant that no tradition or authority was safe; it gave a green light to rebellion. In this time of violent liberation, one could wear the badge of "hooligan" with pride. Recalling his school years in that turbulent period, Khanin had sought to convince his friends of this by recasting history so that they too might have an explicit role in shaping it:

> Who was Columbus? A hooligan who set off down an unknown path.
> Why did the ships of Vasco da Gama sail along the shores of Africa to
> the enchanting lands of India? Because in his veins flowed the blood of a
> hooligan. Who are they, the great inventors, whose tempestuous nature
> cannot be satisfied by today's world? Hooligans! Revolutionaries who
> have died in prison and exile, while cherishing hope for decades on, they
> too are hooligans, honored hooligans.[10]

To ensure the continuation of such an illustrious bloodline, at age fourteen Khanin titled himself the "hooligan general" and lived out the perennial schoolboy fantasy. With forty peers he formed Profeskhul, the Professional Union of Hooligans, whose sole objective was intimidation of teachers and other students. It had nothing to do with a Marxist revolution (it refused membership to females and a rival group was to become the Komsomol); its charter was simply defiance of authority.

The revolution could be a vanity boost for youth, even if, as in Khanin's case, they did not initially identify themselves with the Bolshevik cause.[11] They heard proclaimed at every stage that they were the generation chosen to lead the world to a communist future. Such symbolic empowerment led many young people to embrace Nietzschean "superman" complexes.[12] The vindication of antiestablishment attitudes consecrated a revolutionary swagger in and of itself. Quoting Marx was a sign of ideological progressiveness, but rebellion could also be displayed in personal appearance and behavior. To be disheveled, informal, or rude was a statement against bourgeois society, as much as leather coats, revolvers, and red stars. The logic was understandable. With polite speech, modesty, and a well-groomed look discredited as affectations of a bourgeois past, many could find solidarity in the international icons of counterculture: wearing one's hair long, smoking, alcohol and drug abuse, and sexual experimentation. For all its bloody seriousness, the revolution offered youth the chance to play a heroic role before their peers and the world.

Naturally, such behavior by young people distressed older and more disciplined members of the party. More than poverty and crowded living conditions accounted for the gritty appearance of many Komsomol members. Nikolai Semashko, the commissar of health, lambasted the "cult of slovenliness," which showed lack of self-respect; after all, cleanliness revealed a desire for "order" and "discipline."[13] Echoing these sentiments, Aron Zalkind deplored the apathy, laziness, disdain for "serious study," poor hygiene, rowdiness, and a predilection for cards and vodka among young people whom he saw as having failed the revolution.[14] If publicized complaints are an accurate tool for measuring social trends, then universities, just as sixty years before in Russia, were the centers of this new bohemia.[15]

If the October Revolution made the personal political, the reverse was equally true. The pedestal on which youth found themselves was a license for introspection—amplifying the importance of what before had seemed relatively insignificant. A commitment to revolution (or counterrevolution) could be read in the most common appearances and gestures. In the view of many, particularly youth, every act was a potential metonymy of ideological standing, and they bombarded Komsomol authorities with simple questions such as "Can a member of the Komsomol sit in a bar and drink beer with a *kimovskii* pin on his chest?"[16] As Iurij Lotman notes, referring to earlier revolutionaries, the nineteenth-century Decembrists, "everyday behavior ceased to be simply everyday." Now, however, the new self-consciousness encompassed the entire population.[17] Indeed, for Bolsheviks, the heart of their campaign in the 1920s was to eliminate distinctions between private and public. The former, no longer a sovereign domain, was subject to the same criteria as the latter. In theory, nowhere, not even in the bedroom, could one be ideologically neutral. This ideal became the refrain for all who believed that youth had fallen short of expectations. Yet critics of youth could not escape feeding the inflated self-image of many in that generation. If young people's behavior was important enough to criticize, then they themselves, in their own eyes, were that much more important.

In short, Bolsheviks became victims of their own success. No matter what they claimed for their new state, the image of the rebellious revolutionary continued to appeal to certain youth. On the contrary, if revolution was no longer an abstract dream but a real condition, some exploited their license to question social propriety as if it were state-approved. It was difficult for them to distinguish between proper Marxist revolutionary behavior and simple rebellion. Looking to members of Gorky's generation, which exhibited both Lenin-like austerity and wild living, young people could find mixed guidance. Politburo member Nikolai Bukharin admitted that in his younger days under the tsar young people misbehaved, thought "it was fun to walk past the school director with a cigarette," wear hats in the classroom, drink too much, neglect their duties on the job, wear their uniforms incorrectly, and disdain sexual propriety. Yet he argued that such defiance of the status quo—even robbing banks, the grandest gesture of prerevolutionary Bolshevik rule-breaking—aided the revolution. But now times had changed. "Bad" behavior had helped bring the revolution; but now such acts represented "the incorrect transfer of methods for destroying the bourgeois order onto one's own organism."[18] A member of the Komsomol Central Committee used more pungent language: "What was useful then is harmful now. Disrespect for social norms, fighting against the order-obsessed bourgeoisie—that was a holy affair; in the Soviet state an analogous struggle is pure counterrevolution."[19]

Fortunately for him, David Khanin's career as "hooligan general" was short-lived. The civil war demanded real soldiers, and by 1920, at age seventeen, he was a party member and fighting in the Red Army. Having been educated in Marxism at the newly created Communist Academy, he rapidly ascended the ranks of the Komsomol, became at a young age an editor of its journal *The New Shift*, headed its publishing division, and finally, having chosen the winning side against Trotsky, was made a member of its Central Committee. But although Khanin's conversion from rebel to revolutionary constituted a model for youth, his memoirs attest to competing tensions that propelled him to power. The subject that resisted neat compartmentalization in his reformed, ideologically mature state was sexual behavior, specifically the validity of charges of debauchery leveled against his generation. Why must he speak of sex, he asks at the end:

> Is it because we didn't experience love? Because we lived as ascetics? In the name of revolution did we suppress in ourselves explosions of feeling and the flesh?
> No, a thousand times, no! We loved just as other generations. Women of our time can attest at length to the strength of our embraces. Just like previous and just like future generations, the young men who grew up with me gained tremendous pleasure drinking the warmth from the lips of our favorite girl.
> But it is here similarities end.

We didn't put love on a pedestal. We didn't allow it to disrupt our lives, habits and labor. Love was joyous but only to the extent it didn't prevent the civil war generation from devoting its strength to the revolution.

Isn't it strange, then, that this love people called debauchery? When we had to break with our loved one, we did that. . . .

I don't want to defend the excessive "freedom" of morals, when the ideal becomes the "love of the worker bees," who imbibe of such pleasure on every flower. There was such a love in those days, perhaps even more common than before. However this is not a surprise. Caught in a whirlwind, old conventions were falling; the previous understanding of the permissible and impermissible in this area had been shattered.

All the same, with indignation I reject the accusation that debauchery reigned among youth in those years. Our heroic epoch was ascetic. We looked with open eyes upon love, but experienced it only when it didn't interfere with the principal task: revolution. This means that we gave to love only a little of our strength and time.[20]

Khanin could not decide whom he and his comrades had been: they weren't prudes but weren't profligate; when they loved a little, women didn't complain; when they loved a lot, circumstances were to blame; they weren't ascetics but the epoch demanded asceticism; they enjoyed sex but never to the detriment of the cause. Combative, regretful, egotistical, conservative, liberal—amid all these contradictions the only thing Khanin could not accept was the accusation of debauchery, embodied in his reference to Alexandra Kollontai's infamous story collection, *Love of the Worker Bees* (to be discussed later).

Khanin's outburst, curiously following praise of Stalin, captures the unique position of postrevolutionary youth. Countless party declarations assured them of their importance by stressing the connection between age and ideology. Thus Khanin's "we" signified not just a political alliance (members of the Komsomol) but a generation that came of age amid world war and revolution. His laborious defense of himself and his comrades suggests how often they had been called licentious, undisciplined, and disorderly. The language they likely heard can be found in the 1925 diary of the Russian critic Robert Kulle:

Youth are just terrible. Their principles are entirely base. The chaos of their sexual lives is something primeval, from the Stone Age or the time of the [pagan] Polovtsy and Pechenegs. All in all, the country is Polovtsian. In a village the girls must sleep with whoever the "head guy" indicates! It's not rare for a girl to have two or three children. . . . Youth have

absolutely no interests. Late into the night they wander, say, along the
edge of a swamp, bawling their stupid songs—"gukajut i tjukajut."
That's also where the "love" happens. . . . Not a drop of revolutionary
enthusiasm. They couldn't care less about the government and make fun
of the "evil communists," yet at the same time only have primal hatred
for the previous way of life, wanting neither the tsar or landowner
back.[21]

While Kulle lambasted youth and Khanin defended them, both allude to
their image as boorish, apathetic, self-indulgent, and profligate. Such charges
after 1917 helped to enforce the idea that this generation, good or bad, was an
autonomous unit worthy of attention, feeding youth's growing self-consciousness. Revolution gave them a symbolic voice more powerful than students or young activists had ever known before.[22] For both supporters and
opponents, they became the exemplars of the new Soviet culture. As much as
political convictions, age itself could serve as an index of one's value to society.

Yet who or what was Soviet youth? Bolshevik culture might present a
young face to the world, but whose—that of Khanin the hooligan, or Khanin
the Komsomol leader? The paradox reminds us how rapidly the revolution
became contaminated by its environment. Bolsheviks believed that revolution would "trickle down," that it would reshape all facets of *byt* or everyday
life. Otherwise, how could one presume to create a socialist society? But what
was alarming was that the ideal of revolution, as it penetrated various do-
mains, did not necessarily supplant what was present but instead was corrupted in the very course of its descent. However much Bolsheviks believed
that their revolution reflected some pure law derived from the Marxist gospel,
they could not escape a new kind of *dvoeverie,* dual belief. Just as Christianity
absorbed pre-Christian faiths on Russian soil as elsewhere, the October Revolution also took on new colors and flavors as it spread to different classes,
generations, regions, and nationalities.[23] A revolution is a polyvalent phenomenon; no matter what meaning its leaders may give to it, no shield pro-
tects it from penetration and reformulation by other interests.

Confusion over sexual behavior became an immediate barometer of such
contamination. To be sure, one would want to avoid the essentialism in assuming that with youth's natural impulses and curiosities, sex would become
the key domain where the personal collided with the political. Yet what cannot be denied is that many young activists sought to understand their bodies
and behaviors within a new ethos and through a new vocabulary. This was
not just a condition of revolution but of modernism as a whole. Throughout
Europe and America, the modern age had catapulted this generation to new

prominence; never before had youth commanded society's attention to such a degree. With Victorian traditions and ideals discredited by myriad forces of change and shattered in the First World War, a spirit defined by iconoclasm, experimentation, and a commitment to all things new rushed into the vacuum. A similar eruption of youthful self-consciousness occurred in the United States, ironically the ideological antithesis of all things Soviet, with its portraitist being F. Scott Fitzgerald. To be modern was to be consciously against tradition; to be modern was to embrace jazz, film, and the automobile; to be modern was to be young.

On both sides of the ocean, to the dismay of both capitalist and Bolshevik traditionalists, a common thread behind the new mores was a changed attitude toward sex. Admittedly, American youth were less iconoclastic than Soviet. As Paula S. Fass argues, the sexual revolution in the United States "was not a revolt against marriage but a revolution within marriage."[24] Unchaperoned dating, premarital erotic exploration (petting), and recognition of a woman's physical desires gave sex an acknowledged and vital role in the choice of a marital partner. There were no calls for the abolition of marriage in the United States (what the communists were accused of), but in both East and West the emergence of generational self-consciousness was intimately tied to a revolution in sexual behavior and defiance of parental mores.

The sexual questions debated by Soviet youth intensified after the chaotic three years of revolution and civil war. The New Economic Policy (NEP), introduced in 1921, began to encourage national recovery, permitting small-scale private enterprise and ending forced requisitions from peasants, but many saw it as a retreat from the objectives of 1917. Full state control, essential for military victory, had given way to a mixed economy that in turn bred a new "Soviet" bourgeoisie with its own corrupting potential. This modification dampened some of the iconoclastic drive but not the inquisitive spirit. Throughout the 1920s, youth generally continued to see themselves as living in revolutionary times; with the coming of peace, members of a new Soviet society hoped they could begin to construct a truly emancipated life.

Sex as Revolution

If to be modern was to reject the mores of the previous generation, then Soviet society, by identifying itself as progressive, could not avoid the "accursed question" of sex. Khanin's remonstrations suggest that it was an almost inevitable by-product of the promise of liberation: did revolution give citizens added responsibility to preserve their "energy" for the cause, or was it a banner of emancipation that gave people a license to experiment and defy normative conventions in private behavior? The question was not unique to

Bolshevism, but by the 1920s in the Soviet Union it had moved from the hypothetical to the concrete.[25] We do not know how many embraced, in word or deed, the new libertarian ethos, but we hear their voices in voluminous published reports, books, articles, polls, memoirs, and criminal accounts, as well as in letters, diaries, and secret party documents. If viewed collectively, they substantiate that over the decade the very idea of revolution was often used to justify questionable behavior. In short, the turbulence of NEP society extended beyond politics and economics to impact personal life.

It is to such voices that we are indebted for the wave of alarm that gripped many in the party and general population as a whole. If modesty, chaste courtship, and marriage were ideals of prerevolutionary society, what place did they have in a postrevolutionary one? Were not love, passion, jealousy, and respect mere bourgeois conventions? To be an authentic proletarian, therefore, could mean abandoning self-restraint. As a character in Nikolai Bogdanov's *First Girl* (1928) is advised by a friend, it is ideologically superior to address one's sexuality frankly and with a minimum of fuss:

> If desire awakens in you, tell a girl, a comrade, about it directly and honestly. If she wants to satisfy you, then no one's going to judge you. You both have a good time and whose business is it? . . . If she doesn't want to satisfy you, then look for another. Isn't it really all the same, whether a Masha or Dasha quenches your desire. This is the way for man and woman not to burden themselves with chains, the muddle of love and living together; they remain free and able to dedicate themselves to the service of society. That is more natural, simpler and better. If we're preaching new forms of society, then we should preach new forms of sexual relations instead of philistine love and bourgeois marriage.[26]

For those so inclined, the real-life power of such logic to persuade was undeniable, particularly among those young people (as was true for most) whose understanding of the politics behind revolution and "historical materialism" was minimal. Confirmation, unfortunately, can be found in the words of its victims. In a letter from a young female worker to *Komsomol Pravda,* published in 1926, we sense a desperate attempt to fend off both physically and ideologically the advances of a man who proclaimed that the idea of love was simply "bourgeois" and she should "do what nature demands." "Is [love] really just a prejudice meaning that people should get together like animals?" she asked. "Please answer this, comrade, and don't laugh at me because if it's true, then I am ashamed to live. Please tell me if there is love from a Marxist point of view?" The response, predictably, condemned the man's actions: "Our point of view does not reduce love to the naked sexual act. It endows it

with social significance. Attraction to a woman without the feeling of comrade sensitivity, without solidarity of interests, is not love but animalism."[27]
However, in what was a recurring problem for both inquisitive youth and officials, such an answer did not explain ideologically how love and sex should
be related. It was easy to prohibit unacceptable behavior, but what were the
political directives for what to do day by day? The young woman might have
asked further questions: what is "comrade sensitivity," and once it is achieved,
is sex then permissible?

Some feared that for youth lust threatened to displace Lenin as the center
of revolutionary life. The language of Marxism even seemed to invite this imbalance. The more popular Bolshevik rhetoric became, the more it could be
misappropriated. Vaunted class terms, particularly the opposition of proletariat versus bourgeoisie, were often little more than synonyms for "good"
and "bad" and used to advance unabashedly prurient interests. Thus, to the
horror of authorities, youth could apply doctrine too far. Once again, it was
essential to distinguish past from present. In the words of a member of the
Komsomol Central Committee:

> When a nihilist spat on the "family code" of the tsarist body of laws,
> that was a protest assaulting the foundations of tsarist order; when a
> Komsomol member spits on the Soviet marriage law, he tramples on the
> seedlings of the new *byt* and undermines the foundations of Soviet
> society.[28]

More distressing was that revered historical figures could be seen in the same
light. If Karl Marx was faithful to his wife, as most believed, did this make
him a bourgeois philistine?[29] Such misguided zealotry could be found among
literary villains, but, as periodicals and surveys reveal, fiction was not the only
source. A contributor to *The New Shift* argued that because he was a member
of the proletariat, the anointed class, women should not refuse him.[30] Or, as
another reasoned, did not the declared equality between the sexes mean equal
access to sexual gratification? His protest exemplifies how revolutionary entitlement could be equated with satisfying sexual desire: "It's imperative for our
female personnel to drop these stupid prejudices. Are they just planning to
shrivel up or what? There were these times when she would say that though
she would like to, she wasn't giving any. (I think such people are crazy.)"[31]

Over fifteen hundred Moscow students responded to the same survey,
conducted by Israel Gelman and sponsored by the Commissariat of Health.
Published in 1922, it offered the first comprehensive portrait of the sexual behavior of postrevolutionary youth. Although its statistical conclusions may be
problematic (to be discussed later), the candid comments of participants are

invaluable. Men generally reduced sex to intercourse.[32] Many feared marriage as entrapment or, as seen above, could not accept rejection in this new age. Most intriguing are those who used the "logic of the revolution" to resolve an individual plight. A twenty-two-year-old student worker wondered if social planning was putting the cart before the horse. Referring to programs for new mothers, he commented:

> If, for the results of sexual intercourse we have set up so-called maternity wards, then why not build intercourse wards (not to be misunderstood as "tolerance houses") which would consist of the following: put simply, the one desiring satisfaction of one's needs would arrive, register, be examined carefully by a doctor, etc. If necessary I can give you a fully detailed account of this idea.[33]

The notion that the government should assume responsibility for the satisfaction of sexual needs reappeared in a survey conducted by David Lass in 1928. One respondent stated that he simply had no time for love. Because prostitution still thrived a decade after the revolution, the government should offer public brothels (which had been legal in tsarist Russia).[34] Others hoped that salvation would come through technology, that science could relieve men of their longing for women and of their "attendant nightmares."[35] Another asked for a pill that would suppress sexual desire until he was able to support a family.[36] A few had already given up hope: "I don't believe in marriage, only sexual intercourse like two dogs together."[37]

The surveys by Gelman and Lass are useful because they focus on voices that questioned or diverged from the ideal.[38] Their intention, of course, was to highlight incorrect and harmful behavior, which they did on nearly every page. Men like those quoted above were "sexual nihilists" ruled by "blind sexual need that leads [them] from encounter to encounter. The morality of yesterday's bourgeoisie still imprisons both the man of today and tomorrow."[39] Lass was dismayed to discover that even well into the 1920s male students continued to see women through a "medieval mentality," solely as "objects of pleasure." Naiveté and cynicism were still all too prevalent. The comments of one respondent, who reduced the question of sexuality morality to one of accessibility, were sufficient, unfortunately, to cement Lass's point:

> In order to resolve the sexual question, both sexes need to approach it more simply and morally. It is necessary to prove to a woman that scrimping and shame regarding the sexual act are harmful and not healthy. A woman should look at the sexual act just like a man. She

should switch from a policy of defense to one of offense, that is, it is necessary to increase the supply of the female body.[40]

A rhyme that allegedly passed through universities summarizes this attitude: "A rock isn't a mineral just as a co-ed isn't virginal."[41]

Fear over youths' misguided morality spilled onto the pages of *Pravda* in March 1925. Sofia Smidovich, a Bolshevik of eminent pedigree (she had joined the Social Democrats in 1898, had been head of the Zhenotdel, currently served on the party's Central Control Commission, and was married to the equally distinguished party member Petr Smidovich), published a scathing portrait of communist youth as having "the most primitive approach to questions of sex." She describes some of their delinquent attitudes as follows:

> (1) Every *komsomolets,* male worker-student, and young, moustacheless boy can and should satisfy his sexual desires. For some reason this is considered an indisputable truth. Sexual abstinence is characterized as bourgeois.
>
> (2) Every *komsomolka,* female worker-student, and just simply female student to whom has fallen the choice of this or that tomcat boy (why all these African passions have erupted up here in the North, I won't begin to judge) should go directly to him; otherwise she is bourgeois, not worthy of carrying the name *komsomolka* or being a member of the proletarian student body.[42]

Smidovich was aghast at seeing the revolution reduced to sex: "Listen, listen, comrade women! All of these words were overhead in real life. Nothing has been made up." It was heresy to say that abstention was "bourgeois." After years of work in the underground, she could not comprehend how Bolshevik ideals and language could be turned to such an abominable end. Identifying these perversions as "African," a metaphor for the erotic and exotic, meant that for her the virus was foreign and thus false. Smuggled in via literature, film, and music, it was culturally and ideologically alien to the true nature of Soviet youth. The revolution itself could not be responsible for such abominations.

One might assume that *Pravda* would uphold the image of a blameless revolution. But an article, "About Love and Something Else as Well" (1925), ostensibly (but not likely) penned by Kollontai, suggested that the roots of the problem were home-grown: widespread poverty and the demands of balancing work and study led to such "perversions" among students.[43] It attacked Smidovich's portrait of women as passive. This was a disappointing "caricature," given her work in the Zhenotdel. To understand the sexual problems of young people, the article continued, Smidovich need only look in the mirror.

> After all, within the older generation itself there is not less but likely more debauchery. The only difference is that youth do it openly and directly, trying to mask perversions with its own peculiar ideology of sexual anarchism, whereas adults nearly always do it in bourgeois fashion by engaging in dalliances in the guise of a do-gooder and feeding their children old tales about storks, immaculate conceptions, and other junk.

Not only were youth not to blame, they weren't hypocrites. Smidovich may have been chastened by this counterattack. *Pravda* noted that she did not attend a public debate on April 12, disappointing the students who had come to hear her and Semashko, commissar of health, speak on "love, life, and sex."

Pravda readers were evidently intrigued by the question of a sex-ridden society, and the Smidovich issue was reportedly read during lectures and discussed between classes. In May the newspaper devoted sixteen columns to readers' letters that capture the true breadth of opinion among Soviet citizens.[44] Many confirmed Smidovich's portrait and noted her compassion toward young women: "At just the right time you have truly highlighted this misguided understanding of the issue of sex and have given answers to questions that have tortured me and hundreds of other girls. With your help I was able to understand a lot and thus save my youth." Some men were offended that Smidovich portrayed women solely as victims. Girls were just as guilty in the spread of "African passions"; after all, "in no way do [girls] want to be fettered by the chains of chastity; they themselves seek satisfaction." Female readers argued that they weren't ignorant or gullible: a girl "knows better than anyone the value to put on the songs 'young moustacheless boys' sing; she simply tells them to go to hell." In short, they engaged Smidovich on her own terms. What horrified her, some noted, was not an abomination. Social revolution did mean sexual revolution in the most dramatic sense:

> What kind of social order do we have? One based on the systematic destruction of private property. This is what gives it its distinctive qualities. With regard to the family it signifies the systematic destruction of the basis for the family. Contemporary sexual relationships are nothing other than a profound reflection of the economic processes in our country. How youth live today is a revolutionary break from sexual relationships formed on the principle of private property. In the eyes of youth, not

only is a girl who abstains [from sex] bourgeois but one who destroys her youth in the name of prejudices of the past, who preserves herself for the husband/property owner.

Letters such as these—which imply that the source of "African" passions was Marxism itself—were curiously not condemned. Unique for *Pravda*, the one forum where criticism of heretical views would be expected, there was a most peculiar silence. Readers were identified by name, not the usual ad hominem; their voices were introduced simply to be heard—not for rebuke. An almost unprecedented debate unfolded in the central organ of the party: a contentious article by a senior member had been subjected to critical review by average Soviet citizens, with both the positive and negative included. Usually a synonym for intolerance, *Pravda* served solely as a moderator, which suggests confusion in the top ranks as well. Sexual behavior after the revolution was an issue of genuine, vital concern to many Soviet citizens, and party publications themselves demonstrate how resistant it was to glib ideological packaging. This partly explains why public discussion was so voluble and interpretations so varied. If, at its center, the party openly sanctioned disagreement regarding sexual behavior, could one expect greater clarity among the general population?[45]

Most alarming were those who employed revolutionary rhetoric and lopsided logic to mask sexual predation. The sense of entitlement combined with aggressive impulses could lead to abuse. Ironically, new laws and programs intended to liberate women were part of the problem, since men could take advantage of legalized abortion and elimination of divorce restrictions. "Don Juans" (a term popularized by Lenin) could more easily shake responsibility for impregnating women and with fewer pangs of conscience. After all, a woman now had access to free abortion, and if she bore a child she could theoretically receive some state support.

At the end of the decade, in a devastating study entitled *Life Out of Control* (1929), Vera Ketlinskaia and Vladimir Slepkov documented the impact such men could have.[46] Penetrating, judicious, and balanced (an increasing rarity by this time), the report acknowledged the progress that had been made in gender relations, yet it decried the continuing abuses and hypocrisy of those who espoused the progressive line at work while behaving at home as if the revolution had never occurred. It compiled an appalling portrait of male behavior that included domestic abuse, acquaintance rape, alcoholism, sexual harassment, and demeaning attitudes toward women. Some expected women to live as domestic servants with limited employment and educational opportunities; others pressured women to have abortions or abandoned them after they gave birth. Venereal disease was not a primary concern, and love was often disdained as a vital component of relationships. Their preference was for quick sexual encounters with female colleagues or prostitutes.

Ketlinskaia and Slepkov explicitly blamed the Komsomol for failing to provide education about sex, and they were most disturbed when leaders of individual cells exhibited such behavior. "The Komsomol is the school of communism," declared Emelian Yaroslavsky, and its members should be beyond reproach. Alexander Milchakov, head of the Komsomol itself, agreed. In *The Komsomol in the Struggle for a Cultured Life* (1927), he acknowledged that although the rank and file must serve as examples at work and home, "even here not everything is going well."[47] The journals and newspapers published under his tutelage (he became secretary of the Komsomol Central Committee at age twenty-three) indicate what he meant. It was reported that some Komsomol members abused their position for sexual exploitation, and in some cells members allegedly "changed husbands and wives like gloves."[48] One report charged that the Komsomol pin itself had become a tool for sexual conquest: to impress women, a young man had to show that he was more than just a "plain worker."[49] It is not surprising, therefore, that Ketlinskaia and Slepkov noted in a poll taken among Vyborg youth that only 10 percent of female respondents claimed to have a healthy sexual life, and only 6 percent saw men's behavior as morally upstanding.[50]

It would be mistaken to view such transgressions and the misuse of class rhetoric to justify sexual conquest as a conscious subversion of Bolshevik goals.[51] Even the worst of the lot did not see themselves as anti-Soviet. In all their puerile vulgarity, they still identified themselves as true revolutionaries. One critic, exasperated at how class language had been co-opted, lambasted youthful delinquents as "radishes," red on the outside but white (the color of counterrevolution) on the inside.[52] A Professor Zavadovsky suggested: "Our youth [should] take a red-hot poker and burn out of their midst all attempts to disguise animal lust by invoking ideological principles."[53] Less painful but equally impractical was Bukharin's advice: "If you wish to build socialism . . . then you should do exactly that and not something else." To clarify, he added, if you want to make a stool, then you shouldn't dance the *trepak*.[54] No wonder politically conscientious youth were perplexed as to what constituted proper behavior. A certain S. Devenishsky echoed the frustration in many young Soviets' minds:

Of course I'm not inclined to believe in the degeneracy of youth or fall into pessimism. It's clear that right now a new psychology, a new way of life, is only forming; but our older comrades need to help us. It is imperative that they give us an authoritative answer to the question: how should we live now? How can we eliminate blemishes? It's also clear that articles full of officialese and rah-rah optimism don't do anything but cause more harm.[55]

While the Komsomol took the brunt of charges of sexual debauchery, the party itself was not immune. Lev Sosnovsky's compilation of letters from wives of party members, *Painful Questions* (1927), revealed that double standards and exploitation by men were among their chief anxieties. Sosnovsky's stated purpose was to combat the "conspiracy of silence" that widened the gap between a rhetoric of equality and real-life conditions in the USSR. "We don't recognize the archaic nature of relations between men and women only because little is spoken about that subject; most prefer to be silent on the matter. But if we were to shine the light of the projector on that which is called the contemporary family, we ourselves would be stunned by the ugly picture open before us."[56] The complaints are striking in their sincerity and in the women's inability to comprehend this new life which, except for a new parlance, smacked so much of the old. One wife of an "old revolutionary" (in experience, not age) wanted to join the party despite her husband's insistence that she stay at home. She later learned that at meetings he was a vocal supporter of a greater role for women at work and in the party. Another, though her husband agreed that revolutionary times demanded mutual respect between marital partners, found herself left with the domestic chores. She recognized that he was affectionate to her only when she was necessary for his sexual satisfaction. When he left her for another woman, she blamed herself and asked in the new idiom whether her despair was "bourgeois."

For Sosnovsky, the longest letter was the most stunning, not because it detailed the sexual escapades of a female candidate to the party but because it indicated what should be and should not be. Paraskeva Ivanova (a fictitious name) said that she joined the Komsomol as a chance to be "a valued cog in the Great Proletarian Machine building the future." When she became a candidate for the party, she was elated: "Oh, now I am all for the party and all with the party. . . . My head is burning. I am consumed with a desire to give all of myself in every way to be useful, but I have no practical experience." Yet her initiation to said experience, which she also termed "the communist way of life," took an unorthodox turn when Comrade Ganov, secretary of her district committee, invited her one night to a cemetery. He regaled her with stories of fallen heroes. He then moved from fighters for communism to the "new way" of life and her beautiful eyes, then kisses and a declaration of love. She was "absolutely floored":

Spasms of tears flooded my throat. But he's a communist; what does he want with me? But he even has a family, a wife? Or maybe I just don't understand something. Maybe he's right? He's smarter than me. He's older. I told him this. But Comrade Ganov again gave me a lecture: "Family? A communist does not and cannot have a family. What's a family? It's old-fashioned, really old-fashioned. No, we're cultured people. Earlier there was a family, with the Romanovs there were families etc., etc. What's more, I love you and only you. I'm not to blame for that. And by the way your abstaining, your defiance, is all bourgeois. Not too communist of you."

Eventually she gave in, with Ganov as her "teacher" and "classes" held in the field. She concluded ironically: "I mastered all my teacher's lessons brilliantly . . . and sank lower and lower." Then she ceased to protest.

> I justified myself as a worthy student of a worthy teacher. During the secretary's absences and during my own trips away, Ganov's pupil put into practice the new way of life, the new ethics, with checklists, policemen, Komsomol and party members, and in carriages, on wagons, in carts—every place where possible. At a union conference Comrade Borisov, who could be my grandfather in age and service to the party, also gave a good lesson in "the new way of life," for which he presented me with a gift, a textbook on the rational resolution of questions of everyday life, Bukharin's *Theory of Historical Materialism*.

Such a lifestyle, however, led to self-loathing, and by 1924 encounters with "good, honorable" members only disgusted Ivanova. To regain her comrades' respect, she buried herself in work. Foreshadowing what would become a staple of corrective literature, the effect was reciprocal: her peers helped her in her self-purification. She married a Komsomol member and withdrew her application to the party, vowing, "I will join as a Leninist, not a prostitute."

Ivanova's letter is a tale of sin and repentance, and, except for Sosnovsky's role and place of publication, we might dismiss it as apocryphal. There may be dramatic embellishment, but as a journalist and former head of the Central Committee's Agitprop department, Sosnovsky frequently targeted abuse and hypocrisy in his own party. In fact, many editorial and archival letters outstrip fiction in their poignancy and unintentional grim humor. Whatever its source, this letter gives voice to the common complaint of sexual harassment under the cover of social liberation. As another woman observed, the revolution had merely created a new class of exploiters: men. She experienced so little of the officially vaunted gender equality that she could find consolation only in the promises of science. Perhaps artificial insemination would eventually allow women to fulfill their social obligation of giving birth without having to submit to men.[57]

However, not all women saw themselves as victims of corrupted revolutionary ideals. Proclaimed emancipation gave some a sense of empowerment similar to that of young men. In a 1927 letter to the journal *Red Students*, a female student named Biriukova equated the passivity of an acquaintance rape victim, Panteleimon Romanov's heroine in "Without a Cherry Blossom," with a relic of the bourgeois past:

> I feel that girls like us, while we still haven't achieved full equality with guys, still have sense and good vision. The Cinderellas are all gone. Our girls know very well what they want from a guy. Without any particular "worries" many of them sleep with [guys] because of a healthy attraction. . . . And if the heroine holds to the following—"I waited for only one thing, in my mind I asked only for a kiss"—well, we ourselves know how to kiss. We're not objects or simpletons that guys should court. Girls see and know whom they choose and with whom they sleep. And if this is the case, then why all the whining, why all these "but he's to blame" or "he deceived and then dumped me"? You have to look to yourself; "don't blame the mirror if your face is ugly."
>
> The heroine of "Without a Cherry Blossom" accurately portrayed the frame of mind of a girl standing with one leg in the past. We, however, want to stand with two firm legs on this wondrous Soviet land and under a May sky with a guy by our side, breathing in "the scent of grass and flowers."[58]

Biriukova's tone of barely suppressed anger indicates a growing revolutionary sense of personal autonomy. For her, sex was a directly political act. Emancipation gave her the power of agency, defined here by choosing and dismissing her partners. This was proof of her revolutionary standing. Yet agency also included full responsibility for one's actions. Therefore, any suggestion of victimization was for Biriukova a personal and ideological affront.

No wonder that marriage, a bourgeois concept for many young women, was equally suspect. In Gelman's 1922 poll, only 14.3 percent of women, as against 21.4 percent of men, cited it as their "ideal." The reason, one female worker commented, was fully consonant with the revolution's promises: "I don't want to be subordinate to a husband or become his slave." She preferred "short-term romantic liaisons."[59] Women also admitted to the same distractions as men: "Sex, I'm afraid, plays the major role in my life. It usually doesn't interfere with my work, but that's a big struggle"; another reported, "For me sex is extremely important. Its absence ruins my whole mood."[60] One leader of female students requested that any "poor boys" who were sex-deprived should be sent to her group (with address conveniently provided).[61] Women's emancipation was biological as much as legal; they could be equal "to the boys" as victimizers as well as victims.

The revolution may have met few of its promises, yet in this decade women could exercise a new freedom to address their own sexuality, not yet as equals to men but with expectations of equality. This freedom was not welcomed by all, and it was not to last long. Women who expressed such views won the opprobrium of both officials and traditionalist parents; indeed, one of the most vilified figures in the 1920s was Kollontai's fictional portrait of a young woman who took charge of herself and her own sexuality in the name of revolution. Still, where else at this time can one read of the following complaint? If revolution had made open liaisons easier, quantity did not improve quality; increased sexual activity had not increased satisfaction for women.[62]

The Kollontai Factor

The most outspoken advocate of women's empowerment was Kollontai, party official, fiction writer, and polemicist. Aristocratic and highly educated, she was of the same generation as Lenin, Yaroslavsky, and Stalin. From professional revolutionary and sometime confidant of Lenin, she became commissar of social welfare, head of the Zhenotdel, and roving ambassador for the Soviet Union. Her most dramatic contribution was that as a social critic she refused to be silent regarding the importance of sexuality for both men and women. This laid her open to attacks by enemies who drew from the behavior of her literary heroines evidence of personal indiscretions. Never favoring hedonism or sexual license, she was nevertheless accused of both, and in the attacks against her matured the vocabulary that polarized debate for the rest of the decade. She became the scapegoat for youths' transgressions, excesses, and "unnatural" interest in their own sexuality.

Kollontai's principal essays on these topics—"Sexual Relations and the Class Struggle" (1919), "Communism and the Family" (1920), "Theses on Communist Morality in the Sphere of Marital Relations" (1921), and "Make Way for Winged Eros" (1923)—are a prolonged critique of bourgeois ideals and practices.[63] Her message was that there could be no authentic marriage, no love or intimate relationship, in a class-based, property-obsessed society. A wedding was not merely a union of two individuals, but a conflict of economic interests. The woman, generally denied means of self-support, became a husband's dependent; the man viewed her, consciously or not, as property, not substantively distinct from livestock. The family was thus a socially destructive force in which men and women played out these stereotypes, and its interests were set above those of society (the house-as-castle mentality). Yet for Kollontai, even outside marriage real love was impossible in a bourgeois context. Because of economic disparities, there could be no equality of the sexes. Moreover, the cult of private property encouraged jealousy and possessiveness. Within it no woman could be an individual. Kollontai writes:

> We are used to evaluating a woman not as a personality with individual qualities and failings irrespective of her physical and emotional experience, but only as an appendage of a man. This man, the husband or the lover, throws the light of his personality over the woman, and it is this reflection and not the woman herself that we consider to be the true definition of her emotional and moral makeup.[64]

From this blindness emerged the double standard; men were free to seek gratification, but women could not. Given the aspersions cast upon Kollontai because of her relationship with Pavel Dybenko, a peasant seventeen years her junior who became commissar of the navy, it is significant that the litmus test she offered for the double standard was society's inability to accept a woman's liaison with a "lesser" man.[65]

By identifying class and private property as the evils underlying patriarchy, gender discrimination, and the double standard, Kollontai recognized that the law alone could not eliminate these ills. Legalizing divorce, for example, would not deliver women from a host of other inequities. Only in a classless society could there be an equal sexual relationship. The family, by necessity, would lose its raison d'etre. No longer would it be an economic pact, the locus of toil and burden. Communal kitchens, laundries, and child care would relieve women of domestic chores (though she quickly added, "Communist society is not intending . . . to tear the baby from the breast of its mother").[66] In classic Marxist fashion, the family would wither away, to be replaced by the "great universal family of workers." Marriage, an institution of "conjugal slavery," would become "a free union of two equal members of the workers' state who are united by love and mutual respect." This was not mere free love (even today a notion attributed to Kollontai); it simply meant that there should be no formal limits on love. Whether a relationship were brief or enduring, neither partner should be trapped in a situation that one (usually the woman) could not leave for material or moral reasons. Kollontai characterized the ideal state, "love-comradeship," as based on (1) "equality in relationships" (men shedding their egoism, women their slavish suppression of themselves); (2) "mutual recognition of the rights of others" (a partner has no ownership rights over the other); (3) "comrade sensitivity" (the ability to lis-

ten and understand the other).[67] Scorning the conditional, Kollontai presented her convictions not as theory but as prophecy: "These relations will
ensure for humanity all the joys of a love unknown in the commercial society
of capitalism, a love that is free and based on the true social equality of happy
young people, free in their feelings and affections."[68] No matter what legends
or fairy tales have told us, *true* love would flourish only under communism.

While much of her attention was directed to the past and future, Kollontai also spoke to the present, particularly the concerns of youth. Her essay,
"Make Way for Winged Eros: A Letter to Working Youth" (1923), was published in the Komsomol's flagship journal, *The Young Guard*. Here she recognized that in a period of social turmoil, visions of "what will be" might be
inspiring but offered little in practical terms. The grandeur of the revolution
had not displaced sex; indeed, the opposite was true. Contemporary hardships, combined with natural bodily needs, had led to a "sexual crisis" in the
country. The physical and emotional demands of revolution and civil war had
left no room for "for love's joys and pains." Kollontai described this phenomenon as "wingless eros," a condition in which citizens had no time for love,
for it drained energy away from the revolution.[69] Nevertheless, human beings
have physical needs—hence the increase in transient sexual relationships
without emotional weight or obligation. Kollontai was concerned that the
wingless phase would continue and undercut progress toward the love-com-
munism connection. What Soviet youth were often accused of—viewing sexuality as an end in itself—would lead to "unhealthy carnality," spreading
venereal disease and denying love its proper place. Bolsheviks—as we shall see
in the ideas of Anatoly Lunacharsky and others—could be romantics; but
love and sex had to be requalified within Marxist ideology.

Toward this goal Kollontai drew what was in her eyes a logical conclusion,
yet for others it became the single most inflammatory statement on sex made
by a Bolshevik: "The sexual act must be seen not as something shameful and
sinful but as something which is as natural as the other needs of [a] healthy
organism, such as hunger or thirst. Such phenomena cannot be judged as
moral or immoral."[70] Removed from context and misconstrued, the "glass of
water theory," condemned as the equivalent of "just do it," was cited in nearly
every major attack against sexual license in the 1920s. But by calling sex "natural," Kollontai did not mean to deprive the sexual act of consequence, only
to combat the silence that usually attended this issue. Just as one needs food
and drink, so too one has a sexual drive, the satisfaction of which needed to
be acknowledged. By naturalizing the notion of sex, she hoped to remove it
from the bourgeois template of valuation. Only by eliminating traditional
prejudices could the discussion of sex be raised to a new criterion within a
new "communist morality." Without this last qualification, her declaration

might seem a brazen call for licentiousness, but it was never presented or intended in so isolated a fashion. Kollontai always argued that, while natural, the sex drive should always be subordinate to social concerns.[71]

Contrary to the charges soon to be leveled against her, Kollontai insisted that love and sex were to be evaluated only within interests of health and social solidarity. Duty to the collective should define the conduct of a relationship. Indeed, a couple's happiness should be inseparable from the strength of the group. Thus sex without love was wrong, and love itself was not the whole of our lives. Pulling the curtain on old-fashioned romantics, she noted, "The old ideal was 'all for the loved one'; communist morality demands all for the collective."[72]

Like her fellow Marxists, Kollontai believed bourgeois sexual conventions to be degrading to women and saw relief from women's "double duty" (demands at work and at home) in the communal sharing of domestic chores. Forty years earlier, August Bebel's *Woman Under Socialism* (1883) and Friedrich Engels's *The Origin of the Family, Private Property, and the State* (1884) had detailed the causes of the subjugation of women, the double standard, the evil of private property, and the family's hidden misery. Engels memorably concluded, "Since the bourgeois of Protestant countries are mostly philistines, all that this Protestant monogamy achieves . . . is a conjugal partnership of leaden boredom, known as 'domestic bliss.'"[73] On the subject of sex, he argued that only when both partners were on an equal footing could "sexual love" truly flourish. Bebel, affirming the need to satisfy sexual urges, was closer in spirit to Kollontai, even providing her with the famous analogy of eating and drinking.[74] He too believed in the free dissolution of relationships—not a call for profligacy, but something approaching what we today call serial monogamy.[75]

Well versed in these precedents, Kollontai parted company from her Soviet contemporaries only in the depth of her critique. Few explained exactly how political and socioeconomic liberation would affect personal relationships. They could write volumes on present ills, but gave little thought to sex in the future—a reticence that reflected optimism and presumed infallibility more than prudery. The future would be better because it would be communism. For such brevity they could find a precedent in Engels, who, starting a tradition well favored by Bolsheviks, described sexuality in the future mainly in terms of what it would not be:

> What we can now conjecture about the way in which sexual relations
> will be ordered after the impending overthrow of capitalist production is
> mainly of a negative character, limited for the most part to what will disappear. But what will there be new? That will be answered when a new

generation has grown up. . . . When these people are in the world, they will care precious little what anybody today thinks they ought to do; they will make their own practice and their corresponding public opinion about the practice of each individual—and that will be the end of it.[76]

However, Engels was wrong in assuming that closure could come so easily. It was precisely Kollontai's fictional illustration of what might be new that proved hardest for colleagues to digest. "Three Generations," one of three stories in *Love of the Worker Bees* (1923), chronicles the changes in attitudes toward marriage and sexual behavior brought by revolution through the story of three progressive women who rebel against their parents' moral conventions.[77] The first, Marya, left her husband; Olga, her daughter, pursued two sexual relationships simultaneously and has now entered into a common-law marriage with a third man, Andrei. Finally, Olga's daughter, Zhenya, gives new meaning to sexual rebellion. She has slept with her stepfather, Andrei, and is now pregnant (though she is not sure who the father is and plans to have an abortion). The story centers on Olga's appeal to the unnamed author to help her understand Zhenya's action. What upsets Olga most is that Zhenya seems to view sexual intercourse with cold rationality. Her daughter does not love Andrei, yet voluntarily had sex with him. Is Zhenya corrupt, or is Olga herself behind the times?

The author, Olga's friend, does not provide an answer. Rather, the story closes with her meeting Zhenya, where the reader is given the opportunity to "hear" firsthand the new generation of Soviets. For her, sex is something natural, a simple desire to be satisfied with whomever one wants. Her stepfather was a convenient partner or, simply, outlet: "I need Andrei about as much as I need this table here." Given her political activism, she has no time for love; it is an emotional drain that can only foster passion and jealousy, interfering with her work. The story ends ambiguously. On the one hand, Zhenya, like her mother, has gained professional and economic autonomy; she is defined not by her relation to a man but by her contributions to society. Here she embodies something of Kollontai's ideal: she is in control of her life and is not silent as to her sexual feelings. Moreover, her energy is directed to the collective, a point underscored by the final line, where she dismisses the whole discussion as distracting, since "we have work to do." On the other hand, Zhenya is not a mouthpiece for Kollontai, who disapproved of purely physical relationships. Where to situate Zhenya in Kollontai's argument is thus problematic. Still, Kollontai leaves no doubt in the story as to whether this young woman should be valued as a productive member of society. After all, Zhenya states that she loves Lenin more "than all the men I've slept with."

Alas, the affection was not returned. In his celebrated interview with the German Marxist Clara Zetkin, Lenin allegedly pounded the table when confronted with such frivolous questions. They were a distraction when the survival of the Soviet Union and the success of world revolution was at stake. "The Revolution demands concentration," Lenin declared. "It cannot tolerate orgiastic conditions."[78] Youth needed to discipline their bodies and minds; so much attention to sex was counterrevolutionary. Women "who confuse their personal romances with politics" or men "who run after every petticoat" could not be trusted to carry out the struggle. With Zetkin sitting in awe, Lenin assailed Kollontai and the "glass of water" theory; to equate satisfying a sexual urge as one would quench thirst was simply "un-Marxist," a notion that had "made our young people mad, quite mad." "Of course, thirst must be satisfied," he countered, "but will the normal man in normal circumstances lie down in the gutter and drink out of a puddle, or out of a glass with a rim greasy from many lips?"[79]

Most thought not—thereby turning Zhenya into an icon of sexual turpitude, a whore parading behind the mask of revolution. "Sanin in a skirt," came the charge, thus equating her with Artsybashev's protagonist in the eponymous novel of 1907 (which, arguably, was the closest Russia had yet come to de Sade's writing).[80] As David Lass commented from his polling of students published in 1928, Zhenya had abused the freedoms secured through revolution for her own sexual pleasure.[81] Students, he noted, "with their young healthy core," could resist such "many-stringed loves."[82] Yet in attacking a fictional character, Lass acknowledged her appeal. While Lenin's ex cathedra warning circulated widely after his death and became the canonical statement against Kollontai's ideas, something in Zhenya did speak to contemporary conditions—a point supported by many comments in Lass's poll. Indeed, the popularity of "Three Generations" caused critics like Zalkind to see it as a threat; young people might see Zhenya's behavior as "the sexual ideal."[83] Zalkind admitted that monogamy can be dull, but a search for sexual variety could become itself a "narcotic" to which Zhenya had fallen victim: "Apparently, Zhenya suffers from a moderate case of satyriasis [sic], a point which comrade Kollontai, it seems, forgot to remind us."[84]

For many critics, the story's ambiguity—the narrator does not condemn Zhenya—suggested that Kollontai was in allegiance with her heroine. Despite Marxist pretensions, her work was an undercover attempt to restore a bourgeois lifestyle. In a speech before the student body at Sverdlov Communist University, the president, Martyn Liadov, lambasted Kollontai as a Nietzschean holdover, promoting license in the name of revolution. He warned female students against her false theories of gender liberation; they only led to "degradation," returning them to the traditional role of woman as sex object.[85] Yaroslavsky also condemned *Love of the Worker Bees* as bourgeois and individualistic.[86] Others hinted at parallels with Kollontai's personal life by turning her logic inside out. If multiple lovers made a woman "proletarian," one posed, then why not include Cleopatra in that illustrious group?[87] And a doctor pointed out that Kollontai had not merely corrupted Marxist ideology, but sinned against science as well: "Worker bees are drones and, therefore, do not know what love is."[88]

Kollontai had struck a nerve. One attack cited the letters in *Pravda* addressed to Sofia Smidovich, which appeared two years after "Three Generations," as proof that an effort had to be made to combat "Kollontai types" among their ranks.[89] Young minds were too easily swayed by rhetoric presented in their name; they needed protection:

> We should simply ban all this rubbish on the [sex] question, allowing
> only strict scientific studies, discussion, and enlightenment. Otherwise
> we face an unpardonable mockery of youth: instead of therapy we get
> chit-chat with female readers from a "journal for housewives"; instead of
> eliminating the education of "young ladies" and students via poetry and
> novels, we get pseudo-Marxist analysis of "winged and wingless eros." . . .
> No more slander, Comrade Kollontai![90]

In 1924 Finogen Budnev detailed how Kollontai's "dangerous" literature harmed society. The pursuit of autonomy through multiple sexual partners could produce "invalids" plagued by sexual ailments and venereal diseases, or could lead to incest and degeneracy. Citing the commonly held notion that sexual energy was released at the expense of mental and physical development, Budnev warned that female readers could find themselves at age twenty, unlike Zhenya, permanently "emaciated, frayed and withered"; men by age twenty-five could become "sickly, bony, and bald."[91]

Yet Kollontai was not trying to graft illicit sex onto Marxism. In "Make Way for Winged Eros" she provided a taxonomic home and purpose for the protagonist of "Three Generations." Clearly Zhenya was not a role model; she is one of the "wingless," forced to decouple love and sex, but neither is she reckless in her behavior. Sex for Zhenya is less important than party work. At the same time, she is not a drone. Having a potential for love, she may metamorphose into the "winged" stage once conditions have changed. Certainly her bloodline is impeccable. Her grandmother and mother represent the pinnacle of political and personal achievement respective for each generation. Both are women of action who challenge convention in personal relationships. However, both are bound by a certain code. For the grandmother, one cannot love two people at once; for Olga, love has to accompany the sexual act. The endurance of this code after the revolution is what separates Zhenya from her mother.

Reading "Three Generations" through Kollontai's essays puts Zhenya's perceived transgressions in perspective. Of the three women, only Zhenya can be truly free because she shows that full liberation and equality are functions of social, economic, *and* moral change. Unlike her mother and grandmother, she will not live a life of deception or restriction; she can act upon her bodily needs without fear. She is not an egotistical delinquent, but a model of discipline; her emotional energy is not spent in fits of jealousy or passion but of love for the cause. In short, Zhenya has solved the sex problem simply because it neither interferes with work nor dictates her life.

This story occupies a logical place in Kollontai's overall thesis, as do the two other stories in *Love of the Worker Bees:* "Sisters," about prostitution, and "Vasilisa Malygina," about a husband's infidelity. In both her essays and her fiction Kollontai sought to come to terms with postrevolutionary society by castigating the ills of the past, illuminating difficulties of the present, but always pointing to the goals of the future.

However, none of this meant anything to her critics. A useful index of how far Kollontai was scapegoated lies in the misreading of her intentions. Her ideas were not just distorted but twisted into their opposite, and with impressive speed her public image of loyal Bolshevik degenerated into something of a bourgeois witch, casting a spell over youth by arguing that sexual license was the supreme gift of revolution. Such vitriol was necessary cover, because many attackers, in truth, actually shared her goals. Indeed, between volleys of character assassination, assaults against her often advanced remarkably similar proposals. A young member of the Komsomol, S. Shkotov, author of *The Daily Life of Youth* (1925), no doubt relished the opportunity to lambaste a superior as advocate of "bestial carnality" and "profligacy." After all, it put him in impressive company (the preface to his book was written by the prolific commissar of health, Nikolai Semashko). Yet we could also cite Shkotov for plagiarizing his target: "Love," he wrote, "is the honorable comradely and sexual relationships between a girl and a guy or two spouses." Echoing both Kollontai's recognition of a necessary sexual element in relationships and her suspicion of love's permanence, he continued in italics: "*There is not and cannot be an eternal, pure, ideal and non-sexual love.*" If lifelong fairy-tale love is essentially a fiction, then we should have the freedom to enter into and break off relationships throughout our lives. Shkotov hastily added that this was not the kind of free love that Kollontai ostensibly promoted (a different partner each day), rather it was based on mutual respect and common interests. With uncredited borrowing from Kollontai's "love-comradeship" ideal, he even concluded by deploring, like her, the debilitating gender stereotypes of males as superior, females as "harem-girl" objects of lust.[92]

The volume of criticism launched against Kollontai should not surprise us. Even before *Love of the Worker Bees,* she was sufficiently tainted. In 1918 she had disagreed with Lenin over the Brest-Litovsk Treaty, which pulled the Soviet state out of world war. Ominously, her lover and soon-to-be husband, Petr Dybenko, was arrested for treason shortly afterward. (He was exonerated but was executed by Stalin in 1938.) Because of her criticism of party bureaucracy and its growing elitism, in 1922 Kollontai was replaced as the head of Zhenotdel by Smidovich. Kollontai's allegiance with the Workers' Opposition was also a stain. Her support for this movement, which had the temerity to suggest that under Marxism workers should exercise more control, resulted in a permanent career shift to roving ambassador, the ultimate anywhere-but-here assignment, until 1945. Like others of her generation, Kollontai was in a sense too Marxist for her own good; faith in the letter of the doctrine made her a constant victim of realpolitik. Wings and bees were just the latest heresy.

It was also for many the most upsetting. Sex with stepfathers was going too far. The mere suggestion that youth were troubled over questions of sex was in itself slanderous. In seeking to "naturalize" the discussion of sex, Kollontai, it was commonly charged, overemphasized it. Particularly mean-spirited was the thirty-page response from a former close colleague, Polina Vinogradskaia, who skewered her in appropriate literary fashion as both the "George Sand" of the twentieth century and the "Verbitskaia of communist journalism."[93] The first was a convenient metaphor for the shameful woman author who lives the life of her fiction; the second identified the quality of that fiction: "Each story [of Kollontai's] reeks of pornography and the gutter press." Appealing to male colleagues, Vinogradskaia reduced the whole of Kollontai's feminist message to "down with men." "How should we respond," she challenged readers, "to all the unimaginable garbage whipped up by her? One can only ridicule it. Nothing else remains."[94]

Actually, as Vinogradskaia's article itself demonstrated, another path did remain. In what was to become the key methodological step in attacking fictional representations of sexual relations, documentary evidence was marshaled against Kollontai herself. Noting that as ambassador to Norway Kollontai had lost sight of how Soviet youth truly lived, Vinogradskaia cited polls from the Sverdlov Communist University to rescue students from slander: "We know of course that students today devote the bulk of their energy to studies. . . . The 'problem of love' does not play one-tenth the role in our lives as Comrade Kollontai would have it. . . . And even if there is some interest in questions of sex, then their interest is doubled if speaking of materialist theory, tripled if speaking of economics."[95] In the very next issue of *Young Guard* after the publication of "Make Way for Winged Eros," Ilya Lin, a member of the Komsomol, came to the rescue of workers. "Working youth don't think about any sex stuff," he snapped. Those who were doing *that* were "bourgeois fathers and sons." Everyone knew that the "working guy" was different. He "has his favorite girl whom he respects," and "their relationships are simple, without any misunderstandings." In an unwitting echo of Zhenya's own self-discipline and sense of proportion, he concluded that even if workers may be sexually involved, "all that happens unnoticeably. It takes up no time, occupies no space."[96]

A difficult thing, these statistics. A year later and in the same journal another reader came to Kollontai's defense. Not she, but rather Lin was blind to reality, S. Devenishsky charged. "You've got to take off those government-issue glasses, komsomolets Lin! . . . The categorical declaration of Comrade Lin is both amusing and untrue. Of course, working youth don't know of such words as 'eros,' but they know what sexual attraction is and it does occupy a large space. It's really noticeable in recreation halls, clubs, and so forth."[97] Or, as a student commented in responding to a Moscow university questionnaire, "Sex is the axis around which all people rotate."[98] And in answer to the demand that only "scientific studies" should be permitted to address the issue, a Dr. Tsukker stepped forward with an informational booklet, *Questions of the Sexual Behavior of Working Youth* (1926), in which he explicitly praised Kollontai's idea of "love-comradeship" as the way to eliminate bourgeois ills from Soviet society. Unprecedentedly, he also quoted Lenin's words from the Zetkin interview, thus suggesting that the ground between Lenin and Kollontai was closer than was admitted in political or ad hominem attacks.[99]

Zhenya's ascent guaranteed her creator's demise. Kollontai resurfaced in 1926 during debates over a new marriage code, but it was clear her authority had passed. (By then there were only scattered attacks against her and the crown of villainy had passed to others, primarily the writers Panteleimon Romanov, Lev Gumilevsky, and Sergei Malashkin.) Loss of prestige, however, did not mean that the impact of Kollontai's ideas had diminished. Her unwitting achievement was to provide Soviet culture with a sort of anti-canon in the polemics over sex. Her name and work would serve throughout the 1920s—much as Trotsky's did a decade later—as a metaphor for the incorrect, counterrevolutionary line. References to Kollontai's name, "eros" (winged or not), the "glass of water theory," and "Zhenya" became convenient pejoratives used by critics castigating the failings of others. Invoking any one of the four captured in shorthand officials' fears of a corrupted youth. Boiled down to its most simplistic form, here was the recipe for infection: a mistaken author possessed of mistaken ideas creates a flawed character who encourages the reader to engage in the same inappropriate behavior.

Threats to a Fragile Generation

The attacks on Kollontai's work, whether malicious slander or tragically accurate, framed the debate over young people themselves. An older generation could see them as either handicapped by their own iconoclastic enthusiasm or vulnerable to the decadence flourishing in quasi-capitalistic NEP society. Such concern must surely have conditioned Gorky's next contribution to the troubled waters of Bolshevism and sexuality. A few months after Kollontai's "Make Way for Winged Eros," Gorky published "About My First Love" (1923) in *Red Virgin Soil.* With an eye to his own checkered past, he sought to tailor his memoirs for a contemporary audience by drawing a sharp line between rebellion and sexual license. While he would not deny being sexually tempted as a youth, he had been able to resist, he said. At age twenty, he had been infatuated with Olga Kaminsky, a married woman ten years his elder, yet would not consummate their mutual attraction. The reason was clear.

> For me it would have been easier if I were simpler, more direct. But I believed that a relationship with a woman is not confined to the physiological act which I had witnessed in its impoverished, vulgar and animalistic form. That act filled me almost with repulsion, notwithstanding that I was a strong, quite romantic youth who possessed an easily excitable imagination.[100]

Like David Khanin, Gorky assured readers of his masculinity. He continually interrupted his narrative to comment on Kaminsky's physical charms and included such clichés as "All that is beautiful in the world was born of the love for a woman" or, when embracing her, "If I hadn't held on to her so strongly I would've flown out the window like a soap bubble." Nevertheless, the sanctity of the sexual act remained inviolate. Gorky the rebel, yes; profligate, no. A central achievement of his youth, it seems, was that he had preserved his virginity, and, with recourse to the usual trope of the old guard, now believed that restraint had ennobled him. A constant theme in *My Universities*, to which this recollection was appended, is his disgust at the depravity he had witnessed in his travels through prerevolutionary Russia. He underscores the pitfalls into which sex can lead the young and the unwary. However, again like Khanin, he flounders in his own self-created ambiguity. He admits that he met Kaminsky again, and this time abandoned all pretenses to asceticism. They began living together in Nizhny Novgorod, during which time she was his "first woman." Bliss, though, quickly eroded as Gorky launched his writing career and they grew apart. (Her worst crime was falling asleep as he read her one of his stories.) They separated; Gorky became the famous writer-cum-revolutionary and, after marrying Katerina Pavlovna, set himself up for a new scandal with Maria Andreeva in America.

When contradictions and embarrassment infiltrate even the more orthodox memoirs of youth, we can see how problematic the issue of sex was at the time. To be sure, Gorky himself was a paradoxical figure. In the months following the October Revolution, he became the voice of internal dissent on the pages of *New Life,* speaking out against the Bolsheviks' propensity for violence, suppressing freedom of speech and disregarding individual rights. To him in 1917, Lenin was a "cold-blooded trickster who spare[d] neither the honor nor the life of the proletariat." The revolution itself, he feared, had been premature, forced on the people before they had matured culturally and morally, and was thus destroying them in an "inhuman experiment."[101] For such "traitorous" comments, the paper was shut down in the summer of 1918, the same day the Romanovs were executed. Despondent, Gorky soon retreated to Italy where he continued to negotiate a tricky balance between support for the proletariat and skepticism of the Soviet state's policies.

On sex, however, Gorky maintained a strict tone, perhaps trying to atone for his past, and painted himself in the same ascetic colors that marked his hero, Pavel Vlasov, in *Mother.* Yet the threat of "animalism" he so disdained in "About My First Love" struck once more, this time in Sorrento, where his peace was shattered one night by jazz music broadcast over the radio—in his words, it was "a wild shriek, whistle, thunder, howl, shout and crash," like "a horse neighing, the grunts of a metallic pig, or the lustful croaking of an enormous frog." This "chaos" brought to mind "an orchestra of crazies, driven mad by sex and directed by a kind of man-stallion waving a gigantic phallus." The randy words sound uncharacteristic of Gorky, but not perhaps for a sixty-year-old revolutionary forced to recognize that modernism was more than technological and social innovation. Jazz not only sounded like bestial sex, it drove listeners to the same, causing them to "cynically shake their hips in vile simulation of a man copulating with a woman." Gorky withstood the test; indeed, sexual temptation was no longer a question for him. But this did not mean there wasn't a lesson for others. With jazz coursing through Soviet cities, vulgarity again might corrupt the sanctity of love which, he reminded readers of *Pravda,* separated human beings from even "the smartest of animals."[102]

Like this warning, Gorky's memoirs were also written for the present, exemplifying the fear that by its own behavior the new generation was endangering itself and, by extension, endangering the revolution. Ego and energy were a potentially volatile combination in the hands of those surrounded by bourgeois influences or ideological diversions. That the stakes were high became dramatically clear during the Kremlin in-fighting that broke out shortly before Lenin's death in 1924. Dismayed by the rising bureaucratization of the party and its increasing intolerance for internal debate, Trotsky repeatedly warned that a complacent old guard would ossify and inhibit the implementation of true revolution. Most daringly, he proposed that the remedy lay in a synthesis between the new blood of young communists and the wisdom and experience of the old. This was, in so many words, an attempt to block the ascendancy of Stalin (currently allied with fellow Politburo members Grigory Zinoviev and Lev Kamenev). Yet it also endorsed the supposed failings of party youth: initiative, defiance, and a refusal to kowtow to the party hierarchy. What young Soviet—equal parts Bolshevik and just plain revolutionary—would not have been stirred by the summons contained in Trotsky's letter, "The New Course," published, of all places, in *Pravda*?

> It is completely insufficient for youth just to repeat our formulas. They must energize themselves, turn formulas into flesh and blood, and work out for themselves their own opinion and identity; they must be free to fight for this opinion with that courage which comes from sincere conviction and independence of character. We must rid the Party of mass obedience, knee-jerk emulation of authority, uniformity, subservience, and careerism! A Bolshevik is not only a person of discipline; no, he is a person who in getting to the bottom of everything forms his own firm opinion in each case, and he defends it courageously and independently not only in battle against enemies but inside his own organization.[103]

With exhortations such as these, Trotsky became a patron saint in many circles of communist youth. His logic was too savory to ignore: young Bolsheviks could assist their superiors precisely by exercising independence of mind and voice. Challenging one's elders was not just appealing; it was for their own good. "Only the constant interaction of the older generation with the younger in the context of party democracy," continued Trotsky, "can preserve the old guard as a revolutionary force."

The result of Trotsky's letter was a predictable firestorm. Some party members were elated, particularly students, from whom he received substantial electoral support for the upcoming Thirteenth Party Conference, held in January 1924. Yet Trotsky's challenge in "The New Course" destroyed any last chance (if it was not too late already) at accommodation with the Stalin triumvirate that controlled the Central Committee. With his words taken as a summons for generational conflict, Trotsky became simply a heretic and was lambasted in absentia at the conference, with Emelian Yaroslavsky taking a prominent role in the denunciation. Students themselves were subjected to a massive purge.[104] Even this political confrontation could not escape being re-encoded as a sexual one. The year that witnessed Trotsky's final countdown to defeat, 1926, saw the publication of Sergei Malashkin's novella, "Moon on the Right," (discussed in chapter 4), demonstrating that it was precisely the hedonistic students who were enamored of him.

We can never know just how profligate Soviet youth were in the decade following the revolution, how many equated political and social revolution with sexual license, whether a significant number were "radishes," or how many thought Marx was a philistine. Not all were the heroes declaimed by Khanin, yet neither were they the degenerates envisioned by Kulle. Overall behavior was certainly not of the riotous, libertine nature that red scare America feared. But what does matter is the qualitative perception, as the Trotsky uproar confirmed, of a troubled, sometimes deviant, and certainly vulnerable generation. Young communists no doubt believed in the idea of a socialist future, but clarity was the first casualty of revolution. Capitalist bourgeois traditions had been fractured, yet socialist ones were still inchoate. The dangers inherent in this volatile mix were acknowledged by the party early and often, as with the following statement of 1920: "Old, foul norms of the family and marriage have collapsed, and each day brings us closer to their full destruction. Yet there are no upstanding pillars for the creation of new, beautiful, and healthy relations. We just have an unimaginable bacchanalia. Free love is understood by the best of people as free debauchery."[105]

The crisis in society and sexual behavior was connected to a crisis in representation: youth as yet had nothing to turn to that would showcase "the upstanding pillars." This statement foreshadowed how, in that perennial cliché of Russian culture, literature would become the guiding light of reform. But as a valued source of edification, literature too, as we have seen with Kollontai, could just as easily be seen as exacerbating the problem if it diverged, ever so slightly, from a norm that was itself subject to rebuttal and modification. The sheer volume of attention from all quarters of the Soviet media ensured a fractious and sometimes contradictory diversity of opinion regarding the "proper path." As events would demonstrate, even among those in the Komsomol and party hierarchy, unanimity of purpose was conspicuously absent.

What united disparate perceptions, however, was a genuine concern over the sexual behavior of youth. However exaggerated their rhetoric, party officials, doctors, sociologists, writers, and cultural critics feared that sexual excess could jeopardize the ideological and physical health of a generation and thus threaten the advent of communism. And although they may have contradicted each other in the process, they fervently sought to contain the idea of revolution, to keep its meaning pure, and to rechannel the energy unleashed by an ethos of liberation. This would not be an easy task, since it required a strategy for persuading youth to renounce the very spirit of rebellion that gives revolution its romantic sheen. In the Soviet 1920s, social liberation and personal libertarianism were two antagonistic children of the revolutionary spirit. An antidote had to be found to the selfish, hedonistic freedom that some young people assumed had been inaugurated in 1917, a mentality condemned by Bukharin as "spit wherever you want."[106]

CHAPTER 3

Fashioning a Code

The Marxian Legacy

O NLY four years after the revolution, Boris Pilnyak, author of some of the most disturbing narratives of the revolutionary period, introduced readers to a new protagonist, Comrade Ordynina, in "Ivan and Maria" (1921). As a member of the Zhenotdel and the secret police, she appears in the requisite leather jacket with revolver in hand. According to dress code metonymics, this costume confirms her ruthless loyalty to the revolution. Her dedication enables her to unflinchingly execute prisoners in the basement of a jail. With equal sang-froid, she announces her position on sex:

> I understand and excuse those men who have slept with women and then, after getting married, are distraught if it turns out their wife isn't a virgin. This is why. Ninety-nine times out of a hundred a woman giving herself up for the first time brings to it her body and soul—all of which she bestows on the man. The man, before marriage, goes to a woman embarrassed, like a thief, feeling that he is doing something base and dirty and buries his soul deep. Afterwards he is tortured by this theft and washes himself of it. Only to his wife does he come body and soul so as to create, as is most often the case, something holy, chaste, and thereby atone for his past. For him to then find out that she has already sacrificed her soul and sanctity for another is unbearable. . . . I don't belong to those ninety-nine.[1]

As champion of the one-percent minority, a "body only" woman, Ordynina anticipates Kollontai's Zhenya, and critics rushed to save the country from yet another heretic. Pilnyak was excoriated for daring to infuse the revolution with raw sexuality. He was "the Homer of syphilitics," the herald of "Artsyba-shevian obscenity," the merchant of "shameless pornography."[2] A second strike against him was that his style approached that of James Joyce in its density and word play. It was difficult for the average reader to make sense of his writing, except for certain lewd parts of the narrative. Incomprehensible as art yet with its vulgarity clear for all to see, two workers declared that Pilnyak's work was good for only one purpose: toilet paper.[3]

Although critics sought to drive a wedge between Pilnyak and a chaste image of the revolution, his early work captured what the revolution really was: a violent tempest that engulfed all ideological banners and beliefs. If the Bolshevik literary canon preferred the unquestionable triumph of principle, Pilnyak glorified the id. "Ivan and Maria" is a paean to Dionysian release. Its deliberately confused plot and chronology reflect the fury unleashed in the country and among the people by war. The unparalleled brutality of revolution and civil war strips everyone of cover and pretense. Pilnyak's two favorite metaphors for revolution come not from Marx but from nature: the wolf and the winter storm. Sex is but another symbol of pure elementalism. In Pilnyak's work people do not just speak of sex or engage in it; the whole revolution is sexualized. Russia, the once "beautiful woman," is "poor, unclothed, and hungry."[4] Sexuality defines the country's inhabitants, politics, and traumatic experience. It is the one metaphor that can describe all. Bolshevik rhetoric, mangled and misunderstood in Pilnyak's writing, cannot contain or explain bloody anarchy.

Like the nation, Ordynina is torn by a conflict between revolutionary devotion and sexual liberation—a clash typical of her generation. She is a pagan as much as a commissar. A princess before the revolution, she can shed the leather jacket and, dressed all in black, become a Circe who entrances men. A self-proclaimed romantic, she is also a sadist who, when the order comes, arrests her lover and drills his head with a bullet—an act that brings her physical pleasure. In the most provocative lines of the text—indeed, of the whole decade—Ordynina declares Marxism to be blind to the truth of 1917:

> Karl Marx was mistaken. He took into account only physical hunger, not the other mover in the world: love, love as in blood, reproduction. Sex, family, birth—mankind did not err in idolizing sex. Yes, there is physical hunger and sexual hunger. . . .
>
> I feel that the whole world, all culture, the whole of mankind, all things, chairs, cabinets, clothes are infused with sex. . . . I am not alone. Sometimes my head spins and I feel that the whole revolution, the whole revolution smells . . . of sexual organs.[5]

Pilnyak, remarkably, was not alone in making this charge. Others also hinted that Marx was ignorant of sexual realities. In Anatoly Glebov's "Inga" (1930), he is contrasted not with Dionysus but Freud. Teasing his communist colleagues, Nemtsevich, a forty-five-year-old engineer, lets them in on a secret: "You Marxists don't value Freud. Speaking truthfully, if you look at it objectively, does Marx really rule the world? . . . Freud, my friend, Freud. Not class, but sex."[6]

To be fair, these accusations, which bookend the decade, were not entirely correct. In *The Communist Manifesto* (1848) Marx had mentioned sex, but only obliquely. It was not the communists who would collectivize women, he remarked; commodification of females already existed in bourgeois society:

> Nothing is more ridiculous than the virtuous indignation of our bourgeois at the community of women which, they pretend, is to be openly and officially established by the Communists. The Communists have no need to introduce community of women; it has existed almost from time immemorial.
>
> Our bourgeois, not content with having the wives and daughters of their proletarians at their disposal, not to speak of common prostitutes, take the greatest pleasure in seducing each other's wives.[7]

For all its grandstanding, this outburst contributed little. Specifics and bombast operated in inverse reciprocity. The fewer the former, the more the latter. Marx did not attempt to address how the proletariat might behave under a new order; the implication remained only that adultery, seduction, and the objectification of women would disappear under communism. Perhaps suspecting that this was too utopian, he quickly moved on to the more heady subject of nationalism.[8]

Reticence was the specter haunting the Marx-Engels legacy on sexual matters, and this fact did not help Bolshevik leaders make sense of the chaos wrought by upheaval and war. It seems that most were caught off guard when the subject exploded after 1917. Almost waxing nostalgic, Emilian Yaroslavsky noted that before the revolution they had no time or energy for such trivial concerns. Their lives were devoted to underground activity and recruitment; they themselves suffered imprisonment and exile.[9] Much to his chagrin, however, the revolution did not change the fact that human nature would still assert its own. When pressure from both inside and outside party ranks made the "accursed question" of sex too great to ignore, Bolshevik leaders sought to fill the gap, assisted by scores of sociologists, doctors, and other experts. Indeed, Marx's relative silence on the subject gave them near carte blanche to address the issue as they saw fit.

Most chose the most expedient route: a discursive divide and conquer. Whatever questions youth might pose, behavior could always be reduced to the desirable and undesirable, reflecting the binarism of a good proletariat versus a bad bourgeoisie. Lenin provided the backbone for this mentality with his famous dictum to the Komsomol in 1920 that the definition of moral behavior was whatever benefited the revolution.[10] Following suit, Aron Zalkind presented an argument in his compendium, "Ethics, *Byt* and Youth" (1927), that wasted no time with sophisticated strategies of persuasion:

> The natural sciences instead of the bible, talmud, or koran; the [Komsomol] club instead of the church, synagogue or temple; red ties and portraits of Lenin instead of crosses and amulets—all this is new *byt*. To quit swearing, gambling, drinking, fighting; the club instead of bars—all this too is new *byt*. . . . To teach yourself and others proper hygiene with regard to one's body, clothes, place of living, linen, food; a fierce battle with dirt no matter where it may be; to train, strengthen and forge oneself; to organize all of one's physiological processes; to put the brake of class frugality on the sexual profligacy left us by the bourgeoisie and to transfer those reserves of energy to cultural activity; to give up this ridiculous smoking and drinking—all this is the new *byt* of society.[11]

The distinction between good and bad behavior was made sacrosanct by its attachment to class categories. "Proletarian" became shorthand for hard work, devotion to the cause, modesty, self-discipline, respect for others, good grooming, proper speech, and politeness. All else was condemned. In his 1927 dissection of the petty-bourgeois philistine, Mikhail Reisner revealed that whatever the utility of class as a sociological concept, in practice it functioned primarily to demarcate the reprehensible from the acceptable. Essentially anyone who ran afoul of the reigning orthodoxy was a philistine. These included the sycophant, the bureaucrat, the drunkard, the rumor-monger, one who marries for mercenary reasons, the fascist, the kulak, and finally both the extreme individualist and the total conformist. The philistine was both a coward and fanatic; simultaneously an egoist and faceless "screw in the capitalist machine"; an anarchic beast and thrifty rationalist. A devotee of pornography and prostitution, the philistine also worshiped literature "about the sanctity of marriage" and films with "heroes of spousal fidelity and female chastity." He was obsessed with his family yet "did not know love," since bourgeois domestic life was a sham with artificial "sentimentality covering [mutual] exasperation and malice." Philistinism was, in sum, a category for all that was negative.[12]

Class terminology immediately raised the stakes for personal behavior. Days of mere mischief-making were gone; now a student's everyday activities were defined in the same terms used for social conflict, class war, and revolution. It was a new world in which being rude to girls or not wearing a tie could be momentous decisions. Grafting class terminology onto personal life was predictable—for what other language did Bolsheviks know?—and something of a theoretical coup. For the true proletarian, good behavior was a priori; thus, if a proletarian (or anyone with similar class consciousness) did anything destructive or wasteful, the cause for such a departure lay outside the working class. Ideological sin and sexual deviance were the result of bourgeois influence. In a pure environment, the working class would never exhibit unhealthy, degenerate sexual activity. In fact, the indigenous sexual identity of the proletariat was diametrically opposed to that of the bourgeoisie. Mixing the two was akin to violating natural law. In a work written at the request of universities, Zalkind memorably declared, "Sexual attraction to a class-hostile, morally repugnant object is as corrupt as being sexually attracted to a crocodile or orangutan."[13]

The class paradigm also explained why the ideal had not yet been achieved. Everyone recognized that the revolution had not eradicated all vestiges of bourgeois society; indeed, much of the Soviet economy of the 1920s was still capitalist and nearly all citizens had been born in a society dominated by bourgeois values. It was therefore easy to explain sexual excesses and abominations after 1917. Blame could be placed on bourgeois remnants who had littered the Soviet Union with their decadent dress, art, and ideas like free love. Who had fiendishly injected the "revolutionary laboring masses with a sexual narcotic?" Zalkind asked. The bourgeoisie, of course. Sex had become a new opiate of the masses. This was why proletarian teenagers continued to masturbate as frequently as bourgeois youth. (However, others cited a reported decrease in masturbation among the proletariat as evidence of an improved social environment.)[14] "Bourgeois traps" could also explain why male workers still frequented prostitutes, used wives only for their gratification, had affairs, and cultivated a taste for pornography. Only with the advent of true socialism, free of all cultural toxins, class distinctions, and private property, would society receive a clean bill of sexual health.

Even Kollontai could agree with this. Her story "Soon (in 48 Years)" (1922) presented a utopia in which youth have been reformed, physically and morally. By 1970, she predicted, there would be no smoking, swearing, disrespect, or conflict; no hint of Zhenya and, most surprising, no mention of sex.[15] Sexuality itself would be neutralized; people would fall in love and procreate, but these functions would not affect how people thought, dressed, and behaved. Most important, it would not curb productivity. Communism and love were not antagonistic. Anatoly Lunacharsky, commissar of education, in 1925 sang the praises of the romance to come:

> Love constitutes life's great jewel. It makes nature bloom, parade its colors, sing the most wonderful songs and dance the most magnificent dances. We know that humanity, freed from slavery and toil, will not become gray and prosaic. On the contrary, from sexual love will blossom chefs-d'oeuvre of happiness and pleasure, about which men and women of previous generations could not even dream. In the future men and women will create a grand poem of love.[16]

Anxious to combat the image of dissolute youth, many sought evidence that such roots were already forming. S. Shkotov, a member of the Komsomol who had earlier excoriated Kollontai, was ecstatic at how rural youth, in his eyes, had turned the tables only eight years after the revolution. In one village, he reported, vodka no longer dominated social events, rather newspaper reading and political discussions. What was most important, there was fun to be had in all this. "Women who go to Komsomol parties are quite satisfied." Why? Because "one can observe concretely" how the attitude of the opposite sex had changed. "The guys have quit sleeping with the girls."[17] (Some reformers were eager to believe in the idyll of peasant life immune to urban-bourgeois decadence, and in these circumstances doubts that workers could learn from peasants, the most "backward element" of society, in Soviet opinion, were generally overlooked.)[18] For those skeptical of such a portrait, Shkotov saw in Lenin and his wife, Nadezhda Krupskaia, the ideal having come to life: "He lived almost thirty years with Nadezhda Konstantinovna and it would be difficult to find a more happy marriage. That was a true union of two comrades, united by the same work and goals; it was a union based on complete, limitless respect and true love for each other."[19] The first couple of communism exemplified what should be. Indeed, Shkotov's comment about Lenin's marital felicity appeared verbatim in Martyn Liadov's speech to students at Sverdlov Communist University in the same year.[20] Ignoring the rumors of Lenin's affair with Inessa Armand, Sofia Smidovich explicitly contrasted his marriage with that of the stereotypical bourgeois couple: philandering husband and loose wife. The relationship between Lenin and Krupskaia was so strong that it "negated the possibility" of the temptation to wander.[21] Zalkind also assured youth that they could aspire to the same level of achievement: "Comrade Lenin is not a miracle; he is the same as we, only a much higher, concentrated product of history."[22]

Officials had little else to offer beyond extolling the example of the perfect couple (though Lenin, who died in 1924, would likely have been repelled by these accolades). For specific questions regarding the frequency of sexual intercourse, the alarming effects of masturbation, or the "safe" age to begin sexual relations, they could turn for guidance to science and medicine. Intimate relationships were a more nebulous affair, however, involving psychology, sociology, economics, and politics. Sex, it was quite clear, should occur in a loving, committed relationship, exhibited by Ketlinskaia and Slepkov in one of the few optimistic parts of *Life Out of Control* (1929). "Ever since I've fallen in love, and she with me, my strength has increased tenfold," one Komsomol member cheerfully told the interviewers, "I want to move mountains; at work I'm always up in spirits; in the evening we share and advise each other. After all, she's an activist too; we talk about and discuss everything."[23] But whether such bliss required marriage, whether it should be a "romantic" experience, proved stumbling blocks. As Lunacharsky daringly observed, switching to dry prose, "if a man has had to change [sic] several women while at his peak and that doesn't reflect ill on either him or society, then there is no reason to defend monogamy."[24]

While experts might not agree on sexual guidelines for the new social order, all recognized the corruption of what "had been." Few diverged from Marx, Engels, and Bebel in castigating bourgeois conventions regulating courtship, marriage, and sexual mores. Attacks against the "bourgeois inheritance" focused on the vital principle that environment was everything, a conviction at the core of Marx's historical materialism as interpreted by the Soviets. Although Lenin, Stalin, and others would drastically modify the concept for their own purposes, environmentalism remained the mainstay of much Bolshevik thought in the 1920s. Viewed pessimistically, it was determinism made supreme, reducing human beings to victims of their surroundings, both natural and social. Optimistically, it was a tool of broad explanatory power, for in one stroke it dispensed with the nature-versus-nurture dilemma. Translated into practice, it overturned common assumptions of personal motivation and responsibility, leading to dramatic rewritings of the law.[25]

A striking change was the decriminalization of homosexuality. This reform was the product of a conscious libertarian effort that belies the assumption that the party leadership was dominated by puritans.[26] In an illustrated work entitled *Sexual Crimes* (1927), E. P. Frenkel, a high school teacher, captured this sentiment in her first sentence, which asserted that no law should infringe upon sexual expression: "A person has the right to free self-determination in the area of sexual relations."[27] The absence of homosexuality from criminal codes later in the decade was proof for her that only in the Soviet Union did true liberation reign. She cited scientific and legal arguments to the effect that "homosexual intercourse with adults does not violate anyone's rights as the latter are [recognized as] free to express their sexual feelings in any form; the invasion of the law into this area only reflects the legacy of church opinion and the ideology of sin."[28] While Frenkel's idealism outstripped Soviet reality (homosexuals could be persecuted in the 1920s for "violating the public order"), it reflects how a mainstay of Bolshevik thought could empower voices outside the canonical center.[29] Conventional morality that proscribed homosexuality and adultery was to Frenkel the product of a discredited and (at least in the Soviet Union) disappearing bourgeois society.

Man as Machine

Faith in environmental determinism provided authorities with two rhetorical luxuries that made their task easier in addressing sexual behavior. First, questions about sexual mores could be shifted to the socioeconomic domain, to which authorities were more accustomed. Yaroslavsky linked the early appearance of sexual feelings in youth (which was regarded as a primary cause of "abnormal" behavior) with current living conditions: "We must take into account that overcrowded housing plays a huge role in this matter: youth are forced to live with fathers and mothers in the same room where sexual needs are taken care of, directly in the presence of children, right before their eyes."[30] Like Frenkel, he saw an obvious solution: if behavioral problems can be traced exclusively to external factors, they can also be solved by altering the environment. Stimulate industrial growth and thus alleviate cramped housing conditions. In his address to students (cited above), Liadov cautioned that strong sexual urges at a young age were not natural. Such impulses were the fault of bourgeois influences and the debilitating effects of civil war. Relieved of wartime suffering and deprivation, in the 1920s people had fallen prey to "film, theater, and literature" with their overriding message extolling "the pleasure of sexual intercourse." Citing fellow communists now under criminal prosecution, Liadov identified a common characteristic: "Each of them in the past had a series of relationships which in the end undermined their will and forced them onto the path of criminality."

The second luxury was even more comforting. Communism itself would bring deliverance from this "accursed question." Against the bright lights of the utopian state, sexual problems would simply disappear in a grand withering away of doubt, confusion, and tension, as Engels had envisioned. Interpersonal relations in the future would be correct simply because they would occur under communism. Such a presumption of infallibility certainly marks Zalkind, who after devoting several treatises to the subject eventually dismissed the matter with a stroke of the pen. In the near future, he wrote, "the sexual question will receive its complete and ideal resolution." Since the revolution had been victorious, "we will be victorious in this matter as well."[31] As with Yaroslavsky's concerns over inadequate housing, his main thrust was to turn the tables. If communism would resolve all, the answers to questions about sexual behavior lay elsewhere, in the greater application of oneself to the class war. The more attention devoted to the cause, the sooner all could enjoy Lunacharsky's blossoms of love.

Armed in such fashion, Zalkind, Yaroslavsky, and a cohort of others in the party could feel confident in tackling the libertarian currents circulating among youth. Shocked at the defensive claims of a right to privacy by wayward members of the Komsomol, the journal *Young Communist* lashed back: "There should not be any division between an individual member's life and that of the collective. All foreign territory must be annulled."[32] Once again, authorities denied the legitimacy of private concerns by redefining them in ominous terms. The autonomous individual was a false concept in Soviet thought; whether conscious of it or not, one was always the representative of something beyond the self, and by extension one was either an adherent or a foe of the revolution. Lenin's morality speech to the Komsomol, on the surface only a word of advice, was basically a strategic maneuver to redefine youth in this fashion. Never were young people to see themselves as sovereign or their bodies as separate from society's interests; every facet of life, behavior, speech, and dress was either for or against October. In short, while the sexual instinct in human beings may belong to biology, its manifestation did not. What one did, and with whom, was not only shaped by the environment, it affected it as well. Therefore it was false to believe like Comrade Ordynina in Pilnyak's story that sex was a separate hunger, something outside the ken of Marxism. As A. Divilkovsky argued, because the dialectic was all-knowing and all-seeing, nothing was exempt.

> Regarding the question of sex, one cannot make "physiological needs" the supreme arbiter. On the contrary, a dialectal perspective must be observed in these circumstances. Then it becomes obvious that the supreme arbiter is the need to construct socialism in our country of Soviets and to conduct class warfare with slave-owning imperialism in the whole world.[33]

To be sure, he added, it would be ideal if the two needs concurred, but they didn't. And when conflict arose, which one should rule was clear.

Give the times, the notion of a "positive sex life" did not make sense.[34] "Good sex" had nothing to do with individual pleasure but was concerned solely with what benefited society. Under Dr. A. L. Berkovich's plan for the complete "rationalization of sexual behavior," published in *The Young Guard* shortly after the appearance of "Make Way for Winged Eros," physical intimacy had no other purpose than the "creation of healthy, robust descendants." One's choice of partner, method, and frequency of relations were issues of truly strategic significance, since choices made at the personal level were joined in a common pattern of behavior that affected human evolution. Until the present time, the record was quite mediocre. Therefore, Berkovich argued that good, socially forward-looking sex should be thought of as delivering us from former evils:

> The correct resolution of the question of normal sexual behavior should lead to concern over the necessity not only of saving humankind from vices, perversions and diseases connected with the past capitalist-bourgeois state (venery, prostitution, and physical and moral degeneration), but also of finding the proper path to making healthy and improving our race—a concern that points us to the fundament of a new science: eugenics.[35]

Eugenics (a term that had not yet acquired a chilling connotation) was a logical extension of elevating society's welfare over individual demands. The idea of genetic engineering was at this time an intriguing concept for many—including many in the United States, Berkovich noted—for it signaled progress and deliverance from a host of human deficiencies. Just as 1917 ushered in an improved socioeconomic system, the revolution would also lay the groundwork for similar improvement of the human body. Whereas some might protest the prohibition of marriage for those who might impede evolutionary progress ("epileptics, the mentally ill, degenerate types, and others"), the answer for him was clear. Complete rationalization had no room for ethical qualms; what was right and what was wrong should be decided on whether something benefited the greater good or not. Everyone had to make sacrifices; the main thing was not to forget the rewards to come. And, he reminded his young readers, the responsibility for seeing these utilitarian principles through fell on their shoulders. If youth behaved properly there would be a better future. His hopes almost sound as if they came from Kollontai's pen:

> Our communist youth organizations should be the foundries in which are forged new relationships between the sexes, a new ideal of sexual love leading to free unions, based on feelings of passion, friendship, respect, and the conscious acknowledgment of responsibility toward one another, one's children, one's comrades, one's class, and the cause of socialism.[36]

In reducing human beings to breeders of future stock, Berkovich (like many others) did not find it degrading to see people as "cogs" in the greater machine of Soviet society. We recall Ivanova's proud use of the term as she tried to fend off Bukharin-toting communists with lustful eyes on her body. It was precisely her desire to be one with society that underlay her self-hatred after her own fall. Such a definition could be seen as elevating, for who within Soviet ranks did not wish to be productive and disciplined? This machine morality reflected the common belief that the best model for a problem-free, efficient community was the factory. The communist future wed technology with ideology. Just as their revolution would destroy the social conditions that inhibited the establishment of earthly paradise, technology could conquer the material problems. Industrial achievement would eliminate want; mechanized agriculture would abolish hunger; science would conquer disease. The reformation of Soviet citizens would proceed in the same direction. For the most impassioned devotees of the cult of the machine, the human body was itself hampered by waste and misdirection.[37] Forced amelioration, Berkovich assumed, would change the human race itself. If Engels demonstrated that human beings had evolved from more primitive forms through labor, Soviet theorists predicted another qualitative jump. In *Literature and Revolution* (1925), Trotsky envisioned a future organism still known as human but in complete mastery of its bodily functions, with everything internal and external controlled by reason. The new creature would be, in his words, "a superman."[38]

Transferring this concept to the issue of sex was a logical step. Questions about sexual expression and energy could be explained by biology, physics, and economics. The key lay in the human body itself, which was more than a mere organism. As A. Timofeev explained in *Where Youth Should Direct Their Sexual Energy* (1926), we are more creatures of industry than of nature:

> If we are to compare the human body with anything, then it is best to use the most accurate analogy: the machine at work. If a machine, for example, runs on steam energy, then one can stoke it up only a specific limit, beyond which it can be damaged, break down or blow up. The more energy that builds up in the machine, the more it expends. But it does not create reserves; any surplus is not retained. All the work of a machine consists solely of the process of transforming received energy into motion, light, heat and so on.
>
> The human organism is also a manufacturer. Its work is usually expressed both as the production of items for society (beginning with the most vital and ending with those of science and the arts) and as the ex-

penditure of that strength, required for its sustenance. The human heart can serve as an example of this; it begins beating when the baby is still in the womb and shuts down at the person's last breath. Over seventy years of human life it produces a huge quantity of work.

Just like the machine, the human body does not store reserves of energy, but seeks to expend it in some kind of labor. Thus insufficient energy results in an insufficient, slack work; conversely, a large amount of energy (but still normal for the given organism) should express itself in a substantial product, because surplus cannot be maintained for an effective length of time. It strives to exert itself.[39]

Timofeev's guidebook was part of a series entitled "What You Need to Know about Sex," a paean to the mechanics of human life. Although he draws an analogy between the body and the machine, he does not equate the two. This was a reluctant acknowledgment of our physical limitations. Like a machine, the body can expend only a finite amount of energy; however, it has too many outlets of expenditure, both physical and mental. Turning one turbine means less energy for another. Nor are all turbines of equal importance. A few are vital and must be constantly fueled (heart, lungs); those for more specific tasks are used only as needed (such as muscles to grip a hammer). The problem is that the brain, the core of rationality that should regulate expenditure, is still not up to the task. In the future, Timofeev conceded, we may become masters of our internal circuitry. But until we reach that level of "technological self-control," our energy is too often wasted on "the path of least resistance."[40]

The path in question was sexual gratification. In reducing the body to an input-output apparatus and sex to a questionable expenditure, Timofeev and others had on their side not only ideology but also contemporary science. In "The Biological Bases of Sexual Behavior" (1925), Ivan Ariamov patiently explained how the external emission of hormonal production threatened overall fitness.[41] Another put special value on semen because of its allegedly high phosphorous content, an element believed to be critical for brain functioning.[42] Drawing from this, Dr. E. B. Demidovich cast aside pedantry and directly addressed her reader (who was likely surprised by the intentional pun):

> Until twenty-five years old, the organism is growing, and this growth demands material and energy. Yet these are expended in sexual activity as well. What is lost, principally, is the "cream" of that construction material which goes to the brain's development and growth. By engaging in sex so early, you have squandered your own construction material, drained off energy and retarded your growth, just as would any living creature which begins sexual activity without having fully matured. . . .

In this manner your sexual behavior has undermined not only your own strength but that of the working collective as well.[43]

To enforce his point, Timofeev cited the example of Peter the Great, a name guaranteed to attract the attention of young men. Active hormones, he wrote, assure that "a given person has a superior capacity for engaging in sexual intercourse but alongside this they also heighten characteristic gender traits—for example with boys, strength and vigor. A striking example of someone of this kind is one of the emperors of tsarist Russia, Peter I, a great debaucher and exceptionally strong and hardworking man."[44] On second thought, Timofeev added, "It's understood that the reader should not conclude from this example that profligacy, that is, the predilection for sexual excess, always accompanies strength." On the one hand, youth need not fear bodily urges as they matured. Sexual energy is to be welcomed precisely because it is an index of one's physical and mental potential; witness the sloth-like appearance and behavior of castrati in history. On the other hand, advanced physical and mental development could be realized only if that same energy were directed elsewhere. Having argued himself into an impasse, Timofeev ended on a patriotic note: "Youth should subordinate questions of sex, sexual need, and sexual activity to the interests of the proletariat's class struggle. The class struggle demands fighters; class construction demands builders; the proletariat needs youth, strong and healthy, full of civic enthusiasm who do not waste energy."[45]

Timofeev retreated to these platitudes as an uncompromising answer to the dire situation in which youth found themselves. Soviet society was polluted, dangling before the eager eyes of youth the worst abuses of the NEP: "wine, women, and cards." The nouveau riche, prostitutes, free trade, loose lifestyles swept the streets. "Not for nothing have our cities been compared with American ones," Timofeev observed. Worse than external threats were inner dangers. Young people were at the critical "transitional age" between child and adult, when they needed energy most, yet this is when the temptation to "waste" it was strongest. His repeated insistence that unlike "barns" human bodies cannot store energy indefinitely meant that every day was a new struggle, requiring constant vigilance. Socialism would not survive its transitional phase unless the next generation succeeded in mastering its own destiny. Turning from Peter the Great, he closed with Lenin, the icon of rationalized expenditure of human energy: "The most shining example of such people, the true prototype of humans in the future, is the great revolutionary, the one most modest in sexual relations, the tremendous scholar and accomplished skater, the never-tiring activist and excellent chess player: Vladimir Ilich Lenin."[46]

Turning man into a machine required temporarily shelving Darwin, one of the mainstays of materialist thought. Because so many pejorative descriptions of sexual license were drawn from the animal kingdom, decoupling humans from their biological origins was inevitable. It wasn't just that animals were mindless, instinctual brutes; they were slaves to their hormones. For Israel Gelman (who conducted the first student poll in 1922), this alone ensured that human beings would ultimately prevail and transcend their animality:

> A person is not an animal. He learns to master his desires. And this fact presents us with enormous potential to influence his sexual life. Special hygienic-educational work, molding the moral consciousness of a new human, free from social prejudices—all of this will enrich gender relations, make them more truthful and normal and lead to a more healthy human race.[47]

The "voice of nature" can be resisted. Timofeev reminded readers of Tolstoy's Father Sergius who chopped off his finger to thwart (and thus divert) sexual energy following the path of least resistance. This was not the example to follow, but by virtue of our capacity to reason we are not (or should not be) animals. Animals do not struggle with hormones; they expend their sexual energy directly and simply because they cannot control their bodies. Human beings can exercise control; animals are victims of circumstance. Not for nothing did Bolsheviks call capitalists "pigs," "vultures," and "spiders," since their world mirrored nature. What is the free market economy but the reign of chaos and anarchy? The constant struggle for survival forces its inhabitants to live by instinct which, translated into sex, makes for profligacy. This is why, Timofeev noted, "nine-tenths of bourgeois literature" is devoted to "a man chasing a woman."[48]

The Harm of Expenditure

For all concerned—whether university president, government official, doctor, sociologist, or cultural critic—sex was defined in terms of costs: what it costs society as an industrial power; what it costs the body in productive potential. Yet theory had limited power to convince; scare tactics were arguably more effective. For Zalkind sex was a "parasite," a "spider, greedily and mercilessly sucking out a tremendous amount of the body's stored energy."[49] For Yaroslavsky, a promiscuous twenty-five-year-old could look "ready for the rest home."[50] In a lecture to youth, Dr. E. B. Demidovich allegedly came face-to-face with the victims of such devastation. Amid a group of "healthy, strong organisms" in her audience, she noticed a few who showed signs of premature wear. Enfeebled by fatigue, they sat hunched over, with pale faces and vacant eyes. What explains such debilitation in youth, whose internal engines should be at their strongest? She recalled an experience she had as a medical student following her professor on his rounds. As they paused to examine a patient, their conversation went as follows:

"What's the matter with him?"

The doctor on call reported, "Atrophia testiculorum" (atrophying of the testicles).

"Was he sick?"

"Never, not in any way."

"What then is the reason?"

"Sexual activity begun at age fifteen. Coitus (the sexual act) was practiced several times a day."

The results: atrophying of the testicles, loss of moustache and beard, and impotence (inability to have sex) at age thirty.

The patient burst out crying. There was a reason to shed tears.[51]

Back in the lecture hall, another student caught her eye. Demidovich's silent diagnosis of his problem deftly combines Victorian science with Pavlov:

Not far from me stands a young man. His good build, broad chest, pleases the eyes, but his face is pale, his look dull and his movements weak. What has happened?

Was there not in his childhood something constricting his foreskin such as tight pants or some other irritant of his sexual organs? Perhaps his father whipped him and this punishment awakened in the child early sexual desire or maybe his friends taught him to masturbate. A once strong disposition got carried away; abuses began; sexual excitement, sexual satisfaction, shifted from an innate reflex onto the incorrect path of a conditional, acquired sexual reflex. In the masturbator conditional reflexes temporarily suppress innate ones. The organism protests such a perversion, tries to struggle, but fails and reacts with disgust and revulsion at every act of onanism. One wants to go up to him and ask or, if need be, state authoritatively: "Young comrade, you are not alone; . . . nearly all youth, beginning from age fifteen, masturbate for several years straight. Masturbation is harmful when it is abused. The innate reflex is usually stronger than the conditional, and, with the help and advice of a doctor, it's always possible to redirect sexual arousal and sexual satisfaction from the corrupt path onto the healthy one. There are sex consultation centers with doctors and specialists. Go there."[52]

We do not know what Dr. Demidovich actually said in her lecture, but she reports that students "bombarded her with questions." This response confirmed for Demidovich that within us lies an irrepressible "sexual hunger." For the time being, health officials could advise on its measured and thus natural satiation; with regard to the future, Demidovich confidently shared Trotsky's superman vision and Lunacharsky's romanticism. Then there would be "free love" without the current excess and debauchery because the human nervous system would have evolved to the stage where it could handle bodily needs rationally, without loss or suffering.

Concern over the age of sexual initiation and frequency of intercourse understandably ran thick in Soviet health and medical literature, where science, Bolshevik ideology, and the Victorian tradition dovetailed. Guidelines about the first question proved relatively easy to calculate. The accepted age for women to begin sexual activity was 20–22; for men, 22–23. This was the presumed end of maturation, when physical and mental growth had already peaked and the body's "energy" could be expended elsewhere with less danger.[53] The second was more problematic. In *What Is Normal Sexual Behavior?* (1927), Dr. O. Feigin advised that one should have intercourse no more than two or three times a week (which, according to polls, put most people out of danger).[54] Andrei Uspensky agreed that two times was a good number and focused on men, warning of the "peacock" paradox. The more a man attempted to prove his prowess in bed, the more he threatened his manhood. In short, it was worse for men to ejaculate many times in one session than once a day for a week. "Peacocks" risked incurring a number of male nightmares: impotence, premature ejaculation, repeated "day and night" erections, priapism, genital pains, neurasthenia, exhaustion, headaches, dizziness, memory loss, weakness, chronic constipation, loss of appetite, and an irregular heartbeat. Uspensky included a simple formula to ensure safe sex: $1 \cup 3 > 7 \cup 1$, citing an unnamed authority for this wisdom. "One multiplied by three is greater than seven multiplied by one because one sexual encounter, which includes three acts of intercourse in a row, is more harmful than seven separate encounters consisting of only one act of intercourse."[55] At least on the subject of sex, health trumped mathematical accuracy.

A more dangerous abuse was masturbation. Especially dire warnings came from Semashko. A Marxist since medical school in the 1890s, he had served diligently in the underground, spent time in prison, and was now chief medical officer in what was in his eyes the most advanced country in the world. For him masturbation was a "disease" that led to "very serious, widespread nervous and physical disorders."[56] Most classified it as a "perversion" or "abnormality" commonly linked with homosexuality or bestiality. Its damaging effects were dramatized by a poll of Odessa students conducted by David Lass in which one respondent wrote:

> After the act of masturbation, I curse myself for doing such a thing. I become timid, antisocial, pensive. My look on life is rather indifferent. I often feel like sleeping. Moreover, my fantasies take over and during normal intercourse I prematurely ejaculate, making both the sexual act and the woman with whom I'm doing it repulsive.[57]

The confession not only reflects the prevailing mentality regarding the evils of this behavior but effectively illustrates how the student himself has internalized them.

Since masturbation had been regarded as deviant long before the revolution, officials could employ statistics as indices for comparison. Of course, one may question the accuracy of such polls because the stigma attached to masturbation was so strong that the low number of reported incidents is unconvincing. Faced with the statistic that only 27.8 percent of respondents had masturbated, S. E. Burshtyn admitted to some doubts in his 1925 survey of soldiers and students.[58] Burshtyn's frustration points to what is important for our purposes: how this information was used, as with Zalkind's aforementioned delight in finding that ostensibly fewer workers masturbated after the revolution than before. The most enthusiastic statistician was Lass, who divided those respondents who admitted masturbating according to nationality, class origin, and gender, with the following results:

	Males	*Females*
Ukrainian	66.8%	6.8%
Russian	46.1%	11.4%
Jewish	43.0%	11.2%
Workers	47.5%	12.1%
Peasants	62.6%	9.5%
Bourgeoisies	45.6%	17.5%

At first sight, male Ukrainian workers and peasants seemed the greatest deviants. But Lass was able to salvage victory in the face of defeat by simply adding female and male percentages together. In so doing, he could explain the 72.1 percent rating for peasants by pointing to the environment. From early childhood they had seen farm animals copulating, which "fixes their attention on the idea of sex." For Lass this was evidence of the perennial backwardness of rural living. He also noted the high percentage among Ukrainians, but avoided any speculation as to ethnic-national differences. That workers reported a lower incidence (59.6 percent) than the bourgeoisie (63.1) led him to a memorable conclusion: "With regard to onanism, the most healthy element [of society] are the representatives of the working class, in which can be found the best preconditions for a healthy sexual lifestyle."[59]

Not all experts were so old-fashioned in their views. A group of doctors—Uspensky, Feigin, Lemberg, and Sigal—discounted the common belief that masturbation led to serious physical harm, such as paralysis, retardation, or loss of memory. Lemberg argued (logically) that its harmful effects were overblown, since it would be hard to find anyone who had not masturbated at some point. Feigin was even more direct. In *The Most Important Abnormalities of Sexual Behavior,* he disputed Lass's conclusions as to the likely cause of low self-esteem experienced by his students: "Assertions that onanism causes mental deficiency, cirrhosis of the spinal cord, loss of memory, and so forth are not only incorrect, but are in reality harmful themselves: they almost always scare beyond measure the very person who does masturbate and lead to thoughts of despair, suicide, etc."[60]

Nevertheless, some ideological patriotism infiltrated these doctors' conclusions. All four concurred that even though masturbation did not pose grave physical danger, a healthy socialist society could not tolerate it. Masturbation was a self-indulgent (for many, repulsive) waste of bodily energy. No procreation, no chance, in Demidovich's words, of "sexual glands" serving as "factories to manufacture material for the creation of new human machines."[61] Masturbation epitomized narcissism and self-absorption; it cultivated the Soviet Union's worst internal enemy, individualism. "From the moment he begins masturbating," warned Dr. B. V. Tsukker, "a person becomes ballast for the collective. He brings harm to his own body and at the same time makes himself useless to society."[62]

The remedy was to eliminate environmental factors that led to "abnormal sexual excitement." Dr. M. Lemberg closed *What Is Necessary to Know About Sex* (1927) with a five-step prevention program:

> (1) Never, in any circumstances, use alcohol (wines, vodkas, beers and so forth).
> (2) One should sleep on a hard bed and, upon waking up in the morning, get out of bed quickly. There is nothing more harmful than lying in bed for a long time without sleeping. That causes sexual arousal.
> (3) One should not consume too many meat products. Beef should be eaten once a day, toward dinner (and no more than half a pound). Supper should be taken three hours before retiring. Right before going to bed it is imperative to relieve one's bladder.

(4) One's imagination should not be inflamed by reading erotic literature (light novels), telling indecent stories, or looking at pornographic pictures.

(5) One should not lead a sedentary life. As much time as possible should be spent outdoors. In this regard walks, gymnastics, sports, and other fresh-air activities are useful.[63]

Sigal warned in addition against stimulants such as strong tea and coffee, while Feigin leaned to therapies: psychotherapy, hydrotherapy, and electric shock therapy. Stating that "war must be declared against masturbation," Uspensky took the battle straight to the enemy. The regimen for youth should include cold baths, sports, and loose clothing; to be avoided were wool underwear (which "scratches" the genitals), belts (which force blood into the lower abdomen), soft beds, and sleeping with hands inside the covers, lying abed in the morning, and sharing a bed (even with someone of the same sex). Also banished were suspect books and movies, alcohol, sweets, rich foods, and, if the sexual impulse were too strong, he recommended limiting food intake generally.[64]

The perennial nostrum was abstinence. Yet all self-appointed guardians of morality found their task complicated in the 1920s by the rumor that abstinence itself was harmful. Soviet officials and doctors attacked this canard on ideological, physical, psychological, and cultural grounds. Yaroslavsky extolled abstinence as reminiscent of the heroism demanded by revolution. It had been forced upon his generation by the isolation of prison, the hardship of exile, and by revolutionary work. Their sacrifice was rewarded by the triumph of 1917.[65] Semashko in turn offered young people a direct challenge. Until the state could rectify all environmental ills, they must take responsibility upon themselves: "And so all of you students, both women and men, since our government is so impoverished, there is only one conclusion: abstain!"[66] If patriotism failed, Uspensky, Timofeev, Feigin, Sigal, Abramov, and Gorinevsky had physiological evidence to prove that abstention was good for the health. It prevented premature aging, Abramov argued, because "products of sex glands" were retained in the body, keeping it young.[67] Gorinevsky outright declared that resistance to sexual urges "brought great pleasure."[68] Mindful of industrial productivity, Feigin pointed out that the very fight against desire steeled the body and sharpened self-discipline: "In this struggle a young man matures and forges his will. Victory over the most powerful instinct creates confidence in oneself, in one's strength, in one's ability to resist that sudden impulse which can hinder our achieving the greatest goals in life."[69] To women he was less generous. Abstention was good only up to age thirty, after which it took its toll: "This is why old maids become petty, fusty and peevish and are suspicious of everything around them."

Enter Freud

A tinge of nostalgia colors these studies, suggesting that the grand engine of energy conversion—the revolution—was behind them. Numerous polls substantiated the belief that revolution and civil war had discouraged interest in sex through enforced, subconscious sublimation.[70] Needless to say, NEP inspired nothing of the sort. Dreams of a "communism to come" often paled before the immediate pressures, enticements, material hardships, and emotional depressions of postrevolutionary life. After 1922 models of sublimation came not from grand historical events but from the lives of famous individuals. Youths aspiring to greatness could take comfort in the fact that, according to Timofeev, "documents confirm that Leonardo da Vinci was a virgin almost to the end of his life."[71] Others might find solace that Beethoven, an "unattractive man" in Ariamov's words, transferred his capacity for sexual love into artistic creativity. Therefore "genius and abstinence," the latter concluded, "are closely connected."[72] Newton and Kant were also cited as distinguished examples.

Exhortations for abstinence rang most heroically—and humorously—with Alexander Pushkin. In the autumn of 1830, isolated from his fiancée, Natalya Goncharova, by a cholera quarantine, he wrote in an unparalled burst of energy two chapters of *Evgeny Onegin*, *The House in Kolomna*, *The Little Tragedies*, and *The Tales of Belkin*. The greatest Russian poet could not be ignored, and he sometimes rivaled Lenin as the model to follow. Without a proper outlet, Pushkin's "strong sexual appetite," Ariamov declared, "was transformed into the highest of mental processes, into creativity."[73] This was an assertion of the tallest, and most truncated, order given his notorious reputation as a romantic, seducer, and rake, one who violated with passion and enthusiasm the guidelines for proper sexual behavior later enunciated by the Bolsheviks. Justice was served with the timely publication in 1923 of Petr Guber's *The Don Juan List of A. S. Pushkin*, a gossipy exposé of the poet's "life of the heart" that noted in its opening sentence his "enormous reserves of energy."[74] Through memoirs, letters, and observations of contemporaries, Guber revealed Pushkin's sexual "profligacy," his innumerable flirtations and affairs, and his illegitimate children. As if in response, Timofeev reluctantly acknowledged that Pushkin "paid dearly for the sexual excesses of [his] youth,"[75] whereupon Uspensky, still seeking to retain the poet's good standing, could only comment that Pushkin "wrote his best works during those times when because of venereal disease he had to refrain from sex."[76] Quite the example, indeed.

Given their acclaimed faith in sublimation, Soviets were openly indebted to Freud.[77] Much of the same language and metaphors used in his studies written before the First World War reappeared in the 1920s. Uspensky credited him for providing the principle through which to understand Pushkin's production while in quarantine, and Freud's definition of sublimation in "Civilized Sexual Morality and Modern Nervousness" (1908) could serve as the backbone of Soviet tenets. Like Lenin, Freud also took a moderate position: one should neither be monk nor Don Juan.[78] The celibate was always consumed by "struggles against libidinous temptation," whereas for the hedonist "love became worthless, life became empty."[79] Moreover, in Freud's analysis the impact of the social environment on sexual behavior loomed large, extending far beyond infancy. "Civilized sexual morality" (which Soviets preferred to call simply "bourgeois morality") was brutal, blind, injurious, and patently hypocritical in setting a standard higher than most could achieve. No one was born "neurotic" or "perverted." For Freud, both neurotics and perverts possessed strong, but self-destructive, sexual instincts. The former conformed to cultural standards, but they were crippled by the expenditure of energy demanded by suppression. Perverts did not suppress impulses but paid the social costs of nonconformity. With society's demands in perennial conflict with the individual (Marxists made the same critique of capitalism), there was no escape from the dilemma: they were damned either way.[80]

Zalkind, a self-styled "communist psychoneurologist," led the push to wed Freud and Marx. He had a foot in both camps. A party member, he began writing on psychoanalysis before the First World War while still in his twenties. In 1924 he openly assumed the mantle of ambassador of psychoanalysis with the publication of "Freudianism and Marxism" which sought to eliminate "superstitions" surrounding Freud. This article, published in *Red Virgin Soil*, introduced readers to fundamental concepts such as the conscious and the unconscious, the pleasure principle and reality principle, catharsis, displacement, suggestion, and transference.[81] To bring Freud into line with his own strict beliefs, Zalkind was relatively silent about the centrality of sexual desire in Freud's work. In fact, that Zalkind could explain Freudianism with little reference to sexuality proved that for him it had a minor place in his overall psychoanalytic scheme. In an impressively circular argument, Zalkind tailored Freud for his own purposes, then convinced himself that his interpretation was the true Freud. In short, Zalkind claimed to know Freud better than Freud, who had made "serious mistakes" in emphasizing sex. For Zalkind sex was the spider that "swells and blows up as it parasitically gorges on the juices not belonging to it but stolen from other areas." Never retreating from his faith in external forces as saviors of the internal, in bold print he

declared that society was most qualified to relieve its citizens of the danger of
built-up sexual energy: "A well-organized social environment is the best antisex pump."[82]

Zalkind capitalized on the tolerance of Freudian ideas in the party. Much
of this interest was motivated by a suspicion of bourgeois subjectivity, which
determinists could not stand. (No "free will," no "free choice," was Zalkind's
mantra.) Top leaders such as Trotsky, Karl Radek, and Bukharin were favor-
ably disposed toward psychoanalysis, and Freud's works were printed by the
state's own publishing house, with every volume eagerly grabbed up.[83] Yet, as
was typical in the 1920s, few of Freud's theories enjoyed unanimous support.
Painfully aware that his revolution had only provoked heightened interest in
both Freud and sexuality, Lenin debunked both in the same breath. While
Freudian theory might sound "educated" and even "scientific," for him, it was
"ignorant" and "bungling."[84] More explicitly, in *Freudianism: A Critical
Sketch* (1927), Valentin Voloshinov sought to correct the record. If Zalkind
hoped to de-sex Freud by conscious omission, Voloshinov soberly noted, removing the sex from Freudianism was to deprive it of its "soul."[85]

Voloshinov and other critics could have saved ink, effort, and energy by
merely directing readers back to Freud. While very general principles could
be gleaned from his work that were acceptable to party leaders, such as sublimation, when it came to details regarding youth and abstinence, little of
Freud could remain in the Bolshevik camp. In 1908 he had already debunked
the notion that average youth might aspire to creative genius:

> It may be said that the task of mastering such a mighty impulse as the
> sexual instinct is one which may well absorb all the energies of a human
> being. Mastery through sublimation, diverting the sexual energy away
> from its sexual goal to higher cultural aims, succeeds with a minority,
> and with them only intermittently; while the period of passionate youth
> is precisely that in which it is most difficult to achieve.[86]

According to Freud, for a young man to abstain from sexual activity past age
twenty was a sure path to injury.[87] Even the most precious of ideas for Bolsheviks, that of the "mechanized" human being, was suspect:

> It is indeed said that the struggle with such powerful instincts and the
> consequent strengthening of all ethical and aesthetic tendencies "steels"
> the character; and this, for some specially constituted natures, is true. . . .
> But in the great majority of cases the fight against sexuality absorbs the
> available energy of the character, and this at the very time when the
> young man is in need of all his powers to gain his share of worldly goods
> and his position in the community.

And to the chagrin of Pushkin devotees, Freud concluded, "An abstinent artist is scarcely conceivable."[88]

Bound to the Past

Soviet beliefs regarding sexual behavior were a tenuous amalgam of precedent and projection in which Freud in truth played only a minor role. The traditions underlying the arguments about sexuality in the 1920s bridged many centuries and vast ideological differences. From the Judeo-Christian heritage to contemporary socialism through industrial capitalism, there was no one exclusive line of precedent feeding into Bolshevik paradigms. This debt to the past was never fully acknowledged, but Bolsheviks could not help internalizing, consciously or not, a plethora of other ideas. This is why their pronouncements can seem contradictory to us, why they sound so curiously ultramodern and archaic at the same time. Each thread of influence found a new voice somewhere in the revolutionary environment, revealing, if only fleetingly, how much the Bolsheviks were tied to the past. Currents of libertarianism, for example, could find partial support in Bebel and "free love" movements from the previous century. Operative metaphors, like sex as a spider, were already clichés. The conception of the body as a machine enjoyed widespread currency long before 1917; and in questions of health, the obsession with regulating the expenditure of sexual energy was a fundamental Victorian concern. Viewing sex as a destroyer or distraction from more important areas of life resurrected Pauline tenets, whereas anxieties over masturbation echoed—mutatis mutandis—earlier fears, such as those of Nicholas Cooke who in *Satan in Society* (1870) simply pronounced that those who masturbate "will die and go to hell."[89]

In Bolshevik rhetoric we can see the hopes, fears, and prejudices shared by both right and left, secular and religious, in the Western world as a whole. The value placed on quasi or full asceticism, for which the Bolsheviks later gained the reputation for being "ignorant" and "prudish," was not peculiar to them. Besides the Russian philosophical and intellectual tradition (as detailed by Engelstein and Naiman), the most direct line of influence came from nineteenth-century progressives in Western Europe and America obsessed with the perfectibility of the human being—a goal to be achieved by eradicating or suppressing all the irrational, inept, inefficient aspects of corporal existence. A smoothly running body necessitated meticulous care, which generated widespread hysterias regarding pain, aging, dirt, constipation, nervous exhaustion, and corpulence.[90]

Another progressive tenet that circulated widely in the West as well as in the Soviet Union was that maintaining oneself in good physical health was a social obligation. Progressives often exhibited suspicion of all pleasures, sometimes even more than religious moralists. Personal fitness, raised to a public concern by doctors and social theorists, could be guaranteed only through individual self-control and discipline. "Every surrender to impulse," it was commonly feared, "threatened a person's sanity."[91] Thus sports and other means of sublimation could save citizens from vice. Masturbation, as might be expected, was a "pointless and prodigal waste of limited and valuable resources leading, figuratively and often literally, to impotence. It constituted loss of mastery over the world and oneself."[92] Failsafe remedies such as hard mattresses were, by the 1920s, standard fare. For the Bolsheviks to have believed differently—*that* would have been truly revolutionary.

On sexual questions, the Soviets had internalized the dominant mentality of the Victorian age—"the gospel of thrift in semen"—that joined the progressive and conservative camps.[93] Just as socialism needed strong (primarily assumed to be male) bodies, so did capitalism. Based on the same scientific premises, the methodology and reasoning were the same: one should save the body's "capital," just as one saved money in the bank. In the capitalist ethos, wealth came only to those with a high moral and physical aptitude. It was a reward earned by sublimation, self-discipline, and denial. By the same token, the necessary attributes for gaining wealth—prudence, thrift, hard work, restraint, or modesty—also characterized the political revolutionary. The right and left shared common enemies: idleness and succumbing to physical appetites that drained the body's energy and intellectual faculties. For the Victorians, anything that distracted from the pursuit of wealth was suspect, particularly if it wore a petticoat: "No romance must interfere with the solid worship of Mammon," declared one proud Englishman at the turn of the century.[94] Substitute Marx for Mammon, and one graduated to the Soviet ideal. Indeed, the benefits of denial were expressed in the same language. What "braced the character" in Victorian England "tempered" or "forged" the Soviet citizen.

To be sure, following Max Weber, the capitalist ideal was an internalization of the Protestant ethic. As Matthew Arnold confirmed, "money-making" and "soul-saving" were directly connected, for they both depended on the same kind of personal reformation and both, in their own way, enriched the person.[95] Though few Bolsheviks would admit it, the radical revolutionary was no different. If one were religious, continence was the path to heaven; for the acquisitive, it was the way to wealth; for the communist, the path to victory. This is why little in Zalkind's often cited "Twelve Commandments of the Revolutionary Working Class" would have upset either the clergy (Protestant, Catholic, or Orthodox) or the "respectable" Victorian:

    I.   Sexual behavior should not begin at too early an age.
    II.   Abstinence is necessary until marriage.

III.   The sexual act is only the final stage of a deep, mutual affection and attraction to the object of intercourse.

IV.   The sexual act should only be the final link in a chain of deep experiences connecting the two lovers.

V.   The sexual act should not occur frequently.

VI.   One should not change one's sexual partner frequently. There should not be much variety in sexual behavior.

VII.   Love should be monogamous and monandrous.

VIII.   With each sexual act, one should always think about the possibility of pregnancy.

IX.   Sexual selection should not take place in line with class, revolutionary-proletarian purposes. Intimate relations should not include elements of flirting, coquettishness or courting, or other features of the specifically sexual.

X.   There should be no jealousy.

XI.   There should be no sexual deviance.

XII.   In the interests of the revolution's goals, the [working] class has the right to interfere in the sexual lives of its members. In all respects the sexual should be subordinate to the social, never hindering but always serving the latter.[96]

The twelve dicta capture how scientific-medical and ideological-moral approaches to regulating sexual behavior could seamlessly overlap.[97] However, it would have been blasphemy to acknowledge the Bolsheviks' debt to a bourgeois-capitalist moral heritage. Knowing that religion was anathema to most Soviet youth, Zalkind masked the inheritance by stating that only now were the facts being told, only now was sexual behavior being defined in proper, proletarian fashion. He denied that his commandments represented "new shackles" or "new enslavement under a revolutionary-proletarian label." Claiming "full scientific backing," he declared that the communist future would be characterized by "greater sexual modesty, fidelity, and frugality."[98] It was the church, with its superstitious reliance on sin, that was hypocritical and ridiculous.[99]

Conflicting Routes to Overcoming Tradition

The dominance of the ascetic ideal was not absolute. Diverse in their sources, Bolsheviks and their sympathizers were diverse in their views. As of yet, however, they did not have the theoretical instrument to compress various currents into a single doctrine or the real power to suppress discordant voices. There was disagreement in the party and with nonaligned or less explicitly ideological doctors who assumed the authority to speak on sexuality.

The proliferation of studies by the latter ("right under Moscow's nose") was particularly vexing to Semashko, who berated the "bacchanalia of publications" on the sex question that were full of nonsense and likely penned by "nymphomaniacs."[100] It was the fate of "popular topics," he lamented, to attract stupidity.[101]

These conflicts reflected notable challenges to doctrine. Dispute, for example, over the root causes of homosexuality threatened the legitimacy of the environmental principle. Seconding Zalkind and Lass, Lemberg argued that homosexuals were outside the proletarian norm: "Same-sex love was widespread in antiquity, but in our days homosexuals can be found among actors, artists, musicians, and writers. Undoubtedly in these cases poor examples and [doing what's] 'in fashion' play a great role."[102] However, some argued the opposite. Most tolerant was perhaps E. P. Frenkel, cited earlier. Others decisively claimed that homosexuality was a biological, not cultural, phenomenon.[103] Gelman, the earliest empirical analyst of sexual behavior among Soviet youth, was also sympathetic. He regretted that his questionnaire had not specifically referred to homosexuality (some questions had been removed by reviewers). Nevertheless two female respondents still felt compelled to address it. Their unsolicited responses led him to conclude:

> The times have already long passed when homosexuality was viewed as a moral perversion demanding, in the interests of correction, criminal repression. Science has now determined with indubitable accuracy that here we are dealing primarily not with flawed will, not with a crime, but with a sickness that is caused by deep psychological and often physiological changes in the person which cannot be corrected. The entire world of the lesbian or gay man is perverted; the normal sexual attractions that exist in the normal person are alien to it. Normal sexual relations do not appeal to them and are even tortuous. Only in perverse sexual attraction does the homosexual gain not only full physical but also psychological satisfaction.[104]

To be sure, homosexuality was still a defect and its practice "perverse," but Gelman argued (unsuccessfully) that it was simplistic to see it as the result of cultural influences or voluntary choice. Thus homosexuals should not be persecuted. Unlike with "deviants," such as the "Don Juans," Gelman spared the two women any condemnation. With the exception of whom they slept with, he noted, they were the same as everyone else, including their capacity for work.[105]

Another divergent voice, yet one still faithful to the revolution's assumed goals, was heard in M. Shchekin's treatise, *How to Live the New Way* (1925). Hypnotized by the remarkable future promised by communism fortified with technology, Shchekin believed that all world barriers—physical, national, psychological—would eventually fall, making the globe one large, cheerful neighborhood.[106] His vision was an intriguing synthesis of strict collectivism (he favored the musketeer's slogan, "All for one, one for all") with libertarianism. Only the iconoclastic spirit of the libertarian could shatter the laws that divide and the conventions that separate. True communal living without true openness and equality was impossible. Shchekin railed against all barriers that impeded free movement and communication, that covered or concealed. Condemnation included walls in offices and homes, and even clothing:

> The impact of nudity on health, particularly if one gets accustomed to it gradually, is so unquestionable that it constitutes one of the fundaments of a healthy society. It goes without saying that in summer months, and in warmer climates all the time, people should be naked (without all sorts of fig leaves, which would play a tremendous role in the eradication of various venereal diseases—the primary scourge of humanity, threatening its survival). Thousands of catarrhal, skin and pulmonary infections would cease to exist if we were naked because the body would be able to breathe safely. After all, sweat is a poison and one so strong that injecting it under the skin can kill even the most healthy person. The frequent change of clothes only allows sweat to "soak in" and thus poison the blood.

Health-conscious, not voyeuristic, Shchekin assured readers that for the nudist sexual intimacy could coexist with collective living. "For the seclusion required at the well-known hour of love, [the 'collectivized person'] can use special gardens of pleasure, where he and his girlfriend will find the needed comfort." Moreover, full nudity would rid society of sexually transmitted diseases. For disbelievers he elaborated on the anti–fig leaf principle:

> Even now at resorts and sanatoria one can often see that the importance of nudity for health is understood; people look suspiciously at those walking around clothed and mentally ask themselves: "Why isn't he naked? Does he have some disease?" If people in summer and winter (inside in the winter) walked around naked, the spread of skin and venereal diseases would drop like a rock because for the most part the sufferer's body would be visible. The Grim Reaper's terrible diseases would lose their primary weapon: treacherous concealment.

In addition to reducing disease, nudism would prevent the improper expenditure of sexual energy, since it could not be hidden, and alleviate the crisis. A libertarian, not a libertine, Shchekin predicted,

> [In the future] healthy bodies will not be carriers of hidden infection; human sexual selection will take its proper course. The exhausted debauchee will scare others off with appearance of his body, whereas the healthy, normal person will only attract. A healthy attitude to the naked body will be cold water on clamped-up sexual feelings, and the ubiquity of nudity will have less of an arousing effect than does today "the leg of a ballerina, dressed in a partially bared pink outfit, raised at a right angle (or 45 degrees) on lovers of art." "The forbidden fruit" will lose its artificial piquancy. The attitude to nudity will be just as healthy as with animals (the wild ones, not corrupted by humans) which are far more restrained and know the natural norms of sexual behavior.

In his defense of nudism, Shchekin cited Lenin's moral code (anything that benefits the cause is just) and made it the cornerstone of his program: all cultural conventions are relative. Embarrassment and shame about nakedness were social constructs and thus easily overturned. Their removal would usher in an environment that would allow true, unfettered love to flourish—Eden before the Fall regained:

> With regard to feelings of shame, it should be noted that for naked savages it is shameful for them to be seen in clothes (just as if we were to be seen without) and in the future it will be shameful to be dressed when underneath one can hide only disease and malformity. Shame derives exclusively from custom and customs change.

Shchekin closed his discussion of nudism with a paean to the past that may be unique in Soviet literature:

> The ancients had cults of sexual organs and were correct in doing this since the two most beautiful spots on a person's body are the forehead, the emblem of how far man has advanced, and the sexual organ, the emblem of the master of that achievement.

We may laugh at Shchekin. A contemporary reviewer, M. Golman, questioned his sanity and noted that his book would attract readers because "the issues of *byt* and sex are of great interest not only to youth but to adults." But we have to take Shchekin seriously. In his fanaticism he represents many others—perhaps quacks and eccentrics, but loyalists—who justified their views in the name of revolution. If bourgeois society stood for shame and concealment, how could one not fight for full, uncompromised freedom? Shchekin's use of Lenin shows how open and expansive the leader's doctrine could become in the hands of those who sought to apply his theories to current problems. Shchekin's treatise indicates what could be expected from the devout: via Lenin's dictum, one could argue for any number of goals, such as communal kitchens, laundries, day care, that would bring efficiency, benefit the collective, and promote utopian ideals. Only Shchekin's extended paean to nudism, a comprehensive cure-all for a host of social, psychological, and bodily ills, separates him from the other theorists quoted above. Salvation and liberation were his sole motivation, and he published his treatise, *How to Live the New Way,* at his own cost in an amazing print run of five thousand copies.

Within the party itself, the "psychoneurologist" Zalkind was a source of embarrassment and target of scorn. A popular lecturer, he was a master of both sensationalism and alarmism, with a propensity for animal metaphors (e.g., the orangutan and the spider). Semashko, a popular rival, ridiculed Zalkind's use of weighty terms like "communism" or "marxism" to dress infantile ideas in the robe of erudition and infallibility.[107] If there could be a limit to praise of Lenin, Zalkind crossed it by describing the recently departed leader as "a psychophysiological apparatus stuffed with colossal energy, wielding an unlimited source of energy and action, boundless strength for the push ahead, and inexhaustible, formidable reserves." One shocked reviewer noted that such "empty phrasemongering" was the key to Zalkind's success in spreading "sheer nonsense."[108] Unimpressed by big words and neologisms, another reviewer commented that if masturbation was of particular concern to Zalkind, it showed in his prose, which was nothing less than "mast-verb-ation."[109]

These discordant voices were united only by a common desire for an ordered, perversion-free environment. Yet was the future to be a disciplined factory of human machines or the more idyllic paradise favored by Lunacharsky? Were its roots to be cultivated in the countryside, that is, furthest from the bourgeois contamination of the city, or were the urban barracks, the heart of proletarian life, the proper place? Debate over the original source of corruption echoed the classic split between agrarian and urban socialism. It was reflected in literature, which ranged from exposés of the brutality of village life to morality tales in which the hero finds redemption only by leaving the city. In short, attempts to address questions of sex in life and literature were cobbled from a range of voices and traditions, making the decade rich in comical search and error yet scarred by misunderstandings and in-fighting. Such confusion also helps to explain why the sexual revolution, understood more as a period of inquiry than activity, finally came to an end.

Authorities could agree only in the abstract, as reflected in their use of language. Drawing on relatively coherent, scientifically justified, or morally established principles for understanding sexual behavior, they offered little unique to this legacy. Where they, the most prolific Marxist writers on this issue, made their mark was on *how* the subject of sex should be defined. Marx, Engels, and Bebel had already established that sexual behavior was a function of class, yet nowhere in their work do we find a detailed biological-ideological dissection of sexuality. This would be the Bolsheviks' contribution. In the Soviet Union the devil and sin were replaced by a new concept. Regardless of one's preferences or habits, whether one were a Don Juan or a monk, whether heterosexual or homosexual, all could now be aligned along a continuum with two poles: proletarian and bourgeois/philistine. The proletariat was immaculately conceived, with sin or deviance the result of the machinations of the latter. This distinction underlay Lenin's insistence, in his interview with Zetkin, that young Soviets needed "clarity, clarity, clarity." The language was accessible; the logic incontrovertible. To attack the bourgeoisie was to move toward resolving issues of sex. With one elegant sweep, class rhetoric reduced the maddening complexity of the "accursed question" to digestible form. No more vacillation or trepidation over this most personal and problematic aspect of life. The simple class paradigm seemed to overcome the ambiguities of the Bolsheviks' mixed inheritance and, for many on the outside, enforced the image of their unanimity of belief and practice. Bolsheviks were out to simplify the world, and, discursively at least, they did it most admirably on sexual questions. The challenge was to translate this clarity into action.

★ CHAPTER 4

Confusion and Backlash

The Problem of Theory

FRESH from her attack on Alexandra Kollontai in 1923, Polina Vino-gradskaia was likely in high spirits. That few ventured to defend *Love of the Worker Bees* must have assured her that her broadside was on target and that Soviet students were not truly concerned with sex. Who understood youth better? Kollontai was fifty-one and had been posted to Norway as ambassador; Vinogradskaia was twenty-five but already sharing the confidence of Krupskaia. Who then was more attuned to the problems of everyday life? *Byt* was Vinogradskaia's newly discovered expertise in which she believed she could never err because Marxist ideology always provided the correct answer. "For our party," she declared, "all questions [relating to *byt*] have been theoretically and programmatically resolved long ago." Therefore, there was a simple solution to all the sexual "garbage" Kollontai had dragged up: it was time for the state to realize its ideals through law and proclamation.[1]

For all her hubris, Vinogradskaia was not mistaken. As theoreticians, Bolsheviks reigned supreme. There was no issue that could not be dissected and explained through a Marxist lens. Yet already by 1923 Trotsky was casting a wary eye on such jingoism. As one of the more incisive, honest and consequently Cassandran observers, he warned in *Pravda* that theory had jumped far ahead of daily life, sometimes "by decades," sometimes "by centuries." Vinogradskaia's faith in theory was itself the problem, he believed, since it demonstrated that while Bolsheviks could project the future, they could not remedy immediate problems on the street by rhetorical sleight of hand. An eminent theorist himself, Trotsky knew that theory was safe territory, that it could explain anything. This was the very danger. Recognizing that translating ideas into practice would be the greatest obstacle on the domestic front, Trotsky saw in Vinogradskaia's appeals to the state a mistaken belief that an "enlightened bureaucracy" could resolve social problems.[2] "The state, even the most active and dynamic," he pronounced, "cannot remake *byt* without the powerful initiative of the masses."

Trotsky's call anticipated by a few months his more fiery appeal for "democratic" initiative in "The New Course," cited in chapter 1. It also led Trotsky immediately into a quandary. To stoke democracy below was to question the role of the party itself, so he doubled back, asserting that workers might know about their own conditions but needed party-provided theory to put it all together. This was why, for all their spontaneous potential, workers did not themselves build the child care centers they needed or why communes failed: they were not prepared to understand their obligations. Therefore, Trotsky believed, although workers needed enlightenment to become independent, the guiding light of initiative should come from the bureaucracy he so scorned.

Such voltes-face reflected the basic tenet of Bolshevik principle: only the party knew what was best for the people, that spontaneity must be tempered by consciousness. For this reason, Trotsky could not help contradicting himself. He had to extricate himself from the environment-is-all belief, a circular trap that threatened its adherents. It was too much a recipe for passivity, an opiate as much as religion once had been. Don't worry, do nothing, things will take care of themselves—what message was that for a revolutionary? How could the environment improve if people did not rise above it, if they did not themselves become the engine of change? Trotsky had to retreat from Marxist determinism to the Russian revolutionary tradition as the practical answer to real-life problems: internal discipline, the steeling of character—what had distinguished Chernyshevsky's fictional heroes in *What Is to Be Done?* (1831) and the real-life martyrs of the People's Will—that was the key to socialism. Here was the true cradle of Trotsky's superman, a creature in command of and transcending his environment.[3]

What Trotsky critiqued he himself could not avoid; no materialist who simultaneously favored conscious, planned revolution could escape it. The emerging debate over *byt* was a clear sign of how easily Bolsheviks could become tangled in their own ideological web. Trotsky tried to have it both ways—recourse to the environmental explanation, or individual will, depending on the problem at hand. Certain phenomena were better explained as products of environmental forces; but personal relationships and sexuality were better defined in individual terms. Trotsky was at least open about his flexible understanding of Marxism. There was little else he could do, since after 1921 the revolution took an introspective turn, giving more and more attention to the individual. The iconoclasm expressed in the overthrow of tsarism and the Provisional Government eventually ran out of steam and it-self became suspect, as the Soviet state assumed the mantle of control. De-struction could never be permanent; it eventually had to yield to its opposite. Moreover, the failure of Marxism to take hold in other countries meant that the Soviet Union was more and more on its own, and this raised the question as to whether its citizens were up to the task. Official acknowledgment that the country was beset by economic problems, that the environment was not up to par, threw responsibility onto the individual to withstand its destructive influences. Since everyone had been born before the revolution, the ability to overcome one's origins became a test of ideological purity and revolutionary strength.

This was the theme of Aleksandr Tarasov-Rodionov's novel, *Chocolate* (1922). His protagonist, Zudin, a police officer, sees the nation's greatest threat not in a foreign invader but "in ourselves! In our internalized attraction to the past: to past lifestyles, to its fashions, to its habits. That's where our en-emies are! . . . We should not expect help from the heavens; we are gods our-selves!"[4] Zudin proves the truth of these words when his divine intentions succumb to the inner demon of sex. His downfall is Elena Valts, an abused former ballerina whom he employs as his secretary out of pity. He is immedi-ately entranced by her "chocolate eyes" and "lace stockings," introducing to literature the principal symbol of the anti-Soviet femme fatale. The descrip-tion of Zudin's seduction illustrates how traditional sexual imagery elided with the new machine mentality. In Elena Valts's presence, he is engulfed by "currents of electricity" that "melt him like wax."

> Zudin felt a flood of fragrant, soft, warm, sultry lava of delicious milk chocolate covering him entirely, filling his mouth; spasms choked his throat. This was not Valts but a frightening, lustful machine, a generator of terror, its driving belts flailing and booming. He stood next to it, a step from its clanks and clangs, but the machine continued to buzz; it called and beckoned him with its tender, plaintive drone. It beckoned and called: forget the sooty, dirty factory, come closer, closer to me.[5]

Tarasov-Rodionov sets up in Zudin a conflict between two machines, that of the sexual drive and that of the body as factory. Reluctant to betray his wife, Zudin tries to resist: "But Elena, you don't understand, there resides in me—how can I explain?—class devotion. . . . In it I find all my strength and from it I imbibe the highest personal satisfaction." But it is too late for patri-otic outbursts; his wife has already become ensnared in bourgeois fetters be-cause of Valts's gifts to her, chocolate and silk stockings, and thus Zudin is arrested for accepting bribes from the enemy. He denies conducting "orgies" in his office and attempts to prove his loyalty by citing the number of prisoners he has executed, but in his colleagues' eyes, he has already failed the test. "These women," one of them concluded, "are the cause of ruin." Clarity, once again, must triumph: "The masses will never understand [your] lengthy justifications. They understand only one thing: yes or no!" Though he is innocent (he took no bribes and had resisted Valts's sexual advances), Zudin must be executed because, as his prosecutors explain: "We are protecting [the people] from the unproductive expenditure [of energy] and in this manner increasing by a thousandfold and directing to its necessary purpose the wellspring of our class strength."[6] In a final monologue, Zudin expresses hope that his death will be a lesson about the evils of temptation. "Chocolate," symbol of the bourgeois past, must be rejected; one should think only of the Soviet future. As he awaits execution, workers march past singing "The Internationale."[7]

Unlike later works of socialist realism, *Chocolate* does not represent men of the party as invincible. Sexual temptation is one of the gravest dangers. Externally it subverts their authority; internally it destroys their self-control. Tarasov-Rodionov amplifies the warning by making Zudin one of the old guard, of the supposedly "pure" generation. A party member since 1903, Zudin had served in the underground and braved Siberian exile under the tsar. (The author himself joined in 1905 and in 1938 met the same fate as his protagonist.) These laurels make his story all the more poignant. If such a background was insufficient to protect Zudin from temptation, what could be expected of real-life youth who have not enjoyed prerevolutionary character "forging"? The common perception was that the trauma of 1917 and civil war, fighting and dying as revolutionaries, had forced young people prematurely into adult roles. Peace and reconstruction left them adrift, lacking outlets for their awakened energy and enthusiasm. With too much "chocolate" still around, how could they escape what happened to Zudin?

The call for personal responsibility was therefore embedded within environmental-determinist arguments. Semashko admitted that youth could turn to their elders for theoretical answers, but for practical solutions to day-to-day problems, they had to rely upon themselves.[8] They must learn restraint and sublimation; they must stop smoking, swearing, and drinking to excess. Others were more specific. S. Shkotov, who had praised the idyllic purity of rural youth, cautioned against adopting or succumbing to the seductive ways of Elena Valts: "Young women should cast off the mask of a lusting animal and stop artificially inflaming the sexual instincts of guys with all that lace and fancy trimmings, powders and paints."[9] To balance the charge, a Professor Gorinevsky in a letter published in *Pravda* advised men "to treat women with respect, as comrades without trying to inflame their sexual instincts."[10] (Assigning blame to one sex or the other was a common theme of debate. In literature, there was far less forgiveness toward women.)

Criticism from Within

The diversity of opinion reflected not only Bolshevism's attempt to balance contradictory paradigms, determinism and voluntarism, but also that there were competing interpretations of each. It made for a lively but crowded stage, and it ensured that criticism could be open and incisive. Following Trotsky's lead, challengers often came from within the Komsomol itself. Two notable critics were Viktor Kin and Ippolit Sitkovsky, who ridiculed the advice currently being peddled to youth. Representatives of Khanin's generation, those who came of age during NEP, Kin and Sitkovsky were schoolmates from the Tambov region, a hotbed of peasant insurrection during the civil war, where they had worked for the Komsomol underground. After victory, they never lost their combative spirit and swagger. (Kin was the inveterate jokester; Sitkovsky was known to parade around the city, Borisoglebsk, with Marx's *Das Kapital* thrust in his belt to shock passers-by.) Like Khanin, they both ended up in Moscow and rose in the Komsomol hierarchy. Kin graduated to *Pravda*, and Sitkovsky to the Komsomol Central Committee, where he was known just by his first name, which was itself a pseudonym. His real name was Isaac Ioelson and Kin's was Viktor Surovikin. (In the footsteps of Lenin, Trotsky, Stalin, Kamenev, and countless others, no true revolutionary seemed complete without a nom de guerre—even when its necessity had long passed.)[11]

In 1927 Kin and Ippolit attacked the leaden banality of the ultra moralists. In their view, commandments from above were off-target and inherently flawed. People could not—and should not—live by the tenets of a modern-day Leviticus. In the journal *Young Bolshevik,* Kin noted how difficult it was to make proscription sound appealing. He described meetings where officials spoke only of do's and don't's: "Don't chase women, believe in God, spit on the floor, swear, drink vodka, or smash windows." The only positive instructions were a meager "bathe and clean regularly." This prompted Kin to offer a new regimen for youth:[12]

Monday—clean your teeth
Tuesday—don't swear
Wednesday—bathe
Thursday—no women
Friday—get a rope and nail because it's time to hang yourself

In his self-help guide for Marxists published by the Komsomol entitled *The Right to Love* (1927), Ippolit was more provocative. Displaying rare wit (including supporting "footnotes" by the typesetters), Ippolit took to task Smidovich and Zalkind, among others, for their excessive theorizing. The latter, mocked by Ippolit as the "apostle of the Twelve Commandments of Communist Love," found his thesis that cross-class love was the same as making love to a crocodile reduced to folly:

> Well said! The beautiful words here about "the morally repulsive" are pointless. If the object [of love] is repugnant and thus all the more disgraceful, then it will be rejected regardless of any class situation. . . . How easy it is to take common sense to absurd levels! One is curious to know how comrade Zalkind feels about Marx, who spent his whole life with a woman of another class—Jenny von Westphalen, that is, a crocodile—and he really loved that "reptile." Or perhaps comrade Zalkind is in company with those who consider Marx a philistine in his domestic life? If that's the case, then we have nothing to talk about.[13]

Like Kin, Ippolit poked fun at dry Marxist theorists who called love a "bourgeois" affectation. As his title—*The Right to Love*—indicates, he agreed with Kollontai in extolling love; if it is just a function of glands, then what separates us from dogs? Communists should embrace, not reject, a higher concept of love. Taking a cue from the romantic side of Lunacharsky, Ippolit declared that "love is a great, necessary, and beautiful feeling to which the communist and Komsomolets alike have a full right." The mechanized ideal, no matter how attractive, ignores the importance of a "person's emotional enrichment."

Ippolit manipulated both sides of the debate, parodying that which, all the same, his work expressly asked for: "A communist not only has steel eyes and an iron voice, as literature presents him, but a living, beating heart to which the human is not alien." Behind this ironic cover, he also daringly suggested that propaganda should not always be accepted at face value: "The same hot blood as with other people runs in the communist's veins. . . . I don't turn my nose up at sentimental pleasures; I have a heart and eyes and enjoy looking at a pretty girl, feeling the round firmness of her breast when arm-in-arm, pressing myself to those lips, imbibing the sweet passion in her gaze and dying in her embrace."[14] Ippolit set off another round of the "what is love?" debate, first occasioned by Smidovich in her 1925 article in *Pravda*. For such "bourgeois" sentiments, he was accused in *The Young Communist* (which had published an excerpt from his book) of collusion with Kollontai for undermining the sublimation principle. To give oneself to love, wrote one reader, was "simply criminal."[15] Another dismissed love as a "cult of the parasitical classes," and for this reason communists "must declare absolute war" against it.[16] An essay entitled "Erotic Heresy" by S. Mileiko combined both criticism and a defense of Ippolit. He "doesn't know what he's writing about," Mileiko wrote. "Love and revolution are the best of friends. Love, inspired by revolution, is the best love! Revolution, infused with love, is the best revolution!" Proof could be found in the pantheon of cross-class heroes such as Spartacus, whose love for the patrician Valeriia did not stop him from becoming (to quote Marx) "the greatest person of all of ancient history—a strong leader, a noble character, a true representative of the ancient proletariat."[17] Another anonymous reviewer ("B. R.") came to the rescue of Jenny von Westphalen, not so much a "countess as a revolutionary who shared Marx's views and his fate." B. R. credited Ippolit for his "occasionally stunning humor" and for producing a work that, despite its mistakes, was "one of the best pieces of youth writing" on the subject.[18]

This scholasticism over the question of love revealed the limits of the Marxist doctrine that all human activity could be defined in relation to the revolution. Party leaders and intellectuals were reaping what they had sowed. The very language of revolution set the trap. The year-long debate over Ippolit's *Right to Love* was fueled not so much by disagreement over policy per se as confusion over the word "love" itself. "Love" signified too many things: emotional interest, romance, desire, the sexual act, or just the instinct to reproduce. Yet in the hands of Marxist critics, semantic differences were the battleground for political orthodoxy. By "love," Ippolit meant intense, mutually rewarding devotion, the antithesis of the emotionally frigid machine ideal. He decried the "sexual nihilism" he witnessed among Soviet youth, yet he was accused of propagating the same. For A. Saradzhev, the very title of Ippolit's book was "dangerous"; his idea of love brought him too close to the discredited Kollontai. To argue for such love as a "right" was inexcusable. This was precisely the kind of language that gave the "sexual question" center stage.[19] Saradzhev clearly misread Ippolit's argument, but their disagreement shows the malleability of the period's vocabulary. No better example exists than Lenin's blank-slate doctrine of revolutionary morality—the ultimate in semantic and ethical elasticity—which, as expected, was faithfully cited by all sides.

The same problem of definition arose in the debate over pornography, as reflected in the chillingly comic reception of Andrei Volzhsky's "The Volga Brotherhood" (1925).[20] A story of canonical orthodoxy, it highlights miners gaining class-consciousness, through Bolshevik guidance, as they pass through the necessary stages of proletarian maturation. First, the discontented miners form a secret union; they receive theoretical instruction from a Bolshevik, fight in the civil war, and end by living in an idealized commune five years later. There is not one word, no hint whatsoever, of sex among the communists. What was the story's sin? Three phrases, all pronounced by the enemy and hurled as obscenities at the protagonists: "ram's balls" (as in an officer commanding that his boots shine as such), "screw you" (*edrena mat'*, a euphemism for "fuck you"), and "whorehouse" (where the officers take their leisure).

"The Volga Brotherhood" was attacked in *Pravda* and taken to court at a publishing house in what was called the "first public trial of pornography in [Soviet] literature."[21] Given the prosecutors' charges—equal parts Kafka and Keystone—it is unclear what lesson could have been drawn from this affair. The "pornographic" words in question were said to be part of a sinister plot that "brings grievous harm, corrupting the reading masses, particularly youth." In self-defense, Volzhsky noted that such expressions were common in rural areas and that in using them he was merely being a faithful realist. Foreshadowing the crux of the debate over sexuality in literature, the prosecution countercharged that there was such a thing as too much realism, putting "The Volga Brotherhood" in the same company as "pornography which arouses, causes lust, and which corrupts youth in a sexual sense."

The prosecution closed by attempting to turn condemnation into a morality tale. Had not Tolstoy, it was noted for the record, depicted in *War and Peace* the whole of society "without the slightest hint of pornography?" Why then couldn't Volzhsky in a work thirty times smaller? Perhaps, therefore, he was influenced by Artsybashev and Verbitskaya, or had he read Pushkin's racy *Gavriliada*? No, Volzhsky responded to the first charge, yes to the second. In seeking prerevolutionary pornographic influences, the prosecution could claim that Volzhsky threatened to spread the same virus to a new generation. Worse, he was part of a veritable conspiracy, including the avant-gardists Pilnyak, Isaac Babel, and Nikolay Nikitin. Elsewhere such company would be a compliment, yet in this court, with Nikitin's prose derided as "mixing verbal onanism with the real thing," it was a ticket to damnation.

Fortunately for Volzhsky, sobriety was not in short supply. An older party member, Comrade Svirsky, came to Volzhsky's defense, making the modern argument that words have no meaning outside of context:

Before judging Comrade Volzhsky, we have to establish what pornography is. Unfortunately I have not read his work but have heard what he is accused of. He is charged with using such-and-such indecent words in his work. Permit me to direct your attention to some very decent words but from which you can create whatever pornography you want: bed, pillow, blood. From these three one can make something so pornographic that you'd run out of the room.[22]

Svirsky chastised the prosecution for neglecting the artist's motivation. Yes, pornography exists to "excite a well-known feeling," he continued, but this was not Volzhsky's intention. What should we do with pictures of naked women in museums? What if Volzhsky meant only to capture the speech of tsarist officers? In a work of realism, such language was not salacious. Svirsky concluded by declaring that pornography in the real sense was alien to the nation's literary tradition. For a true Russian realist, it was a betrayal: "In Russian literature there is practically no pornography; it came to us, like many things good and bad, from France. Now, there's a country where there truly is pornography."

Another defense was offered by Artem Vesely, party member, prose writer, and Pilnyak paragon, who applauded Volzhsky's efforts. Russians should take pride in the piquancy of their language, he insisted, which Volzhsky had captured in his dialogue:

> Volzhsky is not guilty. He wrote according to his conscience, and for this he is being attacked? Where is this coming from? From the desire to castrate the Russian language, to make it a gelding instead of a stallion. What's this? Prostitution is tolerated, but not Russian speech? All I have to say is that Comrade Volzhsky is correct. Down with fancy-shmancy Latin. Long live the Russian language.[23]

The trial was as much cartoon as kangaroo. While Volzhsky was vindicated, the court reprimanded him for using "indecent words" and hoped that the proceedings would help to "educate writers." The real purpose of the trial, a judicial travesty with merely symbolic value, remains obscure. The proceedings only highlighted the widespread confusion, particularly among party members, about what was proper in literature. Indeed, the court's own raison d'etre underscored the malleable foundations of Bolshevik ideology. By attacking an innocuous work that merely touched on naturalistic details of contemporary life, the trial succeeded in discrediting the very concept of pornography. The term was gutted of any real value beyond flagging whatever critics disapproved of.

Criticism from Outside

Young people were not blind to the fault lines in official models of sexuality circulating in the 1920s. Confusion about the issue was on full public display. In fact, tension and disagreement from on high only encouraged the personalized, idiosyncratic appropriation of revolutionary discourse by young people that frustrated party leaders and challenged their authority to regulate

Soviet society. At the worst, youth could reverse tack, identifying intensely private or selfish behavior as revolutionary. Such a reversal happened repeatedly in life and was reflected in literature. If officials themselves read contradictory meanings into ostensibly fixed ideological terms, one could only expect even more divergence as one moved further from the center. Young people were not necessarily intentional counterrevolutionaries, nor did they consciously resist the party's hegemonic ambitions.[24] On the contrary, much of what they did was what they thought proper—indeed, expected—since it was a Soviet axiom that one could not perform an ideologically neutral act.

In other words, malleability worked both ways. What made Bolshevik rhetoric so powerful also allowed it to be thrown back in the leaders' faces. The idea that environment controlled everything, for example, was too fortuitous an explanation to remain the property of high-placed theoreticians. Some began to identify the party itself, not merely bourgeois influences, as part of the corrupting environment. This was the point of A. Rozin's article, published in *The Young Communist,* entitled "Who's to Blame?" (1926), its title echoing that of Alexander Herzen's depressing novel of life and love in the nineteenth century. Rozin linked the frustration and despair among young people with the party's failure to correct their behavior. The tactics of shame and scare, of coerced patriotic salutes, were backfiring. Youth could not be helped, Rozin insisted, by burning questionable works or banning provocative literature. Youth needed "clear, insightful, and convincing answers to the questions that worry us members of the Komsomol." Such literature spoke to life, Rozin challenged, whereas the banalities proffered by the likes of Zalkind would never find a real audience:

> It's true that what you put into sausage is what you get. Unfortunately,
> the filling we have is incredibly poor, stale, and less than nourishing.
> Proof lies in our political clubs and our Komsomol popular literature.
> The latter reminds us of those automatic dispensers which if you put a
> coin in spit out tons of paper with ready-made, systematic answers.[25]

The article set off a small firestorm in the Komsomol.[26] Whereas all members subscribed to the proletarian-versus-bourgeois paradigm, their complaints and questions about sexuality revealed that personal experience could not be so easily defined. Lenin's widely touted aphorism that true communists were neither Don Juans nor ascetics fell flat in real life, since this was the kind of anemic advice that enraged Rozin and others. When asked how to apply this guideline to their own experience, party officials stumbled all over themselves, handicapped by self-righteousness. All they could do was to say what behavior was positive and what was negative. A collision of interests was inevitable. Frustrated young people were less concerned with judgments than with finding a means of understanding; yet officially sanctioned discourse, which they sincerely tried to use, pushed them toward the former. The predictable result was increased dissatisfaction on all sides.

Also in 1926, another caustic scandal erupted over young people's impatience with the patronizing tone and glib projections of party proclamations. The uproar began with a published letter from "Lida," a Komsomol member, to Sofia Smidovich, who gained notoriety through the "About Love" exchange in *Pravda* a year before. Because Lida's letter could stand for myriad others, it bears citation in full.[27]

Dear Comrade Smidovich,

I've read your articles about *byt* that have been published in journals and newspapers and therefore have come to the conclusion (which, admittedly, was not difficult) that you know youth *byt* well. I would like some answers to a few questions or, more accurately, advice on what to do. Although I have some answers of my own, I may be mistaken and, in any case, you know a great deal more about life than I and as an older comrade could help out and, perhaps, give me new direction. The problem is that the question of new *byt* is really debatable, with everyone understanding it his own way. Even among members of the party and Komsomol you won't find a single answer.

Below I'll give several facts regarding my life.

I'm nineteen, I live in Uzbekistan, so far from the center. Twice I've had to face this question. The first time was a year ago. In the Komsomol cell I met one member, X, and was suddenly taken with him and saw that this was the case with him too (perhaps to a lesser degree). We would walk home together from meetings and so on. As others do, we would slip into dark corners of the square, a garden or street and, as always, kiss. And then I would go home completely satisfied. But this only lasted for a month. One evening the kissing stopped: "Enough. I can't anymore, I need something more." But I absolutely didn't need anything else. So I answer, "No, we won't do that since I'm still too young and, what's more, it's not worth destroying your life [meaning abortion] on account of a momentary desire."

X says: "there won't be any abortions and I guarantee that I'll live with you seven months." Of course I didn't agree to *such beneficial conditions*. X said then that he would leave me for another and really wouldn't be able to see me anymore. I agreed to the last, since he didn't want to give up his freedom on account of me and I didn't want that.

To be honest, it was hard for me at first. I doubted my decision and was prepared to go back on it, especially as he would say in passing: "It's too bad you're denying yourself happiness." Then he moved away and only recently I met him, as a Komsomolist, in one cell. We walked home together but were so alien to each other like a wall had grown between us. That was the first time; now the second.

In the summer I often visited our Komsomol center and would see a guy there. We had a good, friendly—specifically friendly—relationship, as if there were no difference in gender. But in November the feeling changed and we began to learn about each other not only in a professional, Komsomol sense but a personal one too. But again I ran into the same problem. Once again: "Why do I love him but don't want to satisfy his needs" (although sometimes the feeling was there). I just wouldn't agree and he doesn't want to tie himself up, ruin his life, and so on. Everything's not over between us and we still have a friendly relationship but our get-togethers no longer have the same feeling or innocence. It's always the same conversation: why don't I want to?

Why is it "they" only want one thing and then leave, not even thinking about how I could destroy my life through an abortion and the thought that once I satisfy him he'll go.

Why do they want to have secretive get-togethers out there, on the grass? I'm not planning on dragging them into marriage but simply to live together if I'm cut out to be such a friend in life. After all, I'm not asking for all the comforts, material security, and so forth, but only that we live together and instead of wandering around all over and jumping up at the slightest sound, afraid that someone's coming.

I'm stuck at the crossroads and don't know whether I'm right or not. And what's next? Once again I'll meet someone and once again the same thing will start. What should I do? Either live under the bushes or go and put an end to it all. It's just all so stupid and I don't know who to be mad at, myself or someone else. This is why I decided to write you and share all this, like with an old friend who has experience in life, so that, as is said, I can take it all under advisement.

> With Komsomol regards,
> Lida

Lida's letter described a situation and posed questions typical of many others in the voluminous commentary flooding the media. (The letter had been sent to Smidovich in care of *The New Shift,* a lighter, illustrated cousin of *The Young Guard,* which took the lead in portraying and discussing contemporary *byt.*) Lida gave voice to many young people's sexual anxieties and antagonisms: selfish males against fearful, dissatisfied, resentful females, predatory behavior against low self-esteem, both internalizing destructive feelings. (Lida questions her own worthiness, not his.) She accurately conveys the public perception of gender roles and relationships, and thus her letter was too opportune for *The New Shift* to ignore. The letter was also appealing for its personal touch and, what was more important, the fact that Lida addressed it to a member of the older generation. The editors therefore published her letter in full, along with Smidovich's reply.

Smidovich had apparently learned little from the "About Love" debate of a year earlier, since it was her response to Lida's letter that caused the scandal. She assured Lida that she was right to refuse to have sex. Since women enjoyed "the honored role of reproducer of the human species," intercourse for them was both a greater reward and a greater danger than for men, who were physiologically programmed to consider a woman as a sexualized "animal." Smidovich then dropped the specifics of Lida's questions and turned to larger issues. Having succeeded Kollontai as head of the Zhenotdel in 1922, Smidovich had felt a responsibility in her new role to clean house and save youth, particularly young women. Now, four years later, she recognized that there was still much to be done. She worked Kollontai into her response as the theoretical inspiration for the kind of men who pressured Lida for sex. Kollontai's "glass of water theory" was the antithesis of Smidovich's carefully plotted biological argument. Marriage was not essential for sexual partners (her one concession to the modern age), but a father must help with the care of a child and recognize that a woman wants, first and foremost, a friend and comrade.

Ignoring the similarities between her response and some of Kollontai's beliefs, Smidovich made the usual recourse to the Marxist history of the family (traditionally defined by production relations) and its future ideal (defined by new relations and shared responsibilities between men and women). She believed that the advent of socialism and an improved environment would enable human beings to merge their sexual instincts with society's greater interests. In short, Lida's problem was temporary and could be explained away, once again, by a theoretical exposition of how Marxism would bring future good. Smidovich concluded by responding to Lida's specific questions with general maxims:

> You are sadly shaking your head because your personal question has not been answered. But until you work on resolving the central problem [the construction of socialism], it will be difficult to receive a satisfactory answer [for the questions] in your personal life.
>
> First of all, be firm in your conviction of having made the right choice. Don't make any concessions because they will bring to you nothing but disappointment and sorrow and to society, in which you live,

nothing but harm. After all, the details of your life that you've written about are not the only thing that constitutes our *byt*. A healthy proletarian youth with strong, healthy instincts is growing, a youth without the rot and decay that the cursed, vile, dying bourgeoisie exudes.[28]

A capsule version of core Marxist principles, Smidovich's response ironically offered no substantive answers to Lida's questions. Soon after, *The New Shift* published a fiery letter from Nina Velt (who identified herself as "senior in age and party status" to Lida) lambasting Smidovich for failing to offer any practical advice under the guise of providing proper guidance. This was for Velt the height of arrogance and condescension. Smidovich's favorite words were "should" and "must"; her favorite tense, the future. She could only console Lida by recourse to biology and assuring her that her feelings did not "contradict the interests of our proletarian state." Lida had merely been given the vague directive to do nothing that would bring grief to herself or harm to society. Velt writes:

> Lida will be right if she's not satisfied with Comrade Smidovich's answer. And who would be, when sharp corners are carefully oiled and smoothed, and the question itself is shifted into the glittering but cold sphere of discussion of principles?
>
> Lidas—and there are many of them—will only go look for answers in another place and will learn by their own sweat and from their own small experience. And maybe they'll pay with their lives for the starry-eyed advice of older comrades who don't even give a hint as to [proper] conduct. Let's not argue about principles; here we're all in agreement. It would be better to speak about turning heavenly principles into earthly reality.

Velt's letter rose above the usual polemical tone and in so doing went to the heart of the matter. Velt charged that Smidovich's arrogance, her inability to connect with youth (which so often sabotaged Bolshevik efforts to assume the role of surrogate parent) reflected not so much her personal character as the ideological paradigm itself. Like most authorities, Smidovich was more secure operating in the theoretical domain, where everything made sense, the boundaries of right and wrong were recognizable, and there were no anomalies or exceptions. Smidovich's understanding of Marxism kept her in an ivory tower contemplating a golden future. That Velt didn't have to exaggerate in order to discredit made her attack more poignant. She juxtaposed the words of one of the party's authorities on love and *byt* with those of a young woman seeking advice on the same. The distance between the two spoke for itself: the party's confidence in always having the right answer was part of the problem.

Velt's honest, forthright letter indicated her loyalty to the party. She readily accepted the infallibility of Marxism, but would not let future promises substitute for present needs. (She briefly mentioned Trotsky, who despite his downfall still remained for many a symbol of openness and pragmatism.) She ridiculed Smidovich's simplistic reduction of love to biology; a woman is more than a birth machine. A child is not a necessary element or an automatic result of an intimate relationship; hence Smidovich's opposition to abortion was unrealistic. Abortion certainly was dangerous, Velt conceded, but so too could be multiple births. Moreover, given current conditions, having more than two children would likely make a professional career for a woman impossible; therefore abortion was sometimes an unfortunate necessity. Similarly, some women might need to live separately to avoid male domination at home. Velt's goal was nothing less than full emancipation from complications, whether biological or social—in short, to "give mothers the right to choose the time for and the father of their child."

These three letters did not pass quietly. They were reprinted in one of the decade's most important collections, *Komsomol byt,* an anthology designed to educate youth that reflected a diversity of voices.[29] Echoes could be found elsewhere as well. In *The Right to Love* Ippolit lampooned Smidovich's idealism as "r-r-revolutionary" and (what was more dangerous) containing the kernel of a "neo-nihilist" attitude toward sexuality. For all her references to Marxism, he argued, Smidovich was curiously un-Marxist in reducing love to mere physiology.[30] Obviously enjoying the debate, the editors of *The New Shift* also published letters hostile to Velt. Smidovich nevertheless had the final say, rebuking Velt for her "apathetic" and "ironic" attitude to theory, while praising her for recognizing the practical problems at hand. Only self-discipline and will power, Smidovich concluded, would enable young women to get through these difficult times.

Fading of Revolutionary Zeal

All involved in this exchange noted the impact of currently dismal economic conditions on personal behavior. Even the most ideologically intoxicated could not ignore widespread poverty and deprivation in the Soviet Union, especially among students, as critical factors shaping popular attitudes. For all his faith in the future, in his study of sexual behavior David Lass included the following student's disheartening comment:

Our stipends are nothing, and because of a lack of money we don't go to the theater or movies, we don't buy books or dress properly. We just sit in our rooms, not going out. . . . All nice things in life just pass us by.

We have no future. We're not living but eking out an existence, mind-
lessly counting off the pitiful days. Our material deficiencies very often
drive us to criminal activities because life demands its own.[31]

This bleak picture does not describe the immediate postwar period but was
written a full ten years after the revolution, when the New Economic Program was at its height. Small-scale privatization under NEP had not benefited
everyone, leading to sharp divisions between a new, "Soviet" bourgeoisie and
impoverished workers or government-dependent students. Contrary to expectations, visible class distinctions persisted, exacerbating widespread despair and resentment. This inspired not only petty crime but also the whole
gamut of rebellious activities for which youth were frequently blamed: dis-
trust of the state or the party, drinking to excess, a "nihilistic," carpe diem approach to sex, materialism (the "silk stocking" syndrome, trying to maintain
at least the appearance of better living), and slovenliness. (In one survey of
young Leningrad workers, 42 percent reported washing every day, many
without soap, and less than a third brushed their teeth daily.)[32]

Those like Smidovich and Semashko who rejected the environmental explanation for youth's "filth" and indiscretions were often in the minority. N.
Tutkin's analysis of university life in Moscow, published in *The Young Communist* in 1927, is an appalling picture of half-starved students, with almost
three-quarters of them ill. (Conditions were even worse farther from the center.)[33] Tutkin saw poverty and degradation as explicit reasons for why students resorted to theft or prostitution. He did not condone such behavior,
but sought to jolt readers out of narcotic complacency, the "everything will be
great" mentality. Propaganda was prominent in the early Soviet Union, but
at that time it could not efface reality. Tutkin reminded readers that a year
before *The Young Communist* itself had identified poverty and the ineffective-
ness of cultural-educational institutions as the two primary causes in the rise
of crime among youth.[34] In terms as stark as Velt's, Tutkin laid out his frustration with those who would deny the obvious: "Pessimism is a fact. Suicides
are a fact. Drunkenness is a fact. Sexual depravity is a fact. Infection by [NEP]
ideology is a fact."[35] The Komsomol's own internal reports validated Tutkin's
comments. Drunkenness was the most prevalent transgression among young
people—so much so that some cells in villages had earned a local reputation
as mere drinking clubs (this was an improvement, however, over the image of
Komsomol clubs as the locus of godless orgies).[36]

Despondency caused by material want became associated with an overall
emotional letdown that pervaded Komsomol and party ranks following the
tumult of civil war. Zalkind noted that for many the "revolutionary flame had
died out."[37] Worse, some questioned what they had done, as Khanin admitted in his memoirs. Whatever NEP had done to save the country, ideologi-

cally it was a catalyst for doubt among die-hard communists as they witnessed a new bourgeoisie rising from the ashes of the old. Most alarmingly, postpartum depression was not confined to youth.

The most disquieting portrait in this vein was Fedor Gladkov's novella, *Drunken Sun* (1927), which explicitly combined political ennui with sexual depravity.[38] It is set in a sanatorium in the South where four patients are undergoing water and electric therapy to restore their exhausted nerves and bodies. Sofia Petrovna and Akatuev represent the older generation, party members from before the revolution; Marusya and Maznin, age seventeen and nineteen, are the young Komsomolists. Rather than advancing elevating scenarios such as the old teaching the young, or the young helping the old (following Trotsky's "New Course," all working as a single force for the party), Gladkov presents a sordid picture. What unites the four principal characters is not love of party or country but a shared melancholy and an obsession with sex. (Sexual overindulgence seems to be what landed many of the patients in the sanatorium in the first place.) Sofia Petrovna, after twenty years' experience in the party, is now old and desiccated (except for her "luscious, maiden-like lips"). She remembers the revolutionary past, with its underground work and imprisonment, as her happiest time, when sexual "disruptions" restored her energy for the struggle. Now the luster is gone; only an "epidemic of debauchery" reigns. Her peer, Akatuev, still hopes to reclaim his sexual power as a tonic and eyes young Marusya as the means to a cure. Surprisingly, Marusya grants his wish, and their embrace on the edge of a cliff is rendered by asterisks. More shockingly, she, not he, is restored by their act. When Sofia Petrovna worries that Marusya, like so many other young people, will again overwork herself and have to come in for "repair," Marusya retorts that she now has "the strength of a hundred horses." Conversely, Akatuev regrets his moment of weakness and leaves, preferring the orderly dullness of work to dangerous, listless freedom. Yet it is young Maznin, who has long desired Marusya, who is shattered by the cliff-side encounter. He calls Marusya a slut for having so easily given to Akatuev what she had so firmly denied him. He tries to rape her, but, calling on her newfound strength, she fights him off. The story closes with a reverse gender stereotype: Maznin, abandoned, succumbs to a final fit of hysterics.

From the party's point of view, it would be difficult to imagine a set of characters more damning or a plot resolution more maddening than that of *Drunken Sun*. It not only sounded like a dirge for fighters that once were strong, but also an attempt to besmirch their good name. Readers who recognized themselves in Akatuev no doubt cringed when reading his thoughts. His change of heart at the end could hardly compensate for his role as a scavenger, feeding off the remnants of broken spirits and bodies. Far from presenting the ideal of a well-functioning human machine, Gladkov's characters are abusive, exploitative, sex-ridden, narcissistic animals. They may give lip service to ideological correctness, yet their words have no substance. Their true interest lies in themselves, their emotions and impulses.

While *Drunken Sun* seems to end on an uplifting note with the triumph of Marusya, ideologically it is hardly an affirmative work. It dramatizes real-life conflicts: young men concerned only with sex; predatory sexuality; men's preference for bourgeois-looking women over comrades; the revolutionary spirit dampened by daily routine. Yet these themes have no satisfactory resolution. If anything, only sex is advanced as the true cure for the characters' physical and spiritual malaise. It certainly does more than the "Frankenstein" treatments undertaken at the sanatorium—half-naked bodies with metal cups stuck on them, sparks coming out of the apparatus. All are infected, male and female, old and young. Maznin's animalism is paralleled by Marusya's willing acceptance of a quick liaison with a much older man, both favoring sex without reason, love, commitment, or forethought. And yet while one falls, the other rises. What more conflicted message could there be?

Gladkov's intention in *Drunken Sun* was unclear. An established Marxist who had been arrested and exiled before the revolution, he had become a champion of proletarian literature with *Cement* (1924), a novel of industrial and personal reconstruction.[39] It, too, broached the issue of new family relations and sexual mores. Gleb, the protagonist, returns from the civil war to find his wife, Dasha, transformed into an icon of the newly liberated, independent woman. With hair bobbed and Bebel under her arm, she is no longer Gleb's "sweetheart" but "vigorous, unsubduable, knowing her own mind." She tells Gleb that she has been with men "more than once" in his absence and will no longer submit to a double standard of sexual behavior. After the death of their daughter, nothing remains to keep them together. She consoles him at the end with words that could be found in any number of official speeches and pamphlets: "Love will always be love, Gleb, but it requires a new form. Everything will come through and attain new forms, and then we shall know how to forge new links." The present is uncertain, but all will be well in the future.

Cement also contained its share of dark spots, most notably a rape of a woman by a communist who is never punished, despite the story's emphasis on the trauma suffered by the victim. This is one of many unusual touches that made the novel sometimes ambiguous, but it was, surprisingly, praised by almost all. In fact, such a favorable reception may explain the negative response to *Drunken Sun* three years later; critics must have had their expectations horribly overturned. It was too much for G. Iartsev, an editor of *The Young Guard*, who entitled his attack, "Let's trim the wings of this winged eros." Failing to mention that his journal had published the essay by Kollontai alluded to in his title, he still decided that enough was enough. "Comrade

Gladkov, have mercy! This is not a sanatorium for sick workers, members of the party, or Komsomol, but a legalized brothel. Where have we ended up? According to *Drunken Sun,* all the proletariat's thoughts and experiences come down to one thing: lust for the flesh." He evoked Gladkov's earlier protagonist in *Cement*—"Gleb Chumalov, where are you?"—as a reminder of what the author was capable of and questioned his intentions. Because Gladkov had earlier received the benefit of the doubt with *Cement,* he must have meant *Drunken Sun* to provide "material for arguments and discussions on questions of *byt* and sex because of youths' interest in this subject." But even here a line had to be drawn. "After the life-affirming *Cement* we don't want to accuse Gladkov of decadence, but why go so overboard?"[40]

The question remained unanswered, as *Drunken Sun* disappeared from later discussions of Gladkov's contribution to Soviet literature. It was an obvious embarrassment to the writer and critics alike. Nevertheless, Gladkov was not entirely off the mark. His characters' degraded condition (if not exactly the cause of it) reflected the post–civil war alarm over party members driving themselves to exhaustion. Zalkind declared that a "revolutionary year" was the equivalent of "many years of normal living." This meant that the demands of the sociopolitical calendar outstripped the chronological one: "In five to eight years the organism wears itself out as if it had lived fifteen to twenty."[41] A report from the Central Control Commission noted that overwork, along with the more old-fashioned malaise of unrequited love, was partly to blame for suicides among party members.[42] Lenin's and later Trotsky's fear that the stultifying tentacles of bureaucracy posed a grave threat to the lifeblood of revolution was becoming all too true. In a speech before the Komsomol Central Committee, now preserved in the archives with the stamp "top secret," Sosnovsky pointed an accusing finger at "the soul-crushing frigidity and stifling banality that without exception plague all institutions, Komsomol, union—about the party ones themselves I need not even speak."[43] Even Milchakov, responding to a special commission investigating increased drunkenness and hooliganism in the Komsomol, publicly admitted that the Komsomol clubs, the heart of each cell, were too often boring, dreary places. No more writing resolutions, he stormed; clubs had to be remade to appeal to youth in an intellectual, political, and social sense—though he categorically rejected the attempt by one club to attract members with lectures entitled "Prostitution and Youth," "About Masturbation," and "Is Sexual Abstinence Harmful?"[44]

A Permanent Answer

Yet whatever the party hierarchy gained in honesty was compromised by the proposed cure: give youth more of the same. If young people were turned off by party work, ran the bureaucratic reasoning, it was because the party and the Komsomol did not play enough of a role in their lives. In *Life Out of Control* (1929) Vera Ketlinskaia and Vladimir Slepkov did not hide the depressing results of a poll conducted among Vyborg youth in which only 47 percent indicated that the Komsomol exerted a positive influence on their lives; 13 percent claimed a negative influence, and 39 percent saw no impact. Worse, only 52 percent even answered this question, which meant that perhaps only a quarter of those polled saw the Komsomol as a beneficial institution. Predictably, authorities decided that the only sure way to restore morale, instill greater devotion, and deliver youth from behavioral excesses was to broaden the function of the Komsomol from "observer" to "organizer." Full agency meant that its members should seek and accept greater intervention in their lives by the organization. "It is high time," Ketlinskaia and Slepkov declared, "to cross the 'forbidden line' and rip open the doors of the private home where the Komsomol-individualists gather, where philistine habits often form, where the community spirit cannot reach. The life of the Komsomolist and, in general, that of the young worker cannot be divided into two halves."[45] The solution was to promote success through model behavior and by stepping in forcibly where example was not enough. Those who misbehaved must be corrected; those who were slipping away must be returned to the fold; if a family had problems or was nurturing the seed of philistinism, it must be visited.

Yet the most favored path, the one made necessary by party-first ideology, pushed officials into a corner. Was not the extent of the party's presence in their lives part of what young people, even committed ones, objected to? Indeed, Slepkov had warned in *Komsomol Pravda* that efforts to politicize all facets of life and to hold youth to strict behavioral codes often backfired. Striking a libertarian chord, he asserted that Soviet teenagers should be left alone: "To be young in all of its particulars is not a sin, is not in any way bad and, in fact, is necessary." To live entirely within official guidelines, while theoretically desirable, would make one an "ascetic," a prematurely aging automaton that would burn out and fall prey to "decadent inclinations."[46]

Likewise, *Life Out of Control* also criticizes party policies and intentions as dehumanizing: "The collective should quit handling people as dry statistics but understand them as living Komsomol members."[47] To the chagrin of those advocating greater intervention in personal life, there was also published criticism of the Komsomol stepping over its bounds, dictating when to go to bed, what leisure activities were proper, or how many dates one could have.[48] Even the presumed staples of control were not always free of scrutiny. Referring to recent activities at a Novgorod university, one member noted in *Komsomol Pravda* that searching dormitories for harmful literature (in this casc, Kollontai's *Love of the Worker Bees*) was going too far in the campaign for ideological and moral purity.[49] Youth could be excused their confusion when, alongside crusades against red tape, Dr. B. V. Tsukker openly championed bureaucratic activity as an excellent way to combat sexual misbehavior: "The constant motion until you drop, the meetings, discussions, councils, commissions, and assemblies—all of this helps sexual discharge, that is, energy is expended."[50]

A more expedient, if permanent, escape from conflicting messages, poverty, and depression was suicide. How many chose to end their lives is impossible to ascertain. Nevertheless, the widespread alarm over the current epidemic of suicides among young people is important because, more than any other transgressive act, suicide drove home to authorities the gulf between hopeful ideals and the current chaos.[51] An explanation for why some young Soviets resolved to commit suicide is found in an anonymous letter, never published, but preserved in the Komsomol archives. The author could stand for the prototypical youth for whom the revolution had gone sour, its promises of material abundance broken, its spirit corrupted. For many, the cataclysm had only changed the surface, the discursive coating of life, leaving behind an even worse reality than before. With elusive syntax and punctuation, colliding bureaucratic and conversational tones, and escalating rancor, the letter gives the impression of an exploding monologue. The run-on sentences capture the writer as if he were physically present before his tormenters, shaking a fist of despair and anger.[52]

Comrades!

So as to not create any extra red tape or cause you to warn those who perhaps aren't even to blame for this event, I won't give my address and don't even know how to send this letter so that you won't be able to tell by the postmark, but maybe I'll succeed by getting someone else who is going to a different city to do it. I wish to inform you, comrades who work in the city and in particular on the editorial board of *Komsomol Pravda*, how students are being treated in universities, especially technological schools, as I myself am a student at one, and why I have decided to kill myself all so that you can know how sincerely I express not only my opinion but the opinion of other proletarian students who do not live, but suffer in tech schools.

Already a second week without a penny or piece of bread, I'm doomed to death by starvation and will have to go without food for another month, of course being physically healthy I'm not going to beg for bread on the streets and about work, there is none, not even grunt work, for a month I've been asking daily in offices, organizations, and the labor board and everywhere a refusal, they say they need to give workers work, and my comrades and me, we're just students—"students" don't get work so we're doomed to starve to death and why now, that is at the time when we haven't received our stipends (for the first month it was the usual deficit and for this reason we're already a month and a half without it) and have to go to classes exhausted after a lot of studying and party work (and I'm considered a good worker, both for the Komsomol and society) and we'll get tuberculosis and other diseases, so I've decided to kill myself, starving already 1½ months (I would probably die of hunger anyway) to kill myself, while I can still move and do it myself. I am a peasant by birth, but being with the Komsomol I left home, the usual procedure and once was sent on business by the Komsomol regional office to a technical school. Because I had no place to go and there was no work and also being hungry I began to ask if I could study but they sent me where I didn't want to go and where I ended up was really bad.

What else, there being in my character the need to get to the truth and all the time I tried being twenty years old and found it nowhere. The directors, they're so fat and heavy the chairs break while students go hungry and in rags, no matter where you go to get what you need they tell you to get lost; everywhere it's their own clan and gang, those are not communists in the state apparatus now (I mean the ones put in there by Comrade Lenin and others) but bureaucrats who if you try to see without prior notification, he'll bark at you, won't treat you like a human being or listen to you. All the while we're starving (and so are all those out of work), but these individual people are choking on their own fat: cars, buses, horses, restaurants, theaters, the best cafeterias are all for them; you begin to ask yourself, hey, why all the words and speeches, how does our state differ from the tsarist one: with the tsar there were fewer pot-bellies, now we've got more. It's too bad that 1917 has passed; I'd slice open more than one of their bellies. They are the real parasites, just like bedbugs. . . . Everything's b.s.

Since I'm hungry and no one has helped, neither the city committee, district committee, tech school, bureau of labor, the city council or anybody else, I give my word to *Komsomol Pravda* that when you receive this letter I'll already be dead. (Suicide among students is not the newest thing in our district.) The fact that I am hungry, not having found support or justice and not seeing anything hopeful before me, and since I entered this college not by my own choice and am not allowed to transfer, and this profession disgusts me (I repeat that I ended up at this college only by chance) then why should I continue to suffer now and later.

[Signed]
One of the suffering

I will commit suicide in a way that no one will find out immediately;
I'll say I'm going somewhere.
Everything is just so empty, pitiful and trite

Why the letter was not published is obvious. It was too much even for the relatively open-minded and inquisitive spirit of the newspaper. Significantly, it does not criticize the revolution itself. For the author its legitimacy is unquestionable; he waxes nostalgic for 1917, when he had a license to effect social change with his own hands. That this time of empowerment has passed and he is ruled by fat bureaucrats lies at the heart of his frustration: *they* don't give him work; *they* don't pay him; *they* don't care about him. It is as if the revolution were a colossal bait and switch: promises of deliverance from hunger have turned into a policy of starvation; guarantees of liberation and equality have brought greater inequity and disenfranchisement. The letter exposes, in short, the raw hypocrisy enshrined by NEP: it has become a fraud in which party members, if they are truly loyal, cannot participate.

The first to give a name to suicide was the poet, Nikolai Kuznetsov, who hanged himself on September 20, 1924, also at age twenty.[53] His death was a tremendous blow to the Komsomol, for it was too close to home and could not be washed over as a mere statistic: the family had lost "Kolya," as he was often fondly remembered. Kuznetsov was an official celebrity because the details of his life were tailor-made for the ideal young worker-poet. Like so many others, he had gone from the village to the city. At age fourteen he was working in a factory. Later he joined the Komsomol and fought in the civil war, then moved to Moscow to study and write. Even better for orthodox Bolsheviks was the fact that Kuznetsov's most famous work, the cycle *Komsomol Love* (1923), extolled the two imperatives of male sexual behavior, sublimation of passion and respect for women, for which the critic Dmitry Gorbov proclaimed him "standing equal to the best that post-October literature has given us."[54] This title, however, did not save him from tragedy, as exemplified in a posthumously published poem: [55]

> All day I wander with a cigarette,
> My heart in the paws of despair.
> I'm lost at the intersection
> Of the city square.

To have the poet of proper love end his life did not make sense. Consequently, just as he was a symbol of the right values while living, a lesson had to be made of his death. Kuznetsov came to embody, all at once, the chief explanations for youthful malaise. In addition to his disappointment with NEP—which ostensibly killed the "romantic" in him—the city was blamed for ensnaring him in its "literary bohemia."[56] Given that poets' cafes were dens of prostitution, drugs, alcohol, and libertinism, Kuznetsov had been lured away from the bedrock of his life, the factory. One of the earlier critics of Kollontai, Ilya Lin, lamented the poet's estrangement from his work as if it were the alienation of two lovers.

> In separating with his faithful companion, comrade lathe, he also split from his true friends, the mentors and instructors of the Danilov workers [his factory]. This was the reason for his internal discord and strife. And the further he stepped away from the factory, the more difficult life seemed, and the more his own strength drained.[57]

Isolation from the factory was not merely a Samson-like haircut; it meant that Kuznetsov had severed ties from his other home, the Komsomol. Significantly, his parents were dead. He was an orphan, both literally and ideologically, drifting more and more into himself. For Lin, who claimed to have last seen him at Lenin's mausoleum, such isolation should have warranted both outside intervention and an attempt at personal reformation:

> [Kuznetsov] lost his grounding, the support of the Komsomol, the factory, the motor, the lathe, and his fellows from the cell. And that was our mistake, our sorrow, and our responsibility—the responsibility of the party and Komsomol to tell all poets and artists who come from the ranks of workers: don't lose contact with the factory![58]

The campaign against Kuznetsov-like disaffection received an official imprimatur from the highest echelon of leaders at the XIV Party Congress in December 1925. This was the last real showdown over control of the party, and it ended by delivering a crippling blow against the Zinoviev-Kamenev bloc which, after Trotsky, had belatedly discovered the need for more "democracy" in party governance to thwart Stalin and Bukharin. Although Bukharin's defeat would come a few years later, for the time being the congress was very much his show. Calling in an early session for "iron discipline" in the party, Bukharin led the attack against Zinoviev's alleged factionalism. Later, in the nineteenth session, he turned in the other direction with a speech, "About the Komsomol." From the veritable pulpit of the party, Bukharin assailed the rot in the Komsomol and recommended its cure. He cited as causes the usual environmental factors (unemployment, poor living conditions), faulted the Komsomol's own conduct (overworking its members, boring them with sloganeering) and attacked individuals, primarily the "anarchists" (shorthand for anyone who resisted central control) and the "nihilists" (those who put rebellion before socialist revolution). For the latter he restated his mantra that 1917 had turned the value of countercultural activity upside down. If the state was now good, antiestablishment behavior was now bad. Bukharin pointed his finger at young people's smoking, excessive drinking (acknowledging that in some Komsomol cells 25–30 percent of members regularly got drunk), and free sex, singling out the pro-nudist "Down with Shame" movement and its cousin, "Down with Virginity" as egregious examples. In explicitly political terms, he cautioned that these transgressions should not be seen as separate from Zinoviev's opposition. Factionalism was the primary danger from above; alienation and waywardness came from below. Both threats could be countered by closing ranks, by increasing discipline (that is, by supporting him and Stalin), and by taking a new step, "the rationalization of *byt*," defined as the "introduction of order where before there was chaos."[59]

Bukharin said nothing new, but because of its timing, his speech came the closest to what might be called an official platform after Lenin's interview with Zetkin. Except for the one representative from Leningrad, Zinoviev's power base, in the "debate" that followed Yaroslavsky, Milchakov, and others praised and reiterated the points of Bukharin's program. The congress ended by issuing a special twelve-page resolution formalizing Bukharin's conclusions, with three additional emphases: (1) the problem of youth's vulnerability as pawns in their elders' political struggles (a reference to the support for Zinoviev by the Leningrad Komsomol and Trotsky's earlier flirtation with the organization); (2) the necessity of subordinating the Komsomol to the party (combating the assumption of youth's superior wisdom); and (3) a warning directed to young people to avoid extremes of optimism and pessimism (a controversial doctrine in the campaign against youthful excesses).[60] Bukharin's speech and the party resolution, much reprinted and anthologized, marked a renewed effort to reform Soviet youth.[61] Endorsements came, symbolically both from the old guard (represented by Yaroslavsky) and from the young (represented by Khanin, the rebel-turned-revolutionary).[62]

What electrified Bukharin's broadside was what happened offstage. Two days before his speech, the poet Sergei Esenin had hanged himself in a Leningrad hotel. The dramatic coincidence of the suicide of this "cherubic hooligan" (in Max Eastman's words) during the congress seemed almost providential.[63] Who else but Esenin represented all that Bukharin had targeted? He was the Khanin-like rebel amplified many times, and quite unrepentant. He had welcomed 1917 for all the wrong reasons: "In the years of revolution I was wholly on the side of October, but I regarded everything in my own way."[64] This "I" was Esenin's banner of romantic libertarianism, and in its name he took Moscow by storm in the years after the revolution. If bohemia has two faces, the brooding and the brash, Esenin embraced the latter. By his early twenties he was already an accomplished alcoholic, a vulgar habitué of artistic cafés, and given to exhibitionist pranks with fellow imagist poets. A perennial loudmouth, he was once detained by the police for telling an audience to "fuck off." Indeed, the police station seemed almost his second home (or only one, since he had no permanent residence).[65]

With reports of illegitimate children, bisexuality, and carousing with prostitutes, Esenin's notoriety exceeded even that of Pushkin (who was currently being offered, however awkwardly, as a model of sexual sublimation). Marriage to Isadora Duncan, whose bare feet and rich personal life had already made her an international symbol of art converging with carnality, only added to Esenin's scandalous reputation. The union of an older woman with a younger man recalled Kollontai's reversal of stereotypes, yet similarities ended there. The highlight of their tumultuous relationship was a whirlwind trip to America, full of incessant drunkenness, smashed furniture, and Esenin's abuse of Duncan—otherwise known, in Max Eastman's deft coinage, as a "Bacchical noctambulation" and "Dyonisian demigration."[66]

It is not difficult to see why Esenin had such a cult following among youth. His poetic work, which included such titles as "The Confession of a Hooligan," "A Hooligan's Love," and "Barroom Moscow," was seen as one long celebration of debauchery, drunkenness, and taboo-wrecking. His last poem, a farewell to an unnamed friend, was written in his own blood. The anonymity of this "friend" seemed an open invitation to disenchanted revolutionaries and poets to imagine themselves in his place. Nor was Esenin's popularity restricted to the politically "immature" or "vulnerable." Key figures like Trotsky and the editor and critic Alexander Voronsky lauded his artistic talent (if not lifestyle), and even Bukharin admitted that their praise for his poetry was justified. Esenin's lyrics appeared in prominent journals such as Voronsky's *Red Virgin Soil* and *October*, and collections of his works were often reprinted. Thousands attended his funeral, and countless poems and eulogies were published in his memory.

From the party's point of view, Esenin's suicide could not have come at a better time. It played directly into officials' hands because it fulfilled all their prognostications. Since Esenin showed no remorse for his atrocious behavior, the script called for self-destruction. Whereas Kuznetsov's suicide could enforce the lesson not to separate oneself from the collective, in Esenin's bohemian excesses the Bolsheviks found a profusion of personal, social, and political transgressions. A propaganda machine would have been hard pressed to invent a better poster villain. His life neatly reenacted the cautionary tale in which a village youth comes to the city and is ensnared by decadence. Also damning was his association with Trotsky. Although Esenin never supported Trotsky in the traditional sense, their lives curiously intersected at key times as both fell from grace. As much the cultured intellectual as revolutionary Marxist, Trotsky appreciated artistic talent and lauded Esenin in *Literature and Revolution* (1925). In turn, Esenin pronounced the party leader a "genius" in *Izvestiia*.[67] After the poet's death, Trotsky was one of the first to publish a eulogy in *Pravda,* Bukharin's own stronghold. In his campaign against the growth of deadwood in the state apparatus, Trotsky singled out Esenin as "real" and "fresh." Despite scandal, the poet possessed a "true soul," and his death was caused by the tragic collision of a lyric heart and the raw brutality of the day. Unable to endure the present, Esenin was meant for the future, when "friendship and love, not conflict reigns." If Ippolit could argue that communists had "the right to love," Trotsky declared that the revolution would guarantee not only a "right to bread" but a right to "song" as well.[68]

Eseninism (*eseninshchina*) became an all-purpose epithet, a blend of fact, myth, and innuendo that represented the worst of young people's wayward-ness and assigned to them a common fate. To be sure, most critics and offi-cials were careful not to question Esenin's artistic achievement. Bukharin (closer to Trotsky than to Stalin in his cultural tastes) conceded that "there could be no argument" as to the poet's talent, but went no further. Other gifted writers had written pornographic verse, such as the eighteenth-century poet Barkov. More important than artistic merit was the impact of such liter-ature. Bukharin was frankly "ashamed" at the outpouring of sympathy fol-lowing Esenin's suicide, although he acknowledged that many readers would not share his dismay. In "Evil Observations," he dumped all the skeletons out of the poet's closet:

> Eseninism is disgusting, powdered-up and vulgarly painted Russian ob-
> scenities, drenched in drunken tears which makes it all the more revolt-
> ing. A weird mix of "studs," icons, "big-titted broads," "hot candles,"
> birch trees, the moon, bitches, the lord god, necrophilia, oceans of alco-
> hol tears and the "tragic" hiccup of the drunk, religion and hooliganism,
> "love" for animals, the barbaric treatment of humans, in particular
> women, the pitiful attempt to get "the whole picture" (within the very
> narrow four walls of your usual pub), debauchery raised to a height of
> "principle," and so forth all under the banner of the holy fool and quasi-
> populist nationalism—that's what Eseninism is.[69]

Bukharin's outpouring was an attempt to turn decadence in on itself. It was also part of a clearly orchestrated campaign of denunciation. *Komsomol Pravda,* which in 1925 superseded *The Young Communist* as the Komsomol's primary organ, published letters from "typical" members denouncing Es-enin's poetry.[70] An article about young people who had recently committed suicide noted their common infatuation with Esenin.[71] Orthodox Komsomol poets like Aleksandr Zharov (nine years younger than Esenin) and Aleksandr Bezymensky (three years younger) countered the flood of eulogies from literary circles by editing an anthology of attacks against "literary hooliganism and bohemia"[72] and by labeling Esenin as "poison" and deriding attempts to "whitewash" his name.[73] After a series of gang rapes in the summer of 1926 by Komsomol members, Lev Sosnovsky upbraided his colleagues for only now recognizing the danger posed by the poet and his legacy. In *Pravda* he directly identified the poet as the instigator of these violations even beyond the grave. Esenin's crime was to romanticize hooliganism, reduce women to sexual objects, and enshrine their exploitation (or, as Sosnovsky put it, the "poeticization of pawing"). This time Sosnovsky had the evidence he needed: the poetry itself. By quoting selected lines with the guilty words in bold type, he sought to prove that Esenin's artistic reputation was unfounded, that he was an incarnation of the "pornographic" Barkov. Sosnovsky even confessed to feeling embarrassed to print these offensive lines again, but something had to be done to "dethrone hooliganism":

> **So many girls I've felt.**
> **So many women I've squeezed in corners.**
>
> Drink with me, **dirty bitch.**
> Drink with me.
>
> Drink, scarecrow, drink.
> I'd be better off with **that one there, with the tits**—
> She's stupider.
> You're not the first woman I've had . . .
> There's a lot of you.
> But with such a one as you, a sleazebag,
> It will be a first.

Sosnovsky went beyond criticizing Esenin. Those who praised and supported him were equally complicit, as was the publishing house for posting a banner with his name. He accused the editors of being excessively "permissive," raising a question that is still puzzling: why in a state with the ability to control publications was Esenin's work so often reprinted?[74]

Sosnovsky's attacks revealed that the stakes in the debate had risen sharply. If three years earlier the main concern in the uproar over Kollontai's writing had been a fear of her potentially bad influence, now an exact connection was being made between a corrupt literature and corrupted life. Although the impact of art on life had long been asserted, never had there been such irrefutable "proof." Thus the campaign to de-romanticize Esenin's suicide compressed life and literature into one domain. Esenin's real-life sufferings had generated a poetic voice that had inspired crime and suicide, which in turn only inflated his mythic specter even more. It was a closed circuit in which art and reality did not merely imitate each other; they were ontological siblings. As the futurist Aleksei Kruchenykh observed, where goes the poetry so goes the poet: "Esenin, the poet of suicide, led his own life to that sad but logical end, to suicide itself."[75] The implication was that so too could go the reader. Such a fear drove the critic G. Bergman to call for explicit ideo-biological hygienic measures: if Esenin is an "infection," then "a revolutionary, communist, Marxist inoculation, particular among students, is needed."[76]

Extending the metaphor of inoculation still further, officials believed that if literature could kill it could also save. A. Reviakin demanded that the battle be moved onto the poet's territory: "Esenin's harmful impact cannot be eliminated by decree. . . . Proletarian poetry has to create [its own] artistic product capable of answering the epoch's needs."[77] Bukharin conceded that young people were right to complain of the sterility of propaganda; it only made Esenin more popular: "We serve up shockingly monotonous ideological fare. . . . More often than not the consumer receives hackneyed paragraphs and circulars written with such boring uniformity that they make the unaccustomed person nauseous."[78] In a 1924 Central Committee speech regarding the party's role in cultural affairs, Bukharin had championed market principles—a policy that would become official in a famous resolution the following year—arguing that only "free anarchical competition," true "literary works, not theses," could answer the demands of "diverse" readers.[79] Now he cast down the gauntlet:

> Why does Esenin capture the attention of youth? Why among our youth
> are there groups of "Esenin widows"? Why does a book of his poetry
> often lie underneath the Komsomolist's communist textbook? Because
> we and our ideologues have not touched the chords of youth as has
> Sergei Esenin, albeit in a destructive way.
>
> From this can come only one obvious conclusion. We can't feed our
> youth with horse pills made up of all the same content. A greater variety
> of questions [is needed]! More attention [must be given] to living persons with their distinct psychologies! More attention to life in all its diverse colors, sides, and fantastic complexity.[80]

The fight over Esenin's legacy encapsulated all facets of the party's attempt to connect with and correct youth. The convergence of art and reality may seem a platitude today, but it was the heart of debate then. Yet even in the battle over literature, in which it would seem that party officials shared a common purpose, they could not escape the conflicting signals that bedeviled their own proclamations. Even though Esenin was said to pose a grave internal threat, at the height of the anti-Esenin campaign the state was busy publishing his collected works in many editions, complete with the poems that so offended Sosnovsky. One edition included a foreword by Voronsky (along with Trotsky, Esenin's greatest defender in the party) entitled "About the Departed," in which he noted Esenin's tremendous appeal among peasants, workers, and intellectuals, young and old alike.[81] If anything, the poet symbolized a true *smychka*, a term much paraded by the state to signify its attempts to unite the peasant and proletarian classes under one banner. Also paradoxically, Karl Radek, a member of the Politburo, argued in print that the rash of suicides were not all Esenin's fault, that distressing material conditions were much to blame. Esenin's poem cycle, *Barroom Moscow,* received a favorable review in the Marxist journal *October.*[82] *Pravda*, edited by Bukharin, published a speech given at Esenin's funeral by the proletarian poet Vladimir Kirillov, in which he called Esenin one of "the most talented" poets after Pushkin.[83] Ever unpredictable, Dmitry Gorbov, an ally of Voronsky, made the bold claim that far from advocating decadence, Esenin sought only to expose it.[84] In 1926 *Red Virgin Soil* (whose editorial board included the pro-Stalinist Yaroslavsky as well as Voronsky) published an article by Fedor Zhits, "Why We Love Esenin," asserting that hooliganism was merely Esenin's artistic mask because true artists are by nature "oppositionists." His tragedy was what made his work real; "A happy person has no place in art. His biography is boring and not interesting to the reader." In a strike against poets like Zharov and Bezymensky, Zhits declared that it was because of this "pain and blood" that Esenin was so loved, rather than the "steel nightingales" that crowded the literary scene.[85]

On one side youth were attacked; on the other they were forgiven their tastes and, to an extent, their actions, beliefs, and disbelief. Throughout it all, in questions of ideology, science, and literature, young Soviets were receiving mixed messages—a confusing beginning to the watershed year of 1926 when the debate over behavioral excesses, the failures of the Komsomol, and the corrupting influence of literature came to a head. Indeed, the very resolution on literature at the XIV Party Congress—neither too much optimism nor too much pessimism—became the flash point. Understandable but difficult to translate into action, it gave license to explore but also provided the grounds to attack.

CHAPTER 5

Annus Horribilis

NO matter how divergent their convictions, few Soviets would likely have disagreed with the statement made in *The Young Communist* that in 1926 "on the cultural front we suffered a great defeat."[1] The much publicized debate over a new marriage code reopened old wounds, underscoring how divided the party—and country—was on that issue and many others. In the Kremlin the year 1926 also witnessed the final, failed attempt to curb Stalin's growing power, this time with Zinoviev, Kamenev, and Trotsky on the same side. On campuses the Esenin cult was at its height, and still another writer, the prosaist Andrei Sobol, fell victim to the suicide wave. On the streets "hooliganism" encouraged a national hysteria, with the worst culprits coming from the Komsomol. Despite Bukharin's rampage against sexual promiscuity, the behavior of young people seemed to be worse than ever. As the long, hot summer of 1926 approached, the organizers of a poll conducted among Moscow students warned that "the sexual life of youth is being conducted abnormally due to an absence of sexual literacy."[2] Unbeknownst to three writers, Panteleimon Romanov, Sergei Malashkin, and Lev Gumilevsky, the proof for this claim would fall on their shoulders.

Literature Comes to the University

The storm began with the publication of Romanov's brief story, "Without a Cherry Blossom," in the June 1926 issue of *The Young Guard*. The title was deliberately evocative of Kollontai's "Wingless Eros" (in Russian, *without* is quite close to *wingless*). Instead of Cupid's wings, now the metaphor for sex without emotional attachment is taken from nature; instead of a triumphant Zhenya, we have a victimized female student whose letter to a friend about her "fall" comprises the story. What happens to her is given in the first lines, which shifts the reader's focus to how it came about. The story presents a classic conflict of mismatched expectations: she desires love, he wants sex. In this respect the protagonist finds herself among a distinct minority, even among her female friends. In her words, "Those who seek in love something greater than the physical are laughed at like crippled and mentally retarded subjects." The source of this emotional poverty she traces to the material impoverishment of their lives at the university and to young people's radical skepticism. Just as their language is blunt and informal, so is their attitude toward sex. To romanticize sex would be to endorse the bourgeois lies and deceptions from which the revolution had ostensibly delivered them.

Against this background, the protagonist makes an effort to meet a popular male student who has caught her eye. He asks her if she can "do it" without a cherry blossom sprig. She answers yes, but adds that it is better with the floral sprig and symbolically attaches a blossom to her dress. He responds that he is not interested in "poetry"; he could have sex with anybody. "I always do it without and nothing bad ever comes of it. . . . It all ends with the same thing, so why make all the fuss." She refuses him, but later cannot stand to be alone when everyone else is together. She goes to his room, still wearing the blossom, where he receives her with the brusque greeting: "Well, what's the sense of wasting time talking?" He hangs a note on the door for privacy and turns out the light in deference to her need for "poetry." When she resists his advances, he forces himself upon her. She leaves—with her blossom, like her expectations, "crushed, hanging like a rag." With nothing to counteract the vulgarity of what has transpired except a hint of nature's beauty in the nighttime scent of blossoms, the story has no resolution. It conveys the same emotional desolation that created her loneliness and his contempt for her feelings that enabled him to commit what is today called acquaintance rape.[3]

Three months later, in September 1926, Malashkin's novella, "Moon on the Right," appeared in *The Young Guard*. This story also focuses on the downfall of a female student, Tanya Aristarkhova, presented through her letters and her diary.[4] Malashkin's story is a more substantive exploration of the motivations for student behavior and even provides an ideologically satisfactory conclusion, although it was ignored by many critics. The daughter of a kulak, Tanya hates her father and works surreptitiously for the Bolsheviks. Age fourteen at the time of the revolution, she organizes a Komsomol cell and after the civil war is sent to study in Moscow as a reward for her work. Four years later, Tanya is at Sverdlov University, where she has transformed herself into the quintessential femme fatale, the bane of university officials. (The story uses the actual name of the then-current university president, Liadov.) She receives a visit from Petr, a friend and comrade-in-arms from her village, who is appalled by the new Tanya. She enjoys shocking him by playing the tart: blowing cigarette smoke at him, displaying her "pantaloons" as she sits, and parading before him with swinging hips. She looks at him, she says, as she looked at her "twentieth guy" yesterday. She invites Petr to attend one of their "Athenian Nights," a bacchanalian debauch where women dance in flimsy gauze dresses and dandified men openly fondle them. As the students audaciously sing patriotic songs about being the next generation of communists, a woman named Shurka propositions Petr, telling him that she is "not yet" infected with syphilis. The climax is a long speech by a student nicknamed "little Trotsky" that combines Lenin's "class morality" principle with a bowdlerized version of Kollontai's alleged celebration of sexual promiscuity.

When confronted by Petr, Tanya blames both the other students, whom she calls "radishes," and her own weakness for her moral decline while at the university. In 1923, she had faithfully defended the "old Leninist guard" (the Zinoviev-Kamenev-Stalin bloc) against Trotskyism and had been kicked out of her Komsomol cell. Although she was officially reinstated, her peers taunted her as "bourgeois" for remaining chaste. She had finally yielded her virginity, like Romanov's heroine in "Without a Cherry Blossom," to a member of her Komsomol, then moved on to another, dumped him, and "then without thinking went through twenty-two guys." Surprisingly, Petr responds that this confession makes him love her still more because it shows that she still has a "soul." Life has made her dirty; how can she be purified? The story does not offer the stock remedy found in later works: resurrection through the party. Instead, Tanya and Petr live together for a week as "man and wife." But with "all her juices drunk up and sucked out" by so many previous men, Tanya is emotionally destroyed. When she learns that Shurka has committed suicide, Tanya, filled with self-loathing and believing she can never be worthy of Petr's love, tries to do the same. The diary ends at this point, and the novella closes with the author learning from Tanya's brother that she went north, "led a virginal life," and has reunited with Petr.

Dwarfing Romanov's and Malashkin's efforts, Gumilevsky's novel, *Dog Alley*, published in December 1926, undertook to be the most comprehensive examination yet of the "sex crisis" among youth.[5] It was a veritable roman à clef of real-life voices currently crowding the popular discourse. Characters include a femme fatale, a sexual predator, a sexual rationalist, a model couple, a debauched couple, a junior version of Lenin, a Kollontai-Zhenya type, and an innocent, virginal victim. Whereas "Without a Cherry Blossom" rehearsed the real-life debate about sexual mores among youth and "Moon on the Right" dramatized it, Gumilevsky attempted to resolve it. Good characters are pitted against the bad, and the two sides are cleanly divided by a single criterion: their attitude toward sex. Anything less than absolute abstinence, including masturbation, is not permissible. Sex unleashes a beast, and the function of characters, whether saints or sinners, is to affirm this fact without any of Romanov's neutrality. In *Dog Alley* there is no character development, and changes in scene or shifts in action are relevant only insofar as they bring different voices to the stage. As if on cue, each character has his or her say and then experiences one of two outcomes: the puritans finish the novel chaste, upright, and (literally) basking in the sun; the unbelievers end up in the grave, disgraced or, like Tanya, in self-imposed exile.

Intended to scare Soviet youth into personal reformation, *Dog Alley* recalls the best of nineteenth-century antimasturbation fright literature. Ignorant of subtlety, Gumilevsky also stuffed the novel with melodrama of the cheapest grade. The initial dramatic encounter takes place not on a train but a Soviet tram: Khorokhorin, the student leader of the Komsomol, finds that a woman has placed her hand on his. Though a woman makes the overture, the hard, pragmatic point of view is still his: "In the woman's frank audacity he saw the triumph of the new people over philistines who were blindly occupied with their own petty affairs and who did not notice that right next to them a man and a woman, ruled not by prejudices but the natural desire for each other, clasped their hands as a symbol of embraces to come." In the absence of "prejudices," that is, the bourgeois convention of flirting, Khorokhorin is concerned with only two thoughts: "Do I need a woman today?" and "Is it worth losing the evening over?" These questions are answered by the woman as she leads him from the tram. She is Vera Volkova, a fellow student, rumored to have caused the downfall of at least one professor. Her apartment is (significantly) located on Dog Alley, where she lives alone, free to practice her own credo of sexual liberation. Living with one man would be boring and would interfere with entertaining other men. Upon entering her apartment, the elated Khorokhorin immediately begins to undress, to Vera's express horror. Equal in their initial frankness, they are unequal in expectation of what is to follow, and she ejects him. Apparently the new freedom to choose her own men has not eliminated a prerevolutionary "prejudice" in Vera: a need for old-fashioned passion and romance in addition to sex. Khorokhorin, conversely, is the ultimate glass-of-water practitioner: the physical need for sex must be satisfied or the organism will suffer a harmful imbalance. Indeed, four days after his rejection by Vera his work efficiency drops dramatically.

With the sides drawn up, the remaining three-quarters of *Dog Alley* develops the conflict of behavioral principles through a murder mystery that is suspenseful only for those ignorant of cliché. Though Khorokhorin is ultimately delivered from his enforced, four-day abstinence by visiting a prostitute, he cannot escape the clutches of desire. (Gumilevsky's metaphors for the destructive power of sex include a Dostoevskian blood-sucking, web weaving spider, a wolf, a noose, a swamp, poison, and flypaper.) Vera, whose sexual seductiveness is likened to all of the above, continues to drive the frustrated Khorokhorin mad with lust by alternately enticing and rejecting him. With his "equilibrium" dangerously upset, he selects another target, Varya, whose seduction is a partial reenactment of events described in Romanov's "Without a Cherry Blossom." Khorokhorin forces himself upon Varya at night in a grove where students congregate to engage in sex. His motivations are clear; hers are pitiably innocent: how better to serve the cause, she reflects, than by restoring her leader to full working efficiency? How else can she fulfill her dream of having sex once in her life with the right man in order to provide the state with a superlative baby? Varya finds no pleasure in sex itself, only fulfillment of a sense of duty. Clearly, Khorokhorin is a threat not only to himself, but even to the purest of heart and mind. Varya becomes pregnant but learns that he may be infected with syphilis following his visit to the prostitute. Seeking an abortion, she goes to a midwife instead of the hospital, develops an infection, and dies, hallucinating about Mars.

Varya's sacrifice is doubly in vain. There is nothing left to restore in Khorokhorin, in whom the animal has taken over the human. Only lust the narcotic, lust the enslaver, flows in his muscles and mind. Dismissed from his post for negligence, he confronts Vera, blaming her for his supposed infection. If she had yielded to him that first night, he says, he never would have gone to a prostitute. Horrified, she realizes that she too may have been infected during subsequent liaisons. He draws a revolver, a shot rings out, and Vera falls dead. Thinking he has killed her, Khorokhorin turns the revolver on himself. The best doctor and the best detective are put on the case, one saving Khorokhorin's life, the other solving the murder. It was the disgraced professor, lurking in the shadows, who shot Vera and, at the end, leaves his confession in a suicide note. Following in the footsteps of Malashkin's Tanya, Khorokhorin goes to a small city in Siberia and is never seen with a woman again. It turns out he never had syphilis.

As in any good morality tale, a fall must be balanced by growth. An alternative plot in *Dog Alley* unfolds, a love story between Zoya and Senia Korelev that is a chaste romance conducted without physical intimacy. Denial is not a struggle for the couple, but a source of fulfillment: "Renouncing all pleasures of the flesh for the sake of duty seem to [Zoya] such a simple and understandable thing." The two are happy, content, in control, and model students precisely because they don't have sex. This puts Gumilevsky on a different level from Romanov or Malashkin. Love is not the issue, rather sex itself.

While Gumilevsky later claimed Lenin as his inspiration, a more appropriate model would be Tolstoy. *Any* surrender to the sexual drive, no matter how well motivated (as with the example of Varya) can lead to destruction. Sexual intercourse turns men into rapists or murderers and women into victims of disease and abortion. At the end Korelev, the new leader of the Komsomol, explains all in a speech at Vera's funeral. Following the example of Tolstoy's "The Devil" and *The Kreutzer Sonata*, and with the sun rising higher, Korelev reveals that the real killer of Vera and Varya is not an individual but "simple carnality, the naked animal feeling calling forth from the depths of yesterday's person that primitive wildness, brutishness, by which the stone age man lived."

We need not question why Romanov, Malashkin, and Gumilevsky are not household names of Russian literature. Nevertheless, in 1926 they had an immediate impact on the national consciousness by moving the polemic over sexuality from a primarily theoretical ground to one closer to young people's own lives. The works have a common focus on the university Komsomol; each deals with the difficulty of applying Marxism to a practical setting, such as the misuse of terms like *philistine*. Together they embrace the whole gamut of postrevolutionary debates and problems, from drug abuse, sexual promiscuity, prostitution, venereal disease, rape, abortion, and masturbation, to women's emancipation, the value of marriage, and whether romantic love can exist in a socialist society. Moreover, all three authors present their issues not from an authoritarian height but in a fictional format that would appeal to young people. Both Romanov and Malashkin adopt the first-person narrative voice, an effective means of engaging the reader—not a distant "they" and "them," but an immediate "I" and "we." Romanov deliberately avoids giving his characters names, thus encouraging readers to assume one of the roles— victim, instigator, or silent witness—according to their own personal experience. In one case he seems to have succeeded. A student, Sergei Okulov, noted in a short published response that Romanov's heroine had become virtually a symbol of the times, exemplifying a common, though undesired, fate of youth. She in her fictional anonymity told students more about their own lives and was more realistic, Okulov charged, than the real-life Polina Vinogradskaia and her exhortations to replace love and sex with social work.[6] Finally, with the exception of a few literary-minded critics, no one seemed to care much about the melodrama or the overwrought plot lines (especially in Gumilevsky's *Dog Alley*). More immediately attractive was the heavy metafictional orientation of the narratives: each work portrays not only the problem at hand, but also the characters' detailed opinions of it—indeed, discussing problems seems to be their primary activity. Although these were fictional personages, their value (and their potential harm in the eyes of detractors) was to introduce and illustrate real-life polemics.

The relevance of these three works was enhanced by the deliberate insertion of actual people, events, and places into the plots. Malashkin sets his story at Sverdlov University, with references to Trotsky, Lenin, and the Fourteenth Party Congress. In *Dog Alley* mention is made of Gelman's 1922 poll of students, Kollontai's "glass of water" theory, the Down with Shame movement, and Bukharin's Komsomol speech. Moreover, the novel's primary image of sexual entrapment—the spider catching its victims in a web and "sucking their juices dry"—is a direct allusion to Aron Zalkind's repeated warning. Equally important, the texts encourage the illusion of realism by adopting a documentary format. Romanov's story is narrated through a letter, Malashkin's contains letters and a journal, and Gumilevsky presents *Dog Alley* as a case history of a "true" event occurring in Saratov in 1925.

Romanov, Malashkin, and Gumilevsky succeeded only too well in engaging their readers, and a furor soon erupted. If sex always sells, then no one, not even Kollontai, did it better. Officials were compelled to admit in published and secret reports that these three works of fiction were consistently at the top of readers' request lists. Two lessons quickly emerged. First, fiction had become the primary forum for articulating the real-life concerns of young people; like television, film, or music today, fiction provided a common, accessible frame of reference. Second, the anti-Esenin barrage had had minimal impact on youth; if anything, some seemed to have graduated from one evil to an even greater one.

The resulting uproar was in many respects familiar. Critics could easily claim that once again literature was corrupting its audience. However, much of what else transpired in the flood of attention generated by these three works was new. Attacks were met by an equally stringent defense, one not limited to the authors themselves or a few isolated voices. The battle crossed party lines both internally, as the archival paper trail reveals, and publicly, as critics fought among themselves at conferences and in journals and newspapers. Surprisingly, media organs, no matter how orthodox they might appear, did not necessarily take sides about the relative merits of these three works, but often published the views of opponents and supporters alike. Also unprecedented was the importance given to the voices of young people themselves, no longer a mute mass, subject to definition or castigation from above. They too were divided, and their letters were published alongside those of party officials who had dominated the debate until this time. If ever there was contradiction in the public domain, if ever the Soviet press accurately reflected the depth of confusion in popular opinion, it was here. To be sure, the volatile and chaotic debate over these works was short-lived, but its impact was not. It demonstrated how far Bolsheviks were from consensus regarding not only sexuality but also the course and purpose of popular literature.

How Could It Be?

Party stalwarts were incredulous. Had not the attacks against Alexandra Kollontai already condemned licentiousness? Had not Lenin and party declarations clearly distinguished revolutionary right from counterrevolutionary wrong? Had not the sheer volume of scientific, medical, and sociological tracts defined healthy, proper behavior once and for all? And had not students themselves shown in various polls that their own ideals were sound? With the revolution nearly a decade old, party officials were infuriated: Romanov, Malashkin, and Gumilevsky had forced them back into the breach. Sofia Smidovich, numbed by the realization that her countless broadsides had apparently been for naught, stood up at a conference at the Krupskaia Academy for Communist Education and decried the lewd slander that was again being dumped on the public by these works of fiction. With the authority of the Central Control Commission behind her, Smidovich defiantly asserted, "In our reality we don't witness the degenerate Komsomolists whom Malashkin depicts." Her position was seconded by Ekaterina Troshchenko, who denied any factual basis to "Without a Cherry Blossom"; it was consummate fiction in the worst sense: "In Romanov's story, except for the attempt to impose upon our youth feelings that it doesn't experience, theories that it doesn't hold, convictions that are alien to it, and behavior in which it doesn't engage, there is absolutely nothing."[7]

A few months later Troshchenko took it upon herself to show students how they really lived in an article entitled "University Youth," intended as an antidote to these poisonous fictions. She submitted it to *The Young Guard,* whose editors clearly relished the spectacle, since they had already published the conference proceedings, as well as "Without a Cherry Blossom" and "Moon on the Right." They commented that what merited the publication of Troshchenko's article "was a series of recent literary works which have occasionally given one-sided and unfaithful depictions of [student] life." This was such a brazenly disingenuous statement as to be mockery, a stance not difficult to take, given Troshchenko's vehement corrective. Her "true portrait" of student life was so fantastic that one might ask who was really guilty of creating fiction. After a catalogue of examples of the cheerfulness, enthusiasm, reliability, and productivity of "the student," Troshchenko writes,

> There is really no need to prove the accuracy of this characterization. Just
> go to any party or Komsomol meeting, step into any university reading

room, take a look at any room in a student dormitory, and you will hardly have a different impression. It is doubtful you will find on the face of a young man who spends his evening reading newspapers in his room traces of a night spent in debauchery or defilement. You won't see in the room any signs of yesterday's orgy, and even if you ask any of the students present to do you a favor, that is breathe in your face, you won't smell the slightest trace of vodka. Nor will you succeed in finding beer bottles under their beds; nothing, except worn-out shoes, will be there. Even if your attention is caught by noise coming from behind some doors, upon opening them you will land in the midst of some crazy argument such as who is greater: Tolstoy or Bedny?[8]

Critics rushed to agree with this idealized picture. How can Tanya in "Moon on the Right" be regarded as a legitimate student, one review noted, when "not for one minute" do we see her with a book? When she does not heal herself by working more closely with her class but by running away? "Is this the face of youth? No, a thousand times, no! These are just pimples on its face. And can one just show pimples separate from the face?"[9] Another review, also published in *The Young Guard*, charged that Malashkin had descended into sheer fantasy. "Moon on the Right" was so far-fetched that it couldn't even be considered "pornography." Malashkin had "thought up and packed into the novella a whole series of stories, rumors, and gossip about student life."[10] Joining the chorus of outrage was the head of the censorship division, Valerian Poliansky, who conceded that although students might not always be above reproach, Romanov's "total ignorance" of his subject matter was blasphemous.[11]

Similar disdain was heard in more liberal circles. Most damning was Robert Kulle's philippic against Gumilevsky's *Dog Alley*. To attribute any documentary pretensions to this novella was simply absurd. Gumilevsky was worse than a pornographer like Artsybashev. At least Artsybashev had some literary merit; but his stepchild "exhibits no talent whatsoever."[12] This blow seemed to have hit Gumilevsky the hardest, for he singled out Kulle's attack in his memoirs, written decades later and published only in 1988, twelve years after his death.[13] Even David Khanin, once a "hooligan general" and now head of the Press Department of the Komsomol Central Committee, thought that Kulle had gone too far; fair criticism had descended into "malicious barking." He added ominously, "we have to help Gumilevsky because what has happened to him can happen to every writer."[14]

Of course, it was Kulle himself, as noted in chapter 1, who recorded in his 1925 diary the observation that would substantiate something of a real-life basis for Gumilevsky's characters: "Youth are just terrible. Their principles are entirely base. The chaos of their sexual lives is something primeval." The irony demonstrates how certain critics operated with a very uncompromising and limited definition of contemporary sexual behavior. Artsybashev was guilty of pornography, but not slander, because he had been faithful to life, which was itself debauched at that time. Literature, therefore, would be expected to reflect this reality. However, Gumilevsky, Malashkin, and Romanov (the three were usually seen, erroneously, as acting in concert)[15] were purveyors of smut *and* slander because life after the revolution had changed irrevocably. Hence, any writer who introduced overt sexuality into a text about contemporary life was immediately open to the charge of distorting that life or, in the words of one critic, "hypertrophic eroticism."[16] Worse, attackers identified the authors as the source of the objectionable opinions expressed by the characters. These three works were not merely reproducing voices heard on campuses, critics charged; the ridiculous views of Khorokhorin, Vera, Tanya, and others were really those of the writers themselves. As evidence, Poliansky strung together the most outrageous statements in the text and, removed from context, attributed them directly to the author. What literature reflected was not life, but the writers' own perverted minds.[17]

The best evidence to this effect came from young people themselves, who objected to these unsavory pictures of their lives. We have no comprehensive record of the myriad conversations and confrontations sparked by these three works in dorm rooms, cafes, factories, or at meetings and lectures—only the impression that they were widespread and intense. Evidence survives in published letters to the editor and reports of "disputes" (conferences) which elevated youths' voices in the print media. While none substantiated Troshchenko's dream dormitory, there was no shortage of criticism. Gumilevsky's novel made such an impact on the Leningrad sewing industry, for instance, that its central club scheduled a meeting to discuss it that filled the hall to overcapacity and lasted past midnight. Twenty people gave speeches, all with one clear and unequivocal message: "such works must be destroyed before they influence youth."[18] Some offended readers rivaled Smidovich in the stridency of their protests. Their rallying cry was that of slander. Romanov, Malashkin, and Gumilevsky knew nothing about their lives. Romanov had thrown "a clump of dirt in the face of proletarian students," wrote one reader to *Red Students*.[19] In the next issue following the publication of "Without a Cherry Blossom," *The Young Guard* featured a letter by a young woman, "Comrade I.," who took personal offense at the heroine's passivity.[20] Others objected that casual sex, desired or not, was not as prevalent as depicted. At a regional conference dedicated to a discussion of Romanov's story, with the author present, "Comrade Sapronova" openly declared that "girls don't sleep with guys for one night or one week as it's described there." As proof she offered her own eyewitness experience.[21]

Malashkin's novella, "Moon on the Right," was more inflammatory because of its unflattering focus on the party and Tanya's sordid fall. What do we have here, a female reader queried in *The Literary Guardian*, "a brothel or the Komsomol?" It was simply insulting that Malashkin dared to have Tanya speak as she did of their guiding light: "When she talks about the party, don't you just want to stuff her mouth?" She was immediately seconded by a man who labeled Malashkin "politically illiterate" by offering "parasites" as examples of the Komsomol.[22] Workers at the Rosa Luxemburg State Tobacco Factory in Rostov-on-the-Don gathered to refute the "noise" raised by these three works. All were "almost unanimously condemned"—an intriguing qualification because it could easily have been deleted.[23] More persuasive were those who carped at inaccurate details. Several noted that Tanya had to be a figment of Malashkin's imagination because, truth be told, no student could afford to entertain friends at such "Athenian nights."[24] Also revealing was the comment that Petr, one of the novella's few uncorrupted characters, was an impossible figure because, "saint" or not, could he really have been present at Tanya's party, with its half-naked women, and not feel anything?[25] Moreover, young readers were not blind to gross aesthetic deficiencies. "Moon on the Right" was all platitudes, one woman noted, and artistically poor since Malashkin "tells too much and shows too little." No one, it was added, could accept Tanya's sophisticated style of expression in her letters and diaries as the product of a teenage mind.[26]

Not all readers were disgusted, however. The three works enjoyed popularity equal to their notoriety, and many readers even praised the verisimilitude of the characters and their behavior. If some refused to see a "mirror" in the texts (the preferred metaphor for literature's realistic potential), others welcomed their apparent transparency. A joint letter to *The Young Guard* by two workers, male and female, stated that Romanov's picture of student life was "copied directly from nature." It was even more accurate in its ugly depiction of sexual behavior, regrettable but true: "A guy often takes a girl for a week or just one night and then dumps her without a thought, not caring about the consequences. *This completely stamps the human dignity of a woman as comrade, communist, and Komsomolist into the mud.*"[27] Another collective letter from Komsomolists in the military offered the same observation about Malashkin: "The very heart of the story, the sexual relations between young women and male Komsomolists and, to a significant degree, among party members, is timely and given accurately. Of 'love-stuffed' people like [Tanya] Aristarkhova one can count quite a few among youth, and on this standard of vice our group also 'measures up.'"[28]

Another letter pointedly observed that if proof was needed of sexual behavior gone awry, one need only look at the exposés printed in *Red Students*.

Why else had a new verb appeared in the student's vocabulary: *perekharakhorit*, to outdo Khorokhorin (the abusive student leader in *Dog Alley*) at his own game?[29] (Gumilevsky was already one step ahead in having given his protagonist a name derived from the verb "to swagger.") Young readers were also sophisticated enough to combine praise of the novel with recognition of its obvious aesthetic deficiencies, particularly wooden characterization. The soldiers who disapproved of Malashkin commented (echoing a similar complaint noted above) that if any objections were to made about the unconvincing picture of students on small stipends hosting wild parties, more incredible was the fantastical portrait of Petr in "Moon on the Right." "To see nearly naked women, how they sit themselves down on [guys'] laps, the kissing and to look that whole time just 'at his own knees' you're not going to find such saints in our 'sinful' times."[30]

The response in more established literary circles was somewhat different. Even though individuals questioned the accuracy of the presentation of student experience, most noted that the louder the cry of slander, the more obvious it was that these writers had touched a raw nerve. If "Moon on the Right" and *Dog Alley* were mere caricatures, wrote N. Erlikh, they would have been left on a dusty shelf, unnoticed and unread, like myriad other "imagined" stories. "But the punch was right on target," he continued; "the writers' stories attest to facts of great social significance. They direct the attention of organizing forces to what is necessary [to do], and in that is their irrefutable value."[31] Likewise, an analysis of Romanov by "Iu. L." published in *The Literary Guardian* argued that to call this literature "pornographic" or "erotic" "characterizes more the psychological orientation of critics than the writer himself."[32]

Abram Lezhnev, a colleague of Voronsky and an accomplished literary scholar, devoted no fewer than three separate articles to the Romanov-Malashkin-Gumilevsky phenomenon, defending them all against charges of slander. The widespread alarm they had caused showed there was a "measure of truth" in their fictional portrayals. It cannot be denied, he noted in a review of *Dog Alley*, that "the sexual behavior of youth is abnormal." Lezhnev was apparently among the few critics to actually read the entire novel. He recognized that Gumilevsky, "trying to be an orthodox Marxist," had based the novel on Lenin's teachings and had inserted the leader's words nearly verbatim into Korelev's speech at the end. Maybe elsewhere Gumilevsky had taken things too far, he conceded, but given the importance of the topic it was "better to overdo it than underdo it."[33] *Pravda,* notably, took a more skeptical view: "Women's underwear occupies an unnaturally large place in our literature."[34]

The Writers' Defense

What else occupied a prominent place on the literary scene were Romanov's, Malashkin's, and Gumilevsky's attempts to justify themselves. All were established authors even before the revolution, so they had faced criticism before. They were also aware that after 1917 writing fiction was a more dangerous profession than at any previous time in Russia, which may partly explain why each played up the metafictive angle. Malashkin, himself a party member, knew that "Moon on the Right" was not typical of "proletarian" literature, and in the first lines the narrator, half tongue-in-cheek, half seriously, seeks to deflect criticism:

> Honored readers! I well know that some of you upon reading my novella will say: "why did the author have to use such sickly types when we have so many healthy ones." Others will put it even more bluntly: "Did the author really have to go digging in the dirt, pull out this garbage and show it to us when life around is full of happiness, love and creativity?" The rest will act even more severely than the first or second ones and, perhaps not even reading the work to the end, tell the writer off you know how and in the heat of anger and irritation throw the book out the window, while the editor who published it, despite the fact he's a wonderful person and morally upstanding in all respects, will get doused with a strong salty word in Russian.[35]

Despite his irony, Malashkin's concern was prophetic, since the editors of *The Young Guard* soon received a harsh reprimand from the party. His self-effacing narrator was intended as a reminder that not all students are petty-bourgeois, even if some, like Tanya, are a danger to others (the lesson enforced by her ensnarement and downfall). Needless to say, Malashkin's attempt to anticipate objections was a wasted effort. Just as some readers did not acknowledge the calculated ending of Gumilevsky's novel, most brushed aside the first pages of "Moon on the Right" and accused Malashkin of painting all students with a single brush.

The next step was to abandon the fictional mask. At a 1928 conference entitled "Sexuality in Fiction," Romanov and Malashkin appeared together to defend their controversial works. However, a journalist who covered the meeting was not impressed:

> With the exception of certain individual speeches, the debate was of a petty-bourgeois character. Widely advertised, it attracted a huge number

of the philistine public with a penchant for the bawdy. . . .

In justifying themselves, both authors spoke of the "well-meaning intentions" which guided the writing of their works. S. Malashkin tried to prove that in his "Moon on the Right" he had wanted to point out problems in everyday life and so on, whereas Romanov affirmed that he also wanted to "show what's true and false," [peoples'] experiences, etc. . . .

Regrettably, the debate will be continued.[36]

At another meeting dedicated to a reading and discussion of "Without a Cherry Blossom," Romanov found himself confronted by Komsomolists who publicly rebuked him for slander. While he tried to cover himself by insisting that such "distressing phenomena" did exist in life, he must have been humiliated to be publicly scolded by insulted readers upholding the most simplistic standard of evaluation. Anything they did not agree with was, ipso facto, slander. Empowerment had made some Komsomol youth feel that much more self-important and quick to take offense. Much like angered literary critics, they did not care that the story was fiction; when it came to their portrait and reputation, they wanted only the most affirmative and smiling-face representation.

Romanov, in short, faced an impossible situation: to claim that such "distressing phenomena" were in any way significant would lay him open to the same charge of slander. For readers like those attending the conference, no representation, regardless of how many idealized Komsomol members were included, was acceptable if it included negative tones. Anticipating this response, a month earlier Romanov had published a sequel to "Without a Cherry Blossom" entitled "A Big Family," which was just the kind of thing Komsomolists were used to hearing (and saying) about themselves.[37] The story should have pleased them. It is a letter from the unnamed protagonist (of the "blossoms") written a year later. All that was wrong is now right. She has given birth to son and is no longer an outcast, having found new warmth and comradeship among her friends in the dormitory. (As if for the occasion, the dorm is being renovated.) Yet as with Malashkin's apologetic opening lines, the attempt at damage repair in Romanov's sequel was all for naught. There was no mention of "A Big Family" at the meeting (perhaps the students had not read it yet), nor was it ever acknowledged by Romanov's many attackers. He was always to be known as the writer of "blossoms," not the "family."

Gumilevsky tried to have it both ways in a lengthy defense of *Dog Alley* published in 1927 in the journal *Red Students*.[38] To deflect the charge that his novel had been a direct cause of a vicious gang rape by Komsomol members, he explicitly denied any connection between his literature and real life: "Of course I am not depicting youth *byt*; in general I did not and do not want to depict anything. I am *composing* a novel to be read with interest and ease." However, one paragraph later, after citing the appearance of Ippolit's *Right to Love* and other indications that youth's behavior might be improving, Gumilevsky included his novel among the inspirations for this amelioration. Real-life circumstances of a positive kind had "fully" vindicated his idea and approach. He noted bitterly at the end that ordinary readers had found benefits in his work that professional critics could not.

Red Students immediately put Gumilevsky's words to the test, publishing a rebuttal from an anonymous student who believed it was high time for authors and critics to stop speaking for young people and start listening to them. The writer wore his "real student" identity as a badge of pride, implying that it gave authority to what he had to say:

> One proviso needs to be made. The author of this commentary is not a professional critic and, truth be told, is for the first time publicly expressing his thoughts of a literary-critical nature. Though this fact has its negative sides, it also makes for something quite positive because here is the voice of a real student not one "composed" by an author who is living in the real student world, absent of any "vulgar tendentiousness" and "deliberate sensationalism." He is instead imbued with that world's full diversity, as known to him as a fourth-year student and thought through by him as an active member of student society.[39]

The student, nevertheless, did not deny the validity of *Dog Alley*. "It is impossible to accuse L. Gumilevsky of making up things up." What offended him was the novel's shoddiness. Being a student in the Soviet Union was such a high honor that it demanded an art of the same caliber; if Gumilevsky wanted to wear the mantle of artist, he should write like one. The "long agitational speeches" by Korelev at the end were so forced and indigestible that students should politely decline such "assistance." They were strong and healthy enough to help themselves without the bromide-laden interference by those who claimed to know better. Another letter lashed out at the critics: if Gumilevsky was guilty of condescension for writing spineless fiction, his reviewers were guilty of the same for endorsing sugar-coated depictions of student life. (This was the same student who commented on the use of *perekharakorit* and on the similarities between Gumilevsky's themes and the content of youth-oriented journals; this was also the same student who declared defiantly, "We have nothing to fear in showing our deficiencies.")[40]

In his memoirs Gumilevsky mentions having defended his novel in public. For him these open hearings confirmed the disjunction between professional critics and young readers. The local governing board would usually charge him with slander, yet the questions from the audience (written on slips of paper and passed forward) often contradicted their leaders.[41] In his own defense he cited letters of support from officials like Sosnovsky and mentor in absentia for many Soviet writers, including Gorky himself.[42] For those who questioned his literary talent, Gumilevsky could not resist mentioning Boris Pilnyak, who told him that he had once missed his tram stop because he was so engrossed in reading *Dog Alley*—"that's how interesting it was!" (The qualitative difference between the two writers and Gumilevsky's demonstrated lack of ironic awareness lead one to wonder if he missed it here too.) He also clarified his motivations for writing the novel. His ideological inspiration was the Zetkin-Lenin interview; then, shifting responsibility from his own shoulders, he noted that the novel was commissioned by the Young Guard publishing house (which did not follow through). For him, everything was explainable and justifiable, yet in so arguing he contradicted himself. When speaking of his work's devastating impact on his reputation, Gumilevsky played down its origin and his role in it; yet in speaking of its success with young readers, he freely used the first person.

The Journal's Defense

Gumilevsky's exchange with the student reveals, like the larger conflagration caused by these three works of fiction, how difficult it is to speak of opposing sides, as if clean lines could be drawn in the controversy. Instead, there was much indecision. The Moscow metalworkers who gathered to condemn Malashkin declared, "We don't deny that there is sexual depravity among us . . . but what is written about us, that is a lie!"[43] Since censorship was far less preemptive in the 1920s than it would be later, the task of containing "slander" fell more to critics; yet even as they attacked these works, they had trouble negotiating the gap between reality and theory. Hence Troshchenko, who had provided a near fantasy picture of dormitory life to exculpate youth, argued herself into a box: "Ill conditions exist, but not the kind Romanov describes; they're there, but different; present, but not like that."[44] One workers' journal berated Gumilevsky for not teaching proper lessons in his novel and cited Lenin's words from the Zetkin interview to suggest what was omitted—despite the fact that the novel ends with precisely this message. Allowing fears to dictate interpretations, morally censorious critics essentially rewrote the texts in order to confirm their own anxieties. The predictable result was to make these works appear more harmful and salacious than they actually were.

The Young Guard itself muddied the waters, its editors enjoying the role of provocateur. Since they were primarily responsible for the commotion, they had to justify having printed the Romanov and Malashkin pieces while pacifying critics, which only added to the double-speak and contradiction. The editorial staff had changed since the ruckus caused by the publication of works by Kollontai, Tarasov-Rodionov, and others, but they still stepped on toes. The lead editor was Sergei Gusev, whose credentials included membership in the Bolshevik party since 1903, holding a seat next to Smidovich on the Central Control Commission, and heading the party's Central Committee Press Department. The mantle of young upstart was assumed by twenty-two-year-old Vladimir Ermilov, who quickly found himself pressed into the duty of damage control.

Ermilov's first step bespoke hesitation. The October 1926 issue of *The Young Guard,* the one immediately following "Moon on the Right," published a story by Dmitry Furmanov about soldiers during the civil war. Ermilov wrote the foreword to it, which included a curious digression in Malashkin's favor. The causal link between both works was dubious, suggesting that the editors were aware of the stirring controversy but were not comfortable committing to a full justification for printing "Moon on the Right." After commenting on Furmanov's "psychological orientation," Ermilov abruptly switched focus, noting Malashkin's mastery of the same. The young editor then attempted to set the record straight:

> [Malashkin] resorts to the device of sharp hyperbole in depicting the clearly negative sides of Komsomol and party philistinism (Athenian nights, Isaac Chuzhachek, etc.) which immediately give rise in the reader to emotions of disgust, anger, and repulsion. In addition the reader clearly senses that the author himself is enraged, indignant, and full of contempt. Right away the reader clearly sees that the author at least *does not love* his own creation, the puny, vapid Chuzhachek who stinks of rotten philistinism as he tries to justify his own putrid corruption with tiresome phrases about free love, about the principle of free choice between the sexes, and all the same insipidness that is nothing but petty-bourgeois and philistine attitudes turned inside out.[45]

Ermilov's next step, however, was in the opposite direction. In December 1926 an article in *Pravda* came to Malashkin's defense for having accurately chronicled the problems of "certain segments of students" and "the working masses."[46] Perhaps afraid that this would make his journal, the party-anointed forum for youth education and enlightenment, seem overly pessimistic, Ermilov was quick to respond. As a work of fiction, he argued, "Moon on the Right" should not be employed as a documentary learning tool. That would only slander Soviet youth, serving the interests of enemies at home and abroad. Ermilov noted that he was all for publicizing negative phenomena of Soviet society but fiction itself had only a tenuous connection to reality. If fidelity to life was the criterion, then Malashkin was obviously "mistaken" to locate his story at Sverdlov University, whose students were "the best" in the country. As proof, Ermilov referred to Gelman's poll of students there which revealed that they had admirable ideals when it came to "long-term relationships."[47]

As controversy grew, however, chief editor Gusev himself needed to clarify the journal's position.[48] In "The State of Our Youth" (June 1927), he admitted that Romanov, Malashkin, and Gumilevsky had caused the "latest explosion among youth regarding the problem of sex" (though he had read only excerpts of *Dog Alley*). After summarizing the critics' objections, he carefully rehearsed the main points of the Lenin-Zetkin interview. Gusev agreed that fiction was not reality and cited evidence of students' moral health from polling data. Yet there were undeniable "disorders" among youth, and fiction that revealed such problems were not necessarily counterrevolutionary. The three controversial writers were "useful" for they "have directed our attention to negative phenomena of great social import." It was clear that their intentions were to condemn what they wrote about and they could be faulted only in the limited extent of their criticism: "They insufficiently or do not even at all underscore the contradictions between these monstrosities [in youth's *byt*] and our socialist ideal." In short, while the writers both succeeded and failed, the journal had scored a victory.

The Young Guard practiced what its editors preached. Though other journals did the same, including more orthodox ones such as *The Literary Guardian*, it gave full press to all voices in the uproar.[49] Romanov's and Malashkin's stories inspired letters expressing diverse opinions of leading party members, "unknown" Komsomolists, lone students, and forgotten workers. In publishing them, *The Young Guard* did not single any out as correct or in error; the result instead was to bring into rare contact voices of the young and old, high and low. To cover themselves, the editors were deliberately ambiguous. Letters dedicated to "Moon on the Right" were introduced with the following declaration: "The editorial staff, in full agreement with its readers, believes that even in those Komsomol student circles most infected with philistine and petty-bourgeois beliefs, it is impossible to find the attitudes depicted by S. Malashkin." A few lines later, however, came a counter claim: the novella was "a valuable literary work both in the artistic sense and in the fact that it brings readers' attention to the decadent attitudes which do circulate among recognized groups of students."[50] Both positions, notably, found justification in the letters that follow which is significant since, as would become standard practice later, the editors could have easily effected a one-sided portrayal of response, whether positive or negative. The result was not just an equal airing of pro and contra but also an admission that disagreement was important in and of itself. While not necessarily the case elsewhere, here, even during the years of Stalin's ascent, dialogue was seen as productive.

The Young Guard operated in a complicated and unpredictable environment. Just days before the appearance of "Moon on the Right," the Komsomol's primary publishing house, also entitled The Young Guard, received an official reprimand from the Central Committee of the Party both for "the weak treatment of problems of *byt* among youth and inadequate handling of their questions on culture" and for "allowing individual works of a pornographic nature in the Komsomol press." Under obvious pressure, Milchakov, head of the Komsomol, also sent the same reprimand (marked "top secret" in the archives) to the publishing house. One month later, he found himself writing a similar letter to the journal itself:[51]

> Comrades Khanin and Ermilov:
>   Does it not seem to you that the novella or story of Sergei Malashkin (in the ninth issue of *The Young Guard*) entitled "Moon on the Right or an Unusual Love" represents in artistic terms the usual potboiler and in terms of its content an "UNUSUAL DISTORTION" of *byt* among OUR YOUTH, Komsomolists and, in particular, Komsomol activists?
>   What is the opinion of the editorial staff regarding "moon on the right?"
>
> Al. Milchakov

The editors did not give in so easily, publicly or privately. Khanin, current head of the publishing department of the Komsomol, ensured that "Moon on the Right" would undergo several reprints in book format, a process that continued even after he left his post in 1927. Likewise, Ermilov's personal letter indicates why the journal did not print a retraction but felt justified bringing the dispute over the novella into the open:[52]

> Dear Comrade Milchakov:
>   The editorial board of *The Young Guard* agrees with the fact that Sergei Malashkin's novella, "Moon on the Right or an Unusual Love," is in many respects controversial. It is the role of critics and the collective opinion of the Komsomol and party to indicate various inaccuracies, mistakes, and the like. (In one of the upcoming issue of *The Young Guard* there will be printed responses, letters, articles, and so forth that have been sent to the editorial board; a significant portion of these re-

sponses confirm the opinion regarding the content of the novella which you give in your letter.)

At the same time, the editorial board believes that the publication of this novella in the journal has been useful. *The Young Guard* has earlier published works controversial in many respects (for example, *Chocolate* by A. Tarasov-Rodionov, "The False Ones" by V. Gerasimova, "Affair #301" by V. Strelnikova, and a series of others). These works posed sensitive questions about party-Komsomol life, brought attention to the journal and, with critics' corrections, served in the final result a positive role.

Malashkin's novella is valuable precisely because it has generated a large number of responses and thus has brought attention to the journal as well.

As is well known, in the years 1924–1925, *The Young Guard* lost its previous authority among large numbers of Komsomol activists, party youth, and students, including those at communist universities. Having lost its reader base, the journal dragged pitifully along, publishing chance works by chance authors with no redeeming artistic value and which passed on completely unnoticed thereby driving readers away.

Since the beginning of 1926 a "reconstruction period" in the life of the journal has been under way and has been recognized by a whole series of positive reviews in various organs of the party and Komsomol press (*Izvestiia, Red Virgin Soil, The Press and Revolution, Young Communist, Komsomol Pravda, The Book Peddler* and others). Malashkin's novella will play its own role in inviting attention and interest to the journal as well.

The editorial board would consider unfair characterizing the artistic makeup of Malashkin's novella as "potboiler."

The editorial board would like to use this opportunity to invite you to take part in the discussion of Malashkin's novella on the pages of this journal in whatever form you find suitable (an article, review, letter to the editor, etc.).

> With comradely regards,
> Deputy Editor
> Ermilov

Ermilov was frank about the importance of "bringing attention to the journal," which was losing readers and funding. Indeed, much internal editorial correspondence in the archives for the 1920s consists of complaints about insufficient money. At the same time, his reply was a cheeky personal jab at Milchakov, who had served on the editorial board until March 1926, that is, just before Ermilov's arrival and the beginning of the "reconstruction period."

Ermilov's letter confirms from the inside what we find in the public realm: a lack of coherence and continuity among those who were ostensibly the purveyors of a single ideology. The party hierarchy itself was responsible for this mess. Given the outpouring of edicts and resolutions from above, *The Young Guard* could assume that it had the blessing of institutional authority. The famous 1925 resolution of the Central Committee, "On the Policy of the Party in the Field of Literature," expressly sanctioned tolerance for diverse literary orientations, calling for "free competition" in literature. This was an implied invitation to explore and experiment, short of presenting overtly anti-Soviet material. The resolution contained a direct exhortation to avoid "communist arrogance" (*komchvansto*), found in too many woodenly patriotic pieces.[53] In fact, before the controversies of 1926, media organs had been repeatedly chastised for failing to expose deficiencies in *byt*, for ignoring youth's needs, for drowning them with lifeless proclamations, and, significantly, for driving down circulation and interest in party affairs. Young people's complaints about being left in the cold and the subsequent popularity of Esenin, Trotsky, and detective-adventure stories modeled on Western literature had hit home. One Komsomol Central Committee resolution warned that it was the journals' timid, gutless approach that was to blame for poor attendance at political instruction meetings; what had once been a tolerable participation rate of 80–90 percent had now fallen to 50 percent and, in places, to a perilous 30 percent.[54]

The Young Guard could further claim that its actions were a mirror of its operating license. It had been founded in 1922 by the XI Party Congress "to counter the influence on youth of boulevard literature and assist in the communist education of youth masses."[55] Its inaugural editorial correspondingly cast the journal as "an organ of revolutionary enlightenment" fighting "against all remnants of bourgeois culture and ideology." With its publishing record in both fiction and nonfiction of sex and *byt*-oriented texts, *The Young Guard* did not, at least in this respect, disappoint, as Ermilov implied in his letter to Michakov. It opened its pages to a variety of writers, cultural critics, party representatives, and young readers so that "subject to debate" was appended to many of its pieces. Ermilov, celebrating its five-year anniversary in 1927, asserted that the journal still had a special license to provoke controversy: "One can obviously make a mistake or go too far. But it's better to be mistaken than to offer hundreds of pages of calm, soothing philistine pulp." No one could walk away from the journal unchallenged. "One can argue about individual works," he continued, "yet what is indisputable is [our] general line: no philistine garbage where all corners are smoothed over, but rather to put before the reader the sharp questions of our day, to force the reader to agree or disagree, to react hotly to a piece, to confront the reader, to excite his mind."[56]

Internal correspondence in the Komsomol press archives confirms the truth behind Ermilov's words. Editors had wide latitude to explore and engage; remonstration, when it came, was demonstrably after the fact. In short, the motivations for publishing writers like Romanov and Malashkin were complex and, for that reason, more "ideologically" innocent than as part of a concerted plan to entrap youth. They were ones with which any editor of any culture could readily identify: personal whim and taste, material need and a desire for publicity.[57] (Circulation had dropped from an initial high of 9,000 in 1922 to less than 6,000 by 1926.)[58] Publication was done precisely because it could be. Many party members, including editors, writers, and readers, openly embraced texts that challenged dominant paradigms, awakened audiences, and made them think—not to undermine the party's authority but to improve its relevance and thereby safeguard its primacy. None of those who came out in support of Romanov, Malashkin, or Gumilevsky saw themselves as anti-Soviet or antiparty. On the contrary, they thought they were doing what was asked of them.

It could have been predicted that the topic of sex would test party guidelines regarding editorial content. What other subject could claim, both in literature and in life, such lightning-rod status? There were issues specific to peasants, workers, disenfranchised capitalists, defrocked clergy, national minorities, Kremlin insiders, and the international scene. But there seemed to be only one to which all could relate and have something to say, be it with chagrin, embarrassment or enthusiasm. This fact, combined with the relative tolerance in the media for diverse viewpoints (even Trotsky's downfall did not immediately eliminate him from print), suggests that sex, with or without official license, would erupt as a central topic. As Gusev exclaimed disingenuously after the 1926 causes célèbres, "It's often difficult to say what generates more concern or inflamed passion: the problem of sex or the revolution in China."[59]

A Censor's Plight

This brings us to the most baffling part of the Romanov-Malashkin-Gumilevsky affair. Because Soviet literary culture carries the enduring image of state control of the press, one wonders why these works were not banned. Contemporaries such as Mikhail Bulgakov, Anna Akhmatova, and Evgeny Zamiatin could attest that the censor was not asleep, but of the three scandalous writers only Gumilevsky faced censorship, and only when *Dog Alley* was to be reprinted. His memoirs record his conversation with Pavel Lebedev-Poliansky, head of the party's censorship department (Glavlit) and better known by his journalistic pseudonym, Valerian Poliansky:

In those years writers still had free access to Glavlit for personal interviews with the censors so I went to Pavel Ivanovich regarding the suppression of my novel. He interrupted me after my very first words:

"We already know everything: both Gorky's letter [of support] and
your appeal to the press department. We know that second-hand dealers
are selling your book at fantastic prices, and we've heard that even hand-
written copies have been made. . . . But nevertheless we won't allow your
book. One edition is enough!"

"But why then Malashkin, Romanov . . ."

"That's another matter! And why do you have to print an unsuccess-
ful book," he continued softly as he shifted from giving orders to trying
to convince, "when you already have written such wonderful pieces. . . . I
remember well one of your stories where a peasant goes to ask for a
horse. . . . Where he threatens a portrait of Marx with his fist: 'Now see
what you've done, old man!' What a great story! That's what you should
be doing."

He stood up.

"As for your *Alley*, it won't be permitted!"

Gumilevsky was rightfully bitter for being singled out. If all three were guilty
of slander and pornography, then why was he alone to bear the cost, particularly since his novel was the most pro-Leninist of the three works?[60]

Gumilevsky's complaint of inconsistent standards and unfair treatment
shows that censorship, for all the desolation it wrought years later, was in the
1920s a rickety and jerry-rigged affair with a haphazard sense of what it should
do. (The fact that Gumilevsky could make a face-to-face appeal speaks volumes.) On paper, censorship was an awe-inspiring dragnet that leads to the
impression that the party had omnipotent control over what could appear in
print. In the first pages of *Censorship in Soviet Literature,* Herman Ermolaev
reminds us that one of Lenin's first decrees after October 1917 revoked freedom of the press and that by the end of 1920 "no manuscript could be set to
type without permission" from the responsible agencies.[61] Glavlit, as the
agency became known in 1922, was certainly capable of selective, devastating
intervention but at this time, it was unable to deal with the grand task with
which it was charged. Intentions are never the same as results. As later chapters will show, the decade was awash with works from both private and state
presses that belie Ermolaev's assertion that Soviet literature then "was essentially prudish, particularly by today's standards." To compare it with today is
misleading; it may not have favored "sexually explicit scenes," but the same
could be said of Western literature of the same period, or have we forgotten

the travails of Joyce and Lawrence? Arguably, Soviet literature as a whole was more daring and expressive, given the sheer number of fictional treatments of sexual intercourse, rape, assault, venereal disease, abortion, and illegitimacy.

If one is to speak of state-enforced puritanism, then mention must be made of its slips and blunders. The most stunning had nothing to do with Romanov, Malashkin, or Gumilevsky, but with the publication, beginning in 1925, of Iosif Kallinnikov's *Relics*, a multivolume opus about monks and nuns, in and out of the monastery, up through the time of the revolution.[62] To describe it as an anticlerical piece, as its publisher did, was a serious error in advertisement. It is certainly unflattering to the church, but satire it is not. A farrago of tedious, tawdry erotica fills page after page, overwhelming the work's proclaimed political message. Never before or after this time would such libidinous excess make its way into Soviet libraries. The monks themselves are relieved of the task of seduction; widows and nuns throw themselves at the brethren. Married women are also available for pleasure, having publicly declared that the danger of being caught makes adulterous sex "sweeter." Each summer promises a new cluster of virgins to deflower. With its graphic descriptions of coitus, an abortion scene, twelve infant corpses drowned in the monastery well (products of the nuns' abortions, still-births, and infanticides), and the necessary orgy, the publication of *Relics* (in multiple editions) was a startling anomaly.

Pausing temporarily in his rampage against "Dog Alley Literature," one critic lambasted *Relics* as "an encyclopedia of fornication, showing all existing sexual perversions beginning with pedophilia and ending with masturbation."[63] Placing the action in the corrupt prerevolutionary past and exploiting the new regime's hostility to religion could not redeem this work. Most critics recognized that its purpose was to titillate the reader with by-the-numbers erotica and that the author had not "the slightest literary talent."[64] And most admitted that Kallinnikov had succeeded: "The ghost of unbridled pornography has been loosed and flies towards the consumer who, needless to say, does exist."[65] How this work ever saw print is a mystery. Ionov memorably lamented, "Punishing hand of the censor, where are you?" Semashko in turn cited it as proof that the censorship bureau should "focus its attention . . . on the systematic, serious corruption of youth" instead of wasting time protecting "innocent veteran theatergoers."[66] Clearly, there was little method behind much of the madness of the 1920s. If Glavlit had truly exercised the control that many would ascribe to it, *Relics* would have been buried from the outset.

There was simply too much literature, too few censors, too few concrete guidelines, and, consequently, inconsistent enforcement. Evidence for this comes from the source, Poliansky himself, whose tenure lasted from 1922 until 1930. In a 1927 report to representatives to the party's Central Committee, he proudly listed his department's proscriptive responsibilities.[67] First was suppression of anti-Soviet propaganda and military secrets, while the fifth and last obligation was "prohibiting the publication and distribution of works of a pornographic nature." He had in mind not street-corner "manuscripts" and smutty photographs, but sexually charged fiction, the "boulevard literature" that was "flooding" the literary scene. Here was a direct admission of institutional breakdown, and after this point his report began to take on a decidedly different shade of red: from the patriotic to the embarrassed:

> Despite individual merits of books there is a conspicuous dominance by books of poor quality. Russian belles lettres suffers more often than not from the following deficiencies: a boulevard character, worthless eroticism and pornography, idealistic tendencies, the absence of a class orientation, groundless emotionalism, empty fantasy, the unconvincing portrayal of positive heroes, psychologism not of the best sort, ideological confusion, mystical attitudes, the distortion of Soviet reality, the idealization of old *byt*, political mistakes (but still tolerable in terms of censorship), affirmation of moral feelings, overattention to unhealthy criminality, an overflow of eroticism, [and] a maudlin, sentimental portrayal of the revolution and Soviet *byt*.

Poliansky confessed that a "huge number" of literary works from both private and state presses had been published without having been checked. He was shocked that atrocities like *Relics* and Bulgakov's "Fateful Eggs" had slipped through. He accused the Young Guard publishing house, currently churning out thousands of copies of "Moon on the Right," of printing "pornography," an immediate violation of his own code that should have warranted immediate action. If anything, Poliansky's report was a confession of failure, which was good news to many writers and editors. Glavlit had power, but not consistent or sufficient power to stop what was a hemorrhage of salacious works. In prioritizing his bureau's future efforts, he notably reversed hierarchies: the first proscription was "pornography," followed by "unhealthy eroticism" and "swearing." The last two were "the depiction of the secret police as a torture chapter" and anything "clearly counterrevolutionary."

Nevertheless, Poliansky was not willing to shoulder the entire blame. He criticized other party organizations for insufficient coordination and support. Official tolerance for (relative) artistic diversity, enshrined in the Central Committee resolution of 1925, had forced Glavlit to "walk along a razor's edge." He further claimed that he and his subordinates were not beasts but listened to popular opinion. "In order to maintain balance, one by necessity leans first to one and then the other side. This naturally makes us the target of both. [Hence] the whole time we have been rebuked both in print and orally for unreasonable cruelty which has forced Glavlit sometimes to be softer than it found necessary." We need not sympathize with Poliansky's plight, but we should also not ignore it. His superiors had placed him in an impossible situation as evidenced by a 1922 directive: "Describing dark sides of contemporary Soviet *byt*" was *not* sufficient cause for prohibition if a work as a whole was not "inimical to the Soviet state."[68] Here at the very heart, where power could be exercised in its most literal and direct sense, we find the same wishy-washy vagueness of which many took full advantage. Gumilevsky's assumption of a double standard was likely in error; incongruity in censoring was more a reflection of bureaucratic confusion, overwork, and incompetence than of conscious hypocrisy. Poliansky may have known where to draw the line, and in cases like Gumilevsky's he might score a victory. However, for many in the bureau, the ambiguous guidelines only produced the same dithering cloud of confusion that bedeviled writers, critics, and editors "on the outside."

CHAPTER 6

Life versus Literature

Two Realisms

POLIANSKY'S bad humor over the censor's plight was not to pass quickly. In 1928 the Young Guard publishing house released yet another edition of "Moon on the Right," with a stinging, unrepentant foreword. Innocently titled "From the Publisher," it reveled in the novella's current notoriety, declaring that the public meetings and disputes devoted to it numbered "almost in the thousands." Perhaps exaggerated, the claim was simultaneously a taunt and a defense of the publisher's credo: it was better to engage than to patronize the reader. For the Young Guard publishers, the "principal mistake" made by their critics was to confuse imaginative literature with fact. Malashkin of course wrote fiction. On the other hand, they added, "No one can deny that as a social phenomenon sexual misbehavior and sexual anarchism exist to a significant degree among us. Hence no one can rebuke the author of 'Moon' as if his subject and plot are *made up*. For this very same reason, the accusation against this writer, a communist, that his work is of a 'slanderous' character is groundless."[1]

They were having it both ways. Exercising artistic license for the sake of edification was not criminal, not even unusual, they protested. To betray verisimilitude by moving too far from real life would ignore their mandate to educate, and even betray their Marxist roots. In short, they sought to carve out a special place for works like "Moon on the Right" between fantasy and fact, and in so doing thrust themselves squarely into the debate over the purpose and impact of imaginative literature in the 1920s.

Fiction, but not make-believe; artifice, but still an accurate commentary on life. The claim would seem self-contradictory, yet it merely spelled out what Soviet literary culture had already endorsed. One constant in the debates about literature addressing the sexual revolution, for critics and general readers alike, was that the value of a work—novel, story, poem, or documentary—lay in its ability to instruct. A worker might lambaste "Moon on the Right" as slander, and a student praise its accuracy, but both measured it against their own experience and asked what they could learn from Tanya Aristarkhova's life. This expectation also linked critics from opposing camps, such as Ermilov, the *Young Guard* editor who favored works of provocation, and Poliansky, head of the censorship department, who championed morally uplifting literature. Both were committed to judging a text according to how well it answered the reader's presumed needs. Defined simply, the approach was one of heightened utilitarianism, the primary criterion of socially oriented critics since the nineteenth century, and one not limited to the Soviet Union. More charitably, it was a view of literature as a teacher and a repository for useful knowledge.[2]

Overlapping expectations bring us onto the familiar ground of literary mimesis: a text could be accepted as a reflection of "real life" insofar as its (ever variable) epistemological premises, characters, and events seemed to have a plausible connection to what occurred in the world beyond the text. Yet Soviet expectations for realism entailed far more than a suspension of disbelief and a text's capacity to imitate life. Just as Engels claimed that he learned more about French society from Balzac's *Comédie Humaine* "than from all the professional historians, economists, and statisticians of the period together" (which would become a favorite refrain in Soviet letters at the turn of the decade), most assumed that imaginative fiction was fully capable of conveying fact.[3] What was most important was not a text's formal trappings that made it fiction, but its performative result as a representation of truth. For the majority of Soviet readers, therefore, fiction was never just fiction. In an attack on Malashkin, Poliansky asserted that "the artist should base his creative work on scientific grounds, having recourse, at times, to statistics so as to avoid making incorrect conclusions." Imaginative literature did not exist for its own sake alone: "The artist should incorporate real-life material and not make it up."[4] If fiction was to serve real life, it should be faithful to accepted facts. (In Poliansky's eyes, this meant that Komsomol members were well behaved.) If it did this successfully, then it could stand with equal authority alongside any documentary exposition of the same referent or idea.

Subordinating fiction to these requirements did not compromise its effectiveness or quality. Soviet writers' tendency to frame their fiction in "documentary form," the critic Dmitry Gorbov believed, constituted a vital step in creating "serious" art. Malashkin's use of a fictionalized diary or Romanov's epistolary structure revealed a common intention "to dig as deeply as possible into the thicket of *byt* and social-psychological processes that concern us in our everyday lives as we read in newspapers." Gorbov even argued that fiction surpassed journalism by offering more compelling portraits of "real" people than could be found in media reports. Factualized fiction could produce a "truly realistic art" because it saved writers from the twin evils of strict "sermonizing" and the "narrow subjectivity of personalized observations."[5] It held imagination in check: "The true artist is sincere and simple. He is incapable of 'making up a subject.' He must discover it."[6] Thus constituted, imaginative literature could serve as the optimum pedagogic vehicle, since it combined both fiction and fact, understood as having an authentic connection to real life. Each balanced and monitored the other: the first ensured the second had an audience; the second that fantasy didn't go too far.

Essentially, the entire debate over the treatment of sexuality in literature turned on the question of whether writers had renounced mere "make-believe" in favor of fidelity to truth and fact. Across all camps and factions, realism was the summit of literary achievement, the desideratum. However, then, as now, the definition of realism was notoriously imprecise; there was no consensus as to which "windows on reality" deserved to be framed, which cleaned, and which smashed. Nevertheless, this was the criterion for whatever imaginative literature in the 1920s was granted documentary legitimacy and thus deemed worthy of attention and emulation. No work or author could pretend to cultural authority without being declared realistic. Failure to achieve this designation was generally classified in one of two ways. If a work presented too rosy a picture, it could be dismissed as *plakat*, the kind of formulaic optimism and simplistic thinking conveyed by political posters. On the other hand, a work could be faulted for *bytovizm*, a narrow portrayal of life's deficiencies without any compensating perspective or hope. If such a work included sex, it was usually dismissed as slander and pornography.

In a practical, functional sense, no critic or reader substantively moved outside of this terminological grid to register response. Genre was not at issue; a poem could be just as "realistic" (or "slanderous") as a novel depending on the perceived utility, that is, the perceived truth value of its message. The evaluative system was simplistic but crudely effective. Its vocabulary was readily accessible and highly flexible, able to accommodate all texts, regardless of type, author, content, or ideological stance. For all intents and purposes, the tidy triangle that formed was the deliberate by-product of dialectal thinking. Realism was the necessary synthesis, occupying the ground between a distorting thesis, hyperbolic optimism, and its equally delinquent antithesis, slanderous pessimism.

Yet inevitably there was no agreement over what qualified as realistic. To some, "Moon on the Right" was an accurate portrait of contemporary life. To others, it was an insidious falsification. (No one dared call it optimistic.) For us this is not simply an exercise in scholastics; instead, it constitutes one of the more neglected, yet important legacies of fictional works dealing with the sexual revolution. Their true impact was not on people's actual behavior but more on Soviet literature itself as the 1920s became a testing ground for the limits of what was permissible. The controversy over alleged slander and obscenity in fiction by Gumilevsky, Malashkin, and Romanov became a fulcrum of debate over what Soviet literature should be. There never was consensus or a straight dictate from above defining the proper course of literary art. It certainly was to be realistic and therefore didactic, but for whom and in what way?

Nowhere else but with the representation of sexual behavior was the teething pain more acute, for no one—writer, reader, critic, ideologue, doctor, sociologist—could ignore the subject or remain neutral. For this reason, what was written is sometimes less important than how it was read. Criteria for rejection, strategies for accommodation, conditions of praise—all point to how people understood themselves, their country, their art, and their destiny. To view events then solely in terms, however convenient, of puritan officials versus sensationalist writers is not only erroneous (not all the former were "puritan" and many "sensationalist" writers believed themselves the opposite), it also reduces the picture to a monochrome palette. The conflict was more among critics and party officials themselves about what realism truly meant, that is, about which texts were to be accepted as culturally legitimate sources of knowledge and information. A permanent split arose between two critical orientations, what I will call orthodox realism versus analytical realism, although these are merely provisional designations for readers' and critics' expectations of what a text should do, not descriptions of actual camps, schools, or writers.

Orthodox realism was favored by Poliansky and most of the voices from outside the field of literature itself, such as Semashko, Smidovich, Troshchenko, Demidovich, and Yaroslavsky. Their offense taken at works like "Moon on the Right" was not just disgust over a portrait of a sex-obsessed Komsomol. It was also symptomatic of a fear that Soviet literature was deficient and flawed, unable or unwilling to represent life as theory dictated it should be. For them, Marxism made life and its artistic representation easily quantifiable by carving the world into fixed slices. The role that human beings could play were determined by class, which shaped individual character traits and behavior. The social environment was one of identity politics writ large, but with this fundamental distinction: the characteristic features of each class were preset, immutable, nontransferable, and organized in a strict hierarchy. In theory, one could not step outside one's established identity, that is, exhibit the speech, behavior, or thought deemed representative of another class. The proletariat, for example, could not admit homosexuality; the two were mutually exclusive. This is not to say that Soviet workers never engaged in homosexual behavior, but if they did so they were no longer authentic members of the proletariat. Likewise, anyone who feared that masturbation made him "bourgeois" viewed himself through the same theoretical lens. According to the orthodox approach, Malashkin's mistake was to suggest that Tanya Aristarkhova was both a member of the Komsomol and a patron of "Athenian Nights" orgies. This was a falsification of reality, and her behavior forfeited her rights to membership. To show an upstanding member of the Komsomol (as she once was) engaging in improper sexual activity violated ideology. An "Athenian" (or a Don Juan, homosexual, or masturbator) was a false Komsomolist; that is, anyone capable of such aberrations was never a Komsomolist to begin with but representative of a different type, a bourgeois infiltrator.

Among orthodox critics, such formulas for reality begat their expectations for realism in literature: it was to replicate and enforce social life in its established categories. Therefore, fictional characters were to reify as closely as possible social identities as handed down by ideology. Ultimately, this formula was a recipe for stock characterization and standardized plots, a kind of commedia dell'arte. The simple objective was accessibility; literature should exhibit the same clarity of purpose, execution, and argument to be found in a party edict. Of course, everyone understood that fiction admitted certain nuances and allowed for exceptions that would be inappropriate for an ideological treatise. Indeed, this was a central problem in the debate over whether sex-obsessed Komsomolists represented the "pimples" or the whole face. Likewise, Romanov and Malashkin offered certain plausible motivations for their protagonists' downfall, which ventured onto more dangerous territory. By presenting characters as individuals, not as representatives of predefined social groups with particular behavioral traits, their works eluded clear-cut, class-based definitions. No doubt the absence of doctrinaire content and their use of an unobtrusive authorial stance (that is, epistolary form and first-person narrative voice) explain why some young readers identified with the "reality" of their stories. Hence, orthodox critics found fault with Romanov's and Malashkin's work. Though they would never admit as much, they preferred characters who could step from a literary text into the roles of poster art heroes and villains. All imaginative writing had to exhibit the certainty and coherence of a platform statement, regardless of the author's design. This is not to say that a text was inherently of this nature; rather it describes how a text was treated by such critics. The proper Komsomolist had to embody the chaste projections of a Demidovich, had to embrace the precepts of a Zalkind, and had to live according to Lenin's example. If a writer was careless about adhering to these principles, "reality" had to be rectified and the ambiguity removed. As Ivan Bobryshev declared, life wasn't ambiguous; rather authorial fancy made it so: "A literature that depicts the shady sides but provides no resolution or is incapable of doing it is a decadent literature. The literature of our time, the literature of cheerful people . . . will show the path of extricating oneself from contradictions, of healing the diseases and ulcers, for such a path exists in reality."[7]

Given these expectations for literary art, one might ask why critics and party officials sanctioned any fiction at all. Obviously, despite denunciations of "make-believe," no one was willing to forgo the advantage of poetic license. One could still write fiction, true fiction; now, however, in a new environment fiction should also assume the mantle of documentary authority. Indeed, fiction, for the time being more fungible than official history, might fulfill the pedagogic function even better. It was well suited to rectify contemporary social problems by reducing life to more easily understandable and digestible antinomies. The 1920s was a decade of economic boom and crash, political instability, domestic upheaval, and internal strife. Citizens were confronted by mixed messages and contradictory expectations of themselves and their future. Orthodox critics maintained that the right kind of fiction could provide stable points of reference and lend coherence to a fluid, troubling time. Because this expectation would flourish under socialist realism, it is easy to accuse orthodox critics of propagating a similarly false reality. However, for these critics, secure in their own infallibility, the charge would not have made sense. It would have been unconscionable and defeatist for them not to insist on the validity of set class identities and, by extension, on the existence of strong, stable institutions such as the Komsomol amid contemporary chaos. Therefore, in expecting literature to reproduce characters with such fixed value, orthodox critics sought to resolve the profound crisis of self sweeping the early Soviet Union. They hoped that aesthetics and ideology could find a common ground so that, when done right, this literary realism would become an educational tool that would help to create a new society.

The Young Guardists and the "Living Person"

The other orientation, analytical realism, found a symbolic home in *The Young Guard*. In the 1920s this publication was more than a monthly journal; it also served as a breeding ground for tempestuous, committed Marxists for whom literature was a deadly serious business and compromise a synonym for treason. The Octobrists were founded in its editorial offices in 1922. This was a rump group of writers and critics, including Malashkin, Leopold Averbakh (nephew of Yakov Sverdlov, a key associate of Lenin), the poet Nikolai Kuznetsov (who committed suicide), Aleksandr Tarasov-Rodionov (author of *Chocolate*) and the novelist Yury Libedinsky. Dissatisfied with the airy, abstract, and generally fantastical spirit favored by the Smithy, one of the first self-identified proletarian artistic movements, the Octobrists were born in rebellion and never lost the combative spirit. Their goal was to establish a proletarian hegemony in Soviet arts, and as critics they executed their campaign with such zeal, verbal force, and vulgarity that they have come to symbolize the nadir of Marxist criticism. As the group under successive names stabilized around Averbakh and Libedinsky, their primary target became Alexander Voronsky, the editor of *Red Virgin Soil*, whom they accused of aiding and abetting (that is, publishing) "bourgeois writers." Toward the end of the 1920s, under the aegis of the Russian Association of Proletarian Writers (RAPP), they bullied their way to the top of the critical field, where they remained until the onset of socialist realism. Yet so crude and unprincipled was their tenure—its highlights being the suicide of Vladimir Mayakovsky, the hounding of Boris Pilnyak, and the departure of Evgeny Zamiatin—that some writers turned to socialist realism as a welcome respite from the Octobrists' unprincipled exercise of coercion.

This, at least, is the image that endures, and the Octobrists–Young Guardists have remained to this day a favorite punching bag for scholars, who continue to deplore their impact as demagogues and dogmatists.[8] However, one receives a different impression from their approach to sexuality in literature, for it is among this group of critics, more than any other, that one finds tolerance, open-mindedness, and even aesthetic sensitivity. Like the orthodox realists, the Young Guardists were devoutly Marxist, had recourse to the same authoritative sources, believed themselves to have the interests of youth at heart, used the same criteria for expressing praise and condemnation, and, most important, believed that art's primary role should be didactic. Yet their understanding of how literature could achieve this goal was profoundly at odds with that of many others in the party. While both critical schools believed in mimesis as their operating principle, the crucial difference was how fidelity to life, the connection between text and reality, should be defined. Orthodox realist critics championed a fixed model of life that, when applied to literature, would guarantee a protagonist who in any environment would be impervious to internal vacillation or change. The analytical realists, on the other hand, favored an image of life in flux and thus expected any "realistic" representation of life to be dynamic as well. In Vladimir Ermilov's words, "The alphabet of the dialectic is, at the same time, the alphabet of art."[9] Their rallying cry struck at the heart of the orthodox platform; their goal was to wage "war against cliché, schematism, and naked posterism" and bring to an end the "varnishing" of life and "ra-ra-revolutionariness."[10] With typical effrontery, the Young Guardists did not hesitate to accuse their opponents of pretending to offer realism but substituting *plakat* in its stead, that is, works in which the bourgeoisie was always "bad" and the proletariat always "good."[11]

The Young Guardists viewed realism as a mode of engaging the reader with a portrait of life on which the paint was still wet, a literature that asked as many questions as it answered. To them, orthodox realism was a contradiction in terms. "There is nothing easier," wrote M. Bekker in 1926, "than to dress one's heroes in leather coats, red kerchiefs, adorn them with Komsomol badges, make them irrepressibly happy and then declare them to be the typical members of the Komsomol. The results of such a method are clear for all to see: instead of living individuals, one gets cookie-cutter stamped creations."[12] Schematic literature presented an idealized, abstract picture, but not the intricacies of a life in which real individuals worked, loved, and died. Content to remain in a realm of clear presentation and easy answers, such literature was unwilling to dirty its hands. Its failure lay in its own circularity, replicating the paradoxes of its enabling ideology. It could always explain the general and abstract, yet by adhering to the triumphalism of party proclamation and edict, it lost contact with its audience. "Dirt" was precisely what many readers wanted. And though a sanitized representation of contemporary life would seem to answer the state's needs, in truth, as Ippolit and Kin argued, it doomed literature both as art and teacher. "Poster heroes" were the hallmark of creative immaturity that directly attenuated literature's "artistic and didactic value." In order to effect change and connect with readers, writers had to produce a "living person."

As vague as it was empowering, the "living person" concept became the key slogan of Marxist critics who feared the proliferation of ever-smiling model protagonists. With the same brash voice and logic with which he had defended Malashkin, Ermilov emerged as a vocal proponent of such authenticity. "Down with saccharin," he famously charged; "down with romantic beautification!" Neither could satisfy the needs of a maturing readership because such fiction lacked one essential ingredient: a "p-e-r-s-o-n."[13] To present communists as flesh-and-blood individuals, he believed, required a "psychological approach" that acknowledged the internal conflicts, doubts, and vacillation festering in everyone. Life was fluid, beliefs were being challenged, and temptation lurked around every corner. Communists faced the simple problem of being all too human in a time that asked for supermen. For Ermilov, to recognize this condition was not defeatist. On the contrary, to depict only the extraordinary was the coward's path, since it abandoned hard truths for a marionette-filled Soviet Valhalla. "The proletarian style" was "realistic" even in offering "dirt," Ermilov contended, because dirt could truly be fertile ground for artists. In his words:

> We often encounter a "mathematic" approach to art: this is black, this is
> white, and they must be set in *opposition*. But the artist is not obligated
> to counterpose anything. If you're writing about rot and gloom, then

write precisely about rot and gloom and don't listen to anything by those liberal rosy-eyed guys with their well-meaning chirp-chirping: on one hand, . . . but on the other. . . . These guys don't understand art, although they're writing reviews in a lot of newspapers and journals. If an artist wants to express the idea of decay and ruin, then let him do *just that* and *only* that. But he should *express* it so that the reader, the audience, is not left with the sense of a job half done, incomplete, and artistically unsatisfying.[14]

The emphasized words say it all. Literature could, and frankly should, explore the dark side of *byt* if it was to connect with readers. This was not because Young Guardists were pessimists, as their detractors charged, but because the emphasis on the person automatically shifted their attention in that direction. For if all Marxists carved the world into class divisions, advocates of the "living person" went one step further, dividing the individual internally as well. The Young Guardists would theoretically agree with orthodox critics that as a group and as an abstraction the proletariat was stalwart and supreme, but in the here and now this was often not the case. As Aleksandr Fadeev argued, each person in life, and therefore each character in literature, reflected in microcosm the travails of the class struggle:

> In our view, to show the living person means in the end to show the entire historical process of societal movement and development. Just as social processes are not reflected in each individual's psyche in some direct, mechanical fashion but occur in an exceedingly complex dialectical fashion of a person's interaction with his environment, and just as it is equally necessary to take into account that a person is subject simultaneously to the influence of various classes that affect his psyche, so then is the psychological makeup of the person exceedingly complex, as it is shaped in particular by both unconscious and conscious impulses.[15]

As a common refrain that came to dominate critical discourse toward the end of the decade, the "living person" was employed to justify the portrayal of imperfect characters, conscious of their own weaknesses and doubts. Fadeev, in fact, produced the archetype in his novel *The Rout* (1926), which gave readers an admirable but flawed revolutionary hero. Yet the "living person" was not a stock character. By its very nature the concept symbolized unpredictability. An individual's imperfections were certainly not permanent; victory would come, but one could not claim it prematurely. To do so would be to violate contemporary conditions in favor of a theoretical projection or, in Fadeev's words, to take a character "from a political pamphlet instead of the concrete reality surrounding a writer."[16]

The Debate over *Natalia Tarpova*

"Sexual realism," to resurrect a term coined before the revolution, became a primary vehicle for implementing the "living person" paradigm.[17] As a literary theme and approach, it was supremely emblematic of the communist's internal struggle to overcome competing impulses of the head and heart, duty and body, the collective and the personal. It was the flesh and blood behind what Ermilov claimed to be "the first and principal task" of *The Young Guard*: "the all-encompassing, indefatigable and constant effort to represent contemporary reality."[18] To prove that sexual content could be a barometer for a "living" literature, he turned to his own journal with the first installment of Sergei Semenov's popular novel, *Natalia Tarpova* (1927). Although the novel is set in a Petrograd factory in 1923, it offers no uplifting scenes of industrial achievement or civil war reconstruction. Instead, it is a psychological portrait of the heroine's efforts to understand her own sexuality in a time of proclaimed female liberation and to resolve the perennial conflict between professional demands and personal needs. With its explosive blend of political and sexual implications, the novel inspired a critical battle that erupted even before all three episodes of the serialized work had appeared in print.

Natalia Tarpova is an attractive twenty-four-year-old woman with brains and authority (she is the secretary of her factory committee) who finds herself in the classic revolutionary love triangle. She is physically attracted to Gabrukh, a bourgeois engineer, yet she is equally drawn to the newly arrived Riabev, a traveling trouble-shooter for the party. Each character's sexual profile is perforce a reflection of ideological standing. Gabrukh cannot be anything but a rational hedonist. He is married, but freely pursues other women. Marriage, he believes, has only a social function—to establish a family. It should not inhibit the expression of biological impulses: "I don't see any reason to castrate myself with regard to other women." The proletarian Riabev, a veteran of the civil war, fills the role of party hero. He has come to the factory to sort out the bureaucratic entanglements of local politics that are hampering productivity. He is renowned not for an iron fist but for modesty, honesty, self-discipline, and the ability to demand the same from others. Questions of love and family do not concern him; those issues are for the future and will be solved in the future. Such fortitude, however, does not mean he is an ascetic; like Gabrukh, he finds Tarpova singularly appealing, not for her head but for her hips.

Tarpova herself first appears to be almost a cousin of Zhenya from Kollontai's "Three Generations." Brief physical affairs, unencumbered by emotional commitment or pain, constitute her intimate life. These purely sexual relationships have left her questioning the nature of desire, need, and duty. What of love? What of marriage? What of the party? she asks herself. When Tarpova puts these questions to her brother (a student at Sverdlov University), he answers in hackneyed pamphlet prose and offers numbingly impractical advice: "Quit thinking about these details of *byt*. The proletariat has brought women full emancipation and liberated them from all bourgeois conventions. That's what you shouldn't forget and you should let it be the guide for what you do as a woman!" Understandably confused, Tarpova turns for help to a magazine article about "the new family and new women," but it offers only more platitudes assuring her that new relations will arise in a new sociopolitical environment. She finds no answer to her dilemma. At night she dreams of a constant line of men coming to her door. She quickly locks it, not sure who is Mr. Right. "For whom should she unlock the door?" asks her tortured subconscious. Will he come? What if he does and she fails to open the door? Gabrukh puts her dream to the test. He is egoism incarnate, the class enemy, hostile to the goals of October. Yet this ideological distance makes him forbidden fruit for Tarpova: she cannot love him, but she cannot imagine being without him. And what then of the stalwart Riabev, whose words "ensnare her" in a "soft, silky web"?

Thus laid out, Semenov's love triangle is easily translated into ideological terms. The sexual dilemma is given greater depth by its simultaneous refraction through many other oppositions dividing the characters: proletarian and nonproletarian, party and nonparty, young and old, parent and child. Given the sheer number of dialectical possibilities, Ermilov wasted no time putting his own critical theory into action. He was so confident of his interpretation that after only a third of the novel had appeared, he rushed his essay, "In Search of the Harmonious Person," into print, complete with a graph delineating the cross-connections among the characters.[19] To him, the novel illustrated a sexual dialectic par excellence; it analyzed the issue of sexual behavior without promoting sex in a prurient manner. Tarpova's attraction-repulsion response to Gabrukh revealed that class instinct, not hormones, governed the individual. Although she was intensely interested in him, Ermilov concluded, Tarpova's failure to act on her desires proved the validity of Zalkind's memorable declaration that being physically attracted to a member of another class was like being attracted to a crocodile or an orangutan. Ermilov explained Tarpova's indecisiveness in both psychological and political terms. She is pulled toward Gabrukh by her subconscious instincts; she is drawn to Riabev by her class-conscious reason. In short, it is a triumph of ideology and rationality over hormones and animalism. Ermilov singled out Riabev as the already "harmonious" individual who could serve as the anchor for Tarpova. In him instinct and ideology are united, giving Riabev the ability to control himself and "direct great psychic energy toward a conscious, single goal."

Because the serialized novel was still incomplete, Ermilov could only speculate whether Tarpova would achieve the same harmony exhibited in Riabev. For him, it came down to the simple question of choosing the better man. Unlike his comments on Malashkin's "Moon on the Right," Ermilov's response to Semenov's novel shows that he was more comfortable explicating and celebrating than defending and qualifying. Semenov's novel was qualitatively different from Malashkin's novella, and Ermilov's comfort in handling it was evident in a digression on Tarpova's famous hips and copious citations from the text's more "physical" moments. His essay was unquestionably meant to tweak his opponents, but its tone bespoke confidence in his ideas as much as defiance. A luxuriant tableau of theses and antitheses, of searchers and seekers, *Natalia Tarpova* was to him a signal achievement of "realism"— so much so that the novel transcended its characters and became itself "a living whole" and "an entire developing organism."

Unfortunately, Ermilov's passion for dialectics had got the better of him. Semenov finished the novel according to his own plan, ignoring Ermilov's meticulous dissection laid out in his essay and his expectations for an ideologically happy ending in which Riabev rescues Tarpova. In a curious deterioration of his once "harmonious" character, Riabev falls victim to bourgeois domestication. He acquires a larger apartment so he can live with Liudmilla, a member of the intelligentsia, who gets him to shave his beard and transforms the party hero into a docile companion. No longer does he embody modesty, discipline, and restraint; we learn that his past is marked by many relationships with women. He continues to mouth the standard line that the unresolved problems of today's *byt* "can be solved tomorrow." Yet Tarpova realizes he is but a shell of his former self and rejects his platitudes, much as the letter from "Nina" had scoffed at Sofia Smidovich's ideas in the exchange in *The New Shift*. She demands concrete answers. What Riabev says about tomorrow is "very comforting," she says; "but I want to know what *I should be doing today*. I can't put off my 'unresolved' questions until tomorrow, for I am living today." In response to this challenge, Riabev can only hang his head: "Well, that I don't know."[20] Still in love with Gabrukh, Tarpova questions why differences of political opinion should mean that a man and a woman still cannot be together simply as man and woman. Having set the stage for a climactic ending, with the heroine's dilemmas still unresolved (will Tarpova now save Riabev, or will she put her heart over politics and join Gabrukh?), Semenov surprisingly chooses to end his novel with Chekhovian ambiguity. Tarpova remains alone, asserting her independence and recognizing that loyalty to the party takes precedence over physical pleasure, yet she is left emotionally desolate.

While rejecting the script that Ermilov had laid out for him, Semenov also refused to tailor his novel to orthodox prescriptions. Not only does the party program, as usual, fail to deliver Tarpova from her plight, but also physical attraction is revealed to be a force transcending class. In a blow to both groups, he showed that if ideologically oriented literature had problems making poster heroes seem realistic, then adherents of the "living person" idea had difficulty making a realistic text ideologically upstanding and sound. Most readers and critics of the latter group were willing, however, to ignore this point. A chorus of approving reviews, sometimes only of the first installment, quickly appeared in leading party organs. Applauded for depicting communists as "living persons" and therefore "real," Semenov was also praised for avoiding cheap sensationalism in broaching the topic of sexuality.

Readers also found Tarpova to be a distinct improvement over Tanya from "Moon on the Right." In her, Semenov had united three unusual features of the decade's literature: woman as agent, woman as purveyor of good, and woman as an example to men. She does not find Mr. Right, but she does take the Right Path, and Semenov notably spares her the syphilis-abortion torment generally assigned to female characters who find themselves tempted.[21] That the novel was not strictly about Tarpova's relationships was also fortuitous, since it allowed other critics to comfortably sidestep the entire matter of her private life. Dismissing the "faddish sexual problem" as irrelevant, the Marxist critic Vladimir Friche latched onto the factory scenes as capturing "our life, our world" or, in the words of another commentator, they were "close to reality."[22]

The documentary accuracy of *Natalia Tarpova* was ostensibly confirmed at the source in a compilation of workers' responses to the novel. For some, it was a "mirror" of factory life in which one can almost "hear the machinery"; it was a "healthy and useful book and not market pulp."[23] Others were less forgiving of Semenov's unconventional approach. Some workers deplored as "simply criminal" the novel's failure to portray the collective. Though Tarpova comes to the proper conclusion by rejecting both men, she does it on her own terms, after many mistakes and much inner struggle. This may have been good for the "living person" criterion, but certainly not for the image of the party. Workers expressed even harsher opinions of Tarpova herself: "a prostitute operating under the flag of 'freedom for women,'" or "a highly qualified prostitute covering herself with her party ticket."[24] Offended readers blamed Semenov. A work of fiction that offered lessons on proper sexual behavior obviously had to include controversial and sensitive material in the story, but it should avoid sensationalism or any suggestion of promoting lewd behavior. Like Malashkin, Semenov's mistake was not to keep the subject in proper proportion. After all, orthodox readers left themselves little room for interpretive flexibility: either outright rejection of a text or its assimilation within their own critical assumptions. Here, arguably, the latter response was the more problematic since it entailed an explanation of why the subject of sexuality could occupy the attention of party members for an entire novel.

No doubt this explains certain critics' deliberate misreading of *Natalia Tarpova*. Some closed their eyes to any compensating material, just as they had ignored Gumilevsky's heavy-handed moralizing at the end of *Dog Alley*. In both circumstances, by turning the writers' motives inside out and condemning them as slander, critics revealed that their primary objective was not to interpret the author's intentions but to uphold the paradigm in which they believed. If the party were to remain pure, and if Komsomolists were to serve as models for the future, then sexuality had to be put in its proper (minor) place. As Bobryshev charged, "No one denies the presence of sexual depravity. It exists, but don't use it to push everything else about students' lives into the background. Don't depict it on such a Herculean scale that, truth be told, instead of students one sees only a den of vice of gargantuan proportions."[25] In effect, a substantial degree of misreading—what was highlighted, what ignored—was almost preordained by the ideological paradigm within which such critics operated.

At a more substantive level, criticism against Semenov reflected the general suspicion that met the "living person" campaign and *The Young Guard* in particular. Yet the journal's editors were theoretically doing nothing wrong. In June 1926 (exactly when "Without a Cherry Blossom" appeared), their self-critical approach had received official imprimatur in a Komsomol Central Committee resolution demanding that Komsomol literature should "reflect life in all its contradictions" by neither "painting everything in [positive] red" nor depicting "only the dark sides."[26] The slogan sounded correct, since it was couched in proper dialectical fashion. Yet many saw it as giving young Marxists license to instruct their elders—a presumptuousness that could not go unchecked. "Komsomol avant-gardism," Stalin ominously warned, was a threat to proper authority; "to the inexperienced reader it would seem not that the party is correcting the mistakes of youth but the other way around."[27] Stalin was not mistaken. According to Yury Libedinsky (writing in 1927), the Central Committee had abdicated its leading role in refusing to intervene directly in factional disputes. Hence it was up to individual members to carry the cause forward:

> We have taken upon ourselves the role of party reconnaissance. What does this mean? It means that if we pose [in literature] various questions for which the party does not at this time have precise answers, then we will decide them as we see fit. When the party does come to a decision, then our work will be sanctioned or, if we have committed a mistake, it will point this out and correct them. We must be the ideological skirmishers on this front.[28]

Many began to see *The Young Guard,* despite its claims to the contrary, as part of the problem instead of the solution. The futurist journal *LEF,* a frequent target of the Octobrists, declared as much on the first page of its first issue (1927): "In recent years the cultural situation with regard to the arts has fallen into a swamp."[29] *The Young Guard* had become a purveyor of the boulevard literature it had been chartered to combat. In trying to "excite the mind," it had done its job too well. It inspired too much controversy, too much provocation. The alleged infatuation with sex, evident in the journal's fiction and articles, could be explained by the fact that many of its editors and contributors were the same age as their readers and thus prone to the same immature excesses. Averbakh, for example, was born in 1903; Ermilov in 1904. By 1920, while still in their teens, they had already cut their teeth as editors of the Moscow Komsomol organ, *Youth Pravda.* By 1926 they were veterans, scarred but self-assured and ever combative.

They also found themselves mired in a sensational, illogical controversy in which positions and principles were hopelessly confused. In fact, contrary to their opponents' allegations, Averbakh and Ermilov never sanctioned any and all literary portrayals of sex. To them, Gumilevsky was not of the same caliber as Malashkin or Romanov, who were genuine writers. For Averbakh, Gumilevsky was guilty of philistine sensationalism.[30] Likewise, Ermilov's review of Mikhail Barsukov's *Mauritania* (1926), a novel replete with three NEP couples, the men all party members and the women prostitutes, exhibits similar disdain: "It's shameful and disgusting to wallow in such a stinking, sticky pile of manure; it's shameful and disgusting even to report on the contents of Barsukov's novel in the pages of *The Literary Guardian.*"[31]

Yet their opponents within the party were equally inconsistent in the expression of their beliefs. This was true both of orthodox critics and moderates such as Voronsky and Lezhnev, leading members of the Pereval movement and advocates of an "organic realism" that shunned *plakat* (poster-hero) approaches. While the Young Guardists and Pereval members fought like dogs, their proclamations often shared the same rhetoric. Lezhnev expressly approved of certain works dealing with sex, since this orientation made them "problematic" *(problemnaia)* and this fact alone cemented their "living connection" with contemporary reality. With an eye to aesthetics as much as to ideology, he carefully noted that Romanov, Malashkin, and Gumilevsky were certainly not trail blazers in literary terms; all were quite "schematic," with Malashkin sinning the least and Gumilevsky the most. Nevertheless all three opened their texts up to both the good and the bad, a vitality without which literature would stagnate and decline.[32] Likewise, Voronsky's dismissal of the orthodox Marxist critics would have been warmly welcomed on the pages of *The Young Guard:*

It's no secret that there have arisen among us quite a few overly well-intentioned communist form-masters, that is, people who do not want to and do not see the dark, seamy sides of life here. Such zealots sometimes come blinded from the underground [Bolsheviks from before the revolution] but more often from the sort who are respectfully advanced in biological age but whose communist age more befits a green worker. They are the ones who are the loudest, most fanatical, and most inflexible. Their red hue is so overdone that one wonders if it's not just painted on.[33]

These similarities in outlook are usually seen as evidence that the Young Guardists were cheap plagiarists, but they were quite capable of forming their own opinions, which were often more politically provocative than Voronsky's. The reason for such agreement was that the object of contention itself—realism—was itself impossible to define. The definition changed, chameleonlike, from critic to critic, year to year. It was always assumed to be a literary virtue that no true Marxist could ever renounce, but the proper connection between literature and life remained unpredictable and elusive.

The Facts Are Wrong

The "accuracy" of fiction, the one constant in the debate over this literature, was therefore a paradox itself. From this emerged the slippery yet crucial qualification that the desired realism did not necessarily mean strict adherence to facts. This was the message of "Pornography and Pathology in Contemporary Literature" (1928) by Mikhail Maizel, a Leningrad professor. A literary work should not aspire to photographic precision, he explained; such a work would lack the necessary "perspective" and risk a descent into "naked primitivism," reveling in details for details' sake. Furthermore, if a work of fiction did broach the subject of sex, he warned, using Malashkin and Romanov as examples, the result would be "hypertrophic eroticism," which could have an appalling effect on delicate young minds—like that of "hashish on an addict."[34] Writers would often hear this charge—and not just from orthodox critics.[35] Not only academics but also ordinary readers made this complaint. In language uncannily foreshadowing that of socialist realism, a worker castigated Malashkin for "piling on the facts" and failing to show "the typical," that is, "what is characteristic for a specific class."[36]

Both Professor Maizel and the worker were arguing the same point: facts alone betrayed the reality of Soviet life. Such reasoning would seem to put orthodox realists in a tight spot: facts had to match the Soviet reality; facts that contradicted the desired reality were "false" facts. Strangely, however, many openly embraced the contradiction. Speaking at a conference dedicated to "Moon on the Right," the playwright Vladimir Kirshon boldly claimed that "not every fact was lifelike"; there were good facts and bad facts, and only the good ones were worthy of inclusion in a text that presumed to be "realistic."[37] A text should be a window—in this they agreed with the classic realist tradition—but it was to be a window that revealed a select, expurgated, decorously framed slice of life, with the viewer's position carefully delineated. Otherwise, Yaroslavsky inveighed, the recitation of facts alone tipped the dialectical scales, confusing the most vulnerable readers and only breeding despair:

> Some comrades think it necessary to shed detailed light on facts so that all will know of a threatening danger. But these comrades forget about the danger that reading such details causes in teenagers and children. I've had the opportunity to speak with several specialists, doctors, and psychiatrists, and they have pointed out that portraits of this nature have the most devastating effect on the minds and sexual-nervous systems of children and teenagers. Instead of a serious scientific approach to this subject, some comrades fall victim to panic: let's shout some more about this. But the point is not in shouting but *in how and what one says.*[38]

Ironically, emphasis on the "how" and "what" were what Romanov considered his forte. He styled himself a classic realist, a writer who should "disappear" in the work itself. "Form and language," he declared a year after the publication of "Without a Cherry Blossom," "should play the role of glasses wiped clean, through which the picture is visible but not the lenses themselves."[39] Only authorial self-effacement could enable the reader to engage the text instead of simply absorbing dictated truths. Aware that this was a dangerous path, he justified his approach by consciously echoing the credo of the Marxist editors of *The Young Guard*:

> Every great artist is, at the same time, a great provocateur. He lays the bait and then steps back, making the appearance as if he has nothing to do with it. . . . It is irritating to the intelligent reader when the author's ears stick out from behind each line. Such writers are like those insufferable guides in art galleries who follow you around, forcing their opinions on you when all you want to do is stand alone, eye-to-eye with the picture and contemplate what you find in it.[40]

Romanov's self-defense was based on more than one infamous work of fiction. Before "Without a Cherry Blossom" he had already made a name for himself with a series of stories, anthologized in three collections—*Questions of*

Sex, Stories of Love, and *Letters of a Woman*—that explored troubled relationships, chance encounters, failures of communication, and betrayals after the
revolution. With the publication of "Without a Cherry Blossom" (whose subtitle, "From Women's Letters," put it in the same series), Romanov's approach
finally exhausted the critics' patience. Yet another story about the deflowering
of a lonely, ideologically orphaned, and misguided young woman was no
longer tragic but ludicrous. Some suspected that Romanov's vaunted objec-
tivity was nothing more than intentional obfuscation and his use of the letter
form only a convenient cover behind which he could disavow any salacious
intentions and avoid being blamed for the contents of his story. Where Romanov ostensibly sought to engage the reader, others saw abandonment. The
editor Viacheslav Polonsky castigated him for drawing readers in by posing
all-important questions, but then "leaving them without an answer."[41] No
answer was the wrong answer; readers, being a fickle and easily distracted lot,
especially the young and the newly literate, would never get past the surface
enticement of the sexual content. Hiding one's face was too suspicious,
Georgy Gorbachev observed: "It remains for Romanov to finally define his
position ideologically and aesthetically. Before him are two paths: either
epigonish writing in various genres . . . or creating his own approach to the
new life in Russia, an approach which entails working out a specific attitude
to the goals of and driving forces behind the revolution."[42]

Nonplussed, Romanov switched from defense to attack, using his own
checkered reputation against them in two broadsides published in March and
June 1927.[43] If critics believed that their primary role was to ensure that "the
reader was not without guidance," then what could one learn from the mess
they had made so far? Romanov cleverly offered the answer by juxtaposing
quotations from contradictory reviews of his work. He included both the bad
and the good—precisely his point—and cited his sources. No one could accuse him of "make-believe" this time. Clearly, his critics had no coherent
methodology. Blinded by their own self-importance, they misunderstood the
essential principle behind the artistic representation of life, which he reiterated: the artist's task was not to present facts, but to carefully construct a text
so as to uncover the "hidden meaning" of facts and "teach others to discover
their reason for being and their importance." In pedagogical terms, reading
served to develop analytical tools of thought and interpretation (the process
of "discovery"), not to deliver rote instruction. Contemporary critics themselves had not found the time for such analytic subtlety, Romanov charged,
preferring instead to toss out ad hominem attacks, insults that one would not
dare say to a person on the street but only in the safety of print. It was no
wonder that readers had no need for critics; readers themselves could do a
better job, as shown by their participation in "hundreds of debates." In as-

suming the role of scolding parent instead of teacher-facilitator, critics had locked themselves in a self-constructed ivory prison and risked becoming "shepherds without a flock."

Romanov's boldest reply to his critics took the form of another work of fiction, again published in *The Young Guard*. His five-page story, "The Trial of a Pioneer" (1927), was another exploration of sexual mores, this time among an even younger group than the Komsomol. (The title refers to the party-sponsored youth organization for children and teenagers before they entered the Komsomol.) Pioneer Andrei, age fifteen, has been put on trial by his peers for "systematically debauching" sixteen-year-old Maria. The charge, based on eyewitness testimony, is that he walked her home one evening, carried her bag, held her hand while crossing a stream, read her poetry, and, what was most suspicious, stood with her for some time in the dark at the edge of a forest. Asked what they did there (as the court-commissioned spies were too far away to see), Andrei admits that Maria had shared her troubles with him. A true son of the proletariat could have said nothing worse. The chair promptly accuses him of "dishonoring" the brigade, driving Maria from the collective (did Andrei think himself a "priest" hearing her confession?), sabotaging efforts to produce "well-wrought soldiers" (poetry reading and romantic frippery), and undercutting the struggle for gender equity (his courteous gesture in carrying her bag). Found guilty by a majority vote, Andrei is expelled from the group, while Maria is dismissed with the opportunity to reapply for admission in the future.

"The Trial" exhibits Romanov's customary laconic approach, the story being essentially a record of the court proceedings and observers' commentary. An unobtrusive author, however, does not mean an absent one. Readers would have no difficulty in discerning "hidden meanings," as the story loops together beneath its deadpan facade several jolting reversals of expectation. The charge of "systematic debauchery" against Andrei is suggestive of sexual violation, but there has been none. The innocent encounter between Andrei and Maria was conducted exactly as young Pioneers had been taught to behave, in a spirit of comradeship and mutual respect. The story's only true debauchee is a pregnant cat that lurks about the hearing room. Yet the most mocking reversal comes in the court's reprimand of Andrei:

> You, the son of a metalworker, and you're *courting* a Pioneer. If you needed her for physical relations, you could have said so to her honestly, comrade to comrade, and not corrupt her with all this picking up of scarfs and bag carrying. We require women who are our equals, brother, not the kind who need help crossing a stream.

Proletarian simplicity was what made young Pioneers strong, the chorus of observers confirmed; Andrei's "kind of love is the same as religion, an opiate weakening the mind and revolutionary will." As true soldiers of the revolution, they had no time for romance. This does not mean that at their tender age their bodies had no needs. For the satisfaction of physical desires, they proudly declaimed, "we have our own comrades."

Romanov's upside-down world—where chastity becomes debauchery and true debauchery is found among the outwardly righteous—nevertheless spins on a secure axis. The trial reveals a quintessential witch hysteria, a paranoid society believing itself infallible and falling victim to the very language that authorizes its infallibility. The accusers' vocabulary has outstripped common sense and common decency, admitting no distinction or nuance: anyone who is not with the group, no matter how ludicrous its beliefs, becomes a heretic. Nothing is too trivial to escape its purview. It can be applied to the most harmless situations, just as Romanov found that charges of "pornography" and "slander" could be hung around his neck. After all, was he not the real-life incarnation of Andrei—an individual condemned for doing what was right? Both stood accused of similarly absurd crimes—Andrei for debauchery, Romanov for inspiring it—and in both cases the prosecutors seem cut from the same cloth. With bald crudeness, appalling hyperbole, boorish reductionism, and petulant finger-pointing, Andrei's peers sound uncannily like Romanov's critics. Ominously, the story seems to suggest that the Pioneers were the symbolic offspring of Romanov's critics, since who else was teaching youth to think and speak like this?

"The Trial" was published with the inevitable editorial disclaimer that Romanov, for all his "welcome intentions," "reveals his inadequate knowledge of this [Pioneer] *byt*," and therefore readers were invited to respond with comments and suggestions. This request was a deliberate ploy. Sergei Gusev's analysis of responses, "The Trial of P. Romanov by Pioneers," was almost twice as long as the story and functioned as its sequel. Knowing full well the kinds of letters *The Young Guard* would receive, Gusev now could give Romanov's symbolic message a real-life foundation by lampooning the actual hysteria caused by a story about hysteria. He quickly dispensed with complaints about Romanov's ignorance in allowing a pregnant cat to wander into such a serious meeting. They missed the point entirely. Authentic literary realism had nothing to do with verisimilitude but with all-important "facts."

Gusev's true target was the critical environment that had spawned an obsession with finding "slander" in anything that did not "conform to a pretty paper schemata." Those who protested against Romanov were "condemning themselves"; they, not he, were the true falsifiers of life by "closing their eyes to facts" that made up young people's *byt*, even at the younger level of the Pioneers. Charges that Romanov was inaccurate or that he had "exaggerated" proved that the message of his story could not be denied. Sheer fantasy, as had been argued before regarding "Moon on the Right," was one thing; exaggeration, however, was intended to raise consciousness of what already existed. In so many words, Gusev revealed that the discourse of realism was a semantic game. For the practitioners of proto-socialist realism, only facts beholding to "official optimism" counted. Anything else, no matter how irrefutable, was "to be covered up, played down, or painted over." This tendency, Gusev argued, was "most harmful," particularly among those who had assumed "responsibility for directing social institutions" like the Pioneers and the Komsomol. Those who saw no evil through rose-colored glasses were leading youth into a dangerous form of denial in which no problems would ever be solved because their existence could not be admitted.

Fiction, a Culprit in Real-Life Horror

If the discourse of realism was but a semantic game, it was one in which the purblind had a final card to play. The summer of 1926 provided critics with two sordid events that with minimal effort could be pinned on the likes of Romanov, Malashkin, and Gumilevsky. Both received national publicity; both involved the Komsomol; and both featured a young woman victimized by rapacious, lust-crazed men. For many, here was unequivocal proof that "problematic" fiction focused on sex was not merely slanderous but a direct cause of moral collapse among youth.

The first was an exceedingly brutal gang rape of a young woman in Leningrad by over two dozen workers. The victim not only suffered indescribable psychological and physical trauma but also contracted gonorrhea. She was the paradigmatic victim: a virgin who had come from the village to study and improve her qualifications as a worker. Her attackers, aged seventeen to twenty-five, represented a cross section of Soviet youth—civil war veterans, proletarians, rural transplants, members of the Komsomol—debased by pubs, NEP decadence, political indifference, and an acute lack of moral instruction. For the nation it was an unimaginable crime; some of the rapists were shot, while others received prison terms. It also received unparalleled press attention. Naiman, the first to dissect coverage of the Chubarov gang rape (named after the alley in which the woman was abducted), emphasizes how officials fed public outrage in order to justify greater intervention in youth's lives.[44]

The Chubarov case was regarded as a new low in viciousness that illustrated the threat to the nation posed by current attitudes of "sexual nihilism." As one of the prosecutors declared, even if this gang represented an extreme criminal minority, the moral condition of Soviet youth had deteriorated to a critical level. Almost ten years after the revolution, who was to be their teacher, mentor, and counsel: the streets saturated with Esenin's "A Hooligan's Confession" or the state? The battle was real, and if exhortation was not enough, then coercion was next. This is why "an event from everyday life has become a political one, [why] the occurrence of violence has become an occasion for the defense of Soviet life," and why the rape was "an attack against the foundations of the new Soviet society." Though "the names of the living are being crossed out forever," this harsh sentence, the prosecutor concluded, would stand as a permanent lesson "for youth to see how we punish such criminals."[45]

The second nationally publicized event was a more conventional sex scandal, but it too was held up as a sign of moral decadence. Don Juan had come to life in the guise of a Moscow mining student and party member named Konstantin Korenkov. His story followed a now familiar script: while still in his teens, Korenkov had helped organize a Komsomol cell in his village during the civil war, then at age nineteen was sent to Moscow to study. The city offered more than books and learning, however, and he quickly gained a reputation among the women. He was intimate with a fellow student, Riva Davidson, for about a year, during which time she had three abortions. He resisted marriage and only reluctantly agreed to share living quarters. ("Living together will interfere with my studies" was an echo of the classic excuse found in fiction.) Cohabitation did not curb Korenkov's sexual behavior; the Soviet Union was a country of full freedom, he insisted, and no one could impinge on his rights. He taunted Davidson with his infidelities, abuse made more painful by anti-Semitic barbs, and began to leave a loaded revolver lying about their room as an invitation to end her misery. This she did, not by taking his life but her own in July 1925.

Davidson's suicide brought Korenkov before an investigating committee. Under questioning, he was unflinching, insisting that he had never loved Davidson, which meant he was not unfaithful to her. He accused the committee of "hounding" and "blackmailing" by implying that Korenkov might have shot her himself. Unable to hold him criminally liable for either murder or Davidson's suicide, the committee nevertheless found him lacking in "communist ethics" and voted to expel him from the party. The sentence was reduced and he was forced to work in a factory to cleanse him of the evil university influence. However, the cure did not work. In June 1926 he was arrested in a robbery that resulted in murder, but his death sentence was inexplicably commuted to ten years in prison.[46]

Not Davidson's suicide but the subsequent murder made Korenkov a national sensation. Komsomol meetings were called to discuss "Korenkovism" *(korenkovshchina),* banner articles appeared by Sosnovsky and Smidovich, and a transcript of Korenkov's trial was published with editorial comments about his villainy.[47] Much was made of what had led to this crime, a descent down a slippery slope that began with rude language and sexual predation. If the Chubarov rape illustrated the pernicious effects of a debased environment, the Korenkov affair represented the failings of the person. Korenkov's actions fit hand in glove with official remonstrations that loss of self-control could have only dire results. Enslaved by his sexual impulses, Korenkov had degenerated into an animal. One element in his decline from Komsomol hero to murderous "bandit" was his disrespect toward women. In this respect Korenkov's villainy represented a more dangerous phenomenon than a vicious gang rape committed by an extreme minority. After all, how many young men were guilty of his initial sins: using obscenities and mistreating women? One female Komsomolist warned that in the "greater part of youth" were gestating such beasts. From on high, Sosnovsky echoed her.[48] Children were not innocent—predatory instincts could develop under the cover of reckless play, then upon maturity these "young wild animals" spread like a virus, infiltrating factories, universities, and party organs. The once "amusing" child could develop into an adult capable of sexual extortion, harassment, and gender discrimination.[49] These tendencies lurked everywhere, and no man could claim to have had a pure childhood unless, it was variously claimed, Lenin had been his sole guide from diapers through adolescence.[50]

As a corrective to such exclusive attention given to Korenkov, Sofia Smidovich, former head of the Zhenotdel, pointed to the self-victimization of Davidson. Suicide was an inexcusable response to her problems.[51] She was a deserter, abandoning a life that could have been full of useful labor and achievement. If Korenkov represented the worst male stereotype, Davidson's permanent surrender—*davidsonovshchina,* in Smidovich's ungainly neologism—was equally culpable, enforcing the impression that women were naturally weak and subordinate to men. Davidson had absorbed the bourgeois tradition that a woman's fulfillment in life could come only through "him." Why didn't she just leave Korenkov, Smidovich asked, or, more to the point, why didn't she turn to the true pillar of support in Soviet society, the collective?

This last suggestion was critical. If Korenkov and Davidson were the antitheses of the "new type" of Soviet citizen, their peers at the collective level had also failed. That their dorm mates knew so little of the couple's private life, that they did not even try to intervene—a neighbor heard the shot but didn't bother to check what happened—was itself criminal, a "bourgeois, philistine washing of one's hands." Such negligence was the "most distressing point," upsetting the image of dormitories as the ideal place where private life, for the good of society, should be made public. Despite living together, students and workers had merely replicated the worst of bourgeois illusions: home as castle. "In each dormitory room there flows an isolated, individual life that differs little from the philistine lifestyle flourishing in a well-furnished room. Nowhere is to be found the pulse of an organic whole but only people mechanically collected together who do not even try to investigate the lives of their neighbors whether of the same hall or sometimes even in the same room."[52]

The first commentaries on the Korenkov and Chubarov crimes made no mention of the possible influence of contemporary literature on these disturbing events. They hardly could, since chronology was not in their favor. "Without a Cherry Blossom" appeared in the same month as Korenkov's arrest and nearly a year *after* Davidson's suicide. Likewise, the Chubarov assault occurred in August, a month before publication of "Moon on the Right" and many months before *Dog Alley*. For later critics, however, the need to assert a direct influence of fiction on life trumped an uncooperative calendar. In 1927, Viacheslav Polonsky presented a clean line of causation, from Kollontai, through Malashkin, to the Chubarov tragedy. It was the perfect melding of theory, art, and reality: a perverse idea (the glass-of-water approach to sex), spread by bad literature, begetting crime. "Moon on the Right" was the bridge between a corrupt theory and its implementation. Fiction became a blueprint, an advertisement, a how-to manual. Malashkin's story illustrated "in living form" what Kollontai's theory implied and thus inspired the Chubarov gang rape. "It is one step from 'the glass of water' to Chubarov, and [Tanya] Aristarkhova's salon is but a way station on that path," Polonsky concluded.

At least Polonsky did not accuse Malashkin of a conscious intention to corrupt. As editor of the liberal journal *New World,* he had himself suffered in a political scandal when literature came too close to life (Pilnyak's rendering of Frunze's death in "Tale of the Unextinguished Moon"). Polonsky believed that Malashkin tried to write a "communist book" that did not seek to promote Kollontai's ideas. Malashkin's error was to focus on the negative, abandoning the essential "distribution of light and dark in art." This only whetted the reader's appetite: "The clumsy treatment of sexual depravity can sometimes lead to its increase, just as the improper extinction of a fire can sometimes facilitate its spread."[53]

Constructive criticism aside, Polonsky's argument was emotional instead of empirical. It failed not only the simple test of chronology but of causation as well. No evidence was given that the Chubarovites (or Korenkov either) were directly inspired or corrupted by literature; if the courtroom description of their lifestyles is to be believed, reading was not one of their signature activities. Nevertheless, with the rhetoric of scapegoating, evidence became irrelevant. Gumilevsky, Malashkin, and Romanov had inflamed a moral panic among critics, and the Korenkov case was too good an example to ignore.[54] Khorokhorin, the most egregious fictional symbol of sexual depravity, became Korenkov's notorious counterpart. They could be spoken of as if issuing from the same seed. A bourgeois-inspired literature had infected bourgeois-inclined youth, just as the bourgeois-inclined youth had inspired these writers. Since literature and life were mutually dependent, if either failed, the blame fell on the other. To combat Korenkovism, youth had to read less of the likes of Khorokhorin; to ensure that literature spoke less of such villains, writers needed to concentrate on youth who were the antitheses of Korenkov.

Gumilevsky unwittingly provided additional evidence that literature and life fed off each other. The coincidence of alleys, as in the title of his novel and the site of the Chubarov assault, was too symbolically rich. Gumilevsky vehemently denied any connection, since his work was published after the event, but to no avail. As I. Bobryshev patiently explained in *Komsomol Pravda*, the working class marched along a straight, true road. Parallel to it, running in the opposite direction, was the bourgeois one. Alleys were the connection between the two, allowing "bourgeois filth," like the Chubarov gang, to spill onto the proletarian street. Writers such as Gumilevsky, with their "stupefying exaggerations" of debauchery, were pushing youth off the righteous path. "Alley literature" (a category that included Esenin and Gladkov's "veiled Chubarovites" in *Drunken Sun*) explicitly refused to "look at the facts" and show students as they were, upstanding and cheerful. "Dog alleys have no place on our proletarian streets," Bobryshev exclaimed. They should be cleaned and closed off. Chubarovites should be shot and literature supporting them handed over to the censor.[55]

Since censors were failing in this task, others stepped in to fill the void. Critics' insistence on how the Komsomol should behave—intervening and expelling harmful elements—provided the script. Following his dictum that "not every fact was lifelike," Vladimir Kirshon collaborated with Andrei Uspensky on a play about the villainous Korenkov. It was entitled *Korenkovism* (1927) and was published by *The Young Guard* in the issue following "Moon on the Right." (Kirshon, incidentally, was a student at Sverdlov University from 1921 to 1923, when Gelman's poll was conducted. Perhaps this play was an attempt to rescue the reputation of both his generation and his university.)

Since Korenkov already embodied the Don Juan, the authors of *Korenkovism* changed little except to supply an all-important moral corrective at the end. In the play Kostia Terekhin and Nina represent the ill-fated couple. They are lovers, but he has reduced her to a domestic servant, has forced her to have three abortions to preserve his freedom, and openly cheats on her while falsely

accusing her of the same. The circle of "failed" characters includes Leonov, a
decadent poet who drinks because "Esenin did"; Petr, who attempts suicide in
despair over the "nepmanization" of the revolution; and Liza, who favors free
love because "it gets boring drinking out of one and the same glass." However, the play makes a significant change from the real-life mining institute by
providing right-minded Komsomol peers and a social climate hostile to such
corruptions. Liza is rejected because she wants every woman to be a "public
thoroughfare," whereas Leonov cannot publish his poetry because editors demand "real life" instead of odes to disreputable student behavior.

After Nina's suicide, the Komsomol immediately convenes a meeting,
where the defiant Terekhin curses the group for "digging in his dirty laundry."
He is quickly silenced. One woman says that Nina should have shot him instead of herself; another (echoing Smidovich) pronounces the entire group
guilty for not having stopped him earlier. A repentant Petr realizes that the
party has an obligation to intervene in personal life. "For who are we? Are we
not the party? We all live together, one next to the other. Are we not therefore
obligated to help if something's not right with somebody?" The truculent
Terekhin is expelled from the Komsomol. In a later version of the play, Kirshon and Uspensky make a further change. Nina does not commit suicide,
but is murdered by Terekhin, thereby resolving the ambiguities of the real-life
case.[56]

Another attempt to rectify an imperfect reality and to repair the reputation of mining students was *Sexual Depravity on Trial* (1927), a fictional,
scripted court case by Dr. E. B. Demidovich, the physician who had warned
of the evil effects of masturbation. The depraved protagonist is Semyon
Vasiliev, a twenty-six-year-old worker and party candidate studying in a *rab-
fak*. He has abandoned his common-law wife, Anna Vtorova, three months
pregnant, on the pretext that if the Soviet Union is the land of freedom, he
enjoys a special right: "I live with her, I love her; if I stop loving her, I leave."
It is an unusual trial, for no law has been broken, only moral decency is at
issue, which was also at the heart of the Korenkov-Davidson case. Yet if for
Korenkov his past experiences could only be alluded to, Demidovich demonstrably brought onto the stage each of Vasiliev's previous victims. Like Dick-
ens's ghosts in *A Christmas Carol*, four women appear in court to reveal the
tragic personal and social consequences of his libertine career, including
syphilis, child abandonment, and abortion.

Vasiliev's principal accuser is Anna's brother, Mikhail Vtorov, an exemplary mining student, described in the dramatis personae as "representative of
the healthy, strong youth." He declaims that the new "freedom of marriage
and divorce" does not preclude a strict code of conduct. When the court asks
about his experiences with women, Vtorov outlines his gentlemanly respect

for women and "comradely relationships" maintained even after the end of a romance. At twenty-three he is still a virgin (hence his physical strength and robust complexion) and controls his sexual urges by participating in sports, hard work, avoiding solitude (protection against masturbation), and, "when nature raises its mutinous head," by removing himself from the company of women. His proud rationale serves to bolster any wavering youth: "I am a member of the party. I need my strength for constructing a new society, and I consciously act so that my sexual behavior does not ruin me, another woman, or a child."

Like other morally edifying works, the play includes ample commentary. To answer the question of blame, the prosecution emphasizes Vasiliev's personal failings, how he has deprived the Soviet Union of not only his own labor potential but also that of his five victims. The defense in turn targets his environment: the deprivations he suffered as a child and his resulting ignorance. Vasiliev himself reconciles the two in a courtroom conversion: "Only here, in this court has the entire evil of my actions been made clear." Subjected to a "proletarian reprimand" and suspension of his party candidacy, he vows repentance, asks for assistance in leading a healthy life, and states he will marry Vtorova if she will consent.[57]

The two plays based on the Korenkov scandal sought to convey lessons more emphatically than mere reality could. Both works tie up loose ends, plug holes, and fill in the picture according to orthodox schemata. *Korenkovism* establishes a connection with Kollontai and Esenin that was not available in real life, whereas *Sexual Depravity on Trial* presents a medical and moral judgment on sexual irresponsibility: the risk of syphilis, the dangers of abortion, and ends with repentance. In his preface to the latter work, Zalkind (perhaps sensitive to criticism of his own plodding treatises) noted that events presented in "lively, dramatic fashion" could introduce troubling questions of sex without "scientific prolixities" that risked boring the reader. A fictional "documentary" drama was the best teacher because it could be tailored to a particular audience and its realistic staging gave it authority.[58]

Scandal Fatigue

The fact that only in fiction could one so tidily resolve moral issues was underscored by the bungled attempt to handle yet another incident of "debauchery" in the aftermath of 1926. This time Vasily Khazov, a young Komsomol student, was the target. In a clear sign that logic had become a permanent casualty amid widespread panic, Khazov had done nothing, had not even a guilty intention—there was only the *possibility* that he might become like a Chubarov rapist or a Korenkov.[59] Incriminating letters had been found in his briefcase, left on a Moscow commuter train. As was not readily acknowledged by his accusers, he had not even written them; they were from friends. The content, therefore, was not surprising. Most of the letters dealt with classes, work, and having fun, and only a few were off-color. The subject of girls did not dominate the correspondence and did not diverge from the boasting and wishful thinking typical of adolescent males: "In class the girls are amazing. . . . Breasts soft as down; lips sweet as melon." In short, there was nothing even remotely scandalous. Indeed, one suggested that boyish hyperbole was just a phase: "What attracts me personally is the beauty of a young woman and in the future an ideal mother, good homemaker, and loving wife."

Ironically, the only reprehensible acts described in the letters were committed by those outside their circle: party members raping a young woman, a girl who attempted suicide by drinking acetic acid, and a Komsomolist who unsuccessfully tried to shoot himself. Nevertheless, by now mere language, not deed, was sufficient to incur the wrath of authorities such as Semashko (representing the medical angle), Aron Solts (the political), Smidovich (the social-ethical) and futurist writer Sergei Tretyakov (the cultural). Evidence came from the students' casual use of obscenities: *bliad* (literally "whore" but serving as the interjection "fuck") and *khui* ("dick" used with similar impact). For authorities, such language grew into an ominous Khazovism (*khazovshchina*), shorthand for a disrespectful attitude to women from which sexual predators grew. "Listen to them; they don't sing any worse than the Malashkins and Gumilevskys," commented one Komsomol member. "Their mistakes don't come from immaturity; they're guys who are completely degenerate, wallowing in the slime of vulgarity and debauchery. My conclusion: tear this weed out of the field!"[60] With Malashkin and Gumilevsky reduced to teenage gossip and Khazhov equated with alleged pornography for his infatuation with Esenin, once again the impression was enforced that no true boundary separated literature from life.

The outcome of the Khazov affair dovetailed with officials' expectations. Khazov was expelled from the Komsomol and publicly humiliated. He admitted his "guilt" and renounced his "egotism": "Now I understand that my personal life is not something individual, belonging to me alone; no, a thousands times, no." He thanked his comrades for showing him the proper path and hoped that the Komsomol would become his "savior." Just as real villains could inspire fiction, the self-abasement and pleas for forgiveness laid out in fiction could inspire the behavior of real people. Khazov's penitence led Semashko to conclude that an optimistic image of youth had firm roots in reality.[61] Yet the full account of what occurred at the hearing, inexplicably published in the same volume, belies such optimism. Before repenting, Khazov offered a series of defenses, from the adolescent "everyone's doing it," to the innocent "we're only human." More incisive, however, was his bold appeal to the environmental explanation for wrongdoing. His excuse, "I am a victim of the remnants of the past," not only suggests his familiarity with the expected script but also hinted that party rhetoric had devolved into malleable platitudes. Aware of being made a scapegoat, of being pilloried on trumped-up charges, Khazov fought back. Angered by the intrusion into his personal life, he bluntly asked: why did authorities not open people's mailboxes? Or was that not a crime? If he was to be condemned, then official hypocrisy should be too. If he was guilty, then the image of youth promoted by the likes of Semashko were lies: "What we have is a lot of posing from girls and guys alike, trying to paint over our sexual desires with blooming, flowery roses." Turning the tables, he commented on a certain Yakubovsky, who had spoken critically of him, "How can we guarantee that his soul is clean or that he does-n't enjoy the services of the boulevard ladies?"[62] In short, Khazov would not let his attackers have it both ways.

The Khazov affair quickly dissolved into the general stew of other post-1926 aftershocks. The guilty, despite inflammatory remarks along the way, had finally behaved according to script, and the source of the virus—"that recent series of books depicting the moral and sexual depravity of youth "—was officially confirmed. Accusers no longer needed to mention Romanov, Malashkin, or Gumilevsky by name. By 1928, for *Izvestiia* the word "moon" alone was sufficient to signify "individualistic instincts" and works of literature that precipitated suicide and masturbation.[63] Titles too could be dispensed with or mangled—Lev Kopelev remembers one dedicated Komsomolist lambasting *Dog Weddings*—it didn't matter.[64] For two years the scandals had dominated literary journalism. Much else had occurred during this time, but no cultural issue claimed such media attention. Referring to the highly inflected character of the Russian language, one critic complained in *Young Communist*, "Newspapers are declining hooligan in all its cases!"[65]

Eventually people wearied of literary scandal. Whether on the side of prosecution or defense, most critics, readers, and writers had had enough. Some, exhausted over the sheer volume of readers' responses and for having to hammer out their position time and time again, began to fear for society's reputation. What would future historians conclude, asked *Komsomol Pravda*, if they attempted "to recreate the image of contemporary youth based on our literature?"[66] On their side, writers were frustrated at being accused of the very evils they thought they had condemned in their works and at having their names tied to real-life episodes of rape, suicide, and murder. A sure sign of the general weariness with the whole furor was a parody published in *The New Shift* by "Pankrat Bulvar" entitled "Moon without Cherry Blossoms or

Love from Dog Alley" (1927), a crude amalgam that mocked not only the banality of the three scandalous works but also the accompanying sensation-alism.[67] The authors were ridiculed for writing pulp in pursuit of fame, yet the piece also suggested that fame does not appear on its own; it must be bestowed by someone. Readers were equally to blame, for to appreciate "Bul-var's" parody they had to be familiar with the originals. There would be no targets for parody if no one had read such trash to begin with.

What "Bulvar" (a likely play both on "boulevard" and Bulwer-Lytton) hinted at, some critics stated more bluntly.[68] It was that the tastes of the "new reader," the NEP philistine, as opposed to the proletarian, was responsible for the current debasement of literature. Others, however, would not toe this easy line. Many worker-readers did enjoy "absolute trash" like the fiction of Gu-milevsky, Kallinikov, or Romanov, despite the last being "a poor writer, mediocre artist, and primitive editorialist."[69] A 1929 published report from Moscow union libraries confirmed that interest in the three controversial au-thors, as well as Esenin, was still very strong. As B. Gorovits conceded, this embarrassing information indicated that controversy and the heavy hand of the censor had only added to the appeal of these works:

> It is exceptionally difficult to protect youth from the influence of Ro-
> manov and Esenin. It's not enough to convince them that these writers
> are not one of us, that in their literature they disseminate ideas harmful
> to the working class. Nor is it enough to limit the number of copies of
> Esenin in the library. A ban, after all, would not convince anyone [of his
> harm] and would only serve to inflame interest. Readers have their own
> demands and from all groups [of them] one finds a positive response [to
> this literature].[70]

More objective critics did not condemn readers for their tastes. To stamp them all philistines missed the point. Instead, critics focused on the writers' popularity as an indication of the serious rupture between the interests of So-viet readers and officially endorsed literature. Readers lined up for the likes of *Dog Alley*, shared these works among themselves, and argued over them, whereas proclaimed classics like *The Iron Flood* were sometimes ignored. Zeleiman Shteiman wondered whether such works had lost their "demo-cratic" roots by spurning "the current, everyday issues of life that so attract and intrigue today's reader." Writers noted for their "revolutionary" spirit and "orthodoxy" offered less appeal, Shteiman charged. Such "literature has little value in the reader's mind not only because writers still haven't learned how to create living persons in place of schematic portraits of established models, but also because the thematics of our literature is too broad—nothing lower than 'global' problems, nothing less than 'general' philosophy." Soviet literature, in short, was a victim of its own idealism, reaching for the heights when the depths had not been conquered. Writers had to create a new literature, one that did not follow the route of cheap sensationalism but broached the "real problems" of the day with compelling characters and themes, one that showed the "contemporary individual in real conditions of contemporary life," one that "revealed the class struggle in the most insignificant corners of the family."[71]

Here was room for consent. Calls came in from all quarters—editors, librarians, Khazov's prosecutors, critics, students—for literature to fight back. Party authorities had made their statement; for them there was nothing to add. Life was better; young people were better. Psychologism was bankrupt; the "living person" concept a symbol of "neurasthenia, decadence, and hooliganism."[72] The new literature would exclude "all Malashkins, Gumilevskys, Romanovs" and their literary kin. Young people should hear the truth about themselves from their own kind. *Komsomol Pravda,* compensating for earlier ambivalence, declared that writers had "the responsibility and duty to oppose this philistine garbage with accurate and artistically convincing depictions of the new type of youth, as he is in reality and not in the imagination of the Romanovs and Gumilevskys."[73] What this meant in real terms was left tantalizingly unclear. Whose "insignificant corner," what family, did Shteiman have in mind? Which depictions were to be considered "accurate and artistically convincing" and upon what criteria? As with so many of the problems authorities faced in the 1920s, it was easier to argue the negative. The recipe for good literature was the reverse image of bad literature. As Bukhartsev explained, Gumilevsky, Romanov, and Malashkin simply "should serve the Komsomol as explanatory aids of how not to write about our youth."[74]

CHAPTER 7

A Canon of Ambiguity

I T is easy to dismiss orthodox critics of the 1920s for their neopuritanism, skewed logic, and panic-mongering. For eighty years, first in the West and now in Russia, condemnation has marked their legacy. However, a closer look at some of the fiction published in the period suggests that their fears about its pernicious impact were not groundless. Stories and novels such as those by Gumilevsky, Romanov, and Malashkin that created such an uproar were not literary aberrations, but part of a flood of works delving into intimate relationships and sexual habits, some of them far more disturbing than the objects of well-publicized scandals. Critics and censors could complain about, but not necessarily stop, fiction that exploited a de facto literary license to explore the salacious, decadent aspects of NEP society. Remonstrations in numerous party and Komsomol resolutions often had little impact. The result was a curious disruption between orthodox critics and their party supporters on the one hand, and the Young Guardists on the other. While the former outnumbered and generally outranked the Young Guardists, more literature at the time seemed to gravitate toward the orientation of the latter. As Shteiman and others made uncomfortably clear, the works that might have corrected this imbalance commanded little respect among readers. There was, arguably, sound reason to strike an alarmist note since much of the literary environment operated with disregard to, or even at odds with, the general principles of some of the party's most prominent cultural spokespersons.

Writers in the Soviet Union could take advantage of this condition to indulge in cheap sensationalism of the Kallinikov kind, offering romance and exploiting sexual content for commercial success. Political concerns were incidental; titillation and suspense were the mainstays. As such, the impact of this literature was minimal, and critics paid little attention to such fiction except to condemn it. However, many works with sexually explicit themes had a somewhat more sophisticated purpose: to use sexual experience, particularly among the young, as a metaphor for searching for one's identity and one's place after the revolution. Sexual behavior could be a measure of one's worth, a demonstration that one had successfully moved from a bourgeois to a socialist mentality. The number of sexual partners, motivations for one's actions, what one expected of relationships, and attitudes toward abortion were all valid measures of character. For men, sexuality conditioned their achievements as workers or students; it challenged their devotion to party and state; and it revealed their character and conscience. Sexual behavior of females could have similarly metaphoric functions, but as a test of character, it conveyed a more ambiguous message.

To be sure, writers employing the subject in this manner could—and would—be accused of including sex for sex's sake, but this was less frequently the case. Instead, sex became a prominent theme in literature because it offered a powerful lens through which to examine the elusive realities of life in a new society. Zalkind, Yaroslavsky, Semashko, and other social critics certainly did not approve of this, but it was an indirect and unintended consequence of their own studies and remonstrations. The more sex was discussed in sociological and medical venues, the more valid it became as a taxonomic tool available to writers. This is why, at least as reflected in literature, resolving the question of appropriate sexual behavior arguably became a necessary rite of passage for Soviet youth. Rare is the character who does not refer to it somehow, if even to assert a commitment to chastity. In their alleged obsession with sex, many writers were only doing what party officials, sociologists, and doctors themselves were doing, but with this fundamental difference: they sought less to judge and regulate and more to use the subject as a literary vehicle for personal search and discovery.

Into the Depths of NEP Society

A notable feature of these works of fiction was to combine an unflattering portrait of the party with a less than encouraging look at sexual mores, as exemplified by Boris Chetverikov's *Aftergrowth* (1924), first published in *Red Virgin Soil*.[1] The title (which in Russian is suggestive of "atavism") refers to all that remains in the wake of revolution—literally, the human vegetation that struggles to live and love amid ruin. It is an impressionistic journey through the netherworld of NEP society where all pretenses are gone, and Chetverikov leaves the reader with no buttress or ideological guide for interpreting it. It is not Lenin but the libido that rules this world. Varya, the main character, works in a center for "defective children" whose inmates are routinely raped

by the institute's director. Adult relationships are little better. When her colleague Kashirtsev is arrested, Varya is called to testify at the Cheka headquar-
ters in Leningrad manned by incompetents mouthing revolutionary
platitudes which they believe give them license to behave as they wish. It is
more the den of Lucifer's minions than guardians of socialism, whose portraits ("thick-bearded grandpa Marx, Trotsky with his mephistophelian beard,
and Lenin with narrowed eyes") adorn the walls. In Leningrad Varya becomes
sexually involved with Eltyshev, a party member disillusioned after the civil
war, then leaves him for another man who has recently left his common-law
wife.

Works of this nature earned a reputation as the source of the "virus" that
so alarmed critics.[2] In August 1926, *Red Virgin Soil* began serial publication of
Nikolai Ognev's *The Diary of Kostia Riabtsev,* a novel remarkable for including references to masturbation and homosexuality. It was an acute illustration
of how heightened self-consciousness among youth was tied to both a new
ethos and growing sexual awareness. Set in 1923, Riabtsev's diary details the
school experiences of a teenager, bristling with outward defiance but torn by
self-doubt, whose bravado suggests that of David Khanin, the "hooligan general" of 1917. The revolution, Riabtsev declares, has irrevocably changed the
status of the young. They are no longer children. Students hold teachers in
contempt and assert their autonomy at every stage. Yet as the diary progresses,
Riabtsev's concern with ideology comes increasingly into conflict with sexual
feelings. He asks a friend about the latter only to receive the answer that sex
is "no problem"; that a guy need only tell a girl that he likes her and if the feeling is reciprocal, then they can "go ahead" like "husband and wife." When Riabtsev tries this line, his startled female companion thinks he is actually
proposing marriage. Perplexed, Riabtsev poses to himself the question no
doubt asked by countless youths: "I must find a solution to the question of
sex because it had tortured me to no end." Literature only aggravates his in-
security. Upon reading Mikhail Artsybashev's notorious *Sanin*, he can't sleep
and, as he puts it, engages in "feem-fom peek-pak." Masturbation leads to
guilt, and he wonders how a Komsomol member, "someone who is marching
at the fore of youth," can be capable of such defilement.

Riabtsev finds a mysterious document concerning male sexuality, yet he
does not immediately reveal the contents in his diary. Nevertheless, one
teacher in whom he confides informs him that "all of that" is sexual depravity, which the Soviet Union is fighting through physical education and lectures. Still unsatisfied, Riabtsev is propositioned by a classmate's older sister
who asks him to meet her in a garden at night. Provocatively dressed, she
teaches him to kiss through a series of "lessons," each of which he finishes in
his room with "f-f p-p." When they finally have intercourse, Riabtsev is ap-

palled by the act, describing it in the same words as his teacher, "sexual depravity." Only now do we learn of the document's contents and the source of Riabtsev's fears. It is the testament of the "morally and physically defective" worker who had begun masturbating at the age of ten. Self-indulgence had led to homosexuality, for which at age thirty-five he fears imprisonment. Filled with self-loathing, he addresses his open letter to "Society," which he believes made him a cripple. He signs his appeal for help with a challenge to others facing the same problem:

> [Signed]
> Your pupil: onanist, pederast, sadist etc.
> Society, enjoy these fruits of your labor. What you've sown you shall reap.
> Don't dare punish us; punish yourselves.[3]

After this interpolated document, presented without comment as if to attest to Riabtsev's fascination and horror at its contents, the diary ends with a reversal: he defends the school administration before an outside inspector, earns the respect of his former "enemies," and receives the love of his close female friend, Silva.

Surprisingly, while the serialization of *Kostia Riabtsev* overlapped with the publication of *Dog Alley* and "Moon on the Right," its graphic attention to sex, particularly its more taboo manifestations, was not subject to the same criticism. The novel was (predictably) praised by Alexander Voronsky, editor of *Red Virgin Soil* (who also wrote the foreword for Ognev's collected works), and by workers' journals, which even recommended it to libraries for its "quite faithful and objective portrayal" of youth.[4] The novel's convincing realism reflects Ognev's own experience in youth organizations and as administrator of several children's institutes before becoming a writer full-time. Responses praised the accuracy of the novel's language, its documentary form, and Riabtsev's energy, patriotism, atheism, self-assertiveness, and eventual acceptance of the educational system. Alexander Voronsky championed him as a "little American" for his aggressive spirit and healthy skepticism, whereas a reviewer for *The Young Guard* saw him as the "embryo of the new intelligentsia" and Silva the "embryo of the new woman."[5] No critic referred to the novel's taboo subject matter. Perhaps the reason for such reticence was that the novel never resolves the question of young people and sexuality and it is difficult to extract a concrete moral from the text. To be sure, Riabtsev's diary presents masturbation and homosexuality in an unfavorable light, but the overall problem of reconciling physical needs and ideology is left hanging.

Ilya Erenburg's *In Protochny Alley* (1927), a little-known work by one of the Soviet Union's most famous writers, was not greeted by conscious silence. Its title at first suggests Gumilevsky's *Dog Alley*, but such a comparison does a disservice to the quality of the novel. Erenburg lived in a Moscow alley during the crucial summer of 1926 and wrote the novel in Paris in the fall. It was published a few weeks after *Dog Alley* appeared in a heavily censored version.[6] The novel provides a view of the capital's underclass with Gogol-like intensity. The party, revolutionary rhetoric, the Kremlin, and red stars are pushed into the distant background, while the primary focus is on crime, drinking, sex, and broken relationships—in short, the empty, desperate lives of typical residents occupying a communal apartment in the 1920s. The inhabitants have no clear idea of why the revolution has occurred. No one dares to question its goals, but the grand ideal is stripped of all luster. The point of view is that of the street denizen who looks with suspicion on those who wash too often or who read *Pravda*, people seen simply as "commies" (*komchiki*). To the people who subsist at this level, the revolution was merely a cataclysmic event that has led to this debased way of life. There is no hope for improvement.

The party, whose only representative has been purged from it, is virtually nonexistent in the novel. Prakhov, a journalist whose emotional life is comprised of tawdry affairs with actresses and secretaries, does not believe love exists. "In truth everything is much simpler: first they say some affectionate things, then they go to bed, and then comes the payment," he tells his old hunchbacked neighbor Iuzik. "How is not important. If it's a wife, then monthly support; if not, then a gift, well, a ring or something, you know, by the script. I don't have time for tenderness, and I don't have any money either. That's all it is." This bleak view of sexual bonds is illustrated by the experience of nineteen-year-old Tanya Evdokimova, who lost her virginity to Sakharov, a married neighbor, and who sees no hope for love in this ugly environment. She is disgusted with herself, fearing that after Sakharov there will be others, lined up like "benches in the park." The cycle of empty sex fills her with self-hatred. "I'm all filthy," she confesses in her diary. Desolate and apathetic, she gets drunk and sleeps with Prakhov, concluding, "It's clear now in my soul I'm a prostitute." Suddenly, Tanya disappears, either a victim of suicide or Sakharov's vengeful wife, whose sanity is in question.

Erenburg alludes to Tanya's literary and cultural environment, which includes lectures about sexuality, a film, *Abortion and Its Consequences*, and articles by Voronsky, stories by Babel and Romanov, and Esenin's poetry. Ominously, she quotes a line from his suicide poem: "In this life dying is nothing new." We learn at the end of the novel that Tanya did not commit suicide. She is now married and pregnant, yet we have no sense that her life has improved. Her husband, an older communist, is so wooden—"he loves me when he has the spare time"—that she wonders if he is even human. She refers matter-of-factly to a scandal like the Chubarov case, currently in the news: "Last week six Komsomolists raped Masha, our courier, and guess what, none of the youth are even angry."

Does Erenburg condemn what he describes? He certainly could have, and we can well imagine what other writers would have done with the same material. But this naturalistic exposé of daily life is so ambiguous that one is in doubt. The striking metafictive angle makes *In Protochny Alley* a dramatic illustration of the discursive entanglement in which youth found themselves: in a work of fiction a young woman reads and is affected by works of actual writers, whose impact she records in her lifelike diary. Tanya's story erases the separation between life and text, consciously playing on critics' fears that literature could have a poisonous effect on youth. With the exception of works by Voronsky, what she reads has been denounced as harmful, and her life mirrors that fiction. Nothing of the literary antidote so desired by orthodox critics materializes. So too is party intervention mockingly discounted. When a commission arrives to fix up the alley, its sole action is a veritable window dressing: painting slogans and putting up posters. Not only are the messages irrelevant, they are quickly effaced by the weather. The distance between the party's lofty rhetoric and people's reality is so great that Iuzik mistakenly thinks that Gogol's *Dead Souls* is a modern work. Because his copy is missing the title page, because its content seems so contemporary, he believes it was written "today" by no less a figure than Bukharin.

The critical response to *In Protochny Alley* was prompt and equally colorful. "Fulfilling the social directive of the emigré intelligentsia," Dmitry Gorbov lashed out, "[Erenburg] has painted a corner of Soviet Moscow without the construction of socialism, without socialist pathos. . . . Having wandered into the rose garden, he didn't see the blooming, fragrant flowers, only the sharp thorns and manure-filled slush fertilizing the garden bed." So desolate was the picture of contemporary urban life that Gorbov believed Erenburg to be suffering from a "hangover" after romanticism's century-long fetish for the grotesque. Just as he chided Romanov for failing to provide a corrective for the ugliness in his stories, he accused Erenburg of ignoring "the medicine for all the diseases" portrayed in his novel.[7] Years later, Erenburg defended his approach much as Young Guardists attacked *plakat,* even though they regarded each other with hostility. He was aware of pressure to show just the good, but he refused to be unfaithful not only to life but also to himself. "I knew it was better to write about more positive types, and it would have been less troublesome," he admitted, "but an author is not always free in his choice of characters. He doesn't look for them; they find him." His kind of realism, he claimed, was that of Balzac, in which flowers "were trampled and covered with garbage."[8]

A similar fate attended the next attempt to delve into students' lives: Vladimir Lidin's *The Apostate* (1927).[9] Focusing on the travails of a proletarian who goes to Moscow to study, it includes the usual complement of motifs—alcohol, drugs, dissolute sex, abortion, Eseninism, suicide, and murder—common to much literature about students. Most critics immediately lambasted Lidin for drawing inspiration both from the literature of Malashkin and Gumilevsky and the life of Korenkov.[10] One even refused to give a detailed analysis of the plot because its retelling would advertise profligate behavior, "for which there is absolutely no need." Another feared that the "inexperienced reader . . . searching for answers to questions [raised] in the book" might absorb the wrong ones.[11] More irritating was the absence of a politically sound conclusion—nothing even remotely ideological penetrates the protagonist's world—an omission that automatically meant failure as realism. No orthodox critic would gainsay the conclusion tendered by one worker: "This adventure story pretends, so it would seem, to reflect contemporary student *byt,* but the result is terrible. Lidin shows young criminals and highlights them vis-à-vis the student masses as typical characters. . . . These types are not only alien to us, they're not lifelike." Was this the picture of students that should be broadcast around the world?[12]

More, however, was to come, as certain writers insisted that this was life. Even the cultural revolution could not stem the tide. Mikhail Platoshkin's *On the Road* (1929) became a landmark in the attempt to save literature from rote ideological scripting.[13] The novel's title is hesitant, as if no end was yet in sight for afflicted youth; its contents nothing short of blasphemous. The party and Komsomol exhibit little of the expected fortitude, vision, or self-confidence. Platoshkin brings us down to eye level, setting the novel in a Moscow factory during the time of the Trotsky opposition. It was published just as Trotsky was expelled from the Soviet Union, yet incredibly Trotsky appears in the background of the novel as a positive figure. His name is invoked by Andrei Gromov, *raikom* secretary and one of the few to emerge unscathed from the factory's sex scandals. At a party meeting, officials even complain that Trotsky has not been given a fair chance to express himself in the press (which was historically true). Indeed, the only attack against Trotsky is delivered by Dmitry, the novel's exemplar of dissolute sexual behavior and bourgeois affectations.

Fond of "living person" dualities, Platoshkin divides his characters into competing halves. First is Panya, the Komsomol cell secretary, who faces the choice, usually reserved for men, between sexual involvement and an independent life. Though pursued by Dmitry, she resists his advances. At the same time, she is also against marriage: "I won't exchange my freedom for anything. What, waste my life drowning in diapers?" Panya eventually yields, becomes pregnant, and decides to raise the child alone. With this added burden, however, her work suffers, and she is replaced as secretary. Deserted by her comrades, she delivers an accusation that nearly matches the Trotsky digression in its irreverence: "You just used a person while she was strong and then dumped her like a useless nag. Who did I do this for? For the Komsomol? And did the Komsomol help me in my time of need?" Because of her poor diet Panya cannot produce milk for the baby, and little "Mitiushka" dies.

Higher up is Andrei, secretary of the regional committee whose struggle is the more conventional one: to obey reason or defer to his sexual needs. With Panya, his true love interest, taken by Dmitry, he opts for Katya, a fellow Komsomol member and devotee of frequent sex. Yet Andrei is ashamed by the exclusively physical nature of their relationship: "I'd just go over and then leave, like going to the bakery for a bun." He tries unsuccessfully to distract himself by studying history, as two Andreis battle inside. "Jerk. This is worse than prostitution," the good-natured one chastises. "Hurry, or she'll be going to sleep!" the more practical one commands. Andrei eventually breaks the chains of lust, just as Panya escapes from Dmitry. The stage is set for a happy union of the two chastened survivors of sexual indulgence, and Platoshkin ends with them posed romantically on the banks of the Moscow River. Yet he closes on a speculative note. No embrace, no marriage proposal, no "Internationale," just Panya's quiet conclusion: "We still don't know how to live. We don't know how to support and care for one another. But we have to. Every person is dear to us."

The most surprising thing about Platoshkin's novel is that it escaped the fate of its predecessors. Despite a surfeit of potential sources of complaint, from the favorable treatment of Trotsky to the less than uplifting picture of modern life, it seems that only the death of Panya's child was a sore point for critics. E. Levitskaia objected that Platoshkin was ignorant of contemporary reality, in which marriage, work, and political duties were eminently compatible.[14] Yet this attack was among a distinct minority among critical responses. The journal *Cutter* pronounced *On the Road* a model of proletarian literature for putting the difficult questions of working youth in the proper perspective; in other words, "not in the boulevard style like the notorious Malashkin and Gumilevsky."[15] The workers' journal *Growth* found in Panya's final lines a "convincing appeal by the author [for workers] to support and be attentive to one another."[16] Platoshkin was praised for avoiding cardboard characterization. The psychological depth and originality in the portrait of Panya made her "more realistic"; "her image is full of life and authenticity," which made her "completely unlike the schematic portraits of the heroines in the works of Malashkin, Gumilevsky, et cetera."[17] In short, orthodox critics did not yet rule the press. *The Literary Guardian* saw the novel as "directed against the famous glass-of-water theory" and in Panya "the prototype of a new kind of politically involved woman."[18] In the next issue Aleksandr Isbakh lambasted Levitskaia's desire for the standard recipe of a varnished life and saw its representation as no different from that to be found in other, ostensibly more objective places. "That which Comrade Platoshkin showed so deeply and forcefully in artistic form we can read every day in our newspapers. Let's have Comrade Levitskaia take a look at *Komsomol Pravda* or *The New Shift*."[19]

Isbakh's counterpart laid bare the hypocrisy of orthodox critics who singled out for attack fiction about contemporary life. In exposing contradictions, in refusing to paint life in monochrome red, these works were not slanderous. Documentary studies like Ilya Ilinsky's "Society's Detritus Before the Soviet Courts" (1926) offered far worse pictures and with the same intent: to show the "bitter truth" of "sexual profligacy in contemporary *byt*."[20] What emerged exceeded anything Platoshkin, Malashkin, or Gumilevsky ever offered: assault and battery, gang rape, a drunk father violating his year-old daughter, an uncle raping his niece. It also was probably a bitter pill for writers. Was there not a double standard in that nonfiction was allowed to do what fiction was criticized for, that is, demonstrating the often harsh reality of life in the early Soviet Union? After all, the cited cases were "not so much exceptions, rather the most repellent reflections of that reality which is sufficiently repellent in and of itself."

This double standard no doubt proved that fiction was more successful than party pamphlets or sociological exegeses in expressing popular attitudes. Discontent was widespread; one need only mention the revelation by one library that a dissatisfied reader had returned one of Stalin's works uncut because it had no pictures.[21] Admittedly this was better than the fate of other unsatisfactory works that were being rolled for cigarettes. Hence, much fiction about sexuality borrowed plots from the highly popular detective-adventure story and sometimes included attention-grabbing topics such as crime, violence, and death. But between bodice ripping and seduction, such fictional works also tackled the "great question" of the time: finding one's place and one's role in postrevolutionary society. This made them more important but also more provocative. Precisely because readers were more apt to cut and turn the pages of such fiction, it paid the price among critics who believed that literature was the cause of the very problems it addressed.

A striking illustration of the close parallels between nonfiction and fiction comes from Ilinsky's study of "society's detritus." Ilinsky discusses the actual case of Olga Rebrova, who gave birth to a son after an adulterous affair. Her husband's insults eventually drove her to poison her child, yet after initially sentencing her to eight years, the court showed mercy and released her, citing the "exceptionally difficult circumstances she found herself in." Olga's true story furnished the plot of Dmitry Sverchkov's "Case #3576" (1927),[22] which fleshes out Ilinsky's bare-bones sketch by presenting it from the perspective of both husband and wife. The result is a deceptively simple yet physically graphic horror story about the price one can pay for yielding to sexual temptation. Whereas Ilinsky faults the husband, Sverchkov blames both parties— Olga for adultery; Andrei for possessiveness, jealousy, drunkenness, and carousing with other women. Both husband and wife are victims, Olga of her husband's torment, and Andrei of propaganda robots. Both are living in a time of moral confusion. Andrei is aware of the party doctrine that women should be equal to men but is unable to tolerate his wife's infidelity. Called to account for his behavior, he chastises social welfare officials in words likely pronounced by real-life readers forced to endure the same stump speeches:

> Excuse me, but I've come straight from work and haven't even eaten. What you want to tell me I've heard already from one old guy who lectures us in evening courses. He's already said everything and it comes out so smooth and pressed like a tablecloth. The only thing is that all of your talk is empty. It's no good for life now; maybe in a hundred years, then everything will be according to your rules. I don't have time to listen to you, if you'll excuse me.[23]

Zhenya

The license assumed by writers in order to address the dark side of NEP society was less a reflection of cheap sensationalism or the "pornographic" influence of Kollontai or Malashkin than a simple intention to render what they saw for themselves or read about in the press. What was published outside the Kremlin net, such as M. M. Rubinshtein's study, *Youth Through Diaries and Autobiographical Notes* (1928), suggests that these writers were on target.[24] Focusing on Moscow students, Rubinshtein's work is remarkable because, unlike the more frequently cited studies by Gelman and Lass, it avoids automatic value judgments. Its lengthy introduction contains not one word about the Soviet Union or the building of socialism. Without overt ideology, Rubinshtein soberly explains why young people cultivate the rebel image. In the age of revolution, their greatest aspiration, particularly for women, was to prove their "independence," to have everything they want and in their own way. Youth's open view on sexual behavior should therefore be seen as a predictable result of "protest against tradition" and not, as so many feared, of bourgeois infection. For Rubinshtein, young people were not victims but sentient agents.

> Youth are not immoral, but they want what's theirs and from this comes their passion and strength. In order to obtain this it is important [for them] not to fall blindly into the clutches of the past. This is why in their eyes the negation of "grandma's morality" enjoys much favor. . . . Youth are prepared to see in defiance, hooliganism, and even highly destructive acts certain positive features. Boldness, protest, rebellion and an escape from the everyday impress them as they themselves strive for what is new and atypical.[25]

The centerpiece of Rubinshtein's study is an actual diary written by a fifteen-year-old girl that was begun in 1924 and ended mysteriously in 1926, perhaps with her suicide. Zhenya's diary reads like a mirror of fiction, almost as if Romanov had written it. Of middle-class roots, Zhenya has a social conscience and rejects the "bourgeois" dream of home and family. She works in a factory, joins the Komsomol, and is loyal to the system, yet she is frustrated that the world around does not match the ideal. "There's a lot of weird stuff in our life. I love the Soviet state madly, but when you see things fundamentally wrong, it makes you angry." Her barbs against bureaucracy sound like Trotsky, but she has not read his work. However, Zhenya is intelligent and an avid reader of Dostoevsky, Hamsun, Esenin, Bezymensky, and Lidia Seifullina—a curious list lacking in the expected names.

In truth, Zhenya does not write much about politics or literature, but of her desperate search for intimacy, friendship, and love. "No one, no one will understand me or caress me but I so madly want affection—the very sun of the human soul. The chill of loneliness destroys all that is beautiful." Her mother, afflicted with a "medieval mindset," is no help. Her diary mentions a fantasy lover, "Sandro," who appears in nearly every entry; a neighbor with whom she is secretly infatuated; a mysterious "P" (who likely gave the diary to Rubinshtein); and a young man whom she calls "the German" who took her virginity before the diary begins.[26] This event frames all that follows, as she had sex for all the wrong reasons. "I wasn't really interested in sex as such but I thought that this would be a step to gaining his friendship. I happily and openly gave my body to him because in spirit I was one with him, but after this very first time he left me, I lost him." Fearing venereal disease, she cries, "What have I done to deserve this?"

A full year later Zhenya still speaks of her sexual fall as a "wound that hurts more and more." Weary of the real world's "depressing monotony," she withdraws into an inner one of art, literature, films, and writing her diary. She takes up smoking, drinking, using cosmetics, and wearing short skirts, imitating the "bad girls" of fiction. She utters sentiments like those of Esenin's poetry—"It's a lot more difficult to live than to die"—a few months before the poet's suicide, an event that she found devastating. "His death makes me feel really bad. My mood is vile. . . . As a person I'm lost to society. . . . I guess I should also hang myself, jokes aside, but this pitiful human spirit wants something. Perhaps life will smile."

It doesn't. By December 1926, now seventeen and still consumed by a need for companionship, Zhenya has sex again with a man who tells her she is his "five hundredth." This admission detonates a bomb of self-hatred in her: "I ought just to hang myself, but I don't have the strength. You're worthless, pitiful, cowardly, repulsive, disgusting, ugly—shut up, please, shut up! Unbearable, disgusting, disgusting, disgusting—shut up, shut up, shut up, I swear!!!" Zhenya's final entry, entitled "About My First Love," is addressed to "P," with whom she has been intimate yet without intercourse. She reiterates her traumatic deflowering two years earlier by the "German" so that "P" can better understand her. Still tormented by her willing cooperation in her own sexual fall, she protests, "I'm repulsive, but all the same I do not see in my beliefs the roots of profligacy. . . . My friend, what do you now think about me? I'm all made of failure but I want so much to be like a person. Please help me and, if you can, be my friend. . . . I hope that I'll be able to earn your respect and friendship." Her final line is "Please just give me some attention."

At least no one could call this slander. Zhenya's testament was more powerful than nearly anything fiction could offer. She had no need for poetic license in order to produce one of the most penetrating analyses of problems facing Soviet youth. Nevertheless, her diary reads as if a staple of contemporary literature. The party and Komsomol play no role in her life; there is no caring, intervening collective as outlined in official ideology. Like the protagonist of "Without a Cherry Blossom," she is the victim of an environment so barren that she takes desperate actions to recover some kind of human warmth. Her plight, like that of Romanov's heroine, is not the result of personal failings but of her surroundings. Yet Zhenya does not blame those who take advantage of her, only herself. Her accounts of sexual encounters, as with Mr. Five Hundred, are rendered in the stylized language of romance literature. Her dialogues with herself recall the splitting of character that was vital to the "living person" concept. Such parallels suggest that she modeled her experiences against this literary background. She doesn't mention reading any such works, though she likely did, given her interest in culture and the arts. With dramatic flourish, she holds the reader in suspense until revealing the secret behind her loss of virginity. At the end, we never know what happened to Zhenya. Rubinshtein only comments quietly that he received the diary from an acquaintance, leaving the impression that "P" provided it, and that he would have done so only if she were dead.

Women Cast Adrift

On the banks of the Oka River the rotting corpse of a young woman washed ashore. It was worm-eaten and had been gnawed by rodents; its eyes were plucked out. Investigation revealed that it was the body of a seventeen-year-old who had left an incriminating diary. She had worked at a factory and lived in a dormitory, but life for her was an endless cycle of boredom and despair. Her classes were of no interest, especially "political instruction." Loneliness led to self-mutilation: "On the 28th of December I shaved my eyebrows. This was so that I could remember when I did it." She daydreamed, wrote Esenin-like poetry ("I'm sick of this life . . ."), and read, though the only book mentioned was one about "the sexual life of youth." Her own introduction to sex was singularly traumatic, as she was subsequently dumped "like a dirty rag." Thoughts of suicide rapidly took over, and she even obtained a revolver, suggesting to an acquaintance that they do it together. Her life became devoid of meaning: "I only eat, sleep, and f—k." She and her roommate then committed the ultimate act of political desecration by stealing a bust of Lenin from the Red Corner. Anticipating her court appearance, she wrote a farewell to her brother in her diary, asking that he remember her. Then abruptly the roommate's handwriting invades, accusing her of prostitution and drawing a skull and crossbones across the page.

The investigator's file included the testimony of four witnesses from the Komsomol and the victim's mother. The first, Nikolai, called the young woman an "out-and-out philistine" and "traitor to the cause of the working class"—though he admitted his interest in her. Sergei, the second witness, confessed that he was intimate with her for a few months, but never saw this liaison as a "lifetime relationship" and thus did not feel responsible for her suicide. Though he left her for another woman, he carefully noted that sex did not make him "neglect his party work." The third, Evgeny, stated that he never had intimate relations with her and actually counseled her about youth's important role in society. A roommate, Dina, testified that the victim was "corrupt" and had begun behaving like a "prostitute." The mother, a peasant with religious beliefs, testified that her daughter "got on the wrong path" and had been unable to handle the pressures of a confusing time when the new ways were still mixed up with the old. The investigator offered no conclusion.

The body could have been Zhenya's, but it wasn't. This account was a work of fiction, Gleb Alekseev's "The Case of the Corpse" (1926).[27] Though appearing two years before Rubinshtein's study, in all essential points Shura Golubeva's fictional life and death follow the same course as that of the real-life Zhenya. Blame again falls on the environment, particularly Shura's Komsomol cell. No one had helped her; the members' testimonies are merely exercises in self-preservation. The party is also useless, its leaders mockingly evoked in the names of public structures: Lenin Dormitory, Stalin Street, and Semashko Clinic. They are omnipresent but impotent figures, and Alekseev echoes Erenburg's criticism of the party's penchant for "papering over" problems. The story ends with no ideological pronouncement or exhortation to self-improvement. The investigator might have drawn a moral, but he is silent, a mute parody of the bombastic "experts" who tie up all the loose ends as in Demidovich's "documentary" courtroom drama. Is the grim description of the corpse at the beginning a commentary on the fate of Soviet youth? Alekseev's refusal to conclude with a warning or a call to action leaves us wondering.

The number of texts that either fail to include the orthodox version of life or, as with Alekseev's later and much maligned *Shadows of the One Ahead* (1929), do so only briefly at the very end, highlight one of the most striking features of the decade's literature.[28] Irresolution constituted at least a general, if not dominant, current, and in this sense was a self-inscribed canon with its own script to follow. This should not necessarily come as a surprise. The 1920s were not the late 1930s, and it would therefore be unsound to ascribe anti-Soviet intentions even to the most a-ideological texts. Irresolution did not necessarily signify condemnation of Soviet principles since the orthodox line was not the only representative voice of the party. Many writers and critics who favored an analytical, question-posing approach in fiction, like Isbakh or Sverchkov, were party members or had an unimpeachable record of pre-1917 revolutionary activity. Those who claimed neither status were nevertheless a whole breed apart from the likes of Arkady Averchenko, the vociferous and uncompromising emigré satirist of the same period. Refusing to have a party official or commissar swoop down and save the beleaguered characters reflected for them how life really was. In their eyes, this constituted true realism, one that matched readers' expectations and experiences, and it was offered with the intent of helping, not hindering, the Soviet Union's projected victory over "bourgeois remnants." Furthermore, if not Marxist themselves, such writers could claim validation from Marxist organs like *The Young Guard* or outside of literature itself, as with Ilinsky's declaration in "Society's Detritus" that devastating portraits of life were not exceptional:

> Of course, exposés of this kind aren't considered popular, but so too obsequiousness and toadyism achieve only a cheap and limited victory. To be able to tell the bitter truth in its entirety to the [working] class is more vital than putting the spotlight on individual members who have

gone to pieces. Even with a large pitcher, the courts won't empty the sea of monstrosities and diseases that engulf us. Even with revolutionary legislation, there is no other way to eliminate problems in daily life but through patiently and firmly shaping the public opinion of the Soviet democracy not only with regard to issues of political and social construction but to the most important ones of *byt*.[29]

A telling example of the mixed messages Soviet readers were receiving comes with Aleksandr Yakovlev's novella, "No Land in Sight" (1926).[30] Set during the civil war, it is the story of Nadia and Sergei, comrades in the trenches and sexual partners yet for whom love remains taboo. For Sergei, the ideal physical relationship is devoid of emotional commitment, like visiting a prostitute. "You don't have to worry about love or lovers or a bed for two. Just drop in your coin and that's it. Everything else is yours to keep: your time, strength and destiny." Nadia asks, "So that means today I'm the one and tomorrow another?" "Of course," he responds, "What's the difference? Nearly every day we eat lunch in a new cafeteria. People who are doing great things don't and shouldn't have any sentimental sides like with love. To hell with it!" It would be best, Sergei admits, if sex as well as love could be eliminated, so that one could give oneself a hundred percent to the revolution. Nadia responds by showing him her breasts and lures him into bed to prove how vulnerable he is to his sexual impulses.

For Nadia, everyone, including the local nuns who visit the red soldiers at night, can be divided into those who have sex with love and those who do not. Only the latter seem psychologically fit, free from the "pain" Nadia experiences, for example, when she returns from having an abortion in Moscow to find Sergei in the hospital with a venereal disease. Mad with jealousy, she blows off the head of a prisoner she is interrogating because she suspects him of having a callous attitude toward women. (Her comrades only deign to point out that if she's going to act that way, it would be better to kill them outside; head shots are too messy for indoors.) Nadia's inner pain, reminiscent of the *it* tormenting Tolstoy's Ivan Ilych, disappears only when she rallies the troops in combat and orders the execution of another prisoner. Her blood thirst satiated, she begins to fight her emotional side, the distracting passions unleashed by jealousy. She does not need love, she tells herself. "Happiness is a step to weakness." Yet she continues to pursue Sergei, who has been advanced and posted to Moscow, but without success.

"No Land in Sight" provides no answer to a moral paradox. The only characters who seem not to suffer, or, like Sergei, who advance, are able to abandon hope of love. Yet this was the exact reverse of the ideal Leninesque model offered to youth. The novella was one of several works about the chaotic civil war period when casual sex was taken for granted and emotional attachments were threats to fulfilling one's duty before the revolution.[31] However, the story appeared when the "save the youth" campaign began to mount an uncompromising assault against the evils of casual sex. Love was favored and easy sex the culprit. Was Yakovlev on the side of amoral civil war norms or postwar idealism?

Yakovlev's bleak drama of sex without love revealed the darkest side of an unromanticized portrayal of the civil war, when the myth of victory by the oppressed masses had turned into a grim picture of alienation, emotional starvation, and the consequent loss of sexual inhibition. This theme, almost inexplicably, did not run its course until socialist realism was firmly in place. As late as 1930, one can still find fictional portraits of civil war youth rendered in precisely the same terms. In Galina Serebriakova's "Morning Dew" (1930), sex is the primary focus of a story about a group of young Komsomolists scattered throughout the country by war.[32] No one would question their ideological loyalties; they are surprisingly mature, despite their youth, but duty is always qualified by the needs of the flesh. The main character, Valentina, only fifteen, finds herself in a threatening environment. During a bombing attack, a red soldier invites her into his hut as though offering protection, then attempts to rape her. When she complains to her superior, he scoffs at her scruples and implies that she should have known better, as if to say, "What did you expect?" The sexually abandoned Kaleriia describes for Valentina her own sordid introduction to sexual feelings, an episode with twisted Freudian implications. When she was eight years old, her father had shot himself in front of her and her uncle rushed to calm the hysterical child. When he kissed her, the tickling of his beard sent an "electric shock" through her body and a jolt of "real female passion" that she cannot forget.

Valentina is in love with twenty-four-year-old Adolf Talge, a confident youth who lectures her from Engels's *Anti-Dühring*. She is surprised and disappointed when, in the callous spirit of the times, he baldly proposes sex: "Maybe tomorrow I'll ship off with the regiment and die from a bullet or typhus. You see, ever since I've wanted you I haven't been able to work like before. . . . You should have sex with me; . . . what's it to you? Be a man." Valentina refuses, pointing out that if their love is true, he can wait until the war is over. Yet despite the remonstrations offered by the iron Bolshevik, symbolically named Virginia, Valentina ultimately offers herself to Adolf out of sympathy for his "physical" sufferings. Surprisingly, now he refuses, and Valentina falls victim to typhus and hallucinates about sex. Upon recovering, she learns that Adolf shot himself after becoming infected with syphilis. As the story ends, Valentina is preparing to go to Moscow to study—an ominous ending for the decade's literature.

Whither Femininity?

Though Valentina would seem to have the fortitude to survive the travails of a Moscow university, Serebriakova never puts her to the test. Instead, we are left to consider how her potential has been forfeited because of a lack of proper guidance. Virginia's antisex remonstrations were certainly of no use; Valentina politely hears her out and then offers herself to Adolf. To whom, in or outside the text, could she turn? From the Soviet pantheon Kollontai had lost authority; her reputation, unfairly earned, was no better than that of Malashkin's Tanya. Lenin's wife, Krupskaia, was held up as an ideal, but by this date she was too far removed from the experiences of young women to be of any help. The prospects were quite dim for a realistic role model to save Valentina from the tragedy likely to befall her in the capital. She would be on her own.

Central to Serebriakova's story is the assertion, echoed across the decade's fiction, that women faced far different pressures than men. Women's lives lagged painfully behind official efforts to ensure equality between genders. This failure to deliver was damning because Soviet society saw itself as the most progressive in the world, particularly in terms of women's social and economic status. Yet however ambitious Bolshevik plans to achieve gender equality might have been, on most counts they fell short, and because of this policies of the 1920s have been roundly criticized by scholars today.[33]

Less frequently remembered, however, is that this failure was openly acknowledged. Bolsheviks might have been self-defeating idealists but at least here they were not hypocrites. Smidovich, for example, was not one to believe fully the official propaganda regarding promises of equality for women. For her, the two primary reasons behind women's collective plight were both ideological and material-economic.[34] Ingrained traditions and prejudices had survived the revolution and resisted the most strenuous efforts to raise the social consciousness of men (and women) on this issue. This was why so many female activists and fictional heroines regarded marriage with suspicion. Washing, cooking, and cleaning the home were still the exclusive province of women, even among ostensibly enlightened party members.[35]

Moreover, because of limited resources, the state's utopian goal of shifting all domestic chores to the public realm would long remain a dream. It was in part for this reason that abortion had been legalized and why it remained central to so much of the period's literature.[36] To raise a child while remaining a fully functioning member of the Komsomol or party was portrayed as a fundamental problem for women. The demands of motherhood could lead to bourgeois self-absorption, another dangerous possibility. At the same time, abortion was expressly denounced as a solution to this predicament, no matter how men or material necessity might pressure women into having one.

In fiction abortion was unfailingly (and realistically) portrayed as a harrowing experience, as illustrated by a short dramatic sketch published in *Red Students,* simply entitled "Abortion" (1927).[37] The entire story takes place in a gray, morgue-like clinic. Inna and her partner, Abram, have come to terminate her pregnancy, concerned that a baby would detract from the performance of her work. While waiting to be examined, Inna witnesses what could be her fate. She sees an unconscious woman, lying on a table, from under whose "thighs spread a red, bloody circle." The doctors fail to revive her and she dies. Inna then witnesses a birth, also described in graphic detail, after which the mother is herself reborn: "The aged features of her face had disappeared, she had become young again and an indescribable joy brightened her face and lips." With this image Inna's own fears disappear; she realizes that she will not allow a child to disrupt her studies or devotion to the party. She is confident that "she can do it all, and that happiness made her heart beat and a smile never left her lips."

Such confidence, however, was not a common experience for many young women who felt that the revolution had left them behind. The question of identity—what role women were to play after 1917—became acute. Women were given far less attention in the Komsomol than men, not only because of male prejudice but also because they were in the minority, accounting for less than a quarter of the total membership in many cells.[38] This discrepancy put them at severe risk. As the critic Troshchenko warned, women were more likely to leave the protective shell of the collective, neglect their duties, or simply quit the Komsomol if domestic pressures increased.[39] Their small numbers also meant that male members of the Komsomol often sought companionship among women still "infected with old prejudices," that is, "bourgeois" and "philistine" women. As attested by numerous complaints, this set the stage for jealousy and competition, refracted through both sexual and ideological lenses.[40] Many noted that men even preferred the look and behavior of the class enemy. Women thus fell victim to another double standard. On ideological grounds men would criticize the "aristocratic" or "bourgeois" look of women dressed according to current fashion (using cosmetics, wearing silk stockings and short skirts), yet on the streets, away from the cell meetings, this is what attracted their attention. The paradox, as embodied in Chaikina's outburst in Gladkov's *Drunken Sun,* was painfully simple: damned if you do, alone if you don't. "Now counterrevolution hides itself in prettified, painted up eyes and feminine tenderness. My husband got himself one of those, and I got a kick in the ass out the door." When another retorts that theoretically women have gained from the revolution, Chaikina explodes:

Equality? While a man is in power there can't be equality. They're the ones who shout "equality!" but walk all over us even more than under the tsar. They're crushing our souls! A human mockery! Crippling us for life! All they need are dolls, angelic tenderness, a chirping pigeon, a resourceful whore who can always turn them on. They don't need from a woman a comrade at work, no way! What's a woman and mother now? Someone who does political work? She's not a woman or a man but sexless. Look at what they want—those right there! (She flicked her hand in the direction of the broads.) Reactionaries! Killers! They shout "Down with prostitution," yet they're the ones who beget them, pretending that it's only hearth and home, a comfortable little corner to live. Stinking philistines![41]

While Chaikina refuses to give in to the "counterrevolutionary" look, in real life many others surrendered to the pressure, "starving themselves," in Troshchenko's words, in order to afford the current fashions. Clothing, particularly stockings, became a central motif of young women's dilemma. Much as in the West at the same time, silk, light-colored, or patterned stockings were *de rigueur* in fashionable women's attire, but a female thus adorned ran the risk of reproof.[42] Reflexively in fiction, women's legs generally proved the undoing of male communists, as Zudin discovered in Tarasov-Rodionov's *Chocolate*. Georgy Nikiforov, in *By the Lamplight* (1929) took the motif to its logical end, reducing women on the street to "legs":

There were legs in fine silk stockings bared to the knee; legs particularly young and firm. There were legs a bit on in age, tired calves shaking, squeezed painfully into thin shoes; there were legs that brazenly let themselves be known, walking by with confidence, catching the eye and shouting their presence. It was clear that they were searching for someone, asking for something. There were business legs too, running along quickly, paying no attention to others and immediately lost amidst those done up in silk stockings.[43]

Ideologically conscious women were caught in a trap. To negate one's femininity by dressing like a man, cutting one's hair, swearing, and smoking was unequivocally criticized by party and Komsomol officials. Conversely, fancy stockings and cosmetics played into the stereotype of a prostitute or seductress. Both looks connoted a sexual predator. The former symbolized a carefree, aggressive, distinctly "masculine" attitude toward sex, whereas the latter, attacked by Kollantai as "doll-parasites," were capable of entrapping men "for whom two years ago there existed only one great goddess—the Revolution."[44]

Semashko, the commissar of health, tried to rescue women from this Scylla and Charybdis with his treatise "Is Femininity Necessary?" (1924), in which he roundly castigated both female types. The bourgeois "hourglass" woman should, in his view, "nauseate" any true proletarian or peasant by reminding them of the decadent values of their oppressive masters. On the other side, the masculinized woman violated "the natural selection" by which both sexes had distinct roles to play. Women, he noted, have special features and character traits that define them. They possess special "emotional qualities"; after all, only females give birth. Arguing that emancipation and social equality should not erase this special distinction between the sexes, his advice was therefore simple: "The best that is in a woman, a woman needs to retain." One shouldn't forget, he concluded, that Marxism would eventually resolve all with a grand gender-splicing synthesis: "It's unknown what type of person will obtain in the future. Most likely he will inherit the best qualities of the male and female character. But in the meantime, 'femininity' in this sense of the word still holds our favor."[45]

Such rhetoric only underscored the confusion most experienced with this subject. The simple question—how Soviet women should dress and behave after the revolution—was met with bromides and prejudice. A certain V. Kuzmin, in "About Femininity" (1925) built upon Semashko's Marxist approach, declaring that the matter of women's social role was essentially a cultural construct.[46] From the mythological Amazons to women in the modern bourgeoisie, he could demonstrate that femininity had many and various definitions, depending on class and cultural context. However, the power of social environment won out when he claimed that because of centuries of oppression, a woman's brain was "not as developed" as that of a man, just as her hands and feet were smaller. (He noted certain exceptions: Clara Zetkin, Rosa Luxemburg, George Sand, Marie Curie, and, of course, Nadzehda Krupskaia.) But arguing against Semashko, Kuzmin would not allow for an eventual diminution of gender distinctions. "Trying to eliminate the natural difference between a man and a woman" was "a death sentence." Given the malleability of sex-role concepts, the revolution could and should foster a new kind, one that shed old stereotypes of female passivity, "lamblike" tenderness, and tear-shedding as well as the woman's function as a "bedroom toy." A woman should not wear masculine clothes—"never in human history was there ever such a thing"—instead, capable of physical and emotional strength, they should be important members of the working class without losing their inherent qualities.

Meetings convened to discuss the issue of women's attire threatened to drown participants in the murky waters churned by Semashko and Kuzmin. The only concrete position upon which all could agree was that "a proletarian likes beauty . . . the real kind, not the fake one." When asked how this vague guideline applied to women's appearance, they shrugged their shoulders. Nevertheless, the questions women asked about wearing specific garments suggested that they were trying to create their own individual identity as females, shunning the cookie-cutter standardized image preferred by theoreticians. Some noted that trousers were more practical for performing physical labor and, citing Bebel, argued that apparel for all workers should be designed for maximum efficiency. Kuzmin's intransigence in opposing masculine attire for women was criticized as "bourgeois"; the demands of the task, not gender, should determine a worker's dress. At the same time, the editors of *The New Shift* (in which these opinions were published) noted that women's biological functions, notably menstruation and pregnancy, should be accommodated by their clothing. Only one proposal found favor with them—a woman "should work like a man while in woman's clothes"—and on this they declared the question closed."[47]

Literature proved incapable as well of resolving the "femininity" debate.[48] Its offerings were generally as limited as those declaimed by Semashko and Kuzmin. Writers preferred to traffic in the same types, of which the easiest to paint was the prostitute-seductress.[49] The results could be comically inept, as with Nikolai Nikandrov's *The Path to a Woman* (1927), a two-hundred-page hulk excoriated as a "pile of dirt."[50] More often, though, the attempts to portray threatening women were numbingly predictable, such as Natalia Shad-Khan's *Parasites*, published in the same year and by the same press.[51] The novel opens with Khvalynin, a communist hardened by prison and exile before the revolution, entranced by the stockinged legs of Tenny, a cut-out, pin-up "doll-parasite."

> He caught himself thinking about how good it would be to lie down next to her right now and embrace her body, the beautiful shape of which showed clearly through her dress. . . . All powers of reason fell silent before the voice of his blood, that instinct calling a man to a woman who was weak but strong in her own weakness.
>
> Having admitted that feeling, he understood that he wouldn't fight it; instead he would think of a way in order to satisfy it.

Needless to say, satisfaction doesn't present a problem, for without Khvalynin's downfall there would be no cautionary tale. The rest of the novel proceeds in like fashion, never deviating from the standard plot of cross-class romance. Khvalynin marries Tenny out of lust, she marries for economic stability—a mismatch in which Khvalynin finds himself ensnared in a bourgeois nightmare of perfumes and parties. Inevitably, Tenny is unfaithful, has an abortion, and contemplates suicide. Khvalynin breaks free only at the end, safely abroad and away from her spell.

Shad-Khan clearly intended *Parasites* as a warning; on nearly every page the narrator speaks of the pitfalls that await the unwary and undisciplined. Although the foreword by Dmitry Sverchkov (author of "Case #3576") claims that a reader cannot put the novel down "until the very last page," this was a lone opinion. A reviewer for *The Literary Guardian* wondered if Sverchkov had actually read *Parasites*. Its didacticism is so transparent and its construction so tiresome that it serves merely as a blueprint of extant stereotypes. As for any last-page anticipation, the reviewer could only state—and here it is easy to agree—"What a relief when the novel ends."[52]

The Search for a Female Role Model

That Shad-Khan could offer nothing more than a reduction of *Dog Alley* illustrates how quickly literature had fallen into a rut, churning out snakelike Veras by the dozen. There were some strong female characters in current fiction, what Troshchenko called "Soviet Joans of Arc," but they were few in number or appeared in compromising contexts.[53] As in "Morning Dew," iron virgins tended to be secondary characters whose appeal, as noted by readers, paled before that of the more dramatic femmes fatales and psychologically complex suicide victims. When triumphant women did gain center stage, they were often disappointing exaggerations, as in Aleksandr Neverov's "Marya the Bolshevik," or brief, such as Anatoly Glebov's "Inga," or weighted by tragedy like Seifullina's "Virineia," or lacking in correct political orientation, as in Anna Karavaeva's *Homestead*.[54]

Yet different problems attended Vera Ketlinskaia's novel, *Natka Michurina* (1929), a conscious attempt to combine a positive image of women with an endorsement of the supportive role of the Komsomol.[55] The heroine, feeling an absence in her life that neither factory nor Komsomol work can fulfill, is seduced by "Petrukha" Sizov, the secretary of her cell. He entices her to his apartment where, in an almost exact replay of the protagonist's deflowering in "Without a Cherry Blossom," she allows herself to be seduced, falling "under the control of his lips, his hands, and his body." She wants Petrukha to love her, but he is devoted only to fulfilling a biological need for sex: "I'm a man. It's a simple necessity to have women. You should understand that." Natasha becomes pregnant and is pressured into having an abortion (given in explicit, painful detail) because Petrukha does not want the distraction of "all the diapers," and if they were to marry Natasha would risk becoming a "philistine housewife." Although Petrukha has other women, when Natasha becomes pregnant again he accuses her of infidelity. She is embittered by having to undergo a second abortion, begins to trust no one, finds hypocrisy in the Komsomol, and neglects her work.

Petrukha tries to have Natasha expelled from the Komsomol, but suspicion begins to fall on him for causing her deterioration. Others in the group ask whether they too are culpable; have they not also been negligent? A formal meeting is called, attended by party officials, to discuss all the raw issues raised by Natasha and Petrukha's liaison: male hypocrisy regarding women's equality while allowing all domestic chores to fall to them; the difficulty of balancing a career with motherhood; the destruction wrought by free love theories; and the benefits of marriage. Petrukha is found guilty not only of mistreating Natasha and pressuring her to end her pregnancies, but of pretending to be a good and moral communist, doing everything in the name of the Komsomol to disguise his misdeeds. Meanwhile, Petrukha asks to be allowed to prove he can once again be a good party member. Natasha is encouraged to return to the fold by Boris, who finds her appealing but defers romance until she is rehabilitated. Perhaps one day, he decides, "if within the collective family of comrades, she finds in him—in Boris—a friend for life, then he will be able to love her." At the end, as they walk off together in the falling snow, he proudly declaims: "Everything turned out correctly, just as it should turn out."

Natka Michurina was remarkable not in ideological content, which was unexceptionable, but in its critical reception. It was an obvious corrective to the "slander" found in other fiction and to scandals like the Korenkov case; it defended the Komsomol as a supportive institution; and it featured a strong female protagonist, yet reviewers were lukewarm in their praise. The critical establishment was still too diverse and too vocal about its autonomy to genuflect before works that merely promoted the official line. Some found the novel more palatable than "Moon on the Right" and "Without a Cherry Blossom" and praised the author's restraint in refusing to "indulge in the piquant details" of her characters' sexual lives.[56] At the same time, however, for others Ketlinskaia's simplistic and overly determined narrative failed the test of realism. A hot-tempered reviewer for *The Literary Guardian* pronounced its plot "schematic," its conclusions "readily foreseeable," and its structure "weighted down with outside commentary."[57] Indeed, as another pointed out, in her attempt to correct earlier works about contemporary problems of love, duty, and sexuality, Ketlinskaia relied on the same clichés as the works whose example she sought to avoid.[58]

The mixed response to *Natka Michurina* was likely a slap for Ketlinskaia, who was no older than her heroine. Born in 1906, at age thirteen she was already working for the Red Army, and at fourteen she entered the Komsomol and was sent to Leningrad to study. She worked in a factory, engaged in agit work, and in 1927 joined the party. There could be no mistaking Ketlinskaia's intentions, since the novel appeared in the same year, 1929, as *Life Out of Control*, the dramatic exposé of the deficiencies of the Komsomol coauthored with Vladimir Slepkov (see chapter 1). Although Ketlinskaia claimed that her novel was based solely on one Leningrad Komsomol cell, observed at first hand, its parallels with the Korenkov affair (which also occurred in Leningrad) and with other works concerned with contemporary *byt* are too obvious not to suggest additional, deliberate modeling. In *Life Out of Control* Ketlinskaia explicitly complains of the influence of Romanov, Malashkin, and Gumilevsky on the morals of young people—they were all part of a bourgeois "poison" spreading unhealthy erotic feelings and (in Romanov's case) fostering a "special attraction to luxuriant underwear." Even if the characters of *Natka Michurina* succumb to the excesses of postrevolutionary life, the novel ends with the emergence of a disciplined character, shows how to control sexuality and other temptations, and restores the Komsomol to its proper role.

Georgy Nikiforov's *A Woman* (1929), a novel both daring and irritatingly conventional, exhibits the difficulty of presenting a simultaneously realistic and ideologically uplifting portrait of the Komsomol.[59] *A Woman* is a bildungsroman centering on nineteen-year-old Favsta, cast adrift after the death of her mother. Sonya, her father's mistress, later her stepmother, introduces Favsta to the pleasures of the body and tries to persuade the girl that beauty, not intellect, can conquer men. Being an introspective young woman with "a warehouse of unresolved questions," Favsta resists Sonya's advice. However, because of her bourgeois roots, she lacks the proletarian instinct that should point her in the right direction. Nor is she a member of the Komsomol, so there is no family of comrades she can turn to. She is yet another literary orphan whose plight combines that of the heroine of "Without a Cherry Blossom" and that of Zhenya, the young diarist featured in M. M. Rubinshtein's study—vulnerable young people looking for answers but finding none. "Things aren't right," Favsta confesses, "I'm like a wingless fly caught in a glass jar. I want to break free to that place where all of life is clear."

Favsta is an avid reader, but books cannot free her from her prison. Finding no support or guidance in fiction, she turns to actual women as role models. Here too she is disappointed. There is her friend Sima, who rejects love but not sex, and Sverdobova, who meets her husband only once a week so that marriage will not interfere with her work. Sonya, now Favsta's stepmother, is obsessed with female beauty and embodies the cult of self. Nikiforov includes a daring hint of homosexuality when Sonya makes a suggestive advance toward the half-naked Favsta, but is repulsed. Shortly thereafter Favsta attempts suicide upon learning that her father is having an affair with Sima. Aleksandr Briakin, a brigade leader, takes over the narrative at this point. He is attracted to Favsta but is unsure whether love is compatible with fulfilling his political duty. His superior, Nikita, a lifelong party member, cannot answer this question; he too is conflicted and also attracted to Favsta.

Time passes, and the narrative returns to Favsta some years later. She is a member of the Komsomol, emotionally and ideologically mature. Yet her work teaching literacy and inspecting workers' barracks does not save her from loneliness. Aleksandr has turned away from her, and she shares only a tender platonic relationship with Nikita. She wants to forget her "silly" past, but it returns in the form of a suicide letter from Sonya, who encloses an extra packet of morphine for her use. Favsta, distraught, is momentarily tempted but is returned to duty by the morning whistle calling all to work. As she throws the packet out the window, she catches sight of Nikita. She rushes to join him and breathlessly expresses her reconciliation with love and with life: "For ages I've looked for you, Nikita." His strong silence indicates that nothing more needs to be said.

Nikiforov was a minor writer, but one not lacking in originality. *By the Lamplight*, cited earlier for its synecdochic digression on legs, included a surprisingly favorable cameo of Trotsky, "dear leader of the Red Army," in which he delivers a forceful speech. *A Woman* also touches on a near-taboo subject, lesbianism, which, when it appeared at all, was usually under cover of a medical or sociological study. Nikiforov also refused to present cardboard figures; every major character is flawed in some way. The novel as well is built on a clever twist. The title (which in English could also be *Woman* or *The Woman*) signals closure, and though there is in the sense of plot, the narrative focus nevertheless reopens the question regarding female role models. It acknowledges literature's deficiency while doing little to actually resolve it. Perhaps Favsta is an example of the new woman. By the end she has arrived at the ideologically correct position, and for this the novel was praised by reviewers in minor journals.[60] However, most critics were unimpressed, finding no motivation for her change.[61] One reviewer for *October* found the novel ridiculous: "Nikiforov believes that it's enough to center the narrative on an attractive heroine, stick a hammer in her hand, and surround her with lathes and other workers so that, gift-wrapped in this fashion, it will pass as a truly proletarian, contemporary novel."[62] *A Woman* pandered only to an audience of "impatient" readers who refused to look beyond the "surface" of social problems and who expected fiction to do the same:

> A woman? What demands do we put on her? What is she supposed to do? What about her work and, most significantly, what about love? Here's the answer: 1. Work honestly and frequently (but don't let this

mar your beauty or your delicate feelings as, for example, with Favsta);
2. Be sincere and strong in your love (but don't let this love mess up
your life; be sure to connect with your husband by phone [once a week]
like Sverdobova, and if you want a child, give birth but quietly without
all that trouble like Solomina [who inexplicably appears halfway through
the novel with a baby]). Following this wise recipe, which helps resolve
all personal conflicts, a woman, of course, can ensure that her loving
husband will still be able to work and fulfill his social duties while at the
same time be able herself to enjoy love tenderly and free of trouble.

October's simultaneous derision of readers who wanted schematic portraits and the writers who would provide them underscores how mismatched
expectations could be. When a potential role model surfaced, many critics
would jump to discredit it as lifeless. Boris Guber, for example, rejected Yakov
Korobov's *Katia Dolga* (1926) outright because the heroine was unconvincing.[63] In the first thirty-five pages Katia mutates from an ignorant peasant to
a staunch representative of the party, championing the plight of women and
having had only one extramarital affair. Her stunning transformation, ac-
companied by a chorus of sunswept, chirping nature, left Guber aghast:

> While reading *Katia Dolga,* one realizes that it's impossible to call Ko-
> robov an artist. He is distinctly lacking in descriptive ability. There are
> no colors, sounds, or smells on his boring pages. . . . Korobov not only
> doesn't create any new images of people, he is unable to handle the old
> ones. Practically all of his characters live not as humans but solely as
> names. They are whipped up according to the familiar and facile recipe
> of the tendentious laboratory. If a communist is good, then he's 100
> percent good, and if bad then an incorrigible villain.[64]

Hostility to fiction that served up ideologically correct portraits of
women came from two camps, in many respects sworn enemies: on the one
hand, the Young Guardists and those associated with "proletarian" journals
like *October*, and on the other, the Perevalists such as Gorbov. Instead of unconvincing, inspirational models, they all favored protagonists who could express doubt and indecision, who could be both dutiful and decent yet flawed.
In "The New Woman in Literature," Gorbov cited as positive examples characters who presented an "organic, living image" such as could be found in
"No Land in Sight," *Drunken Sun,* "Moon on the Right," "Without a Cherry
Blossom," and "The Case of the Corpse."[65] This was approximately the same
canon championed by the Young Guardists; indeed, their journal published

two of them. They continued to uphold the "living person" objective, encouraging writers to offer more psychological depth, ambiguity, and complexities of motivation and character.

The competing interests that made the decade so ripe for controversy also explain why no clear answer was forthcoming to what was a simple question: why the dearth of proper role models for women? It was a case both of mismatched definitions of "proper," as with the inconclusive debate over femininity, and of "role model" itself in literature. What typically garnered praise in journals, the dynamic yet deficient "living person," did not guarantee success with readers (not to mention the orthodox critics). Works in which a female character was presented as a complex being, with sexual independence, too easily disappointed readers with traditional tastes. At one readers' conference, for example, female workers could not accept Dasha in Fedor Gladkov's *Cement* because she was too unfeminine. One commented: "Although she is a politically conscious worker, she should be a woman in all respects. She simply destroyed [her husband's] life." Their preference was for a Manichean world with promiscuity and adultery, particularly with regard to women, banished to one side. This explains the suspicion elicited by Seifullina's Virineia, one of the stronger characters in early Soviet literature. Readers were disturbed by a woman of flamboyant, independent spirit who was not bound by conventional ideas of chastity. The judgment of female peasants who read the novel was that, despite her ideological fortitude, in the end she was a "slut."[66] In short, the more authentic the character from a realist point of view, the more likely she would appear in tragic or problematic colors and thus negate what many readers were looking for. Political wholesomeness and sexual openness were emerging in the latter's eyes, much as with the likes of the orthodox critics, as antitheses. Something had to give, and at the turn of the decade it became clear what.

CHAPTER 8

Sex and the Revolution

New Reality/New Realism

IT remains an essential though often underappreciated fact that Soviet politics and literature, particularly at this time, did not march as one. The period's fiction included some strange creatures that were far from being anomalies. Although by 1928 Stalin had solidified his position as the head of the party—he had already crushed Trotsky, Zinoviev, and Kamenev and was now poised to inaugurate the first five-year plan—works published in that year continued to underscore the painful distance between contemporary life and promised ideals. Literature focusing on youth and sex excelled in testing the viability of party rhetoric by lowering it into the chaos of the fictional (yet realistically conceived) everyday. Only in the more contrived texts did the party emerge triumphant or unscathed. And even if an author's message could be called ideologically correct, the driving force in *byt* narratives was usually negative social phenomena or the exposition of a failed ideal. Villains were not necessarily cartoonlike Khorokhorins; often what they had to say was more compelling and intelligent than the politically sound views offered by their red-draped counterweights.

Such disillusionment is clear in Ilya Brazhnin's *Leap* (1928), a novel whose title signifies leaving the island of individualism for the mainland of collectivism. Unremarkable in its sex-saturated plot, it stands out for giving space to sharp criticism of the party and the Komsomol. Grisha, a member falsely accused of rape and murder, launches into an eight-page diatribe that symbolically hits all the points of youth's dissatisfaction in real life. He attacks the party for promoting an all-consuming, life-depleting bureaucracy; for its inability to move from the abstract to everyday reality; for sacrificing love and other positive emotions to the cult of the machine; for disregarding the demands of the individual; for crushing all that is bright and cheerful in the name of duty. In a towering rage (and in such terms that one wonders how Brazhnin's novel got past the censor), he accuses the Komsomol of "raping" the victim's spirit:

> You proclaim yourselves the apostles of justice and human kindness, but how do you treat the person? You don't even notice him. Yes, you simply don't notice him. Entranced with the grand scale [of your efforts], you blindly walk right past him, this living, suffering, despairing person, though he is right next to you, under your very nose.
>
> Your short-sighted collectivism clouds your vision. You don't see people as individuals and consequently cannot know a person or understand what is human. With all-important airs, you discuss Comintern resolutions about the Chinese revolution but won't even ask the comrade next to you why he doesn't look well, what's bothering him, and whether he's hungry.
>
> You, the official priests of people's welfare, are inhuman. All personal emotions have died in you. Your "solidarity" makes you deaf and blind to true human suffering and thus makes you inhuman.[1]

Three years later, such sentiments would not be found in fiction. In 1931 in *The Young Communist* L. Bernstein proclaimed victory in the "serious battles" with ideological opponents, "from Esenin to Panteleimon Romanov." His declaration of triumph was neither premature nor inaccurate. Soviet literature was quickly turning away from crushed cherry blossoms, enchanted moons, and dangerous alleys. Already the mood of the 1920s seemed qualitatively distinct from and inferior to the present. Works that had been allowed to be published only a few years earlier, such as Vikenty Veresaev's short story "Isanka" (1927), met with a withering review when it was reprinted in 1930.[2] Its explicit portrayal of two adolescents fearfully stumbling toward sexual intimacy seemed obsolete, and the reviewer saw no relevance to contemporary life. "After all," came the criticism, "isn't the new generation of youth raised in the spirit of comradely equality between husband and wife in bearing the family burden? . . . Isn't sexual abstinence at this young age the natural result of healthy, normal conditions, and early sexual behavior solely the result of the social perversions of the capitalist system?" Since life was now different, so too should be its literature. If before Veresaev had not provided a conclusive ending—readers are never told whether the pair will overcome their doubts and fears, or whether their relationship will grow in a positive way—writers now could no longer get away with such ambiguity. They were to provide answers, the reviewer declared.

Let's even assume that the realist Veresaev is correct, and the problems of *byt* among youth are not resolved properly in a large number of cases because of the bad situation students can find themselves in to this day. How should an artist, the materialist, the dialectician, handle this fact? He should see in which objective conditions of our reality there exist the precursors for its resolution, where our development is going, and whether there is in our *byt* the embryo of what will become the future relationship between the sexes.[3]

A new, forward-looking realism was emerging, together with a resurgence of a more traditional, quasi-ascetic code of behavior, that made the 1920s seem distant. In 1931 Bernstein spoke of the debates of the previous decade— one could nearly count the difference in months—as if their issues were no longer part of the living present. In the 1920s, he explained, "questions of the new family, marriage, and the problem of sex were hotly debated. So too were the minor but still relevant arguments over ties, silk stockings, etc. Each of us can recall how often these questions were on the agenda at Komsomol meetings. Each of us remembers the spirited and passionate debates over 'Moon on the Right' and 'Without a Cherry Blossom.'"[4] All the confusion, challenges, scandals, and disputes were now history. Youth had passed their trial by fire.

The difference between Brazhnin's novel of 1928 and Bernstein's 1931 victory declaration leaves us with an essential question. What had happened? Why did indecision, contradiction, and contumacy seemingly come to a full stop only years into the next decade? How could sexual behavior, one of the preeminent topics of early Soviet literature, have become a virtual nonissue by the mid-1930s? It would be easy, but incorrect, to blame this change in attitude solely on Stalin. This would be the least satisfactory of answers, for it ignores other factors of the cultural ethos and discursive environment that put an end to the short-lived sexual revolution in Soviet literature. As long as the debate over realism persisted, writers and critics could always find justification for including sexual topics in fiction. Only with the resolution of this conflict would it be possible to decouple, once and for all, revolution and sex and thus commit the latter to the realm of the taboo.

Realism became the focal point of contention because underlying its many definitions lay competing political conceptions of what the revolution meant. The dispute between orthodox critics and the Young Guardists was never merely a difference of literary opinion; its roots were more profound: to claim that the revolution's ideals constituted the present or to acknowledge said ideals but to disavow their current manifestation. For orthodox critics, the revolution was not a haphazard event; it was the most significant chapter

to date in the great historical plan embracing past, present, and future. It bestowed on its children proleptic powers that united the real and the ideal,
since the design of the latter was already foreknown. Authentic literature had
an obligation to make this ideal part of the everyday world, to ensure its visibility in all contemporary records, whether fictional or documentary. In the
eyes of orthodox critics, texts that achieved this union of present and future
were not guilty of falsifying reality. On the contrary, realistic writing was by
nature forward-looking and thus necessarily endowed with a positive message. Truth and ideological correctness were reciprocal, which provided them
with solid grounds for their exhortations to produce uplifting portraits of
youth. After all the harm that had been done by ignorant, misguided, sometimes malicious writers, the image of Soviet youth needed to be readjusted
and returned to its "typicality." That there could be disagreement or even dis-
sension on this point was for critics as puzzling as it was maddening. What
conceivable reason was there for writing anything except to communicate a
single Marxist truth?

   This was the primary framework through which the inclusion of overt
sexuality in literature constituted blasphemy. Prudery certainly played a role,
but sexuality was threatening in a different way. Perhaps more than any other
subject, sex tore away the protective shield orthodox critics and their party
supporters had sought to construct around the image of revolution. If
brought into contact with such an intensely personal and, for that time, eminently confusing issue, it could no longer remain a sacrosanct domain, bereft
of ambiguity. Sex profaned the revolution by lowering it, by making it com-
monplace and thereby open to question. The revolution, many believed, was
above and beyond such speculation. Soviet Marxism could speak on the issue
of sex, but it should not be represented through this volatile issue. The revolution and sex were distinct, one high, one low. This wall had been shattered
in the 1920s by the volumes of *byt*-centered literature, dragging the revolution
out of its temple into a gutter of wanton filth. Scattered attempts at repair had
been made in the wake of Kollontai's provocative ideas, Esenin's suicide, and
the scandals stirred up by Malashkin's, Romanov's, and Gumilevsky's fiction.
Yet these attempts proved indecisive and had been rebuffed with audacity and
elan from within the ranks of the party itself and by critics who published in
its primary organs. Only in the 1930s, because of a changing cultural land-
scape and an emerging consensus as to what was acceptable in Soviet literature, could a full assault on these unhealthy influences be launched.

Kolosov and the "New Person"

   In her 1929 retrospective on the representation of Soviet youth in literature, Ekaterina Troshchenko took the lead in trying to restore the notion of

revolution to its proper place, above personal needs and contamination by individualism.[5] Only twenty-seven when she published her study, she could boast a worthy record in the Komsomol, first in Ukraine and then, like so many others, after her transfer to Moscow. Her first comment on the portrayal of sex in popular literature was the broadside against the unrealistic depiction of dormitory life in "Without a Cherry Blossom" (see chapter 4). Troshchenko's zeal and anger arose from firsthand experience as a student at a Moscow university, where she evidently escaped the fate that befell so many other young women in the capital, at least in fiction. Literature was her specialty as a student, then as a critic and budding poet, and she brought to it a passion that put ideology first. The shining heroes of the revolution were real to her, for they were fulfilling historic destiny; she saw life unfolding according to their prophecy and their plans. Like a devout member of any faith, Troshchenko genuinely felt that a true and lifelike portrait of society would be an uplifting one, since an optimistic picture conformed to her understanding of reality as defined by her understanding of Marxism. If literature was to be realistic, it should show how things must be.

Troshchenko had found one writer whose work had already met this stringent definition: Mark Kolosov. His name means little today, but in the twenties and early thirties Kolosov's fiction generated an astonishing amount of praise from all quarters. Yet nothing in his slender brief of short stories would seem, at first, to warrant the laurels showered upon him. Kolosov tackled such perennial themes as adolescent angst, discontent, and conflict, though with a special twist for the politically serious reader. In "Thirteen" (1923), the protagonist Vanka is distraught over the fact that he still must wait a year before joining the Komsomol; providentially, an anodyne comes in the form of a dream in which Lenin hands the boy the cherished ticket. Kolosov took on the issue of Lenin's death in "A Mourning Crape" (1924). In this story, Pavlik, serving on a ship, realizes that the crew cannot pay proper respect to the deceased leader without honoring his portrait. Pavlik steals a length of black crape from the portrait of the commander's father (who has recently died) and he and his comrades ease their pain by singing songs and reading together beneath the newly decorated picture of their own deceased "father." In "Broadside" (1924), Petka recognizes that political journalism comes before "the girls." While mounting the newspaper on a public board, Petka unflinchingly pounds in the nails with his fist when he cannot find a hammer. Like a parent caring for a child, he carefully wipes the dust from the pages with his handkerchief. When rain begins to fall, he rushes out to save the paper, only to find his comrade in the arms of Tanya. This prompts a rebuke: "The newspaper's dying, yet you're just out looking for some romantic adventure." And so on.[6]

While "Thirteen," "A Mourning Crape," and "Broadside" together amount to a mere ninety pages, the critical acclaim they inspired would befit a major literary achievement five times their length. Kolosov's contribution to Soviet literature was to produce what had eluded so many others: an ideologically uplifting portrait of the Komsomol that was seen to be simultaneously realistic and thought-provoking. Prefiguring Troshchenko's resurrection of his stories was a critical reception that had long honored Kolosov as a saint and savior of Soviet literature. In 1927 a reviewer for *The Young Guard* (somewhat unexpectedly) described his stories as "pieces of flesh and blood torn from Komsomol *byt*." Kolosov was said to possess a novelist's psychological depth for "penetrating to the heart [of today's young worker] . . . depicting him in all the concreteness of his experiences, predilections, and proclivities."[7] His stories' "greatest merit," noted another reviewer, was their "verisimilitude and the fact that his characters are not copied from some *plakat* or done according to cliché; all of them are living persons, given with all their virtues and shortcomings." Vanka, Pavlik, and Petka flow from Kolosov's pen as "organic, instinctual" communists, thereby ensuring their "artistic integrity."[8]

Critics found nothing programmatic, wooden, or schematic about Kolosov's writing. He did not "idealize" his generation, declared *Red Virgin Soil*; instead he portrayed it "truthfully, without dressing things up."[9] The political and pedagogical import of his stories was thus unprecedented, offering to date perhaps the "best prose" yet written about Lenin.[10] Critics were confident of his artistic pedigree. Kolosov obviously learned his trade by studying "classical literature," affirmed *The Literary Guardian,* and his stories were thus "distinguished by the influence of its best models."[11] Some claimed that his talent ranked him with Gogol and Babel.[12] Not surprisingly, Troshchenko found in him the exact embodiment of her conception of the ideal writer. His work exemplified the perfect harmony between ideology and art precisely because the art was wholly dependent on Marxist truth: "The communist orientation flows from within the aesthetic essence of his stories, and without this they would not be literary products."[13] He seamlessly integrated the two so well, declared another critic, that his stories illuminated "the path to the great literature of the future."[14]

The modern reader can see the true character of Kolosov's writing as lying in another direction. Although critics denied that his writing was schematic or idealized, that was exactly what he excelled in, and the excessive praise from critics tells us more about current interpretive criteria than about the work itself: realism *über alles*. No matter how stiff Kolosov's heroes and villains, no matter how "unliving" they actually were, because they were eminent models for youth orthodox critics could not fail to bless them as "realistic." Here we see that realism, less a term of critical analysis with all its "flesh-tearing and blood," was rather the indisputable mark of success, indicating what was ideologically desirable. The critics' enthusiastic comments make it clear that Kolosov's alleged verisimilitude derived not from what he did, but from what he did not do. His stories were free of "doubt, vacillation, and despair"; their ideological orientation was "clear and fixed," avoiding the all too common path of showing the Komsomol in its "most unattractive, perverted form."[15] In fact, as Petr Kogan argued (in the same issue of *The Young Guard* in which "Moon on the Right" appeared) that precisely because Kolosov's stories do not deal with "love, jealousy, or relations between genders . . . they are marked with the stamp of realism."[16]

The non sequiturs in the critical commentary about Kolosov's work reveal how strenuously critics sought to encode propagandistic *plakat* literature in a more acceptable vocabulary. He always "reaches for the sun," one concluded, and this is why his writing is "not tendentious."[17] Because these stories were so "artistically well done," another noted, they could serve as "sociological" documents about contemporary life. Lunacharsky observed that whereas the Komsomol is not a "monastery," Kolosov deserved praise for presenting the institution in more or less the same colors. Such double-speak was necessary to rescue the ideal of the revolution from the confusion it had created, to restore it to its sacral potency, occupying a realm of belief that allowed for no equivocation or ambiguity.

Lunacharsky did leave the distinct hint that the claims made for Kolosov were a high-stakes game of semantics. In a protracted discussion of his achievement, Lunacharsky argued that Marxist theory, not life in its totality, dictated what was real and therefore what was valid for inclusion in a literary work. Without this grounding, a writer would produce a flawed product. To rely solely on oneself might make for an original portrait of life, yet it would be inherently "distorted" by subjective emotion and self-absorption that produced "atypical" scenes and characters. Herein lay the primary reason, Lunacharsky believed, for the flood of "pessimism" infiltrating contemporary literature. Marxist theory alone illuminated the truth of life. This meant, in simple terms, that any writer hoping to present an authentic account of reality had to subordinate its representation to the proper party perspective. To be sure, Lunacharsky hastened to add, this did not mean that the Marxist writer "distorts" facts; this was impossible, since the only facts that were authentic were those enabled by Marxist theory itself. In sum, a literary work should proceed from a preset plan: "The goal of the Marxist writer should be, as much as possible, to offer conclusions based on observation and given in artistic form that reinforce his overall beliefs, for all of us cannot fail to be endowed with the conviction that in all and sundry our party views constitute the purest, the clearest, the most objective truth of life such as humankind has ever had."[18]

Lunacharsky seemed aware that this circular logic explicitly sanctioned a license to produce nothing but formulaic optimism. Nevertheless, he turned this to Kolosov's advantage, essentially declaring that his vital contribution to Soviet literature was to produce *plakat* camouflaged as its opposite. According to Lunacharsky, the easiest thing for a writer to do was to focus on the "corruption and debauchery" in the Komsomol. Negativity was the simple result of turning off one's ideological headlights and allowing subjective whim to take control. The "truly difficult" task was what Kolosov had done: "to depict the beautiful in the life of the Komsomol in such a way so that it doesn't come out as if from a copy-book or from an official mandate on prosperity, or sound like rose-colored compliments and self-aggrandizement." And if we are inclined to agree with Lunacharsky that masking formula as nonformula does deserve special recognition, then we should join him in "congratulating" the author: "Kolosov's stories are living pieces of Komsomol life. Every time you read them you take away something edifying, a certain plus, particular colors of life, and with all that you say: yes, that's how it is; that's how it should be."[19]

Lunacharsky's final words anticipate the language of socialist realism. His delicate theoretical balancing act, arguing that "to be truthful" is to be "true to the Komsomol," brings us onto the same epistemological grounds that would later allow reality to be shown "in its revolutionary development." It also explains why Kolosov attracted a veritable cult of fawning critics, why his work was praised by publications that normally disagreed. Though his most celebrated stories were written in 1923 and 1924, with each reprint they could be trotted out on cue, like dogs in a circus, to counter the latest disparaging image of the Komsomol in more problematic fiction. Iartsev used him as a counterweight to Gladkov's *Drunken Sun,* just as the ever-compliant Mark Bekker did in a 1927 attack against the plethora of negative works published the year before. In another article published in 1929, Troshchenko crowned Kolosov's work as the highest Soviet literary achievement to date, declaring that "after Kolosov not one author has brought anything to our literature that could enrich us in terms of a deep, all-encompassing, organic understanding of . . . communist youth."[20]

Troshchenko's reason for making this startling claim was to censure the publication of Nikolai Bogdanov's *First Girl* (1928), another work of naturalism that recalled the controversial publications of 1926. This is the story of Sanya, a Komsomol member who, as a reward for her heroism in the civil war, is sent to Moscow, where she promptly becomes involved with several men, infecting each with syphilis.[21] At the end Sanya pays the price, shot to death by an uninfected comrade who disguises the murder as an accident. Yet Sanya does not play the typical role of parasite-seductress. Bogdanov deliberately clouds the picture. As we discover from her "diary" appended to the novel,

Sanya views her disease as punishment for embracing free love in its literal, hedonistic sense. Her confession, along with the fact that she sought medical treatment, elicited the sympathy of some critics who explicitly contrasted the complexity of her character with the "boulevard exercises of Gumilevsky, Malashkin, and Romanov."[22] For Troshchenko, however, there was no difference. Bogdanov's Komsomolists in *First Girl* grew from the same bad seeds of sexually obsessed and ideologically skin-deep youth that she had attacked before. Troshchenko was astonished that Sanya's motivation for depicting her inner thoughts was her anxiety about venereal disease and not, as with Kolosov's heroes, dedication to the revolution. Sanya's priorities, and thus Bogdanov's as well, were upside down. Troshchenko was disappointed that the political context of the novel appeared almost as an afterthought, that its action and message could have been set in any time or place. This deprived the revolution of any special value. This "sin" explained why Bogdanov's representation failed "to convince" the reader.[23] Since Kolosov had already delineated the true character of Soviet youth in his fiction, Bogdanov's inability to do the same made his characters more the products of a flawed imagination than of reality.

Troshchenko's criticism clearly shows how realism, the muse to which virtually all writers who sought to address the problems of youth swore allegiance, was increasingly defined within the narrow limits of ideological correctness. For this purpose Kolosov was an invaluable example. In 1932, even as the term "socialist realism" was making its first official appearances in Soviet discourse, V. Zlobin cited Kolosov's now dated story "Thirteen" as an exemplary portrait of youth, all the while reminding readers that its characters were not "stiff heroes or hackneyed clichés" but "living Komsomolists."[24] Kolosov's broad applicability as a model was a simple function of the fact that he wrote what orthodox critics wanted. Booze, sex, drugs, dirt, obscenities, silk stockings, adultery, rape, and abortion—all were gone. His Komsomol— the collective sigh of relief is almost audible—was the most hygienic and curative of institutions, one that not only makes a boy a man but also, without fail, makes him a junior Lenin. Moreover, since Kolosov was born in 1904 (the same year as Ermilov), his writing about youth had autobiographical authority. No one could claim that his vision was distorted by age or detachment. Orthodox critics finally had someone from the source, a "voice of the new generation who sees things differently."[25] This welcome contrast was what would make him in Lunacharsky's eyes "the most Komsomolist of all writers."

In 1929, the year in which Troshchenko awakened readers to Kolosov's achievement, he and Valeria Gerasimova collaborated on a made-to-order play entitled *The Test*.[26] This work was a unique accomplishment, ostensibly bearing the mark of "true proletarian artists": the ability "to see the future today."[27] Critics were eager to compare the behavior of the protagonist, Chuprov, with official party directives.[28] Yet once again, despite the cardboard nature of their characters, Kolosov and Gerasimova were praised across the board for not making them marionettes.[29] Proof positive came in the endorsements of Komsomolists who attended public discussions of the play. Confirming that *The Test* "fully answered" their needs, young workers almost unanimously championed it as an accurate portrait of the people they encountered in their own cells.[30]

The Test gave currency to another concept, the "new person," that was soon to replace the "living person" ideal. The pantheon of young communists whose portraits Kolosov had been producing for years were all exemplary representatives. Kolosov and Gerasimova did not coin the term; it had circulated quietly in the press for a few years, signifying the stalwart youth who had outgrown, by-passed, or otherwise survived the temptations of NEP society. "New people" had always been present, but their existence had been overshadowed and often forgotten. Much as with icons of proper female behavior, such estimable characters were generally ignored until the final chapter of a work, at which point, flattened by such a heavy ideological iron, they failed to rise from the page. As M. Rafail noted in a 1928 booklet dedicated to the subject, literature and the press had spent so much of their energy exposing the weeds in the Soviet garden of youth that they had forgotten to fertilize the healthy crops. Despite this neglect, the seedlings had still blossomed into healthy cadres and were now demanding their place in the sun. It was time for the hero to replace the hooligan as the primary figure in Soviet literature for youth.[31] The "living person" had been tried and had failed, tumbling into a pit of solipsism, passivity, and perversion. Nothing like this could ever befall the "new person" because, as with the example of Chuprov, it was proudly noted, his "behavior is not determined in any way by narrow, selfish personal interests."[32] As the old communist in *The Test* proclaims, the uniform trait of Chuprov and his new generation was "unshakeable devotion to our great cause." They embodied precisely what Troshchenko had been asking of literature: to represent characters who completely subordinated the personal to the political, yet who were convincingly realistic.

There was another distinguishing trait of the "new person." Turning upside down Kollontai's infamous "glass of water" remark about the natural need for sex, Rafail pointed out that the "new person" "had acquired a new natural desire—political work—and satisfying that need was just as necessary as drinking, sleeping, and eating."[33] In *The Test,* Kolosov and Gerasimova emphasized this devotion to work. Relatively early in the play, Maika pronounces the lines that we have come to expect from positive heroes:

VIKTOR (*nervously*): Maia, you know, this sounds funny . . . but I, I
think, that . . . I love . . . you. . . . (*stumbling*) That is . . . I'm very
sexually attracted to you.

MAIKA (*decisively*): Well, Comrade Viktor, the question of love has been
removed from my agenda—for quite a long time, seriously speaking.
Now it is filled with work. (*Pause*) We politically conscious girls don't
have time for love.[34]

However, Maika is a bourgeois in proletarian clothes, and her declaration
against love is just one of the covers she employs to infiltrate the Komsomol
ranks. She believes that it sounds right, yet she is behind the times. In her
mouth the lines sound dated, like her ubiquitous red kerchief, and by 1929
they truly were. In a sign of what was to come, the "new person" had transcended even the need to deny love. Serving as the true example, Chuprov is
completely de-sexed, having evolved to the point where women, romance,
and sexual intercourse are nonissues. Critics finally had an ascetic who, unlike
Rakhmetov in Chernyshevsky's *What Is to Be Done?*, had no reason to explain
or defend himself.

Ironically, within the whole Kolosov phenomenon the only truly honest
voice was that of the writer himself. In a 1932 authorial manifesto, he provided readings of his various works, effectively reducing them to the moral
medicine tablets that they were by patiently explaining that each story was
composed with a specific lesson in mind. He more or less admitted, with apparent pride, that he was a hack, striving "to create a gallery of Komsomol
types corresponding to the demands which our party presents at every new
stage in the struggle for communism."[35] The resulting decade-long accumu-
lation of accolades allowed him to endow himself retrospectively with
prophetic powers. From his early stories to *The Test,* he sought only to capture
those traits that would define humankind in the future, as promised by Marxism.

The End of the "Living Person"

The rise of the "new person" coincided with the demise of the "living"
one. Yet it would be mistaken to attribute this change solely to the canonization of a realism that would not tolerate vacillation or ambiguity in its characters. The psychologism inherent in the "living person" paradigm proved its
undoing. The final act, the last significant attempt to endorse the truth-seek-
ing communist as realistic portrait, was penned by Yury Libedinsky in *Birth
of a Hero* (1930).[36] This novel was the veritable swan song of the "living person," cementing once and for all the unsuitability of this concept for Soviet

literature. After all, what was the typical reader to do with a novel which memorably opens with a party member, Shorokhov, spying on his bathing sister-in-law? The first dozen pages are his internal contemplation of sexual desire, and for a third of its entire length, the novel rarely ventures beyond posing a question, one key to Shorokhov but surely not high on the agenda of his real-life comrades: will he sleep with Liuba, his dead wife's sister, or not? When the answer comes in a graphic wake-up scene of the two together, Shorokhov can only see himself as a victim of fate. "What happened was what was supposed to happen." Humane and complex, he is nevertheless a mis-guided individual trapped by passivity. At work looms Eidkunen, a human automaton devoted to order and abstractions. They are balanced opposites, each regarding the other with disapproval. Shorokhov sees Eidkunen as a pas-sionless robot, unable to accept emotion yet with an unhealthy, "philistine" obsession with his family. On the other side Eidkunen sees Shorokhov as an eccentric in need of guidance—particularly when Shorokhov admits that his first recourse to understand the world is not Marxist doctrine but lies in him-self: "He always tried from a sense of common humanity to put himself in the position of anyone on whom he had to pass judgment. He could justify any crime by assuming the point of view of the one who had committed it and laughed at Eidkunen who always wrapped himself up with theoretical con-structions when venturing into the field of ethics and problems of everyday life."

Yet despite his capacity for empathy, Shorokhov is oblivious to problems in his own family. His thirteen-year-old son, disgusted with the behavior of those around him, calls Liuba a "bitch" when he discovers her in the arms of another lover and vows to build special homes to shelter all children of dys-functional families. Meanwhile, Liuba, pregnant with Shorokhov's child, leaves him and marries another man. After giving birth to Vladimir (a name chosen to honor the recently deceased Lenin), she invites Shorokhov to visit his new son. Only in the final pages does Shorokhov wake from his slumber, ready to do battle with all that Eidkunen represents. "Never had he been armed with such strength and knowledge as he was now, and he looked with cold bitterness at Liuba as one does an enemy." Shorokhov makes a vow to save the child from destruction by Liuba and her kind.

The critics were stunned. What had become of Libedinsky, civil war vet-eran, party member, and writer of demonstrated ability who had already be-queathed to Soviet literature such classics as *Tomorrow* (1923) and *The Commissars* (1925)? A group of workers at a factory meeting at first refused to believe that Libedinsky was the author of *Birth of a Hero*. The critic Ivan Vinogradov cried: "A leading worker, an old Bolshevik for whom the dark and tender dimples on Liuba's large hips are more important than work—

that simply is ridiculous."[37] Shorokhov did not drink or beat his wife, but other than that he had few redeeming qualities. Fatalism, lack of self-control, and egoism made him an inept father, a poor husband, and a nonentity in the party. Others commented that the title made no sense. Shorokhov was a hero in name only, certainly not in action. Genuine heroes did something, yet like a modern-day Don Quixote, Libedinsky's hero waged all his wars in his head. It was not clear that Shorokhov was truly ready to eradicate the Eidkunens that plague Soviet society. But if this were true, then why didn't Libedinsky show it? Why end the novel where it should have begun? What example was set by Shorokhov? He realized the truth only after neglecting his work and his family, after a long period of passive self-absorbtion.

Yet Libedinsky's title was nonetheless accurate in that it describes the emergence of a new Shorokhov from the old, as he becomes aware of the conditions that hinder personal growth and by extension the growth of society. He was not, however, a new person in the Kolosovian sense, or at least we have no way of judging because the novel's emphasis was on process, not the result. The negative, therefore, dominated. As N. Svirin noted, "In his exclusive attention to uncovering the pitfalls of Soviet reality, in his attempt to reveal the gaping contradictions, garbage, and refuse of the past that hide behind a shining, lacquered exterior, . . . Libedinsky somehow forgets about the necessity of showing the growth of new socialist ways and of our achievements."[38] The novel's message was hypocritical: Shorokhov's self-absorption and sex drive had blinded him, not the Eidkunen virus of zealous commitment to order and bureaucracy. If he could have driven Liuba from his mind for a minute, he might have noticed something good in the socialist reality that surrounded him.

Elsewhere, readers in a Rostov library charged that if Libedinsky intended to "rip the mask" of bureaucratism from the face of the typical communist, he succeeded only too well, "ripping off the face as well."[39] Another critic was irritated by so much introspection: All readers got was "the debris of analysis, self-analysis, and analysis of that self-analysis," or worse, life's problems reduced to the seduction of a young sister-in-law.[40] If this was Libedinsky's idea of what constituted a hero, commented one worker, it was "one which we can do without."[41] Fellow novelist Tarasov-Rodionov noted that as a hero, Shorokhov was "stillborn."[42]

Critics felt that Libedinsky's mistakes were not deliberate, that he did not consciously intend to malign the party. It was their "duty as comrades," Tarasov-Rodionov observed, "to point out clearly his errors and faults." *Birth of a Hero* was the predictable outcome of an unhealthy obsession with psychologism and the "living person" ideal. It was doomed from the start epistemologically, ideologically, and artistically. A strict focus on the person was misguided, substituting subjective whim for the firm grounding of class identity. This violated "the laws of reality" by upsetting a primary Marxist tenet: class determines consciousness.[43] The more Libedinsky delved into Shorokhov's mind, the more this internal world replaced the external, becoming in effect Shorokhov's reality. That perceived reality, passed on to the reader, was distorted, "unreal." It was only his truth, not truth that "serves the needs of the proletariat."[44] It revolved solely around "I, a capitalized I."[45]

Shorokhov's subjectivity was idealism at its worst, showing why he could sympathize with any criminal. He had lost the class bearings that would normally dictate his proper responses and was cast adrift in a world where, as with the "living person," "the boundaries between enemy and ally disappear."[46] Here lay the roots of his passivity, his incapacitating pessimism. He could not see anything positive in Soviet reality without (as Lunacharsky put it) the proper class lens. Moreover, Shorokhov's unhealthy obsession with Liuba vindicated the charge made earlier that the "living person" was generally a slave to lust. If introspection begat a world shaped by one's own laws, then it could not fail to give license to "internal hedonism."[47] The path from ideological to sexual transgression was preordained.

The condemnation of Libedinsky's novel effectively finished the "living person" as an ideal for writers of fiction. The deficiencies of *Birth of a Hero* were "the logical end" of such a theory.[48] Libedinsky was not accused of debauchery, but his work evinced the same negativity and weakness embodied in his protagonist. It also demonstrated Libedinsky's ignorance of the proletariat; workers had no use for the novel. It "broke from the class struggle" and thus smacked of "petty-bourgeois" inclinations.[49] Once a strong warrior for the cause, Libedensky had surrendered his pen to vacillation and indecision, bewitched by a false god. For a true Marxist at the beginning of a new decade, not only was the truth already set, there was only one road to it—not to be explored but affirmed. Libedinsky's belief in the "living person" undermined this foundation and came close to heresy by suggesting that the revolution was still bereft of a single, all-encompassing meaning. Thus *Birth of a Hero* constituted a "threat," and its publication was condemned: "It seems that commercial interests have overridden common sense."[50] What would become of the collective ideal if literature suggested that the primary source of truth was within oneself?

Exit Romanov

Libedinsky's misfortune was compounded by the fact that 1930 also witnessed the appearance of Romanov's final, and most inflammatory, installment in his near decade-long examination of postrevolutionary mores.

Unlike the frequently reprinted "Without a Cherry Blossom," *Comrade Kisliakov* (1930) made only one appearance, but this was enough to effectively end Romanov's front-rank status as a writer of *byt*.[51] He had tried to redeem himself in "The New Comandment" (1928), a story about a party member's resistance to the sexual temptations of a bourgeois coquette. It received little notice, undoubtedly because it never advanced beyond cliché.[52] In *Comrade Kisliakov* Romanov reverted to his former position, producing a novel that was a stunning exercise in courage bordering on stupidity. Like *Birth of a Hero,* it focuses on a protagonist's struggle to adapt to new times, but, as almost always with Romanov, the plot turns on the question of sexual relations. It was such a devastating portrait of contemporary society that even readers abroad were shocked. A reviewer for *The New Statesman* remarked, "It is one of the mysteries of Soviet government that Romanof's [*sic*]books are allowed to be published. . . . The enforced intimacies, the hideous lack of privacy, the gross stupidity of its rulers, the dreadful struggle with poverty, are all displayed here passionately and with an imaginative power that we expect from Romanof."[53] The author later claimed that he intended *Comrade Kisliakov* as pro-Soviet satire—that it was meant to expose the false face assumed by displaced intellectuals eager to demonstrate their allegiance to the state—and perhaps this was true. Yet the novel unleashed a flood of angry accusations that Romanov was in the service of the "enemies of the USSR." Unlike what happened in 1926, no critic dared to defend him this time.

The novel's title character, shorn of "Comrade" at the beginning, is a museum official and member of the intelligentsia who regards the barbaric behavior of the ascendant proletariat with disgust. He and his wife share a room in a crowded communal apartment marked by a "perennially occupied" bathroom and a band of children who mock him for his antiquated beliefs. Privacy is nonexistent. When guests come, they open a bottle of wine surreptitiously in their small room so as not to be accused of hosting an "orgy." They speak in whispers of their stratagems for survival, with the usual refrain being "I'll do just enough so that I don't land in jail." Kisliakov also must struggle to survive at the museum, which has been taken over by a one-eyed communist veteran, Polukhin, bent on "proletarianizing the personnel" and turning the place into a shrine to Marxism. This plan threatens the last sanctuary of the intelligentsia, for at least here, cultivating artifacts of the past, "they could take pride in the fact that not in the slightest were they compromising their conscience" or "inflicting violence"—an assertion that force and immorality were the exclusive domain of the party.

Kisliakov decides not to resist. He finds it frightfully easy to mouth the words and adopt the attire that ensure acceptance. He buys a bust of Marx, begins to berate the intelligentsia and praises the Bolsheviks for uniting the people. Pants tucked into boots, he smokes with the Komsomolists, sets about reorganizing the museum, plans marches for Soviet holidays, and earns the honorific title of Comrade, which "now sounded like music to him." And when in a ritual purge Polukhin is dismissed, Kisliakov immediately turns on him, for which he is to be rewarded by being made vice-director of the museum. Yet the real motive for conforming, he admits to himself, is fear of losing his job. He is a chameleon, changing color but remaining a class enemy within. He feels secret sympathy for the victims of the collectivization campaign: "The communists are squeezing the kulak. But it's ridiculous to oppress a person just for the fact that he works for himself and does a good job at it. Most likely they are simply decent, hard-working peasants and not really kulaks." Only with his old friend Neznamov, who refuses to collaborate with the Bolsheviks, can Kisliakov shed his proletarian facade. Yet the ease with which one can replace the other only aggravates him more.

Leading a double life at work, Kisliakov also lives a false one at home. He is sexually tempted by Neznamov's wife, Tamara, a stage actress intent on remaining bourgeois in an increasingly proletarian world. Entranced by her silk-stockinged legs and short skirts, Kisliakov has a brief affair, whereupon his wife divorces him. Still obsessed with Tamara, he becomes furiously jealous when she begins to frequent a foreign film director who proclaims that any Russian woman could be had for "three pairs of silk stockings." Tamara plans to leave the country with her new lover. Kisliakov realizes her betrayal too late and in a violent rage stabs her to death.

Comrade Kisliakov effectively finished Romanov's reign as one of the premier writers of contemporary Soviet life. Nothing in the novel indicated that affairs in the Soviet Union—political, social, or marital—were on the right track. "Except for a dying intelligentsia, women's legs, and a perenially occupied toilet," claimed one reviewer, "Romanov cannot see anything in our times."[54] If his earlier stories appeared ambiguous or tentative, in *Comrade Kisliakov* he showed his true colors. His vision was attacked as retrograde, his characters spoiled leftovers from the nineteenth century. He had no "living understanding, no living knowledge" of "postrevolutionary Russian culture"; "thirteen years of revolution have meant nothing to him."[55] Perhaps he did not mean to approve of the deeds of his protagonist, a parasite, fraud, adulterer, temporizer, and murderer, but he failed to present an alternative, not even among the communists in his novel. For years Romanov had enjoyed the privilege of a "problematic" writer, always "running along a knife's edge" in his examinations of the "accursed questions" of the day.[56] Yet by now he should have assumed the responsibility of presenting what was good and bright in modern Soviet life. Even a realistic writer had to include true "heroes."[57] Instead, his novel was pure slander, degrading the party as cut-throat, destructive, and mechanical, portraying workers as uncultured, squalid louts, and belittling the sincere attempts of members of the intelligentsia to "re-forge" themselves.

In ad hominem attacks, critics berated Romanov as an arrogant "apologist of philistinism," imagining himself superior to the reader but mouthing only banalities.[58] With only "a primitive, vulgar, truly philistine level of culture,"[59] he was an advocate for the "beliefs of the class enemy." On this last point, the evidence was against him, as indicated by its success abroad. The novel, pub-lished in England without his permission and suggestively titled *Three Pairs of Silk Stockings*, was sold alongside the work of Boris Pilnyak, already con-demned as a traitor to the revolution, as a portrait of "the true modern Rus-sia."[60] Eugene Lyons commented that the novel received a similar reception in the United States, where readers believed that through this novel they ex-perienced "the flesh and blood" of life under socialism.[61]

Such galling praise from abroad was cited widely in the Soviet press. Ro-manov was accused of leading a bourgeois "counterattack" in literature, of having "conducted a raid" through the back door. "By means known only to him, [he] succeeded in twisting the greatest epoch in the cultural history of humankind into his own decrepit, provincial-philistine world view."[62] Though the word was not spoken, it smacked of treason. Romanov's charac-ters were said to be "all candidates for the Shakhty trial,"—a reference to a sham trial in 1928 in which "bourgeois specialists" were falsely accused of working for capitalist countries and a number were executed. The whole af-fair was orchestrated to impress two vital points: the threat of foreign infiltra-tion and potential treachery of all Soviet citizens who could not claim proletarian or peasant origin.[63] If Romanov himself was no better than his characters, if he had become a tool of the "whiteguard press," then he too was guilty of the same domestic subversion.

Romanov's belated attempts at self-defense signaled how much the cul-tural face of the Soviet Union had shifted in a very short time. In 1927 he had thumbed his nose at critics with "The Trial of a Pioneer"; now he was repen-tant. In letters to *The Literary Gazette,* he expressed his outrage that the mes-sage of *Comrade Kisliakov* had been kidnapped and misrepresented by the "whiteguard press." He sincerely apologized for writing a "politically mis-taken" book. While his purpose had been to expose "kisliakovism," he had erred in focusing only on what interested him, leaving out the rest of society, thus yielding "an unfaithful picture of reality." In so many words he con-firmed Lunacharsky's thesis that the writer who relies only on himself is guilty of self-absorption and violates the true, Marxist vision of life. Romanov asked for "more patience and friendly guidance" from literary critics. After all, he argued, "one who makes no mistakes is one who does nothing."[64]

Tolerance, however, was a rapidly fading quality. *Comrade Kisliakov* proved unique in uniting normally quarrelsome critics. They could temporarily cease their internecine bickering for a collective condemnation of such a monstrous work. *Birth of a Hero* at least offered some room for debate; its protagonist lacked sexual self-control, but he did not fall to the depths of Kisliakov. Kirshon cited this difference in a last attempt to save Libedinsky's reputation.[65] The latter had erred unconsciously and unintentionally, whereas Romanov was a wolf in sheep's clothing—outwardly loyal to Soviet goals but inside, like Kisliakov himself, a "reactionary." In short, there was a fallibility to which Marxists could be prone and then there was plain sedition. The wrangle over Libedinsky, Kirshon believed, obscured the real threat, "bourgeois literature" and the "class enemy" at home. Critics seemed proud to have exposed Romanov's duplicity and to have halted his slanderous assault on the Soviet Union. Although the publication of *Comrade Kisliakov* revealed a lapse in "proletarian vigilance on the cultural front," the damage was controlled.[66] Unlike *Birth of a Hero*, *Comrade Kisliakov* would never see reprint in the Soviet Union.

The Birth of True Heroes

These two novels nevertheless remained tied to each other as examples of failed and thus anti-Soviet writing. In actuality, however, only Libedinsky's novel was a "threat" in any real sense. Romanov was popular but powerless, advancing no artistic theory or creed that might seduce other writers. He could be roundly condemned without arousing a backlash. Not so with Libedinsky. With the onset of the Cultural Revolution in 1928, the Young Guardists' authority in cultural affairs had gained a dramatic edge. The militant proletarianism that engulfed Soviet society at this time vindicated their long-standing plan, originating among the founding members of *October,* to cleanse the arts and popular literature of all nonproletarian elements. Two years earlier, through unrelenting and particularly coarse attacks in the press against "bourgeois" elements, they had gained effective control of FOSP (Federation of Organizations of Soviet Writers), to which most literary groups belonged, including Pereval, LEF, and the Union of Writers, home to many fellow travelers. In 1927, the final defeat of Trotsky had its literary reverberations when Voronsky was dismissed as editor of *Red Virgin Soil*. At once fellow travelers lost their greatest sponsor and Marxist defender, and the rest found it increasingly difficult to claim ideological legitimacy in an environment defined by a narrowing identification of the party and the proletariat. In 1928, Averbakh, Libedinsky, Fadeev, and others formed the Russian Association of Proletarian Writers (RAPP), with the goal of establishing a "proletarian hegemony" in literature by driving offstage or co-opting many journals and literary groups.

With its obvious lust for power, insistence on ideological conformity, and shrill lambasting of "bourgeois" writers, RAPP guaranteed itself a unique place in history as an object of scorn both from Western and later Soviet critics. Condemnation is still the preferred tone, yet this should not obscure the fact that within this organization could be heard the voices that sought to protect Soviet literature from an onslaught of Kolosovian puppets. In other words, RAPP's political militancy did not always translate into literary uniformity. It was for this reason that in victory, RAPP ensured its own defeat. Not only, as seen from the outside, was its autonomy an increasing impracticality given the rise of centralized power behind Stalin, but also internally, its very methodology—no matter how much framed by a Marxist lens—was predicated on inquiry into the internal contradictions that plagued Soviet society and its members.[67]

Of the myriad literary currents born in the 1920s, RAPP was the last, the most controversial, and the most powerful. In the spring of 1932 it was forcefully disbanded (along with all other literary groups), and two years later, at the first congress of the Writers' Union, socialist realism was officially enshrined as the sole cultural policy of the Soviet Union. Although this chapter in literary history is far more complex than can be addressed here, the salient fact is that the resolution of cultural-political in-fighting at the turn of the decade spelled the end of the sexual revolution in literature. Regarding this change, the fate of Libedinsky's *Birth of a Hero* is most instructive, since its excoriation, in many vital respects, reads as a dress rehearsal for socialist realism.

The principal charge against Libedinsky was that his novel was retrograde, unable to keep pace with the new tempo of Soviet life as exemplified by the industrialization and collectivization campaigns. While the country was moving in one direction, his attention drifted in another, disqualifying any claims of realism. To be sure, Libedinsky argued that despite social advancement real-life prototypes of his characters still existed and should be exposed, and a few supported him. This was the same argument that all writers who addressed negative *byt* had employed in the 1920s; indeed, it was the staple of *The Young Guard*'s mission. Yet now this rationale sounded anachronistic. Verisimilitude and truth, as Ivan Bespalov argued in 1930, were not the same. They could even be opposed. Life always presents the artist with various realities; accuracy or truth is obtained by choosing the right one, the one that depicts "new persons, the seedlings of socialist construction." The proletarian artist, for Bespalov, must do more than reflect the surface of reality, for the proletariat is remaking the world. "This assumes the existence of an ideal, not yet completely manifest, but in accordance with which the proletarian artist evaluates the world." The most Libedinsky and his "living person" approach could achieve was verisimilitude and this is why, Bespalov commented, he "fails to capture reality." Only a select facet of contemporary life, that which contained the "seedlings" of the future, was the true reality. In so many words, Bespalov was repeating the position of orthodox critics before, yet now the jump could be made to the key premise that later would underwrite the principle of socialist realism: portraying reality just in its current manifestation was a contradiction of the truth. "If the contemporary realist stops at the representation of life as it is and does not see what it is becoming," Bespalov concluded, "he unavoidably distorts and betrays reality."[68]

However oxymoronic this assertion, critics used it to attack Libedinsky's vision as mistaken, a charge they could now prove. Like his protagonist Shorokhov, Libedinsky was blind to the simple but stunning fact that "our [Soviet] reality is giving birth to hundreds and thousands of heroes."[69] At the beginning of the 1930s with the first Five-Year plan in full stride, society was making terrific advances in industry and agriculture, offering writers myriad success stories of personal sacrifice and achievement. To neglect them was ignorance at best, treachery at worse. Such triumphalism had been heard before, but in isolated fashion. Now there was a colossal shift in the public press to highlight a positive view of Soviet life, which left little room for the parade of debauchers, syphilitics, rapists, prostitutes, drug abusers, suicides, and home wreckers who had tramped across the previous decade's literature. RAPP was not directly responsible for this impression, but the excesses that emerged under cover of the "living person" paradigm and its near inability to uphold even a minimally uplifting image of Soviet citizens—especially in the party—left them on tenuous ground. Criticism even came from some of Libedinsky's colleagues. Ermilov had to admit that he led readers into a minefield and abandoned them without a map.[70] Workers who spoke out at public meetings were weary of the endless procession of broken lives and sex-obsessed people in literature; such portraits, it was felt, were incompatible with life. Libedinsky, said one group, "did not succeed in showing living people of our time because one can't show an actual, living Bolshevik only in the cross-section of love or family affairs."[71]

Libedinsky's demise began in crude, humiliating spectacle. If only publication of *Birth of a Hero* could have been delayed a few months so as to miss the Sixteenth Party Congress in 1930. The previous congress of 1927 spelled the end of political opposition by Trotsky, Kamenev, and Zinoviev. Now, a near all-embracing orthodoxy was coming into its own, as the heretics of ideology, philosophy, culture, and the arts were paraded before the Soviet people. Each field had its demons to be exorcised: Bukharin, Rykov, and Tomsky in the Politburo itself; kulaks in agriculture; wreckers and saboteurs in industry; Deborin in Marxist philosophy; Pereverzev in literary criticism. Libedinsky took the lead among literary offenders, symbolically dragged on stage by Aleksandr Bezymensky, an original member of the Young Guard and author of its anthem in verse. He was also a member of the Litfront, a splinter group of Octobrists who had been ousted from power by Averbakh, Ermilov, Libedinsky, and others when they took control in the mid-1920s. At the congress Bezymensky had his revenge, using what poetic skills he had to ridicule Libedinsky and defame RAPP. His "speech," delivered in rhyme, reported on the strength of communist character, the "Bolshevik miracles" wrought by the party, and the triumphs of "word workers." After a break for applause, he continued:

> Every day
>   gives birth to heroes
> Of blast furnaces,
>   mines,
>   factories,
>   and farms.
> But a writer,
>   to be sure ours,
> Gives us in "Birth of a Hero"
> Slobbering
>   sentiments
> Over the problems of a woman's charms

From the audience came cries of "That's right!" Yet Bezymensky was not finished.

> And other
>   honest ones have said forthright,
> Speaking of themselves and friends,
> That concentrated
>   s-e-l-f a-n-a-l-y-s-i-s
> Is more valuable
>   to us
> Than devotion to the fight.

Bezymensky finished by quoting passages from Libedinsky's critical articles and laying full blame on him for Soviet literature's stunted growth.[72]

Litfront plastered RAPP and *Birth of a Hero*, and though it too would soon be extinct, its criticism that psychologism and the "living person" had

imperiled Soviet literature never ceased to carry weight. Bezymensky's claim
that life itself was generating Soviet heroes forecast a decisive turn: literature
should solidly affirm what should be. *Pravda* took the lead by suggesting that
writers could not do the work alone. Its headline for May 18, 1931, "The
Country Must Know Its Heroes," launched a campaign that represented a
crucial reversal of previous practice. If in the 1920s fiction like Kolosov's had
been used to compensate for a disappointing reality, now the opposite was
true. Reality had surpassed the powers of fiction to infuse Soviet citizens with
spirit and hope, and the party's central organ was going to prove it. In this and
successive issues of *Pravda* came a flood of short profiles of exemplary workers. Their biographies revealed no internal conflicts, no vacillation, no love,
no emotions, no mention of families or related personal problems. As with
"Comrade Sarkin," these heroes seemed to have no life outside their work:

> AWARDED THE ORDER OF LENIN, Comrade M. G. Sarkin was born in
> 1883. He began working in industry in 1898. He has a thirty-year experi-
> ence in optics. In 1915 Comrade Sarkin became a mechanic at an optics
> factory. In 1919 he became a foreman and then leader of the GOZ sec-
> tion.
>   Com. Sarkin was the first in the Soviet Union to organize at the fac-
> tory a series of complex production procedures which freed the USSR
> from foreign dependence. All of his inventions and rationalized method-
> ologies brought the factory significant economic benefit.
>   Despite his grave illness, Comrade Sarkin, sparing neither strength
> nor time, systematically worked on the improvement of productivity and
> ABLY RUNNING HIS SECTION NOT ONLY FULFILLS BUT ALWAYS OVERFUL-
> FILLS THE PLAN. He is also an active participant in factory meetings and
> in the political life of the factory.[73]

Pravda offered workers like Sarkin as "positive examples" for all to follow
and poignantly contrasted their inspiring accomplishments with the media's
propensity to focus on the negative. "Our progress often remains in the shadows. We are efficient at criticizing the remnants of bureaucracy, backwardness, and Oblomovism, but still are not able to show with what heroism the
proletariat is building a socialist economy." *Pravda*, like other major print organs, undertook the task of shaping official reality by showing what was ostensibly happening in real life. "The firm decision of the party and state to
honor the best inventors, shock workers, technicians, etc., has not been reflected in our press in sufficient measure so as to lead millions to new, still
greater victories. And this is because until now the press has not shown heroes
as they should be." Attuned to the prolonged debates over realism, *Pravda*

staked its ground in the middle, eschewing the overly personalized portraits characteristic of RAPP's doctrine and the always discredited *plakat*. "Without falling into individualism, these shock workers should be shown as part of the working class. This task should be undertaken avoiding varnish, aestheticism, and excess but at the same time they should not remain faceless."[74]

This was a campaign with which no one dared to disagree, and RAPP immediately aligned itself with the slogan by claiming that its goal had always been to depict real heroes. But it could not countenance the poster heroes that *Pravda* and soon others were passing off as realistic. Though chastened, Libedinsky again stepped forth and, now believing himself in line with these new tenets, justified the proper approach as portraying the formation of the hero—in short, the path taken by Shorokhov. "The shock worker should be shown in all the complexity of the class struggle which is going on in the Soviet Union, in all its diverse colors. And such things should not be shown through the method of the naturalist. One should not show them following the sole assumption: I want to depict reality and so for that I will only employ positive facts."[75] Still upholding its members' preference for complex characters, RAPP even published a series of parodies in *The Literary Guardian*, complete with recipes for "hero portrayal."[76] It was a brave attempt to graft its method onto a new official line, and it sounded the death knell for the organization.

With the "heroes" campaign, the essential props for the establishment of socialist realism fell into place. The battle over what constituted "Bolshevik" reality—that is, the only one that was accepted as the truth—had been won. Real life in the Soviet Union was heroic, earth-shattering, and unprecedented, and it was here for all to see. In one fell swoop the rug was pulled out from under the Young Guardists, who for years had successfully parried orthodox critics by declaring that Kolosov-like characters were pure fantasy if compared with how people actually lived and behaved. Now the reverse was true. By 1931, in the Soviet Union at least, the present and the heroic age had miraculously merged, giving artists a new world to portray.[77] Before they had always faced a dilemma: be a Homer and produce heroes that exist only in myth; be a realist and produce only tragic characters. Socialist realism was to be the synthesis of thesis and antithesis in portraiture. If one is "true to life," argued E. Dobin, "then the picture that obtains is heroic for such are the qualities of the avant garde of the working class building socialism."[78] It was a closed, tight circle that could be refuted only if one were to claim, which by then no one would dare to do publicly, that the Soviet press was printing lies. And on this basis the whole gamut of artistic sins—cliché, schematism, *plakat*— could be dumped permanently on the advocates of psychologism, for who, if not they, was now trafficking in make-believe?

The case in point was Libedinsky's Shorokhov who was allegedly not accepted by workers and party members as one of their own. With this logic the socialist realist mindset, its language, its principles, and its program, were secure. *Pravda* laid out the guidelines for how protagonists should be depicted, flattening and narrowing the range of acceptable behavior to a fixed set. All that was a "problem" before—irresolution, the question of role models, the polemics over the personal and sexual—was brought to an end. Realism was to be inherently optimistic but at the same time "typical." A narrative did not have to end happily—after all, martyrs for the cause were always useful—but a story should provide a satisfactory closure. The role of the writer was to transmit, not challenge, accepted truths; literature was no longer to be a forum of debate, but a site of confirmation and demonstration.

The canonization of a new reality and new literature was as much a fact of exclusion as affirmation. Socialist realism emerged by the process of negative example, purging the cultural environment of all the detritus, debris, and delusions flung up by the initial chaos of revolution and nurtured by much of the literature of the 1920s. *Birth of a Hero* served admirably in this role, for its story, its characters, its motivating philosophy became a border delineating the permissible and the forbidden. Its deficiencies demonstrated what needed to be expunged from literature: pessimism, passivity, psychologism, ignorance of the collective, absence of a Marxist approach, dysfunctional families, pornography, the demon theories of Freud, Deborin, Voronsky, and Bergson, and the demon ideologies of menshevism, idealism, formalism, and Trotskyism.[79] Until the appearance of Libedinsky's novel, polemics over the "living person" and psychologism had been more theoretical in nature. Now orthodox critics and the party had prima facie evidence. *Birth of Hero*, in short, provided irrefutable proof of the failure and danger of the "living person."

The Debate Ends

Sexuality as a primary theme of literature virtually disappeared after 1930. The attack on Romanov closed the door on those "outside" writers (non-Marxist, fellow travelers) who had taken advantage of an open environment to produce provocative works. The attack on Libedinsky slammed it shut. After 1930 there was really no way, epistemologically or aesthetically, to justify what had been a legitimate topic of literature just a few years before. Capitulation came quickly. In 1931, Libedinsky published in *Pravda* an uplifting story about a hard-working young man.[80] The next year, after the forced disbanding of RAPP, Averbakh, Ermilov, Libedinsky, and Gladkov lined up at the organizational meeting of the new writers' union to admit their mistakes and pledge allegiance to socialist realism, still a floating term defined more by what it was not than by what it was. Ermilov, displaying the chameleon skin that protected his career as an establishment critic for decades to come, bowed his head lowest. "It's as if the party has opened our eyes, showing us all the riches of Soviet literature, and like a wise master tells us," he stated; "people of the party who shut themselves up in little groups, you only see a part of what is happening in the country's literary economy. It's bigger, richer, more diverse and luxuriant than you think."[81] Romanov too was present, and his turnabout was no less surprising. Visiting factories and the like had purged him of his desire to be an outsider, a "hermit," he said. He no longer wanted to be a fellow traveler, but one of the group, primary and central, building communism.[82]

Sexual relations would always remain a topic of fiction under Stalin. Contrary to a common assumption, libido was not denied or dismissed as a "bourgeois remnant." Most realized that the heroes paraded before the country in 1931 were too stale, too skeletal to serve as a true model for any literature, regardless of its political motives. Consequently, even with the onset of socialist realism an author could create characters who were sexually alive, with this crucial qualification: sexuality was not to be presented as a problem, a source of anxiety or trouble in and of itself. Under socialist realism, sexual and emotional intimacy were to be seen as part of normal human experience, but not inflated in importance as they had been in the previous decade. There was always room for anomalies, such as Andrei Platonov's "Potudan River," showing that guidelines for what was permissible were never absolute. The change was already evident in the genre of industrial novels that captured the literary imagination in the early 1930s, providing a bridge from the cultural revolution to socialist realism in fiction. Vasily Ilenkov's *Driving Axle* (1931) makes references to adultery and workers' wives who complain that their husbands work too much, but these are minor elements in the novel. In *Time, Forward!* (1933), Valentin Kataev reveals that his hero, Margulies, has a love interest only at the end, after a world record has been set in pouring cement.

The most risqué of the genre was *Energy* (1932), by Fedor Gladkov, author of the notorious 1927 novella, *Drunken Sun.* Critics rebuked him for nonstandard language, an occasional accent on nudity, and a protagonist, Miron, given to objectifying women sexually. But even on these points, *Energy* was qualitatively different from literature of but a few years before. Sexuality is no longer threatening; indeed, it is sometimes painted in a healthy, positive light. There is no conflict between Don Juans or femmes fatale; Miron is not Khorokhorin the conqueror. His kiss of a woman's hand generates the kind of lines that stick in our memories as classic examples of Soviet prudery: "Licking someone's hand is gross and unhygienic," he is told. "You don't respect yourself enough and particularly women as comrades."[83] Few would deny that Gladkov had hoisted himself from the muck of *Drunken Sun,* and the rush of critical accolades, including praise for the accuracy of his new work and its depiction of the "birth of the new person," made it clear that critics found this novel to be miles away from all the "dog alleys that we remember appearing in such numbers a few years ago."[84]

By now the stage was more or less set for the crowning statement of Bolshevik asceticism. In the 1934 classic of socialist realism, Nikolai Ostrovsky's *How the Steel Was Tempered* (1934),[85] the new communist Pavel Korchagin brushes off the usual dilemma posed by a concerned parent with lapidary words of wisdom: "Mama, I've sworn to myself not to chase girls until we've knocked off the bourgeoisie in the whole world." His advice did not dovetail with how Soviets in real life and fiction truly behaved, but the essence of his statement lay elsewhere. No longer would the media besiege readers with articles on "the problem of sex" or "the accursed question." Pavel's conclusion and the commensurate change in Soviet literature were as things should be.

That sex disappeared as an issue should not strike us as unexpected; if anything, the opposite, a continuation of dialogue and debate, is what would have been truly surprising. There is a reason why sexual revolutions tend to occur in times of political and social breakdown and why conflict and questioning of standards tend to dissipate once the initial upheaval runs its course. The revolution of 1917, as with so many others, gave birth to multiple interpretations. It was a divided cause from the beginning, a mix of interests that could unite along a broad front, as during the fight for survival during the civil war, but that would split and collide with astonishing speed when confronted with lesser issues. The revolution spoke in many tongues. Some were louder, more authoritative than others, but together they constituted a tower of Babel. The variety of Marxist approaches that treated the issue of sex, whether in literary or other formats, was daunting. Each was marked by confidence and often self-righteousness, but together all show that there was no cohesive understanding in this regard. In the 1920s, there was consensus in the most general sense but divergence in specifics. There was no fixed norm or single party line against which heresies and schismatics could easily be identified. This was to be the achievement of Stalinist culture.[86]

Marxist revolution came to Russia in many colors, and this diversity was what had to go. The situation was not unlike that of early Christianity before the consolidation of the church proper in the third and fourth centuries. There were gospels and other authoritative texts to which all could have recourse, but there were also apocrypha, sacred to some, anathema to others. In the absence of a uniform doctrine, contradictory messages could all claim to be loyal to the fundamental cause. However rough this analogy, it is not without precedent. In 1883, in a veiled lament over the state of the political left,

Engels compared contemporary socialism with early Christianity. Both "swept through the masses in the form of different sects and, for the most part, in the guise of mutually contradictory individual views." Somewhat presciently, he observed that such differences were also reflected in sects' respective sexual attitudes, ranging from the promiscuous to the celibate. This led Engels to note the "curious fact [that] in every major revolutionary movement, the question of 'free love' comes to the fore," since some consider this to constitute "revolutionary progress."[87]

The Bolshevik Revolution would see this prediction come true. It gave birth to sectarianism that for some could not be divorced from the question of sexual behavior—not strictly because it was sex, but because sex represented an emblem, however variously defined, of liberation and emancipation for the individual. And just as early Christianity would not have survived without the canonization of a single orthodoxy, so too with the Soviet Union. The funneling of diverse voices into a more homogenous one was a predictable and necessary stage, whether the commanding voice was to be that of Trotsky, Bukharin, or Stalin. In this, the fate of the sexual revolution was no different from that of other cultural issues. It fell victim to a natural process; the reduction of revolutionary zeal to a single line. As others have argued, this diminution was likely fueled by pressure from below, as many grew tired of experiment and perceived excesses, even if practiced by a distinct minority.[88] The disappearance of sex as an issue, like the dissolution of RAPP and the emergence of socialist realism, signaled that the 1920s, and the revolution as a whole, were over.

The response to this change in climate was not to eliminate sex per se from fiction (there were no true Paulinists in Stalinist culture) but to dim the spotlight on the subject. Many were made uneasy by so much attention to an area of experience that seemed undignified, unworthy of inclusion in the canon. Moreover, sexuality could be threatening, both personally and ideologically. A fundamental characteristic of fiction about sex was that it foregrounded the subjective individual, that it highlighted inquiry and speculation. This emphasis, along with the conscious choice not to show the best and the brightest, made it incompatible with Stalinist culture. That is why the sexual revolution in literature was doomed to defeat, and those who might have expected another outcome—that somehow the Soviet Union should have evolved into a society hosting enlightened discussions of sexuality—are thinking backwards, assuming that today's standards of openness were available seventy years ago. The recriminalization of abortion in the 1930s, for example, did nothing more than realign the Soviet Union with other Western countries. This is not to condone what happened under Stalin, but to suggest that some of the changes that occurred between the 1920s and

1930s were part of a normal cultural process. To condemn the Soviet Union for not instituting a more tolerant view of sexual behavior in the decade, to ridicule its officials for obscurantism, is empty criticism. For what country could at that time, irrespective of political system, make such a claim? When dealing with the topic of sex, the Soviet Union's preferred language was that of Marxism; the West's, primarily that of a Judeo-Christian heritage. Yet both attitudes, morally and medically speaking, were essentially cut from the same cloth. If anything, it was the Soviet Union, at least in the 1920s, where sexuality as a driving force in human life was spoken of more frequently, more openly, and—if it can be said—more accurately.

CHAPTER 9

Conclusion

TRAGEDY is not without its comedy. In 1932, as the sexual revolution was being erased from the menu of acceptable topics, the inveterate parodists, Ilya Ilf and Evgeny Petrov, penned a brief lament over the impending wave of neo-Victorianism that threatened to engulf Soviet arts.

> A strange conversation took place in one of the paneled rooms of Publigov.
>
> EDITOR: Dear Konstantin Pavlovich, I looked at your poster. . . . Just a minute. I'll lock the door so no one can hear us.
>
> ARTIST: *(Smiles grimly.)*
>
> EDITOR : Konstantin Pavlovich, you know I didn't expect this from you. What have you drawn? Look for yourself!
>
> ARTIST : What's the problem? Everything matches the theme "Communal Dining Is the Way." A young waitress is serving dinner in the factory cafeteria. Maybe I messed up the lines? *(He hurriedly declaims.)* "At home there's garbage, dirt, and fleas—here there's borsch and cheese. At home the stove, scraps, and smell—here the cheese is swell."
>
> EDITOR : No, no . . . everything there's fine. But what would you call this?
>
> ARTIST : A waitress.
>
> EDITOR : No! This, this right here! *(He points with his finger.)*
>
> ARTIST : A blouse.
>
> EDITOR : *(Checking to make sure the door is shut.)* Don't play around. Tell me, what's under the blouse?

ARTIST : A chest.

EDITOR : So you see it too. Good, because I noticed it immediately. That chest has to go.

ARTIST : I don't understand. Why?

EDITOR : *(Embarrassed.)* It's too big. I'd even say huge, comrade, huge.[1]

With its humorous references to enforced ideological correctness and its title hinting at Savonarola, "Savonaronosey" slaps at editorial buffoons and their cowardly, ignorant mangling of culture. The official crusade to straighten out and clean up the arts soon extends to film and stage performances, where women are desexed or otherwise masculinized. It is a ramshackle invasion, utterly lacking in serious moral justification, smacking only of monkish prudery in its most obscurantist and intrusive vein.

While written in jest, the feuilleton was also a symbolic echo of what many literary artists had faced in the previous decade: unmerited attacks on their work as slander. Ilf and Petrov mocked official attempts to sterilize Soviet culture by painting such efforts in the worst and most stereotypical colors. "Savonaronosey" was part of a series of such parodies, all targeting the "heroes" campaign and the insufferable ways in which writers were pressured to produce them. How could such irreverence be tolerated? After all, the feuilleton was published in a leading organ, *The Literary Gazette*, months after the disbanding of RAPP and at a time when the new face of Soviet literature was becoming clear for all to see. None of this would seem to make sense, given what we might assume to be the conditions in a controlled environment. Five years earlier, one could have expected such daring; Ippolit and Kin had already demonstrated that. But how can we reconcile this with our usual understanding of Soviet literature in 1932?

The publication of Ilf and Petrov's feuilleton is but one episode that points to the unpredictability of the cultural environment in the early Soviet Union, especially on sensitive topics such as sexuality. Consider the plethora of consciously ambiguous texts like Gladkov's *Drunken Sun* or Erenburg's *In Protochny Alley*; the abomination of Kallinikov's *Relics* or Barsukov's *Mavritania*; the whole uproar in 1926 over fiction by Gumilevsky, Malashkin, and Romanov (which often exceeds credulity); incisive studies of youth like Rubinshtein's, devoid of any ideological coloring; the bare-all revelations of Ketlinskaia, Slepkov, Ilinsky, and others; the fantastic dreams of salvation through nudism; youth's demonstrative voice of protest, their active participation in debates; the Young Guardists' determined challenge behind the scenes and in the public view to push through texts and positions that clashed with established ones; indeed, the inability of the party to speak in one voice, open for all to hear, whether on cultural, sociological, or biological matters.

None of this makes sense if we view the environment through the traditional lens where Kremlin proclamations would deny such diversity, where our assumptions of party control would suppress it, and where censorship would shut it down. Harriet Borland's statement a half century ago that "under the First Five-Year Plan, Glavlit . . . saw that no ideas which were out of line with Party policies reached the masses," and Ermolaev's recent confirmation that at this time there was "no tolerance for works inimical to the Marxist concept of communism" bookend a standing belief that precludes anything of the above nature from entering into our understanding of cultural praxis in the revolutionary environment.[2]

Any surprise then we might feel when encountering what actually circulated in the 1920s is a factor of our own distance from those events, one made extreme by our reluctance to examine what lies behind the canon, by the encrustation of presumptions that do not admit, accept, or acknowledge anomalies. As Arlen Blium confirms in his 1994 study of Soviet censorship in the decade after revolution, since its inception Glavlit exerted "total control" over literature—so much so that his descriptions of Soviet practices are framed throughout with pointed references to Orwell's Ministry of Truth.[3] The resulting portrait again brings to life the classic totalitarian model of power in which the party was everywhere, its finger on every pulse, its viselike grip on every throat. True public expression was an illusion, and literature was merely the puppet of the state. Average citizens had little if any real agency. They were essentially voiceless before the power of the state, its police organs ready to destroy anyone who spoke up, its propaganda machines driving citizens into a pit of falsehood and deception. According to this scenario, first Lenin, then Stalin, was the master manipulator, and behind them at every step was the ever compliant party.

Today only a shrinking number still uphold this view. The tendency now has been to engage Soviet culture in its greatest breadth, to uncover forgotten corners, blights, and disturbances. Ideological change and theoretical innovation have simultaneously paved the way. The empirical density of what we now know about the period has been bolstered exponentially by greater access to resources in the former Soviet Union. The initial, pre-glasnost push to dethrone the totalitarian paradigm has now come fully into its own as the end of the Cold War has presumably freed us from deep-seated prejudices and surely eliminated the need for critical studies to pursue, acknowledged or not, the political agenda of confirming the abject nature of Soviet cultural practices. For history, this has proven most innovative in the study of Stalinism, particularly in exploring the lived experience of average citizens.[4] More strikingly, poststructuralist theories and the embrace of interdisciplinary approaches have allowed for provocative juxtapositions of material previously seen as inhabiting separate realms. Historical and literary texts are no longer seen as pure entities, once arrayed for or against the party, but are situated, rightfully, in a web of other discursive orientations. For the study of literature, as demonstrated in the work of Katerina Clark, Thomas Lahusen, and Evgeny Dobrenko, this has spelled the end of the party-versus-writer model, the preferred terms being that of negotiation, dialogue, and internalization.[5]

Formally acknowledged or not, the work of Michel Foucault has encouraged us to focus attention on factors that lie beyond the state's visible sources of control and coercion—the police and censors that have usually been the objects of study in the Soviet context. The traditional image of power, which Foucault terms "juridico-discursive," represents a force of restriction and repression that we see operative with Blium's portrayal of censorship (where power equals the opposite of truth). Its defining features are that of "limit and lack"; its relationship to sex, for instance, is solely negative, constituting "rejection, exclusion, refusal, blockage, concealment or mask." "Where sex and pleasure are concerned," Foucault continues, "[juridico-discursive] power can 'do' nothing but say no to them. . . . [It] employs nothing more than a law of prohibition. Its objective: that sex renounce itself. Its instrument: the threat of a punishment that is nothing other than the suppression of sex. Renounce yourself or suffer the penalty of being suppressed."[6] For Foucault, however, in his example of nineteenth-century Western society, the opposite was true. There was a manifest "incitement to discourse" that made sexuality more visible than ever before, but this visibility was channeled through the interests of the state (as with the legalization and thus regulation of prostitution). Sexual behavior was also regulated by the medical profession and the emerging field of psychology, with their common obsession with perversions, bodily hygiene and health, and the welfare of society. The sexuality that was "created" as a result of these forces is simultaneously controlling and controlled; it demands categorization and cataloguing and thus legitimates inspection and intervention. Power produces discourses of sexuality that speak through the individual subject and in the process construct it. Thus in addressing sexuality, whether as a topic of judicial, social, biological, or cultural concern, a person or an institution unwittingly reifies and empowers the mechanisms of control—even if the purpose is to protest.

By turning the power paradigm inside out, Foucault and related schools allow for a more comprehensive understanding of how individuals can participate in their own subjugation. Power's interests are upheld within and by the social body. Power is not imposed from above, as traditionally understood, but structures relations as those relations construct themselves. As Dobrenko demonstrates, this model helps explain why Soviet writers willingly (or naturally) produced literary works that supported the precepts of the state. The doctrine of socialist realism did not necessarily force them to create fantastic portraits of life; censorship, or the threat thereof, was not at issue for the majority of writers by the 1930s. They matured in an environment in which, despite intense theoretical disagreements among literary schools, the substance of their rhetoric was more similar than anyone recognized at the time or even today. With limited exceptions, the role of the literary artist was defined in terms of utility, accessibility, and the necessity of providing closure; real differences were primarily a question of methods and limits. Bolstering his analysis with portraits of many now unknown writers, Dobrenko shows how the average Soviet author internalized these precepts; they became an "organic" part of his or her artistic profile. Therefore, becoming a true Soviet writer was predicated on these conditions—a process we can see even in the case of Gumilevsky, no matter how his contemporaries reacted to his fiction. In the 1920s, the discourse of realism embodied two competing orientations defined by the same goal: edification. By the beginning of the next decade, it essentially reflected only one. Once the controversies of the 1920s dissipated, the typical writer had no need for a censor; the official horizon of experience became one with its artistic representation. Just as with critics like Troshchenko, Mark Kolosov's fictional world constituted the "real" Soviet Union.

The Foucault model has undeniably opened up rich perspectives for investigation. At the same time, however, it can compromise its utility by limiting the use we are allowed to make of them by a priori defining and thereby restricting their potential meaning. This is a criticism that has long followed Foucault himself. In Edward Said's words, his "theoretical overtotalization" exhibits a "disturbing circularity."[7] Others have noted that the tendency to view power as an all-consuming monolithic force actually reduces its value as a critical tool. It becomes "universal, essential, eternal" and thus functions as little more than "a kind of transhistorical *episteme*."[8] Dobrenko avoids this tendency by recognizing that such discursive constraints on writing did not impact all artists in the postrevolutionary environment. He focuses on how a self-censoring mechanism emerged among mainstream Soviet authors, but without implying that there were no exceptions to this phenomenon. His complex picture of Soviet literary culture of the 1920s demonstrates why the emergence of socialist realism was neither an anomaly nor an abrupt imposition from above, and why it was not, as commonly assumed, an abomination in the eyes of many writers, critics, and consumers. Socialist realism smoothed the "sharp corners" of revolutionary culture that either displeased average readers (whose tastes were often ignored by avant-garde experimental writers), threatened the state (as when literary groups like RAPP assumed too much authority), or discouraged writers themselves (when subjected to the vitriol of self-appointed guardians of proletarian hegemony).[9]

Such subtle complexities call into question Eric Naiman's use of Foucault's theories to describe the atmosphere surrounding the issue of sexuality in the 1920s, particularly with regard to literary production and reception. According to Naiman's *Sex in Public: The Incarnation of Early Soviet Ideology* (1997), in Bolshevik culture the significance of sexual question was exaggerated in order to mask and justify the intervention of the party into private citizens' lives. Making sex a public issue served a purpose. To speak or write on sex, to think of oneself in sexual terms, was allowed through a Bolshevik discursive filter that was inherently puritanical, tyrannical, and devoted to reducing individual autonomy. Inciting public discussion of sexuality made participants visible before the party and thus subject to its purview. They were, to borrow Foucault's memorable words, "always-already trapped," which is why the party, the Komsomol, and its press organs devoted so much attention to the subject. With no voice able to be heard outside of this discursive web, the success of this campaign was guaranteed. The more sex was made "public," the more people were victimized. Naiman's theory is not flattering to readers, who have little role to play except as dupes, drooling like Pavlov's dogs when the bait of sex is dangled before them.[10] For authors, the picture is only slightly better. While Naiman avoids the state-versus-writer standard, his sweeping discursive brush turns them into unconscious tools of the state. If they published on the subject of sex—no matter if out of genuine concern, for publicity, or for money—they willy-nilly drove the process in that their work was seized by critics and editors who sensationalized it, whetting appetites even more. As for editors, their motive was not, he emphasizes, "to *sell* as many copies as possible." Instead, it was "to attract as wide a readership as possible into the net of Party propaganda," with *The Young Guard* playing a notable role in this "enterprise of seduction" by devoting its pages to the most provocative items. Finally, to ensure obedience to the master plan, key words, slogans, and images were "beaten into the heads of the masses."

The undeniable benefit of the Foucault model for the early Soviet Union lies in its reach. In rendering social intercourse as a closed, controlled circle, it conflates a complex cultural praxis to an easily navigable circuit. Yet the importation of this model wholesale to the Soviet context gives rise to an unintended by-product. Quality of speech in the 1920s becomes irrelevant; only its quantity matters, since even protest, complaint, or exposé are co-opted and transposed to serve the state's interests by justifying further intervention. The resulting picture essentially eliminates ambiguity; genuine chaos becomes a theoretical impossibility, unable to exist in its own right, since all voices operate with their value prefixed. Power, always in the seductive singular, compels us to script their roles. It ascribes to party members a unified plan; it automatically homogenizes readers, and by necessity makes all public forums, especially journals, purposeful agents of entrapment. In short, it makes the conspiracy scenario almost a foregone conclusion.

At the beginning of *Sex in Public* Naiman does admit that within the "process of ideological entrapment . . . the Party and the Komsomol were never in total control." Similarly, in applying Foucault to the same historical context, Christopher Read asserts in *Culture and Power in Revolutionary Russia* (1990) that there was an "extraordinary vacuum at the centre of cultural policy. Nobody in charge of it had much idea of what it was for and continued to discuss it in agitprop terms and through the wielding of rather crude class slogans."[11] However, neither Naiman nor Read fully explores the ramifications of these disclaimers. Recognition of multiplicity is displaced by a theoretical position that cannot admit the same. What we witness in their attempts to contain unpredictability and anomaly within presumptions of near total control by power echelons is a fundamental tension between the theoretical demand that cultural praxis evince a single direction and recognition of elements that compromise such univocality. When Naiman discusses conflict, it is not one of competing discourses but usually the political infighting at the very top—as, for example, in his reading of the aftermath of the Chubarov rape against the background of Zinoviev's and Kamenev's struggle with Stalin. For Read, the same tension leads to a problematic backstep. We are asked to accept that there was a vacuum and, elsewhere, that there wasn't:

> The influence of central control in the early 1920s has been much underestimated. The assumption that there was a loose form of toleration and drift in cultural policy, even a vacuum, until the mid to late 1920s is quite wrong. The essential difference between the civil war and NEP periods in culture is not one of attack followed by relaxation; it is rather the replacement of arbitrariness by greater organization.[12]

Read continues to assert that central organization became so overwhelming that even in the 1920s "party hegemony (though far from complete) had spread to such an extent that the fledgling civil society of post-revolutionary Russia had been effectively eliminated." So great was official intervention that while Read acknowledges differences between the 1920s and 1930s, ultimately for him "this is not saying much."

Ironically, the first substantive use of Foucault to address sexuality in Russia questioned his applicability. In *The Keys to Happiness: Sex and the Search for Modernity in Fin-de-Siècle Russia* (1992) and in a follow-up article, Laura Engelstein underscores the problematics of transferring a model derived from relatively stable Western democracies to the peculiar exigencies of the late imperial–early Soviet context.[13] With Naiman's and Read's attempts to wrestle choreographed control out of confusion, we can see the prescience of Engelstein's warning. Through Foucault, Naiman and Read must privilege the absolute reach of power; however, because they are dealing with an emerging police state, they must map the exercise of power in a strict hierarchical format. The result is a hybrid image of power endowed with specific agency and intention, which necessarily contradicts one of Foucault's central tenets. Foucault stipulates that power remains the "great anonymous"; unlike Machiavelli, he would "do without the persona of a prince," concentrating instead on the relations of power embedded throughout society. The invisible ubiquity of power assumes the absence of a central director and a central direction for its expression (except, perhaps, for its own expansion). For this reason, no matter how much Foucault's own vocabulary highlights the "strategy," "machinery," "intentions," and "calculation" of power, by insisting on its "non-subjectivity" he avoids leaving the impression of a specific, behind-the-scenes institution that manipulates discourse. This absence, it seems, is precisely what the early Soviet context tempts us to restore. If the question at hand is how discourse is constituted and deployed, then the party is an entity of almost irresistible explanatory appeal. In its name, power and subjectivity are reunited, for who would gainsay its desire to dictate, subjugate, and control? Its seeming omnipresence almost compels us to return to "the prince" and identify a sentient, coherent, all-enabling center of power.

For purposes here, sins against Foucault do not matter. The distortion of his paradigm when applied to the early Soviet Union is almost unavoidable. Rather, the resurrection of the party in hybrid fashion reveals how new theory, unwittingly, can sometimes serve old politics. Hence, while Naiman expressly claims to have freed himself from "old [ideological] glasses," his view of Soviet society as tyrannized by a Bolshevik discursive net arguably operates in concert with—though obviously not equal to—the more traditional one that has ostensibly passed its prime. Both assume that Soviet society in the 1920s was held hostage by a near-omnipotent center. If Igor Kon, representing the traditional approach, argues that "repressive sexophobia was an instrument of totalitarian control," now we have irrefutable proof of express sexophilia, yet this view is pressed into substantiating a similar image of the state. In fact, when transferred to this environment, Foucault's model inevitably runs the risk of creating an extremely inflated image of party power. It adds to the verticality of power traditionally associated with the police state a supreme horizontal reach that ensnares the rest of society. Mutatis mutandis, the Leviathan is brought back to life but in a form more potent, controlling, and oppressive than ever before imagined. Instead of merely constricting speech, for Naiman the state exercised in the 1920s a "discursive terror" that was a prelude to the more bloody one of the 1930s."[14]

At issue is not whether the Soviet state employed disciplinary power to control the individual through its discourses; one would be hard pressed to refute this. Instead, the question that arises is the scope, the unanimity, the success, and the ascribing of intention in this plan—the implication that social and cultural institutions, their representative press organs, and literary critics all worked deceptively in concert toward a single goal. In attempting to contain the political and ideological ruptures of the 1920s, the Bolsheviks were not necessarily as cunning or effective in their means of control as we might expect. Coordination and conspiracy are not the first words to come to mind if one examines the whole of Soviet discourses on sexuality, from the party to medicine, social analyses, and literature. Instead, the picture is more one of rancor, vacillation, incongruity, disagreement, uncertainty, and self-inflicted infirmity. If Naiman's assumption of a "discursive terror" in the 1920s is accurate, one would expect this hypothesis to be strengthened as more archival and empirical data is uncovered.

Arguably, however, the opposite is true. Not only did the Komsomol often act at odds with the party, but also both entities were fractured within themselves. The Young Guardists' constant and divisive intervention, indeed the whole authentic debate over realism conducted on the back of *byt* literature, only confirms the profound fault lines that ran throughout institutions in the 1920s. The behind-the-scenes exchange at the Komsomol's flagship journal—which we cannot dismiss as a ruse since most of the internal correspondence was "top secret"—hints that the motivation for publishing provocative works had less to do with a "scripted entrapment" and everything to do with capitalist principles of raising revenue and circulation. Similarly, the quantitative breadth and qualitative depth of literature on sexuality published then suggest that the party did not have the power over the printed word it believed it should have or that we might ascribe to it. In word or proclamation, it seemed all-powerful; in action decidedly less so. Why was this the case? As was admitted then, there neither was a central plan nor, despite censorship, the means to implement it.[15] Although it is tempting to assume the presence of a unified strategy for controlling what appeared in print, only in the broadest sense can we speak of a singleness of purpose and intention within "institutions of power." All Bolsheviks could unite around the platitudes extolling a strong state, healthy and loyal citizens, economic productivity, an orderly society, and so forth. Yet once we move from handsome slogans to the nuts and bolts of everyday experience, it is exceedingly difficult to see the Komsomol or the party organization in terms of univocality. Private conceptions, public assumptions, and party intentions were often one great mess.

In this book I have sought to stress the more muddled features of the 1920s in order to counterbalance the smoothness of the picture that obtains if we concentrate solely on one discourse of the most controlling, oppressive, and insatiable kind. Such a focus belies the gulf between intentions and actual results. Sometimes tension and controversy are just that—particularly in the aftermath of the most destructive social revolution the world had yet seen. This is not to say that such control could never be the case. Katherine Binhammer points out that in the revolutionary context of the 1790s, concerns over sexuality could be incited and manipulated into a crisis by entrenched powers in order to enforce certain political objectives.[16] But this is why in the Soviet context we should give equal weight to less official voices, whether from within the party or from outside, as with the views of countless unnamed youths. It is one thing to argue for the existence of a ruling order that deliberately incites a phenomenon, and another to describe power echelons as trying to contain a phenomenon that erupts for reasons not entirely accountable within an overall strategy.

The lure of the party so defined—possessed of one mind and endowed with nearly unchecked power—may reflect more than the pull of internalized tradition. Such an image of the party in the 1920s offers unquestionable heuristic value, since it provides a sort of base line from which to situate and hierarchize the plethora of voices and positions. Yet whatever we might gain by naming the "great anonymous" we risk losing in the very clarity of the picture that emerges. Upholding the party as a homogenous, unidirectional institution discourages consideration of how schemes issuing from the center failed, how officials repeatedly stumbled over themselves, or how writers and readers were often anything but compliant. Lost as a result is an empirical sense of how the party's plans, consciously drafted or not, might have been thwarted or compromised. The paradigm of party-equals-power as now given does not account for a post–1917 environment that, alongside a push for centralized control, also gave free rein to widespread iconoclastic and libertarian discourses. Thus little is made of the fact that youth were genuinely interested in sex and, in this revolutionary and therefore liberating climate, now believed that they could ask questions that previous societies, in their view, had long denied, papered over, or otherwise diverted. Their voices, seconded and sometimes encouraged by elements in the Komsomol and party itself, suggest that a real crisis was brewing in the 1920s, as the revolutionary spirit threatened to disintegrate into fragments of competing interpretations and definitions of freedom. To be sure, there were attempts to orchestrate opinions and official responses; as Naiman demonstrates, the Chubarov affair stands as a salient example. Yet this was a specific intervention that does not represent the larger picture. It should be situated against the entire background of what occurred. Also, there was an overall desire to rein in the behavior of youth. This was simple damage control and was to be expected. Regardless, however, such impulses by authorities rarely translated into clean, effective, top-down manipulation. After all, if the party was so powerful at that time, why, in the end, did it have to resort to old-fashioned, "juridico-discursive" taboo and proscription to solve the "problem" of sex in literature?

The risk in upholding the party as the exclusive agent of power is that we can fall prey to the Bolsheviks' own rhetoric and assume that discussions of sexuality could be initiated by or enabled only under the aegis of the party. No doubt many Bolsheviks would have wished for such control, but it would be premature to grant them this in the 1920s. Ermolaev's and Blium's conception of the devastating impact of censorship on literature in the 1920s relies more on assumptions about what censors were officially authorized to do than what actually occurred. Symptomatically, Ermolaev's attention is drawn more to later emendations of provocative or questionable works of fiction, not acknowledging the critical fact that, for all the censor's power in theory, these works did appear. This happens in part because in studying a political environment in which central control was regarded as indispensable, we may internalize the ethos and mentality of the time. That we must refer to the party in the singular, that we usually capitalize it, only enforces the image of a united, all-powerful body. If we concentrate primarily on the party, if we bury ourselves in its proclamations, assuming that its discourses dictated actual outcomes, if we accept its words as the equivalent of deeds, if we begin to catalogue people and events along the spectrum of Marxist ideology, we may replicate the same categories of signification. As theorists, Bolsheviks were quite adept at carving the world into either-or, for-or-against dichotomies, and they are today routinely condemned for this habit of thought. Yet in a curious twist we often follow suit, unconsciously translating the goal of Bolshevik discourses and signification practices into the real thing.

The party deserves our attention for what it did do—not what it said it could or should do. This need for closer scrutiny is more pressing when our understanding of the party's role in Soviet culture is largely derived from a dissection of its own decrees and directives. This is the focus of Karl Aimermakher's work on the party's impact on literature from 1917 to 1932.[17] There is nothing wrong with this approach—except when we assume that power on paper was the same as that exercised in real life. Aimermakher finds proof in "party congress resolutions and circulars" that in the second half of the 1920s the party had succeeded in bringing publishing houses and journals under its control. Read also assumes that party organization at the top in and of itself translated into greater control over culture. We need only recall Poliansky's admitted failures as a censor and the whole body of fiction published in the second half of the decade—to a certain degree more provocative than that of the first—to seriously question how often a resolution had the impact it claimed to have. Aimermakher further argues that the party cooperated with RAPP on the "hero" campaign because both applauded it in strikingly similar language. This negates the fundamental difference between how the two entities defined the proper hero; after all, it was Libedinsky, of all people, who appropriated its rhetoric to describe and justify his own attempts at hero construction. We also face this apparent unity of purpose between the Young Guardists and orthodox Marxist critics. Both spoke of realism using the same language yet from contrary points of view. Dialogue about the nature and direction of culture in the Bolshevik environment is inherently deceptive, and not because of some Orwellian design. Rather, many used the same limited terminology but infused it with divergent meanings. This is what undercut the widespread appropriation of Lenin's precepts, since they were employed for contradictory purposes throughout the period. For this reason the content of an official decree and its value are relatively meaningless without attention to the context of its circulation and its effect in the trenches of everyday experience. If we rely primarily on party statements to plot the course of cultural production in the 1920s, we only reproduce what the Bolsheviks themselves saw and fall prey to the same delusions of grandeur that plagued them.

To regard the party as the ur-text for understanding the 1920s, we only confirm its traditional image as a single body, a univocal monolith, dictating cultural praxis. Christopher Read advances this concept in order to overturn Sheila Fitzpatrick's idea, stated nearly three decades ago, of a "soft line" in party cultural policy, that is, the 1920s as a period of relative tolerance. This goal necessitates for Read that the party reclaim its position as sole authority and ensures the continuance of the "hard-soft" debate. Resolution seems unlikely because we can always marshal evidence, anecdotal or quantitative, to uphold either side of the argument. That this can be done is significant in and of itself. Perhaps it is time to question whether "hard" or "soft" are really the appropriate metaphors for the decade. There were some clear oppositions, but they do not always match the clarity that "line theory" suggests. With the Stalinist 1930s ever present in the forefront of our minds, we tend to focus on the continuity of either position and not the cracks and breaks. If there is a central narrative to the 1920s, maybe it is not a "hard" line getting harder or a "soft" line being upended, but of multiple, fragmented, intersecting lines. A case in point would be that of the Young Guardists. After graduating to

RAPP, they generally serve as the supreme example of an uncompromising hard line, in Aimermacher's words having a most "corrosive" effect on literature. Yet on the subject of sex we see that they were, so to speak, quite soft.

In seeking a streamlined picture of cultural praxis, we may, consciously or not, compress observations and evidence into whatever model gives the most satisfactory closure. Tacit acknowledgment of a chaotic environment, only to have it squeezed back into familiar shape, reflects more than anything a desire for a coherent, all-encompassing "story" to explain the 1920s. This is what the paradigms of power—old or new—provide and why, I believe, we often defer to them instead of embracing confusion for what it is. In both redactions a bipolar image of the party against the "masses" has proved irresistible.[18] Some related studies, it should be noted, refuse to replicate this division. Anne Gorsuch's *Youth in Revolutionary Russia: Enthusiasts, Bohemians, Delinquents* (2000) provides a balanced introduction to the Komsomol; Michael David-Fox's *Revolution of the Mind: Higher Learning Among the Bolsheviks, 1918–1929* (1997) focuses on students and acknowledges the "messy" and "contested" ways of implementing policy in universities.[19] In *Terror in My Soul: Communist Autobiographies on Trial* (2003), Igal Halfin, while reasserting Naiman's scenario of a scripted environment, highlights competing discourses, reflected in Malashkin's and Gumilevsky's fiction, seeking to redeem degenerate youth.[20] Yet the prevalence of traditional ideas remains an intriguing feature of studies of Soviet Russia in post-Soviet times and suggests that scholars still engage in what Caryl Emerson and Gary Saul Morson diagnose as "totalitarian semanticism."[21] This means striving to link every text, event, or phenomenon to some grand systematic motivation, such as assigning to "disorder" and "messiness" a rational cause. Studies of culture that define all facets of life along a single dimension, be it power, subversion, resistance, or whatever may be current for the day, risk falling into this hermeneutical circle. There is more to the criticism that Foucault's privileging of power distorts the conditions it seeks to describe; it also can lead us to a dead end. If power defines all, if it is the sole bedrock of social interaction, if every discursive and behavioral act is thus catalogued—there is no "orgasm without ideology" David Halperin quips, not entirely in jest—then we risk falling into a methodological impasse.[22] For all our acknowledgment today of the constructed and contingent nature of cultural phenomena, when power becomes the all-consuming objective of study, when all human actions are filtered through its exclusive value structure of domination and resistance, the resulting frame becomes essentialist since everything is prefixed and prefigured. I offer this as a description not of the present, but of the potential that looms. Indeed, a sign that this power paradigm and derivative schools have already become the standard is that we employ them more and more as if there is no reason to question their operative vocabulary. This is the sign of real "power" for the paradigm has naturalized itself, graduating from theory to axiom. The former requires sustained proof; the latter behaves as an accepted truth.

The irony that emerges from attempts to understand early Soviet culture is that, much as with the Bolsheviks themselves, spontaneity, the unforeseen, or the inexplicable can upset our paradigms and reveal their limitations. If, like Zalkind eighty years before, we allow the safe ground of theory to substitute for empirical conditions, then we risk following the same path of reductionism, for entirely different purposes. Kirshon's incredible claim that not all "facts" are legitimate should stand as a warning. When we uphold a paradigm without question, we wipe our boots free of mud at the door. Its rules establish what evidence is valid; its goals purge the object of study of whatever doesn't make sense within the framework. Perhaps this is a result of a continuing need to demonize Soviets in the 1920s, to present them as brutal and blinded by assumptions of infallibility, possessing backward, mistaken ideas. There is truth to this, but the same could be said of countless other times and places.

With the Soviet legacy quite sour almost everywhere today, it is easy to forget that many people, especially those from the lower party ranks or outside the party but sharing its ideals, were motivated not by a Machiavellian need to control but by a sincere desire to understand and to alleviate desperate social conditions at the time and to aid those perceived to be in trouble—no matter how flawed the medical or social reasoning. Many books and pamphlets of medical advice and works devoted to social reform were conspicuously free of any overt ideology. In Platovsky's and Golosovker's works, medical advice and explanation dominate exclusively. Nor should we forget Frenkel's tolerance or Rubinshtein's compassion. We should recognize too that Kollontai, Ketlinskaia, Slepkov, Smidovich, and countless others took to heart the voluminous appeals for help and information from thousands of bewildered youth. At meetings, interviews, and Komsomol club gatherings, they witnessed firsthand the cavalier attitudes and callous behavior that often led to abuse, suffering, and tragedy. Perhaps the most striking evidence comes from the transcripts of the debates in 1925 and 1926 surrounding the proposed change to the family code that would recognize de facto marriages as equal to registered ones. The proposal was disseminated throughout the country for discussion—by one estimate, there were 6,000 village meetings devoted to the subject—with delegates returning to the Central Executive Committee of the RSFSR. Participants at meetings at this higher level were apparently levelheaded, morally principled individuals, even at times possessed of a sense of humor. Significantly, the overriding motivation for all viewpoints, whether for or against, was concern for the "weakest," a felt need to protect those who might slip between the cracks and fall victim to exploitation if the amendment were accepted (which it was).[23] The party ranks may not have been filled with humanitarians, yet neither were all party members the cold, calculating deceivers who tend to populate studies today.

The controversy over sexuality is but one phenomenon of this period to suggest that Bolshevik culture had many lines and many lives, some of which were traditional, and others radical departures from the norm. Dan Healy's insistence that in revolutionary Russia there was a "diversity of views" about homosexuality operating in a "discursive vacuum" should be extended to the social environment as a whole.[24] To qualify this, we can still have recourse to Foucault if so desired. In *The History of Sexuality* he granted that before the rise of centralized monarchies, there were "dense, entangled, conflicting powers." We would do well to acknowledge that revolutions can precipitate the same confusing pluralism, no matter if ultimately they devolve into the kind of authoritarian states with power of which old-style monarchies could only dream. Sometimes power is weak, sometimes it is seriously threatened by the multiplicity of forces and interests that arise in any transitional period. In the Soviet 1920s, the issue of sexuality was a domain of public and private life where this was acutely felt, as it drove home to the Bolsheviks a fundamental flaw in their enabling mythology: the class paradigm had less application here than elsewhere. To borrow Alan Sinfield's observation from a different context, this decade readily defines a period when "the dominant ideology had not quite got its act together."[25]

Even when enthroned, centralized power does not always function as we assume it should. It would be fitting to end this story of the sexual revolution in Soviet culture not in 1932, but a few years later, when Stalin was at the pinnacle of his authority and power could be exercised in crude, naked fashion without any need for subterfuge. What happened to those who had muddied the previous decade with their tracts, treatises, and fictions on sexuality, especially Romanov, Gumilevsky, and Malashkin? The answer is, surprisingly, nothing. Although Romanov died in 1938, it was from natural causes. Gumilevsky, having learned his lesson, never again wrote on sex; indeed, his personal archive is purposely quite silent regarding the reception of *Dog Alley*. But he continued to be quite prolific, only this time producing literary portraits of academics, not students, for the series "Lives of Distinguished People." From the point of view of the state, here he found his true calling, In a personal letter, Stalin praised his book *Russian Engineers*.[26] Gumilevsky died in 1976. Malashkin, after appearing at the First Congress of the Writers' Union in 1934, disappeared from print for more than twenty years before attempting a comeback with several nonscandalous historical novels. He lived to the age of one hundred, dying in 1988 just as the Soviet Union under per-estroika was beginning to officially recognize again the tumult of the 1920s. Kollontai, of course, was remaindered to near permanent exile as roving am-bassador; she died almost a year to the day before Stalin in 1952. Bogdanov continued to produce into the 1970s, even revising *First Girl* in 1961. Ketlin-skaia received a Stalin Prize for her novel on the siege of Leningrad and died in 1976, after devoting many years to literature and journalism. Lidin com-bined a literary career with teaching and stayed thirty years at the Gorky In-stitute. That these writers did not follow Pilnyak, Babel, Tarasov-Rodionov, or Ognev to their death in the purges is a mystery.

A similarly mild fate befell the Young Guardists. Of those playing a cen-tral role in this study, only Averbakh was executed, even though he was the least appreciative of open sexuality in literature. Ermilov showed true chameleonlike behavior, switching from rebel in the 1920s to reactionary in the late 1940s where he distinguished himself by a most undignified stint as a literary critic. Fadeev followed the same path, becoming a member of the Central Committee and head of the Writers' Union until the shock of the thaw drove him to suicide in 1956. Libedinsky demonstrably turned his at-tention away from questionable heroes and in the 1940s and 1950s devoted himself to churning out heroic portraits of the more standard kind. Con-versely, the Perevalists met with disaster—Voronsky, Lezhnev, and Gorbov all losing their lives in the 1930s. Most of the former Octobrists who opposed the "living person" campaign and led the charge against Libedinsky came to the same end. As for the orthodox critics, Yaroslavsky, after an initial misstep in the 1930s, saved his neck by serving as a historian for Stalin, the kind who had no qualms about fudging facts, and earned a memorial spot on Red Square after his death. Troshchenko survived the 1930s only to perish in the Second World War. Kirshon died in the purges, while Zalkind beat the NKVD to the punch, committing suicide in 1936 after psychoanalysis became a heresy.

The collective fate of these individuals—in part quasi-miraculous, in part tragic—is at odds with what we might expect. The reasons why something did or did not happen under Stalin are usually murky. This is even more true if we step back to the 1920s. The decade had its rightful share of downturns and uplifting moments, of the horrific and the ridiculous. On all sides the participants in the debates over sexuality could be gruesome bullies, madden-ingly opaque and brazenly self-serving. Yet at the same time, particularly as one moves further from the Kremlin, they could be inspiring, perspicacious, and prophetic. We might always search for a single cause to explain such a convoluted, bizarre period. But no one paradigm can provide the answer. This perhaps is its most useful lesson for us today.

Notes

Abbreviations

Titles of journals and newspapers are abbreviated as follows, with the Russian equivalent and the translation used in the text.

IuK	*Iunyi kommunist*	*The Young Communist*
KN	*Krasnaia nov'*	*Red Virgin Soil*
KP	*Komsomol'skaia pravda*	*Komsomol Pravda*
KS	*Krasnoe studentchestvo*	*Red Students*
LG	*Literaturnaia gazeta*	*Literary Gazette*
MG	*Molodaia gvardiia*	*The Young Guard*
NLP	*Na literaturnom postu*	*The Literary Guardian*
NM	*Novyi mir*	*New World*
NP	*Na postu*	*The Guardian*
P	*Pravda*	*Pravda*
S	*Smena*	*The New Shift*
Z	*Zvezda*	*The Star*

Places of publication

L	Leningrad
M	Moscow
M-L	Moscow-Leningrad

Archives

TsKhDMO	Tsentr khraneniia dokumentov molodezhnykh organizatsii (Center for the Preservation of Records of Youth Organizations), incorporated in 1999 into the Rossiiskii gosudarstvennyi arkhiv sotsial'no-politicheskoi istorii (Russian State Archive of Socio-Political History).

1. Introduction

1. E. J. Hobsbawm, "Revolution Is Puritan," *New Society*, May 22, 1969, p. 807.

2. Vera Sandomirsky, "Sex in the Soviet Union," *Russian Review* 10.3 (1951): 199–209.

3. Walter Benjamin, *Moscow Diary*, trans. Richard Sieburth (Cambridge: Harvard UP, 1986), 55.

4. David Lass, *Sovremennoe studenchestvo* (M-L: Molodaia gvardiia, 1928), 56.

5. On the new codes, see Wendy Z. Goldman, *Women, the State, and Revolution: Soviet Family Policy and Social Life, 1917–1936* (NY: Cambridge UP, 1993), 48–57, 103ff.; Barbara Evans

Clement, "The Effects of the Civil War on Women and Family," in *Party, State, and Society in the Russian Civil War*, ed. Diane P. Koenker, William G. Rosenberg, and Ronald Grigor Suny (Bloomington: Indiana UP: 1989): 105–22.

6. On questions of gender, sex, and political movements before 1917, see Richard Stites, *The Women's Liberation Movement in Russia: Feminism, Nihilism, and Bolshevism, 1860–1930* (Princeton: Princeton UP, 1978).

7. Laura Engelstein, *The Keys to Happiness: Sex and the Search for Modernity in Fin-de-Siè-cle Russia* (Ithaca: Cornell UP, 1992).

8. On the reception and impact of Tolstoy's work, see Peter Ulf Møller, *Postlude to "The Kreutzer Sonata": Tolstoj and the Debate on Sexual Morality in Russian Literature in the 1890s*, trans. John Kendal (New York: E. J. Brill, 1988).

9. Engelstein, pp. 383–88, 404ff., rejects the contemporary reading of these works, seeing more sophistication and ambiguity in their authors' designs. For a critique of Engelstein's reading of *Sanin*, see Eric Naiman, *Sex in Public: The Incarnation of Early Soviet Ideology* (Princeton: Princeton UP, 1997), 47ff.

10. Aleksandr Yakovlev, "Bez beregov," *Sobranie sochinenii*, vol. 3 (M: Nikintskie subbot-niki, 1926), 45–46.

11. Eve Garrette Grady, *Seeing Red: Behind the Scenes in Russia Today* (New York: Breuer, Warren, and Putnam, 1931), 111–12.

12. Maurice Hindus, *Humanity Uprooted* (New York: Jonathan Cape and Harrison Smith, 1929), 93.

13. V. F. Calverton, *The Bankruptcy of Marriage* (New York: Macaulay Co., 1928; rpt. by Arno Press and the *New York Times*, 1972), 241.

14. Hindus, 132–33.

15. Calverton, 249.

16. Ella Winter, Red Virtue (New York: Harcourt, Brace, 1933), 132–33.

17. Calverton, 278. See also Fanina Halle, *Woman in Soviet Russia* (New York: Viking Press, 1935), 139.

18. Hindus, 116.

19. Ibid., 98.

20. Halle, 177.

21. Hindus, 97–98.

22. Jessica Smith, *Women in Soviet Russia* (New York: Vanguard Press, 1928), 138.

23. Hindus, 98.

24. Commonly known as the 1926 Code (when the draft was written), it became law in January 1927.

25. Calverton, 258.

26. Winter, 124.

27. Klaus Mehnert, *Youth in Soviet Russia*, trans. Michael Davidson (New York: Harcourt, Brace, 1933).

28. Royal Baker, *The Menace Bolshevism* (Detroit: Liberty Bell Publishers, 1919), 28.

29. Ibid., 28–29.

30. Samuel Saloman, *The Red War on the Family* (New York: J. J. Little and Ives, 1922), 84.

31. Baker, 28.

32. Saloman, 81–82. Her refusal to translate *The Kreutzer Sonata* was published in the *Nation* 50 (Apr. 17, 1890) and reproduced in *Critical Essays on Tolstoy*, ed. Edward Wasiolek (Boston: G. K. Hall, 1986), 162–68.

33. "Bedrock of civilization" is from Ernest J. P. Benn, *About Russia* (New York: D. Apple-

ton, 1930), 73. "Saturnalia of the reds" and "ever hungry hopper of the free-love mill" are from Saloman, 71, 62.

34. Rene Fulop-Miller, *The Mind and Face of Bolshevism* (New York: Alfred A. Knopf, 1928), 118.

35. Walter Lippmann and Charles Merz, *A Test of the News*, special edition of *The New Republic*, Aug. 4, 1920, p. 3.

36. They even made it to Hoolinsky, a nonexistent city whose name rang so well with "hooligan." See C. M. Roebuck, *The Natural History of a Lie* (London: British Socialist Party, n.d.).

37. See William C. Bullitt, *The Bullitt Mission to Russia* (New York: B. W. Huebsch, 1919), 50, 59. Although the only contemporary reports in the Soviet Union referring to the Saratov decree debunk its authenticity, it still retains the status of historical fact. Clements (105) uses it as such, as does Stern. Both cite A. Kharchev's *Brak i sem'ia v SSSR* (M: Mysl', 1964), 139, which in turn refers to a Prague publication, *Sotsializatsiia zhenshchin* (1918). However, to my knowledge, no source from that period and from within Soviet Russia, has ever officially confirmed it.

38. Smith, 99.

39. On the emergence of sexuality in Russia as an object of scholarly study, see Jane T. Costlow, Stephanie Sandler, and Judith Vowles, "Introduction," *Sexuality and the Body in Russian Culture* (Stanford: Stanford UP, 1993): 1–40; and Eliot Borenstein, "Slavophilia: The Incitement to Russian Sexual Discourse," *Slavic and East European Journal* 40 (1996): 142–47.

40. See Richard Stites, "The Sexual Revolution," chapter XI in *The Women's Liberation Movement in Russia: Feminism, Nihilism and Bolshevism, 1860–1930* (Princeton: Princeton UP, 1978).

41. Mikhail Stern, *Sex in the USSR*, trans. Mark Howson and Cary Ryan (New York: Times Books, 1980), 30; Mark Popovsky, *Tretii lishnii* (London: Overseas Publications Interchange, 1985).

42. Igor S. Kon, *The Sexual Revolution in Russia: From the Age of the Czars until Today* (New York: Free Press, 1995), 55.

43. Naiman, 239.

44. Ibid., 97.

45. Ibid., 115.

46. Ibid., 102.

47. Ibid., 102–03.

48. Ibid., 26.

49. F. R. Ankersmit, *History and Tropology: The Rise and Fall of Metaphor* (Berkeley: U of California P, 1994), 179.

50. See Robert F. Berkhofer, Jr., *Beyond the Great Story: History as Text and Discourse* (Cambridge: Harvard UP, 1995); and Nancy F. Partner, "Historicity in an Age of Reality-Fictions," in *A New Philosophy of History*, ed. Frank Ankersmit and Hans Kellner (Chicago: U of Chicago P, 1995): 21–39.

51. *Sex in Public* is now perhaps the most influential reading of the subject. See, for example, Igal Halfin, *From Darkness to Light: Class, Consciousness and Salvation in Revolutionary Russia* (Pittsburgh: U of Pittsburgh P, 2000), and *Terror in My Soul: Communist Autobiographies on Trial* (Cambridge: Harvard UP, 2003); and Eliot Borenstein, *Men Without Women: Masculinity and Revolution in Russian Fiction, 1917–1929* (Durham: Duke UP, 2000).

52. Naiman, 25.

53. Emblematic here would be Richard Stites, *Revolutionary Dreams: Utopian Vision and*

Experimental Life in the Russian Revolution (New York: Oxford UP, 1989). See also *Russia in the Era of NEP: Explorations in Soviet Society and Culture,* ed. Sheila Fitzpatrick, Alexander Rabinovitch, and Richard Stites (Bloomington: Indiana UP, 1991); on the plethora of voices immediately surrounding the revolutions of 1917, see Orlando Figes, *A People's Tragedy: the Russian Revolution, 1891–1924* (New York: Penguin, 1996); Anne E. Gorsuch, *Youth in Revolutionary Russia: Enthusiasts, Bohemians, Delinquents* (Bloomington: Indiana UP, 2000); Orlando Figes and Boris Kolonitskii, *Interpreting the Russian Revolution: the Language and Symbols of 1917* (New Haven: Yale UP, 1999); and Mark D. Steinberg, *Voices of Revolution, 1917* (New Haven: Yale UP, 2001).

54. Of those works addressing the sexual revolution directly, emblematic here would be Vladimir Brovkin, *Russia After Lenin: Politics, Culture & Society, 1921–1929* (London: Routledge, 1998), esp. chap. 5. While concerned more with issues of gender than the sexual revolution per se, both Goldman's attention and that of Elizabeth A. Wood in *The Baba and the Comrade: Gender and Politics in Revolutionary Russia* (Bloomington: Indiana UP, 1997) focus on the negative effects of Bolshevik policies.

55. Dan Healy, *Homosexual Desire in Revolutionary Russia* (Chicago: U of Chicago P, 2001), is an exception. In his analysis of the previously hidden gay subculture of this period, he underscores the diversity of views within the party regarding homosexuality and the resulting conflicts. Brief statements favoring ambivalence include Lewis H. Siegelbaum, *Soviet State and Society Between Revolutions, 1918–1929* (New York: Cambridge UP, 1992), 154ff.; and Mark Banting, Catriona Kelly, and James Riordan, "Sexuality," *Russian Cultural Studies: An Introduction,* ed. Catriona Kelly and David Shepherd (Oxford: Oxford UP, 1998): 315. The thesis of this book was introduced in Gregory Carleton, "Writing-Reading the Sexual Revolution in the Early Soviet Union," *Journal of the History of Sexuality* 8 (1997): 229–55. I thank the journal for permission to use that material here.

2. A Revolution Comes of Age

1. Maksim Gorky, "Gorod zheltogo d'iavola," *Sobranie sochinenii v 30–i tomakh,* vol. 7 (M: Gosudarstvennoe izdatel'stvo khudozhestvennoi literatury, 1950), 7–19. While *Mother* was written primarily in the summer of 1906, when Gorky and Andreeva moved to the Adirondacks, he began work on it while traveling to the United States.

2. Tovah Yedlin, *Maxim Gorky: A Political Biography* (Westport, CT: Praeger, 1999), 49.

3. Gorky, *Mat'*, *Polnoe sobranie sochinenii,* vol. 8 (M: Nauka, 1970), 295.

4. Gorky, "O pervoi liubvi," *Polnoe sobranie sochinenii,* vol. 16 (M: Nauka, 1973), 217.

5. Gorky, notes to "Gorod zheltogo d'iavola," 522.

6. This account of Gorky's trip and quotations are taken from Alexander Kaun, *Maxim Gorky and His Russia* (New York: Jonathan Cape & Harrison Smith, 1931), 569ff.; see also Ernest Poole, "Maxim Gorki in New York," *Slavonic and East European Review* 22 (1944): 77–83.

7. Gorky, *Sobranie sohinenii v 30–i tomax,* vol. 5, 484.

8. This tension is distinct from that of spontaneity and consciousness. There revolutionary discourse operates from the outside to channel energy; the inflation of the individual, however, is internal to this discourse. *Mother* is used as illustration of this dialectic in Katerina Clark, *The Soviet Novel: History as Ritual* (Chicago: Chicago UP, 1981), esp. chap. 1.

9. The symbolic connection between youth and revolution dates back to the 1860s and the fiery manifesto "Young Russia." See Abbott Gleason, *Young Russia: The Genesis of Russian Radicalism in the 1860s* (Chicago: U of Chicago P, 1980), 171ff.

10. David Khanin, *Universitet moego pokoleniia* (L: Priboi, 1930), 13.

11. Figes comments on the spirit of revolution as marked by "self-assertion," regardless of the politics involved (368). He also notes that General Brusilov, before the October Revolution, observed that soldiers identified "anarchistic freedom" with the Bolshevik cause (380).

12. K. Moskatov, "O bytovykh boleznennykh iavleniiakh v komsomole," *IuK* 19 (1926): 40–46. See also Isabel A. Tirado, "Nietzschean Motifs in the Komsomol," in *Nietzsche and Soviet Culture: Ally and Adversary*, ed. Bernice Rosenthal (Cambridge: Cambridge UP, 1994): 235–55; see Bernice Rosenthal, *New Myth, New World: From Nietzsche to Stalinism* (University Park: Pennsylvania State UP, 2002), 117–232. On the early history of the Komsomol, see Tirado, *Young Guard! The Communist Youth League. Petrograd, 1917–1920* (New York: Greenwood P, 1988). For the most comprehensive analysis of the Komsomol in the 1920s, see Gorsuch, esp. chap. 4, focusing on the excesses of militant youth.

13. Nikolai Semashko, "Bor'ba vsiakomu neriashestvu," *KP,* June 18, 1926, p. 1.

14. Aron Zalkind, "Etika, byt i molodezh'," in *Komsomol'skii byt*, comp. I. Razin (M-L: Molodaia gvardiia, 1927), 166–68.

15. On student radicalism in the 1860s, see Gleason.

16. As reported in Tur, "Dela lichnye," *IuK* 19 (1926): 55. *Kimovskii* is the adjectival form of the acronym, *kim*, Communist Youth International. On the potential for minor behavioral infractions by students to be viewed as treason, see Michael David-Fox, *Revolution of the Mind: Higher Learning Among the Bolsheviks, 1918–1929* (Ithaca: Cornell UP, 1997), 109.

17. Iurij Lotman, "The Decembrist in Everyday Life," trans. C. R. Pike, in Ju. M. Lotman and B. A. Uspenskij, *The Semiotics of Russian Culture*, ed. Ann Shukman (Ann Arbor: Dept. of Slavic Languages and Literatures, University of Michigan, 1984), 83; see also Lotman, "The Theater and Theatricality as Components of Early Nineteenth-Century Culture," trans. G. S. Smith, in ibid. Trotsky also noted the "theatricalization of *byt*" in "Sem'ia i obriadnost'," *Sochineniia*, vol 21 (M-L: Gosizdat, 1927), 39–43 (rpt. from *P,* July 14, 1923).

18. N. I. Bukharin, "Vospitanie smeny" and "Za uporiadochenie byta molodezhi," rpt. in *Komsomol'skii byt*, 26ff.

19. Ippolit, *Pravo na liubov'* (M: Molodaia gvardiia, 1927), 27.

20. Khanin, 128.

21. R. Kulle, diary entry for August 26, 1925, in "Mysli i zametki. Dnevnik 1924–1932 godov," *Novyi zhurnal* 186 (1992): 206–07.

22. I speak of symbolic power; before the revolution, activist students exercised more real "street" power as reflected in their clashes with the university administration and the state. However, after the revolution students assumed the state to be their ally, not enemy. See Samuel D. Kassow, *Students, Professors, and the State in Tsarist Russia* (Berkeley: U of California P, 1989); and Joan Neuberger, *Hooliganism: Crime, Culture, and Power in St. Petersburg, 1900–1914* (Berkeley: U of California P, 1993).

23. In *Revolutionary Dreams*, Stites provides the most comprehensive analysis of this phenomenon in a wide array of cultural dimensions.

24. Paula S. Fass, *The Damned and the Beautiful: American Youth in the 1920s* (New York: Oxford UP, 1977), 75.

25. Stites, *The Women's Liberation Movement,* dates the split among socialists between the two views of sex—libertarianism versus asceticism—to the debate between Enfantin and Bazard in 1831 (379). Naiman analyzes this split in Chernyshevsky's *What Is To Be Done?* and its legacy for Soviets, arguing that "Chernyshevsky's grandchildren, the old Bolsheviks, would deny vehemently that they were ascetics, or indeed anything but materialists, while preaching the virtues of asceticism" (37).

26. Nikolai Bogdanov, *Pervaia devushka* (Nizhnii-Novgorod: Molodaia gvardiia, 1928), 164–65.

27. Ia. Okunev, "Chelovek za bortom," *KP,* June 16, 1926, p. 1.

28. Ippolit, *Pravo na liubov',* 27.

29. Emelian Yaroslavsky, "K postanovke voprosa," *Polovoi vopros* (M, 1925), 2. Marx was not a pillar of marital morality; while he was in English exile his housekeeper bore him a son. Engels lived with the unmarried Mary Burns for years. One wonders whether the truth would have hurt Soviet authorities more than youth's comical charges. See W. O. Henderson, *The Life of Friedrich Engels,* vol. 1 (London: Frank Cass, 1976), 203; for citation of Marx's personal life as an example to follow, see Sofiia Smidovich, *Rabotnitsa i novyi byt* (M-L: Gosizdat, 1927), 22.

30. "Novyi byt," *Smena* 17 (1926): 15.

31. Israel Gelman, *Polovaia zhizn' sovremennoi molodezhi. Opyt sotsial'nogo-biologicheskogo obsledovaniia* (M-L: Gosudarstvennoe izd., 1923), 115.

32. A. Saradzhev, "Na 'stydnuiu temu,'" *IuK* 3 (1927): 56, accused youth of reducing all questions to sex.

33. Gelman, 116.

34. Lass, 199.

35. "Novyi byt," *Smena* 17 (1926): 15.

36. Lass, 212.

37. Gelman, 86.

38. See Sheila Fitzpatrick, "Sex and the Revolution: An Examination of Literary and Statistical Data on the Mores of Soviet Students in the 1920s," *Journal of Modern History* 50 (1978): 252–78; on the polls at Sverdlov University, see David-Fox, 113.

39. Gelman, 65.

40. Lass, 211.

41. Ippolit, *Pravo na liubov',* 11. The rhyme approximates the tag opener, *kuritsa ne ptitsa, studentka—ne devitsa,* literally, a chicken isn't a bird; a [female] student isn't a virgin.

42. S. Smidovich, "O liubvi," *P,* Mar. 24, 1925, p. 5.

43. A. M. K., "O liubvi i eshche koe o chem," *P,* Apr. 3, 1925, p. 6. These are Kollontai's initials, but Stites argues that she is not the author (*The Women's Liberation Movement,* 380). Cathy Porter does not list it in her comprehensive bibliography of Kollontai's work, *Alexandra Kollontai* (New York: Dial Press, 1980).

44. "O 'liubvi," *P,* May 7, 1925, pp. 5–6. The following citations are from this piece.

45. Openness was characteristic of journals in the decade. On this feature in the journal *Kommunistka,* see Polina Vinogradskaia, *Pamiatnye vstrechi* (M: Sovetskaia Rossiia, 1972), 56ff.

46. Vera Ketlinskaia and Vladimir Slepkov, *Zhizn' bez kontrolia (polovaia zhizn' i sem'ia rabochei molodezhi)* (M-L: Molodaia gvardiia, 1929).

47. Aleksandr Milchakov, *Komsomol v bor'be za kul'turnyi byt* (M-L: Molodaia gvardiia, 1927), 16.

48. Moskatov, 42; see also Nikolai Pogodin, "Samoubiistvo v Ulu-Teliake," *KP,* June 13, 1926, p. 1.

49. Tov. Iakov, "O korystnom komsomol'stve," *Komsomol'skii byt,* 170.

50. Ketlinskaia and Slepkov, 32.

51. Brovkin, 108–33, argues that sexual misbehavior was an expression of defiance vis-à-vis the party.

52. M. Bekker, "Liubovnaia lirika komsomola," *Komsomoliia* 4 (1926): 68.

53. *Komsomol'skii byt,* 157.

54. Bukharin, "Vospitanie smeny," *Komsomol'skii byt,* 22.

55. S. Devenishshky, "Otvet Il'e Linu," *MG* 4 (1924): 211.

56. L. Sosnovsky, *Bol'nye voprosy* (L: Priboi, 1927), 4.

57. V. O. Klemm, "Tovarishchu Nyne Vel't," *Komsomol'skii byt*, 186–92.

58. Biriukova, "My samy umeem tselovat' (pis'mo devushki)," *KS* 3 (1927): 29–30.

59. Gelman, 85.

60. Ibid., 114.

61. "Novyi byt," *Smena* 17 (1926): 15.

62. Gelman, 114.

63. Citations are from *Selected Writings of Alexandra Kollontai*, trans. Alix Holt (London: Allison and Busby, 1977).

64. Kollontai, "Sexual Relations and the Class Struggle," 245.

65. Ibid., 244.

66. Kollontai, "Communism and the Family," 257–58.

67. Kollontai, "Make Way for Winged Eros," 291.

68. Kollontai, "Communism and the Family," 259–60.

69. Kollontai, "Make Way for Winged Eros," 277.

70. Kollontai, "Theses on Communist Morality," 229.

71. Ibid., 229.

72. Ibid., 231.

73. Friedrich Engels, *The Origin of the Family, Private Property, and the State* (New York: International Publishers, 1942), 63.

74. Bebel admits that he is not the source; he quotes an anonymous author, "Veritas," who states, "The sexual impulse is neither moral nor immoral; it is merely natural, like hunger and thirst: Nature knows nothing of morals" (*Die Prostitution vor dem Gesetz* [Leipsic, 1893], 82.

75. Ibid., 343.

76. Engels, 73.

77. This story first appeared in Kollontai's collection, *Liubov' pchel trudovykh [Love of the Worker Bees]* (Petrograd, 1923). Citations are from *Love of the Worker Bees*, trans. Cathy Porter (London: Virago, 1977), 182–211.

78. Clara Zetkin, *Reminiscences of Lenin* (New York: International Publishers, 1934), 50. The conversation allegedly took place in 1920, while Zetkin's account was first published shortly after Lenin's death. See also Halfin, *Terror*, 136–37.

79. Ibid., 49.

80. Ippolit, *Pravo na liubov'*, 31.

81. Lass, 7.

82. Ibid., 211.

83. Aron Zalkind, *Polovoi vopros v usloviiakh sovetskoi obshchestvennosti* (L: Gosizdat, 1926), 52.

84. Ibid., 52–53.

85. Martyn Liadov, *Voprosy byta (doklad na sobranii iacheiki sverdlovskogo kommun. un-ta.)* (M: Kommunisticheskii universitet im. Ia. M. Sverdlova, 1925), 16–18.

86. Em. Yaroslavsky, "Ob asketizme, vozderzhanii i polovoi raspushchennosti, ili v chem sekret meshchanstva," in *Kakova zhe nasha molodezh'*, ed. S. I. Gusev (M-L: Gosud. izd., 1927), 62–63. This is a reprint of his speech of Apr. 14, 1926.

87. B. Arbatov, "Grazhd. Akhmatova i tov. Kollontai," *MG* 4–5 (1923): 148.

88. M. Lemberg, *Chto neobxodimo znat' v polovom voprose* (L: Priboi, 1925), 34.

89. E. Lavrov, "Polovoi vopros i molodezh' (o nekotorykh itogakh i novykh otkroveniiakh tov. Kollontai)," *MG* 3 (1926): 136–48.

90. Arbatov, 149–51.

91. Finogen Budnev, "Polovaia revoliutsiia," *Na postu* 1 (1924): 243–49.

92. S. Shkotov, *Byt molodezhi* (Ivanovo-Voznesensk: Osnova, 1925), 26–30. See also Smidovich, *Rabotnitsa i novyi byt,* which provides a picture that echoes Kollontai's prescription of the ideal loving relationship (22).

93. Vinogradskaia had worked with Kollontai both in the Zhenotdel and on the editorial board of the journal *Kommunistka.* In her memoirs, *Pamiatnye vstrechi,* she gives a notably toned-down opinion of Kollontai (53).

94. P. Vinogradskaia, "Voprosy morali, pola, byta i tov. Kollontai," *KN* 6 (1923): 179–214.

95. Ibid., 188–89.

96. Ilya Lin, "Eros iz rogozhsko-simonovskogo raiona," *MG* 4–5 (1923): 152–55.

97. Devenishsky, 210–11.

98. "Polovaia zhizn' studenchestva (po dannym ankety odnogo iz moskovskikh vuzov)," *Vecherniaia Moskva,* Apr. 16, 1926, p. 2. The university was not identified.

99. B. V. Tsukker, *Voprosy polovoi zhizni rabochei molodezhi* (Kharkov: Kosmos, 1926), 58–59. Naiman argues that Kollontai's image as sexual liberationist is not accurate, as she "phrased the entire question of communist sexuality in a manner wholly in keeping with the reductive, puritanical discourse" (226).

100. Gorky, "O pervoi liubvi," 217; published in *KN* 6 (1923): 3–25.

101. Gorky, articles in *New Life,* Nov. 7, 1917, p. 86, and Dec. 10, 1917, p. 107, in *Untimely Thoughts: Essays on Revolution, Culture and the Bolsheviks, 1917–1918,* trans. Herman Ermolaev (New Haven: Yale UP, 1995).

102. Gorky, "O muzyke tolstykh," *Sobranie sochinenii v tridtsati tomakh* (M: Gosizdat, 1953): 24:351–56. The article first appeared in *P,* Apr. 18, 1928.

103. L. Trotsky, "Novyi kurs (pis'mo k partiinnym soveshchaniem)," *P,* Dec. 11, 1923, p. 4 (the letter is dated Dec. 8, 1923).

104. See Halfin, *Terror,* 209–30; Isaac Deutscher, *The Prophet Unarmed* (London: Oxford UP, 1959), 121ff.; Sheila Fitzpatrick, *Education and Social Mobility in the Soviet Union, 1921–34* (New York: Cambridge UP, 1979), 94ff.; and David-Fox, 151ff. On the propensity to link his "ideological deviance" with youth's "sexual license," see Katerina Clark, *Petersburg: Crucible of Cultural Revolution* (Cambridge: Harvard UP, 1995), 210–11.

105. S. Ravich, "Bor'ba s prostitutsiei v Petrograde," *Kommunistka* 1–2 (1920): 23.

106. N. I. Bukharin, "Ratsionalizatsiia i uporiadochenie byta molodezhi," *Komsomol'skii byt,* 103.

3. Fashioning a Code

1. Boris Pilnyak, *Ivan-da-Mar'ia* (Berlin-Petersburg-Moscow: Z. I. Grzhebin, 1922), 14; see Naiman, 60–63.

2. P. S. Kogan, *Literatura etikh let* (Ivanovo-Voznesensk: Osnova, 1924), 104; A. Popov, "Proizvedeniia Bor. Pil'niaka," *Rabochii chitatel'* 2 (1925): 26.

3. Lygin and Granat, "Bor. Pil'niak," *Rabochii chitatel'* 2 (1925): 27.

4. Pilnyak, 63.

5. Ibid., 71.

6. Anatoly Glebov, *Inga* (M: Teakinopechat', 1930), 9.

7. Karl Marx, *The Communist Manifesto,* ed. Frederic L. Bender (New York: W. W. Norton, 1988), 72.

8. Of course, this is not all that Marx declared on the subject. For a contemporary Soviet attempt to tie his scattered comments on sex to counter those who sanctioned "sex-communism," see D. Riazanov, *Vzgliady Marksa i Engel'sa na brak i sem'iu* (M: Molodaia gvardiia, 1927). Nevertheless, a sign of how little Marx produced of substance on the subject is evident in the fact that he is seldom quoted in Soviet discussions of sexuality.

9. Yaroslavsky, "Ob asketizme," in *Kakova zhe nasha molodezh'*.

10. V. I. Lenin, "Tasks of the Youth Leagues (Bourgeois and Communist Morality)" (delivered at the Third All-Russian Congress of the Komsomol, Oct. 2, 1920), trans. William G. Rosenberg, *Bolshevik Visions. Part I* (Ann Arbor: U of Michigan P, 1990): 21–25.

11. Zalkind, "Etika, byt i molodezh'," *Komsomol'skii byt*, 79.

12. M. Reisner, "Meshchanstvo," *KN* 1 (1927): 149–63; and see Halfin, 134–35. Gorsuch also discusses the use by youth of *meshchanstvo* to identify the "other," noncommunist (88), whereas Figes and Kolonitskii detail the elasticity of "bourgeois" in the early years of revolution to cover the "enemy"(168–69). See also Sheila Fitzpatrick, "The Problem of Class Identity in NEP Society," in *Russia in the Era of NEP*, ed. Sheila Fitzpatrick, Alexander Rabinowitch, and Richard Stites (Bloomington: Indiana UP, 1991): 12–33; and Figes and Kolonitskii, 114ff.

13. Zalkind, *Polovoi vopros*, 49.

14. Ibid., 6, 34; see also Gelman, 123–24; Lass, 173; and Dr. S. Ia. Golosovker, *K voprosu o polovom byte sovremennoi zhenshchiny* (Kazan: Kazanskii meditsinksogo zhurnala, 1925), 12.

15. Kollontai, "Skoro (cherez 48 let)" (Omsk: Sibbiuro, 1922).

16. Anatoly Lunacharsky, *Moral's marksistskoi tochki zreniia* (Sevastopol: Proletarii, 1925), 43.

17. Shkotov, 48ff.

18. See also V. A. Murin, *Byt i nravy derevenskoi molodezhi* (M: Novaia Moskva, 1926).

19. Shkotov, 33.

20. Liadov, 36.

21. Smidovich, *Rabotnitsa*, 22.

22. Zalkind, "Etika," 85.

23. Ketlinskaia and Slepkov, 55.

24. Lunacharsky, 43.

25. See, for example, *Sobranie kodeksov R.S.F.S.R.*, 3rd ed. (M: Narodnyi komissariat iustitsii, 1925), 558–59.

26. See Healy, 115ff.; Healy also affirms that some "self-identified homosexuals" believed the revolution provided full license to engage in same-sex behavior (111).

27. E. P. Frenkel, *Polovye prestupleniia*, 2nd ed. (Odessa: Svetoch, 1927).

28. Ibid., 12.

29. See Laura Engelstein, "Combined Underdevelopment: Discipline and Law in Imperial and Soviet Russia," *American Historical Review* 98 (1993): 350–51.

30. Yaroslavsky, "Moral' i byt," 43; see also Iv. Ariamov, "Biologicheskie osnovy polovoi zhizni," *Vestnik prosveshcheniia* 9 (1925): 116.

31. Zalkind, *Polovoi vopros*, 14, 16.

32. Tur, 54–58.

33. A. Divilkovsky, "Bolezni byta molodezhi," *NM* 11 (1926): 168–69.

34. Of all the classes Lass polled, the proletariat had the best sex: "With respect to pleasurable feelings that characterize the sexual act, in first place are the workers; in last place—those of the petty-bourgeois class. This can be explained, on one hand, by the fact that the heavy labor of the worker sharpens his ability to feel pleasure. On the other hand, the petty-bourgeoisie possesses variety of possibilities to receive pleasure in other areas. This satiation or heightened sensibility can explain that they are repulsed by the sexual act more often (17%) than workers (12.5%) and peasants (12.7%). Consequently, one can say in general that workers approach the sexual act the most fervently whereas the representatives of the petty-bourgeoisie the most cold-bloodedly" (117). On the perceived opposition between bourgeois and proletarian sex, see Halfin, *Terror*, 105.

35. A. L. Berkovich, "Voprosy polovoi zhizni pri svete sotsial'dnoi gigieny," *MG* 6 (1923): 253.

36. Ibid., 251.

37. Stites, *Revolutionary Dreams*, 155ff.

38. Leon Trotsky, *Literature and Revolution*, trans. Rose Strunsky (New York: International Publishers, 1925), 254–56.

39. A. Timofeev, *Kuda dolzhna napravliat'sia polovaia energiia molodezhi* (Kharkov: Kosmos, 1926), 11.

40. Ibid., 22, 27.

41. Ariamov, 111; see also Halfin, *Terror,* 168ff.

42. O. Feigin, *Chto takoe normal'naia polovaia zhizn',* (L: self-published, 1927), 7.

43. E. B. Demidovich, "Polovaia zhizn' i zdorov'e studenchestva," *KS* 8 (1927): 42.

44. Timofeev, 13.

45. Ibid., 20–21.

46. Ibid., 50.

47. Gelman, 79–80.

48. Timofeev, 20.

49. Zalkind, *Polovoi vopros,* 23.

50. Yaroslavsky, "Moral' i byt," 49.

51. Demidovich, "Polovaia zhizn' i zdorov'e studenchestva," 41–42.

52. Ibid., 41.

53. Zalkind, *Polovoi vopros,* 16; Feigin, 7; see also Andrei Uspensky, *O vrede rannikh polovykh snoshenii* (Kharkhov: Kosmos, 1926).

54. Feigin, 9.

55. Uspensky, 37.

56. Nikolai Semashko, *Nauka o zdorov'e obshchestva* (M: Gosizdat, 1922), 30; see also Halfin, *Terror,* 203–06.

57. Lass, 182.

58. S. E. Burshtyn, *Opyt polovoi ankety v voinskakh chastiakh i vuzax* (Kharkov: PUUVO, 1925), 6.

59. Lass, 173.

60. Feigin, 29–30.

61. Demidovich, 40–45.

62. B. V. Tsukker, *Fizkul'tura i polovoi vopros* (Kharkov: Vestnik fizicheskoi kul'tury, 1929), 19.

63. Lemberg, 38–39. Naiman also cites this list (136).

64. Uspensky, *O vrede,* 46–49.

65. Yaroslavsky, "Ob asketizme," and "Moral' i byt."

66. N. Semashko, "Novyi byt i polovoi vopros," *Sud idet* 7 (1926): 476.

67. Ivan Abramov, "Znacheniia sokraneniia polovoj energii dlia molodezhi," *Komsomol'skii byt,* 288.

68. V. Gorinevsky, "Polovoi vopros," *KP,* Jan. 29, 1926, p. 3.

69. Feigin, 13.

70. See Gelman, 77–78; Lass, 136; Uspensky, *Polovaia zhizn',* 89; Feigin, 13; Burshtyn, 6; A. K. Platovsky, *Polovaia zhizn' sovremennogo studenchestva* (Rostov-na-Donu: Sovet sotsial'noi pomoshchi), 29.

71. Timofeev, 16.

72. Ariamov, 115; see also Naiman, 142–47.

73. Ibid.

74. P. Guber, *Don-Zhuanskii spisok A. S. Pushkina* (Petrograd: Izd. Petrograd, 1923; rpt. M: Evrika, 1990), 19.

75. Timofeev, 20.

76. Uspensky, *Polovaia zhizn'*, 87.

77. Uspensky, *O vrede*, 38ff.

78. Sigmund Freud, "'Civilized' Sexual Morality and Modern Nervousness," *Sexuality and the Psychology of Love*, ed. Philip Rieff (New York: Macmillan, 1963), 16.

79. Sigmund Freud, "The Most Prevalent Form of Degradation in Erotic Life" (1912), in ibid., 57.

80. Freud, "'Civilized' Sexual Morality," 20ff.

81. Zalkind, "Freidizm i marksizm," *KN* 4 (1924): 167.

82. Ibid., 179.

83. Martin A. Miller, *Freud and the Bolsheviks* (New Haven: Yale UP, 1998), 70ff.

84. Zetkin, 45.

85. V. N. Voloshinov, *Freudianism: a Critical Sketch*, trans. I. R. Titunik (Bloomington: Indiana UP, 1987), 129. On Soviets' appropriation and later rejection of Freud's sexual theories, see Halfin, *Terror*, 161ff. and 198ff.

86. Freud, "'Civilized' Sexual Morality," 21.

87. Ibid., 23.

88. Ibid.

89. Stephen Kern, *The Culture of Love: Victorians to Moderns* (Cambridge: Harvard UP, 1992), 106.

90. See Cynthia Eagle Russett, *Sexual Science: The Victorian Construction of Womanhood* (Cambridge: Harvard UP, 1989); and Jackson Lears, *Fables of Abundance: A Cultural History of Advertising in the Americas* (New York: Basic Books, 1994).

91. Barbara Sicherman, "The Paradox of Prudence: Mental Health in the Gilded Age," *Journal of American History* 62 (1976): 894.

92. Peter Gay, *The Bourgeois Experience: Victoria to Freud*, vol. 1 (New York: Oxford UP, 1984), 317.

93. Quoted in Ben Barker-Benfield, "The Spermatic Economy: A Nineteenth Century View of Sexuality," *Feminist Studies* 1 (1972): 47.

94. Peter T. Cominos, "Late Victorian Sexual Respectability and the Social System," *International Review of Social History* 8 (1963): 38.

95. Ibid., 37.

96. Zalkind, *Polovoi vopros*, 47–58.

97. The twelfth commandment advocated the same right to control behavior as the church through doctrinal restriction, confession, penitence, and direct prohibition. Sex was forbidden so often on the orthodox calendar that it was officially permitted only about seventy times a year. Eve Levin, *Sex and Society in the World of the Orthodox Slavs, 900–1700* (Ithaca: Cornell UP, 1989), 163ff.

98. Zalkind, *Polovoi vopros*, 61.

99. Zalkind, "Etika, byt i molodezh'," *Komsomol'skii byt*, 75.

100. N. Semashko, "Nevezhestvo i pornografiia pod maskoi prosveshcheniia, nauki i literatury," *Izvestiia*, Apr. 8, 1927, p. 3; see also Fran Bernstein, "Doctors and the Problem of 'Sexy Science' in the 1920s," in *Eros and Pornography in Russian Culture,* ed. M. Levitt and A. Toporkov (M: Ladomir, 1999): 442–57.

101. N. Semashko, "Kak ne nado pisat' o polovom voprose," *Izvestiia*, Jan. 1, 1925, p. 5.

102. Lemberg, 10.

103. Golosovker, *O polovom byte mushchiny*, 6; *K voprosu o polovom byte sovremennoi zhen-shchiny*, 15–16.

104. Gelman, 118.

105. See Healy on the "multiple perspectives" of Bolsheviks to same-sex love (109, 114); and Banting et al. (319ff.).

106. M. B. Shchekin, *Kak zhit' po-novomu* (Kostroma: self-published, 1925). Citations are from pp. 47–60.

107. Semashko, "Nevezhestsvo," 3.

108. Vlad. Vasilevskii, rev. of *Revoliutsiia i molodezh'*, *Krasnaia molodezh'* 1 (1925): 136–40. I quote Zalkind from the same source.

109. L. Tarskoi, "Ni v chem ne ver' na slovo," *Knigonosha* 42 (1924): 2–3. Tarskoi's term is *slovobludie*, a play on *rukobludie* (masturbation).

4. Confusion and Backlash

1. Polina Vinogradskaia, "Voprosy byta," *P*, July 26, 1923, pp. 4–5.

2. Leon Trotsky, "Voprosy byta," *P*, Aug. 12, 1923, p. 2; see also his "Ot staroi sem'i—k novoi," *Sochineniia*, 21:32ff. (orig. publ. in *P*, July 13, 1923).

3. Trotsky, "Zadachi kommunisticheskogo vospitaniia," 327, 335.

4. A. Tarasov-Rodionov, *Shokolad [Chocolate]*, 4th ed. (M-Kharkov: Proletarii, n.d.), 34 (first serialized in *MG* in 1922).

5. Ibid., 53.

6. Ibid., 186.

7. See Leopold Averbakh, "Literaturnye ocherki," *MG* 10–11 (1925): 207–27.

8. Semashko, "Novyi byt," 476–78.

9. Shkotov, 30.

10. Gorinevsky, 3.

11. On Kin and Ippolit, see *Vsegda po etu storonu. Vospominaniia o Viktore Kine*, comp. S. A. Liandres (M: Sovetskii pisatel, 1966); see also Cecilia Kin, *Autoritratto in rosso* (Rome: Lucarini, 1989).

12. Kin, "Uspekh skandala," *Molodoi Bol'shevik* 5 (1927): 33–35.

13. Ippolit, *Pravo na liubov'*, 22.

14. Ibid., 73.

15. Saradzhev, 55–63.

16. N. Neznamov, "Ereticheskie zametki," *IuK* 13 (1927): 54–63.

17. S. Mileiko, "Ereticheskaia eres' i ereticheskaia liubov'," *IuK* 14 (1927): 57–66.

18. B. R., review of *Pravo na liubov'*, *IuK* 14 (1927): 67–70.

19. Saradzhev, 55–63.

20. Andrei Volzhsky, "Druz'ia po Volge" (M: Rabochaia Moskva, 1925).

21. *Sud nad pornografiei v literature* (M: Vserossiiskii soiuz krest'ianskikh pisatelei, 1926). The trial was held on Nov. 17, 1925. See also G. Moroz, "Poshliaki literatury," *P*, Oct. 25, 1925, p. 5.

22. *Sud nad pornografiei v literature*, 21.

23. Ibid., 31.

24. Gorsuch also argues that not all youth who misbehaved were intentially counterrevolutionary—no matter if their behavior was seen as a challenge by authorities; see esp. 182–83.

25. V. Rozin, "Kto vinovat: k voprosu o samoubiistve," *IuK*: 60.

26. Cf. V. Ermilov, "Ob upadochnykh nastroeniiakh i intelligentskoi fraze," *IuK* 15 (1926): 29–40; and TsKhDMO, fond 1, op. 23, del. 589, pp. 12–14.

27. "Pis'mo komsomolki," *Smena* 9 (1926): 11–12.

28. Ibid., 12.

29. Zalkind, *Komsomol'skii byt*.

30. Ippolit, *Pravo na liubov'*, 34ff.

31. Lass, 31; see also Gorsuch, 31ff.

32. Boris Galin, "K novomu bytu na rysiakh ne poskachesh'," *Molodoi bol'shevik* 7–8 (1927): 84–91; see Naiman, 169ff.

33. N. Tutkin, "Kul'turnaia revoliutsiia i vuzy," *IuK* 14 (1927): 34–39.

34. S. K., "K voprosu o khuliganstve," *IuK* 19 (1926): 47–53.

35. Tutkin, 37.

36. See numerous reports to the Komsomol Central Committee, TsKhDMO, fond 1, op. 23, d. 743.

37. Zalkind, "Otritsatel'nye storony v bytu molodezhi," *Komsomolskii byt*, 167.

38. Gladkov, *P'ianoe solntse [Drunken Sun]*, *NM* 8 (1927): 35 (ellipses in original).

39. Fedor Gladkov, *Cement*, trans. A. S. Arthur and C. Ashleigh (New York: F. Ungar, 1980) (publ. serially in *KN* in 1925).

40. G. Iartsev, "Obrezhem kryl'ia 'krylatomu Erosu' (O 'p'ianom solntse F. Gladkova)," *MG* 1 (1928): 183–94.

41. Zalkind, "O zabolevaniiakh partaktiva," *KN* 4 (1925): 187–203.

42. O. Zortseva, "Boleznennye iavleniia (Po materialam TsKK VKP(b))," *P*, Feb. 18, 1927, p. 6.

43. Speech by Lev Sosnovsky, TsVLKSM (file for Feb.–Aug. 1927), TsKhDMO, fond 1, op. 23, delo 740, pp. 80–84.

44. Milchakov, *Komsomol v bor'be za kul'turnyi byt* (M-L: Molodaia gvardiia, 1927), 17ff.; see also Gorsuch, 62ff.

45. Ketlinskaia and Slepkov, 62.

46. V. Slepkov, "Ne o edinoi politike zhiv komsomolets," rpt. in *Komsoml'skii byt*, 215–19; see also N. Vigilianskii, "O studencheskom byte," *IuK* 11–12 (1927): 74–80.

47. Ketlinskaia and Slepkov, 92.

48. Tur, 57ff.

49. S. Kartashev, "Na predmet devstvennosti," *KP*, June 26, 1926.

50. Tsukker, *Fizkul'tura, 33*.

51. See O. Zortseva, "Boleznennye iavleniia," *P*, Feb. 18, 1927, p. 6. Citing a 1925 report in *Izvestiia*, Halfin notes that 14% of Bolsheviks' deaths were suicides (*Terror*, 109); on suicide as an intersection between life and text at that time, see Anne Nesbet, "Suicide as a Literary Fact in the 1920s," *Slavic Review* 50 (1991): 827–35.

52. TsKhDMO, fond 1, op. 23., d. 588, pp. 27–29.

53. Kuznetsov's death (a year before Esenin's) occurred either on Sept. 14 or Sept. 20; articles at the time cited the later date; however, the biographical sketch in *Komsomol'skie poety dvadtsatykh godov*, compiled by M. F. Pianykh (L: Sovetskii pisatel', 1988), argues that it was Sept. 14 as per the memoirs of V. Svetozarov.

54. D. Gorbov, rev. of *Rabochee serdtse*, 1924, *Knigonosha* 6 (1925): 18.

55. L. Baril,"Pamiati Nikolaia Kuznetsova," *Komsomoliia* 3 (1926): 58.

56. Ibid., 54–60.

57. Ilya Lin, foreword to Nikolai Kuznetsov, *Rabochee serdtse. Stikhi* (M: Novaia Moskva, 1925), 9.

58. Ibid., 10.

59. "Doklad tov. Bukharina," *XIV s"ezd vsesoiuznoi kommunisticheskoi partii(b). Stenograficheskii otchet* (M-L: Gosizdat, 1926): 811–27.

60. "O rabote komsomola," *XIV s"ezd*, 988–1000.

61. See esp. *Kuda idet komsomol. Sbornik statei* (M-L: Molodaia gvardiia, 1927) and *Komsomol na perelome. Sbornik statei* (M-L: Molodaia gvardiia, 1927).

62. See Yaroslavsky, "Za uporiadochenie zhizni i byta molodezhi," *Komsomol'skii byt*: 104–08, and Khanin, foreword to *Kuda idet komsomol,* 3–10.

63. Max Eastman, *Artists in Literature: A Study of Literature and Bureaucratism* (New York: Knopf, 1934), 50. Some now argue that Esenin was killed, a charge not publicly raised then. See, for example, V. I. Kuznetsov, *Sergei Esenin: Taina smerti* (St. Petersburg: Neva, 2004).

64. Gordon McVay, *Esenin: A Life* (New York: Paragon, 1976), 93.

65. Ibid., 127.

66. Eastman, 55–56.

67. Esenin, "Zheleznyi Mirgorod," *Izvestiia*, Aug. 22, 1923, p. 2.

68. Leon Trotsky, "Pamiati Sergeia Esenina," *P,* Jan. 19, 1926, p. 3.

69. N. I. Bukharin, "Zlye zametki," *Octiabr* 2 (1927): 133 (first publ. in *P,* Jan. 12, 1927).

70. See "Protiv eseninshchiny. Pis'mo v redaktsiiu," *KP,* June 15, 1926, p. 2.

71. G. Bergman, "Esenin—znamia upadochnykh nastroenii," *KP,* June 15, 1926, pp. 2–3.

72. Aleksandr Zharov, "Protiv literaturnykh beschinstv," *O pisatel'skoi etike, literaturnom khuliganstve i bogeme* (L: Priboi, 1927), pp. 60–62.

73. Aleksandr Bezymensky, "Protiv 'eseninshchiny,'" *Komsomoliia* 6–7 (1926): 71–75.

74. Sosnovsky, "Razvenchaite khuligantsvo," *P,* Sept. 19, 1926 (rpt. in *O pisatel'skoi etike,* 63–68). He quotes from Esenin's "Poi zhe, poi" (1922) and "Syp' garmonika. Skuka . . . Skuka . . ." (1922).

75. A. Kruchenykh, *Esenin i 'Moskva kabatskaia,'* (M: Author, 1926), 22.

76. Bergman, 3.

77. Reviakin, 18.

78. Bukharin, "Zlye zametki," 136.

79. N. I. Bukharin, "Vystuplenie na soveshchanii o politike partii v khudozhestvennoi literature," *Revoliutsia i kul'tura: stat'i i vystupleniia 1923–1936 godov* (M: Fond im. N. I. Bukharina, 1993): 63–66.

80. Bukharin, "Zlye zametki," 137.

81. Alexander Voronsky, "Ob otoshedshem," in Sergei Esenin, *Sobranie stikhotvorenii*, vol. 1, 2nd ed. (M-L: Gosizdat, 1926): xiii–xxxiii.

82. I. M. Mashbits-Verbov, rev. of *Moskva Kabatskaia* (1924), *Oktiabr* 2 (1925): 142–45.

83. "Pokhorony poeta Sergeia Esenina," *P,* Jan. 1, 1926, p. 10.

84. D. Gorbov, *U nas i za rubezhom* (M: Krug, 1928), 223.

85. Fedor Zhits, "Pochemu my liubim Esenina," *KN* 5 (1925): 216–22.

5. Annus Horribilis

1. S. K., "K voprosu o khuliganstve," 47.

2. "Polovaia zhizn' studenchestva," *Vecherniaia Moskva,* Apr. 16, 1926, p. 2.

3. Panteleimon Romanov, "Bez cheremukhi" ["Without a Cherry Blossom"], *MG* 6 (1926): 8–21.

4. Sergei Malashkin, "Luna s pravoi storony" ["Moon on the Right"], *MG* 9 (1926): 3–54.

5. Lev Gumilevsky, *Sobachii pereulok [Dog Alley]* (L: Author, 1927). On the controversy over Romanov, Malashkin, and Gumlevsky, see Naiman, 99–107; in *Terror,* chaps. 3–4, Halfin dissects "Moon on the Right" and *Dog Alley* in connection with Soviet discourses of sexuality, physiology, and psychology and the redemption of degenerate youth.

6. Sergei Okulov, "Vyvikhi byta," *KS* 3 (1927): 27–29.

7. Ekaterina Troshchenko, "Disput v Akademii Kom. Vospitaniia im. Krupskoi," *MG* 12 (1926): 168–73.

8. Ekaterina Troshchenko, "Vuzovskaia molodezh'," *MG* 4 (1927): 129–30. N. Vigilianskii, "O studencheskom byte," *IuK* 11–12 (1927): 74–80, disputed Troshchenko's assertion: "Our dorms are indistinguishable from the philistine street" (77).

9. I. Novich, "Kholostoi vystrel," *NLP* 1 (1927): 52.

10. R. Begak, "'Luna s pravoj storony' S. Malashkina," *MG* 12 (1926): 165–67. See also I. Sit[kov], rev. of *MG* 8–9 (1926), *KP*, Oct. 15, 1926, p. 4; regarding Romanov, see also I. Sitkov, rev. of *MG* 6 (1926), in *KP*, Aug. 18, 1926, p. 4.

11. Valerian Poliansky, "Pis'ma o literature," *NLP* 7 (1927): 38ff.

12. R. F. Kulle, "Po 'sobach'im pereulkam' literatury," *Vestnik znaniia* 10 (1927): 607–12.

13. Lev Gumilevsky, *Sud'ba i zhizn'*, *Volga* 8 (1988): 104.

14. D. Khanin, "Protiv travli," *KP*, Feb. 17, 1928, p. 2.

15. S. Ingulov, "Bobchinskii na Parnase," *MG* 11 (1929): 80, lumped the three together as a new "Romanov dynasty." But he assured his readers that "the reign of this dynasty will be far shorter than the other Romanov dynasty, which required two revolutions to overthrow."

16. Dm. Bukhartsev, "O pessimisticheskoi 'lune' i pessimizme voobshche," *Molodoi Bol'-shevik* 9–10 (1927): 16.

17. Poliansy, "Pis'ma," 39; see also G. Korotkov, "Literatura sobach'ego pereulka," *Rezets* 15 (1927): 15.

18. B. R., "Golos chitatelia-shveinika," *Kniga i profsoiuzy* 7–8 (1927): 24.

19. M. Gribanov, "Dovol'no klevety," *KS* 8 (1927): 59.

20. "U nas v zhurnale," *MG* 7 (1926): 164–65.

21. B., "S cheremukhoi ili bez cheremukhi," *Molodoi Leninets*, Aug. 11, 1927, p. 2.

22. "O povesti Malashkina: 'Luna s pravoi storony,'" *NLP* 8 (1927): 42ff.

23. A. L., "'Prislushivaites' k tomu, chto oni govoriat," *Kniga i profsoiuzy* 9 (1927): 25.

24. "O povesti Malashkina," 42ff.

25. "U nas v zhurnale," *MG* 11 (1926): 221.

26. "O povesti Malashkina," 42ff.

27. "U nas v zhurnale," *MG* 8 (1926): 171–72.

28. "U nas v zhurnale," *MG* 11 (1926): 221.

29. "Vmesto itogov literaturnoi diskussii," *KS* 10 (1927): 63–67.

30. "U nas v zhurnale," *MG* 11 (1926): 221.

31. N. Erlikh, "Merzost' naraspashku," *Zaboi* 5 (1927): 21–2.

32. Iu. L., "O P. Romanove," *NLP* 21 (1928): 32–34.

33. A. Lezhnev, rev. of *Sobachii pereulok*, *KN* 1 (1927): 256–7; "S. Malashkin," *Prozhektor* 2 (1927): 19. For Gorbov's criticism of Romanov, see Gorbov, "Molodaia gvardiia. Knigi 6 i 7. 1926 g.," *KN* 10 (1926): 234–37.

34. P. Ionov, "Bez cheremukhi," *P*, Dec. 4, 1926, pp. 5–6.

35. Malashkin, "Luna," 3.

36. "Na potrebu obyvatelia," *Chitatel' i pisatel'* 12 (1928): 7.

37. Romanov, "Bol'shaia sem'ia" ["A Big Family"], *NM* 7 (1927): 84.

38. Lev Gumilevsky, "Zakliuchiutel'noe slovo," *KS* 6 (1927): 52–53.

39. Student, "Otvet avtoru 'Sobach'ego pereulka,'" *KS* 7 (1927): 56.

40. "Vmesto itogov literaturnoi diskussii," 63–67.

41. Gumilevsky, *Sud'ba i zhizn'*, 105.

42. On Gorky, see *Sud'ba i zhizn'*, 105; letter of Dec. 15, 1926, and Sosnovsky's letter of Dec. 26, 1926, in *Istoriia sovetskoi politicheskoi tsenzury: dokumenty i kommentarii*, ed. T. M. Goriaeva (M: Rosspen, 1997), 453–54.

43. Berezovsky, 4.

44. "Disput v Akademii," 173.

45. V. Ermilov, "Partiinye obyvateli (O 'Zapiskakh obyvatelia' Dm. Furmanova)," *MG* 10 (1926): 162.

46. Ionov, 5–6.

47. V. Ermilov, "O besplodnom nravouchitel'stve. Otvet tov. Ionovu," *MG* 3 (1927): 166–76; see also David-Fox, 112.

48. S. Gusev, "Kakova nasha molodezh," *MG* 6 (1927): 114–39.

49. See, for example, "O povesti Malashkina," 42–50; and M. R., "Disput o 'Lune i chere-mukhe,'" *KP,* Jan. 13, 1927, p. 4.

50. "U nas v zhurnale," *MG* 11 (1926): 209; see also letters on Romanov in *MG* 7– 8 (1926).

51. TsKhDMO, fond 1, op. 23, delo 588, p. 84.

52. TsKhDMO, fond 1, op. 23, delo 736, pp. 67–69.

53. Originally published in *P,* July 1, 1925; rpt. in *Schast'e literatury. Gosudarstvo i pisateli. 1925–1938gg. Dokumenty,* ed. D. L. Babichenko (M: Rosspen, 1997), 17–21.

54. Resolution of the Komsomol Central Committee: "O politike prosvetitel'noi raboty v komsomole," June 30, 1926, TsKhDMO, fond 1, op. 23, d. 588, pp. 101–11.

55. Khailov, 367.

56. V. Ermilov, "Put' 'Molodoi gvardii," *MG* 6 (1927): 191–95.

57. Ippolit stated that in 1925 *The Young Guard* was almost at "death's door" because of its focus on young proletarian writers who produced "puerile and immature works." He praised the new direction taken in 1926, singling out "Without a Cherry Blossom." See Ippolit, rev. of *MG* 1–6 (1926), *Knigonosha* 31–32 (1926): 10–11.

58. Robert Maguire, *Red Virgin Soil: Soviet Literature in the 1920's* (Ithaca: Cornell UP, 1987), 366.

59. Gusev, "Kakova nasha molodezh'," 114.

60. Gumilevsky, *Sud'ba i zhizn',* 106; ellipses in original.

61. Herman Ermolaev, *Censorship in Soviet Literature, 1917–1991* (New York: Rowman & Littlefield, 1997), 1–2.

62. Iosif Kallinikov, *Moshchi,* 2nd ed., (M-L: Krug, n.d.).

63. Korotkov, 14.

64. B. Irk, rev. of *Moshchi,* vols. 1–2, *Z* 3 (1926): 259.

65. A. Pridorogin, rev. of *Moshchi,* vol. 2, *Knigonosha* 21 (1926): 32; see also N. Fatov, "Antireligioznaia propaganda? Pornografiia!," *NLP* 1 (1926): 48; I. Mashbits-Verov, rev. of *Moshchi,* vols. 1–2, *MG* 6 (1926): 205–6; and Zel. Shteiman, "On zhiv graf Amori," *Z* 4 (1927): 160–66.

66. Ionov, 5; Semashko, "Nevezhestvo," p. 3.

67. "Iz dokladnoi zapiski P. I. Lebedeva-Polianskogo 'O deiatel'nosti Glavlita' Orgbiuro TsK VKP(b)," *Schast'e literatury: gosudarstvo i pisateli, 1925–1938. Dokumenty,* ed. D. L. Babichenko (M: Rosspen, 1997), 29–40.

68. Protocol no. 147 from a Feb. 27, 1922, meeting of the Orgburo, cited by Lebedev-Poliansky in "Iz dokladnoi zapiski," 32.

6. Life versus Literature

1. "Ot izdatel'stva," in *Luna s pravoi storony* (M: Molodaia gvardiia, 1928), n.p.

2. On Soviet writers' internalization of utilitarian principles, see Evgeny Dobrenko, *Formovka sovetskogo pisatelia: sotsial'nye i esteticheskie istoki sovetskoi literaturnoi kul'ture* (St. P: Akademicheskii proekt, 1999), esp. 86ff.

3. Frederick Engels, letter to Margaret Harkness, Apr. 1888, in Karl Marx and Frederick Engels, *Literature and Art* (New York: International Publishers, 1947), 43.

4. Valerian Poliansky, "O povesti S. Malashkina 'luna s pravoi storony,'" *PR* 2 (1927): 98; see Halfin, *Terror,* 107.

5. D. Gorbov, *U nas i za rubezhom,* 175ff.

6. D. Gorbov, *Poiski Galatei,* quoted in G. Belaia, *Don Kikhoty 20–x godov* (M: Sovetskii pisatel', 1989), 170.

7. Ivan Bobryshev, *Melkoburzhuaznye vliianiia sredi molodezhi* (M-L: Molodaia gvardiia, 1928), 121.

8. See Belaia, *Don Kikhoty 20–x godov;* and A. Kemp-Welch, *Stalin and the Literary Intelligentsia, 1928–39* (Basingstoke: Macmillan, 1991).

9. V. Ermilov, "Protiv meshchanskoi krasivosti," in *S kem i pochemu my boremsja,* ed. L. Averbakh (M-L: Zemlia i fabrika, 1930): 134.

10. Yury Libedinsky, "Za chto borivutsia napostovsty," *General'nye zadachi proletarskoi literatury* (M-L: Gosizdat, 1931): 3–36.

11. Yury Libedinsky, "Realisticheskii pokaz lichnosti, kak ocherednaia zadacha proletarskoi literatury," *NLP* 1 (1927): 25–30.

12. M. Bekker, "Problema tipa v komsomol'skoi literature," *Komsomoliia* 3 (1926): 44–49.

13. V. Ermilov, "Problema zhivogo cheloveka v sovremennoi literature i 'Vor' L. Leonova," in *Za zhivogo cheloveka v literature* (M: Federatsiia, 1928): 30.

14. Ermilov, "Protiv meshchanskoi krasivosti."

15. Aleksandr Fadeev, *Stolbovaia doroga proletarskoi literatury* (L: Priboi, 1929), 12.

16. Ibid., 33.

17. A. G. Gornfeld, *Knigi i liudi* (S. Petersburg: Zhizn', 1908), 30.

18. Ermilov, "Put'," 193.

19. V. Ermilov, "V poiskakh garmonicheskogo cheloveka," *NLP* 20 (1927): 56–64.

20. Sergei Semenov, *Natalya Tarpova,* (M-L: Izd. pisatelei, 1933), 427. The novel was serialized in *MG* 1–2, 4–6, 4–10 (1927–1928).

21. I. Novich, "Zametki o romane S. Semenova 'Natalya Tarpova,'" *NLP* 17–18 (1927): 49–55; see also Yu. Pertsovich, "Respublika na ekzamene," *Z* 8 (1927): 140–49, and Aleks. Migunov, rev. of *Natalya Tarpova, Zemlia sovetskaia* 10 (1929): 60.

22. V. Friche, "Literaturnye zametki," *P,* Aug. 14, 1927, p. 6; G. Yakubovsky, "O chem i kak pishet Sergei Semenov," *Oktiabr'* 5 (1928): 217–30. See also S. Pakentreiger, rev. of *Natalya Tarpova, NM* 10 (1927): 220–21.

23. G. Brylov, N. Lebedev, et al., eds., *Golos rabochego chitatelia* (L: Krasnaia gazeta, 1929), 148ff.

24. Ibid., 149ff.; see also P. Neznamov, "Dradedamovyi byt," *Novyi LEF* 6 (1928): 21–28, M. Sh., "Massovaia biblioteka 'Molodoi gvardii,'" 12 (1929): 58–59; and S. Tretiakov, "S novym godom!" LEF 1 (1928): 1–3.

25. Bobryshev, *Melkoburzhuaznye vliianiia,* 112.

26. "O pisateliakh iz molodezhi," *KP,* June 19, 1926, p. 3.

27. Quoted in Evgeny Gromov, *Stalin: vlast' i isskustvo* (M: Respublika, 1998), 78.

28. Libedinsky, "Za chto," 6.

29. "Chitatel'," *Novyi LEF* 1 (1927): 1.

30. Leopold Averbakh, *Kul'turnaia revoliutsiia i voprosy sovremennoi literatury* (M-L: Gosizdat, 1928), 125–28.

31. V. Ermilov, "Ideologiia iz . . . khoroshego doma," *NLP* 1 (1926): 47–48.

32. Lezhnev, "Byt molodezhi i sovremennaia literatura," *KS* 5 (1927): 51–53.

33. Alexander Voronskij, "Literaturnye zametki," *KN* 1 (1923): 292, was defending the writers Arosev, Tarasov-Rodionov, and Libedinsky himself.

34. Mikhail Maizel, "Pornografiia i patalogiia v sovremennoi literature," in *Golosa protiv: kriticheskii al'manakh* (L: Izd. pisatelei, 1928), 170.

35. Bukhartsev, 16; see also I. Novich, "Kholostoi vystrel," *NLP* 1 (1927): 49–54.

36. "U nas v zhurnale," *MG* 11 (1926), 219.

37. "Disput v Akademii," 172.

38. Quoted in Maizel, 169.

39. Panteleimon Romanov, "O sebe, kritike i o prochem," *30 dnei* 6 (1927): 28–29.

40. P. Romanov, "Iz zapisnoi knizhki pisatelia," *Utro: literaturnyi sbornik*, ed. N. N. Fatov (M-L: Izd. avtorov, 1927), 198.

41. Viacheslav Polonsky, "O 'problemakh pola' i 'polovoi' literature," *O sovremennoi literature* (M-L: Gosizdat, 1928), 193.

42. Georgy Gorbachev, "Pisateli, pytaiushchiesia byt' neitral'nymi i kolebliushchiesia," in *Panteleimon Romanov*, ed. E. F. Nikitina (M: Nikitinskie subbotniki, 1928), 94.

43. P. Romanov, "K dvizheniiu ili k nepodvizhnosti?" *NM* 3 (1927): 177–80; "O sebe," 28–29.

44. For details on the rape and prosecution, see Naiman, 250ff.: As a symbolic event, Naiman argues that the rape represented a "hideous parody" in that the collectivist underpinnings of Bolshevik discourse were realized via the rape's "gothic" elements, its motif of sexual communality, its homoerotic potential, and how the San Galli Garden where it occurred was a "distortion of War Communism proletarian Eden." He concludes, "Soviet ideology saw its own 'childhood' fantasies represented in Chubarov Alley and recoiled" (266–86). See also Halfin, *From Darkness to Light,* 146; Borenstein, 68; on the hooliganism phenomenon, see Gorsuch 176ff.

45. *Chubarovshchina: Po materialam sudebnogo protsessa* (M-L: Gosizdat, 1927), 23ff.

46. G. Grebnev, "K delu Koren'kova," *KP,* Oct. 14, 1926, p. 4.

47. L. Lebedev and S. Serov, *Molodezh' na sude: sudebno-bytovye ocherki* (M-L: Molodaia gvardiia, 1927), 21ff.

48. "Delo Koren'kova," *KP,* June 20, 1926, p. 4.

49. L. Sosnovsky, "Delo Koren'kova," *KP,* June 5, 1926, p. 2.

50. Lebedev and Serov, 35; Divilkovsky, "Bolezni byta molodezhi," 174.

51. Sofia Smidovich, "O davidsonovshchine," *MG* 8 (1926): 128–31.

52. Sofia Smidovich, "O koren'kovshchine," *MG* 7 (1926): 97.

53. Polonsky, "Kriticheskie zametki," 178.

54. See P. Nikolaev, rev. of *Chubarovshchina, IuK* 8 (1927): 69–70, which complains that the documents do not go far enough.

55. I. Bobryshev, "Pereulki i tupiki," *KP,* Mar. 1, 1927, p. 3; Mar. 2, 1927, pp. 2–3.

56. V. Kirshon and A. Uspensky, *Konstantin Terekhin (Rzhavchina)* (M-L: Gosudarstvennoe izdatel'stvo, 1927). (This Andrei Uspensky is not the author of *O vrede rannikh polovykh snoshenii,* cited in chapter 2.)

57. E. B. Demidovich, *Sud nad polovoi raspushchennost'iu* (M-L: Doloi negramotnost', 1927); see also Naiman, 108, 132.

58. Aron Zalkind, "Predislovie," in *Sud nad polovoi raspushchennost'iu,* 3.

59. L. Lebedev and L. Rubinstein, *Pis'ma iz uteriannogo portfelia (o poshlosti v bytu)* (M: Molodaia gvardiia, 1928).

60. Ibid., 52.

61. Ibid., 5–6.

62. Ibid., 26.

63. I. Iv., "Bez luny," *Izvestiia* Mar. 8, 1928, p. 6.

64. Lev Kopelev, *The Education of a True Believer*, trans. Gary Kern (New York: Harper & Row, 1980), 212.

65. Ig. Maleev, "Sezonnoe uvlechenie ili dlitel'naia bor'ba," *IuK* 22 (1926): 48–52.

66. "O kleveie na molodezh'," p. 1.

67. Pankrat Bul'var, "Luna bez cheremukhi ili liubov' iz sobach'ego pereulka," *S* 9 (1927): 10, 12.

68. My thanks to Ronald LeBlanc for suggesting the connection with Edward Bulwer-Lytton, author of the famous "It was a dark and stormy night . . . .".

69. Zel. Shteiman, "Pobediteli, kotorykh sudiat," *Golosa protiv* (L: Izd. pisatelei v Leningrade, 1928), 83–114.

70. B. Gorovits, "Chto chitaet rabochaia molodezh'," *Krasnyi bibliotekar'* 4 (1929): 45.

71. Shteiman, 107ff.; see also "Protiv literaturnoi bogemy," *Molodoi Leninets,* Apr. 4, p. 1.

72. Tretiakov, "S novym godom," 1–3.

73. "O klevete na molodezh'," p. 1.

74. Bukhartsev, 22.

7. A Canon of Ambiguity

1. Boris Chetverikov, *Atava: povesti i rasskazy [Aftergrowth]* (M-L: Gosizdat, 1925), first publ. in *Krasnaia nov* 3–4 (1924).

2. See also Ilya Lukashin, *Gorod perepliui* (M: Proletarii, n.d.), which contains a number of sordid elements; by now the party's reputation had sunk so low that "Bolshevik" was slang for "adulterer."

3. Nikolai Ognev, *Dnevnik Kosti Riabtseva, KN* 1 (1927): 94.

4. See Alexander Voronsky, foreword to Ognev, *Sobranie sochinenii,* vol.1 (M: Federatsiia, 1928): 5–19; B. O., rev. of *Dnevnik Kosti Riabtseva, Kniga i profsoiuzy* 5 (1927): 46; Gennady Fish, rev. in *Z* 4 (1927): 167.

5. Ilya Rubanovsky, "O Koste Riabtseve i ego dnevnike," *MG* 5 (1927): 178–84.

6. Ilya Ehrenburg, *V Protchnom pereulke [In Protochny Alley],* in *Sobranie sochinenii v vos'mi tomakh,* vol. 2 (M: Khudozhestvennaia literatura, 1991); it first appeared in *30 dnej* 1–3 (1927) in a heavily censored version. That same year it ws republished as the seventh volume of Erenburg's collected works with most of the omissions restored.

7. D. Gorbov, rev. of *V Protchnom pereulke, NM* 1 (1928): 307; see also Vladimir Friche, *Zametki o sovremennoi literature* (M-L: Moscovskii rabochii, 1928), 46–55.

8. Ilya Erenburg, *Liudi, gody, zhizn',* vol. 1 (M: Sovetskii pisatel, 1990), 460ff.

9. Vladimir Lidin, *Otstupnik [The Apostate],* in *Sobranie sochinenii,* vol. 3 (M-L: Gosizdat, 1927).

10. G. Munblit, rev. of *Otstupnik, MG* 4 (1928): 203–04; M. Poliakova, "'Otstupnik' Vl. Lidina," *PR* 4 (1928): 111.

11. E. Zh., rev. of *Otstupnik, NLP* 15–16 (1928): 106–07.

12. S., rev. of *Otstupnik, Rezets* 22 (1929); see also M. N., "Protiv otkhoda ot kollektiva," *Sibirskie ogni* 1 (1929): 219–20.

13. Mikhail Platoshkin, *V doroge [On the Road],* M-L: Moskovskii rabochii, 1929).

14. E. Levitskaia, "Eshche o molodezhi," *NLP* 18 (1929): 48–50; see also S. Kuper, rev. of *V doroge, Zvezda* 1 (1930): 223–24.

15. V. Druzin, rev. of *V doroge, Rezets* 24 (1929): 1.

16. Anon., rev. of *V doroge, Rost* 2 (1930): 27.

17. B. G., rev. of *V doroge, Kniga i revoliutsiia* 15–16 (1929): 72–73.

18. I. Novich, rev. of *V doroge, NLP* 17 (1929): 64–65.

19. A. Isbakh, *"V doroge* (vmesto otveta t. Levistkoi)," *NLP* 18 (1929): 50–55.

20. I. Ilinsky, "Bytovye perezhitki pered litsom sovetskogo suda," *KN* 7 (1926): 189–203.

21. M. I. Slukhovsky, *Kniga i derevnia* (M-L: Gosizdat, 1928), 139.

22. Dmitry Sverchkov, "Delo #3576," *KN* 2 (1927): 65–85.

23. Ibid., 79.

24. M. M. Rubinshtein, *Iunost'. Po dnevnikam i avtobiograficheskim zapisiam* (M: Publication of the Advanced Pedagogical Courses of the Moscow Training College, 1928).

25. Ibid., 89.

26. Zhenya identifies him as "I.," but to avoid confusion with the pronoun I have substituted "P."

27. Gleb Alekseev, "Delo o trupe," in *Inye rasskazy* (M: Krug, 1926), 129–77.

28. Gleb Alekseev, *Teni stoiashchego vperedi* in *Sobranie sochinenii*, vol. 3 (M-L: Molodaia gvardiia, 1929); for negative responses to it, see R. Kovnator, "Teni stoiashchego vperedi," *Z* 5 (1928): 147–60; I. Mashbits-Verov, "Nastuplenie meshchanstva," *Kniga i profsoiuzy* 2 (1929): 4–7; Aleksandr Virin, "Reaktsiia pod maskoi 'novogo cheloveka,'" *NLP* 4–5 (1929): 61–68; and reviews in *Kniga i revoliutsiia* 7 (1929): 57; *Krasnyi bibliotekar'* 3 (1929): 93.

29. Ilinsky, 203.

30. Yakovlev, *"Bez beregov,"* 5–61.

31. See Vsevolod Ivanov, "Smert' Sapegi" and "Pustynia Tuub-koja" in *Tainoe tainikh. Rasskazy* (M-L: Gosizdat, 1927); Andrei Sobol, "Kniazhna," in *Kitaiskie teni: povesti i rasskazy* (M-L: Zemlia i fabrika, 1926); and Boris Lavrenev, "Sorok pervyi," in *Sobranie sochinenii*, vol. 2 (Kharkov: Proletarii, 1930).

32. Galina Serebriakova, "Rosa," *NM* 3 (1930): 62–99.

33. See, for example, Goldman and Wood.

34. Smidovich, *Rabotnitsa*.

35. See the letter signed by ten women, "Ivanovo-voznesenskie devushki-komsomolki otvechaiut," *KP*, Jan. 12, 1927, p. 1.

36. See Goldman, 254ff.

37. L. Argutinskaia, "Abort," *KS* 7 (1927): 31–37.

38. Ilya Lin, *Iacheikina doch'* (M-L: Molodaia gvardiia, 1925), reports that in August 1924, 36 of 1,000 men and 8 of 1,000 women were in the Komsomol. By April 1925, the numbers were 89 and 16, respectively. According to Lin, there were 25 million young people in the USSR. See also Gorsuch, 96ff. 39. E. Troshchenko, "Devushka v soiuze," *MG* 3 (1926): 130, puts the number of women in the Komsomol at 19 percent.

40. Berezhanskii, "Komsomol'skaia liubov'," *KP*, June 15, 1926, p. 3.

41. Gladkov, *P'ianoe solntse*, 44–45.

42. For a contemporary discussion of the same in American culture, see Eleanor Rowland Wembridge, "Silk Stockings," *The Survey* 52 (1924): 28–30.

43. Georgy Nikiforov, *U fonaria* (M-L: Zemlia i fabrika, 1929), 226.

44. A. Kollontai, "Novaia ugroza," *Kommunistka* 8–9 (1922): 5–9; on imaging the prostitute, see Elizabeth Wood, "Prostitution Unbound: Representations of Sexual and Political Anxieties in Post-revolutionary Russia," in *Sexuality and the Body in Russian Culture;* see also Frances L. Bernstein, "Prostitutes and Proletarians: The Soviet Labor Clinic as Revolutionary Laboratory," in *The Human Tradition in Modern Russia*, ed. William B. Husband (Wilmington: SR Books, 2000): 113–28.

45. N. Semashko, "Nuzhna li zhenstvennost'," *MG* 6 (1924): 205–06. See also Shkotov, *Byt molodezhi*, 33; Healy, 62–63, on how some lesbians took advantage of the masculinized look to indulge in cross-dressing.

46. V. Kuzmin, "O zhenstvennosti," *Smena* 9–10 (1925): 16–17.

47. I. Minaev, "Nuzhna li zhenstvennost'?" *Smena* 9–10 (1925): 15; "Chitateli 'smeny' o zhenstvennosti," *Smena* 15 (1925): 11.

48. On the problems of imaging the perfect Soviet woman, see Barbara Evans Clements, "The Utopianism of the Zhenotdel," *Slavic Review* 51 (1992): 485–96; Naiman also comments on the "desire to be rid of women within the utopian project" (41), with the result that "[in the 1920s] the figurative destruction of the female body and the concern with woman as a limiting origin would come to play an important role in the Soviet discourse of class identity and national survival." In *Men Without Women,* Borenstein also identifies the Bolshevik mentality as one that had no real place for women unless thoroughly masculinized. This current was internalized to the extent that even with prominent noncommunist writers (Olesha, Babel, and Platonov), one can identify feminity in their works as "a nagging, potentially subversive threat to the male order that must be kept at bay at all cost" (162).

49. Naiman, 182 ff., makes the useful observation that this was not limited only to writers; many officials who sought to defend and instruct women often fell into linking them with agents of corruption.

50. Nik. Nikandrov, *Put' k zhenshchine* (M: Moskovskoe tovarishchestvo pisatelei, 1927). "Dirt" comes from A. Derman, rev. of *Put' k zhenshchine, Kniga i profsoiuzy* 10 (1927): 16–17; N. N., rev. of *Put' k zhenshchine,* NLP 13 (1927). See also reviews by Viktor Krasilnikov, *Oktiabr'* 8 (1927): 187; and Gennady Fish, *Z* 10 (1927): 139–40.

51. Natalia Shad-Khan, *Chuzheiady [Parasites]* (M: Moskovskoe tovarishchestvo pisatelei, 1927).

52. M. Altshuller, rev. of *Chuzheiady,* NLP 3 (1928): 71. But see also B. Gorn, rev. of *Chuzheiady, KP,* June 16, 1928, p. 5, and T. P., rev. of *Chuzheiady, Kniga i profsoiuzy* 6 (1927): 51.

53. Troshchenko, "Devushka v soiuze," 129.

54. Anna Karavaeva, *Dvor, Sobranie sochinenii,* vol. 3 (M-L: Gosizdat, 1927).

55. Vera Ketlinskaia, *Natka Michurina* (L: Priboi, 1929).

56. Rev. of *Natka Michurina, Kniga i revoliutsiia* 10 (1929): 58.

57. Deng, rev. of *Natka Michurina,* NLP 10 (1929): 78–79.

58. Rev. of *Natka Michurina, Rost* 2 (1930): 27; but see rev. of S. in *Rezets* 17–18 (1929): 12.

59. Georgy Nikiforov, *Zhenshchina* (Berlin: Buch und Bhune, 1930; orig. publ. Zemlia i fabrika, 1929).

60. B. Boichevsky, rev. of *Zhenshchina, Zemlia sovetskaia* 4 (1930): 244–45; Bolidov, rev. of *Zhenshchina, Kniga i revoliutsiia* 5 (1930): 38.

61. I. Mar, rev. of *Zhenshchina,* KN 4 (1930): 202–04.

62. Rev. of *Zhenshchina, Oktiabr* 7 (1930): 214–17.

63. Iakov Korobov, *Katia Dolga: khronika sovremennoi derevni* (L: Priboi, 1926).

64. Boris Guber, rev. of *Katia Dolga,* NM 7 (1926): 189–90; see also reviews by I. Tereshchenko, *Zvezda* 5 (1926): 206; Mix. Luzgin, *Oktiabr* 10 (1926): 131–32; and M. Bekker, NLP 7–8 (1926): 69.

65. D. Gorbov, "Novaia zhenshchina v literature," *Izvestiia,* Mar. 9, 1928, p. 5.

66. B. Bank and A. Vilenkin, *Krest'ianskaia molodezh' i kniga* (M-L: Molodaia gvardiia, 1929), 78.

8. Sex and the Revolution

1. Ilya Brazhnin, *Pryzhok* (L: Izd. pisatelei, 1928), 282–86.

2. V. Veresaev, "Isanka," *Polnoe sobranie sochinenii,* vol. 12, 2nd ed. (M: Nedra, 1928), 5–50.

3. T. Parishova, "Bez dialektiki," *Kniga i revoliutsiia* 28 (1930): 5–73.

4. L. Bernstein, "Razvernut' nastuplenie sotsializma na front byta," *IuK* 12 (1931): 53–61.

5. E. Troshchenko, "Molodezh' v literature,'" *NLP* 4–5 (1929): 52–60.

6. Mark Kolosov, *Zhizn' nachinaetsia: komsomol'skie rasskazy*, 4th ed. (M-L: Gosizdat, 1928).

7. M. Bekker, "O poetakh i pisateliakh gruppy 'Molodaia gvardiia,'" *MG* 6 (1927): 209; "Mark Kolosov," *NLP* 3 (1927): 34.

8. S. B., rev. of Mark Kolosov, *13 i drugie, Komsomol'skie rasskazy*, *MG* 2 (1926): 186.

9. I. M. Mashbits-Verov, rev. of *Komsomol'skie rasskazy*, *KN* 1 (1925): 312–13.

10. M. Bekker, "Mark Kolosov," *Komsomoliia* 3 (1925): 61.

11. M. Bekker, "Mark Kolosov," *NLP* 3 (1927): 36.

12. M. Bekker, "Problemy tipov v komsomol'skoi literature," *Komsomoliia* 3 (1926): 44–49; see also "Mark Kolosov," *Komsomoliia* 3 (1925): 64; A.V. Lunacharsky, "O tvorchestve M. Kolosova," foreword to Mark Kolosov, *Zhizn' nachinaetsia. Komosol'skie rasskazy*, 4th ed. (M-L: Gosizdat, 1928), 10.

13. Troshchenko, "Molodezh' v literature," 56.

14. Mashbits-Verov, "Literaturnyi molodniak," *Oktiabr'* 7 (1925): 134.

15. Ibid., 133.

16. P. S. Kogan, "O komsomol'skoi proze (Kolosov, Kochetkov, Shubin)," *MG* 9 (1926): 159.

17. Mashbits-Verov, "Literaturnyi molodniak," 132.

18. Lunacharsky, "O tvorchestve," 6.

19. Ibid., 7–8.

20. Ekaterina Troshchenko, "O 'Pervoi devushke,'" *NLP* 6 (1929): 53.

21. Nikolai Bogdanov, *Pervaia devushka: romanticheskaia istoriia* (Nizhnij Novgorod: Molodaia gvardiia, 1928), 251.

22. V. Druzin, rev. of *Pervaia devushka*, *Z* 1 (1929): 195–96; see also V. S., "Pervaia devushka," *Rezets* 27 (1929): 1; Boris Kireev, rev. of *Pervaia devushka*, *Knigia i profsoiuzy* 2 (1929): 39; Boris Grossman, rev. of *Pervaia devushka*, *NM* 3 (1929): 265–66; D. Talnikov, "Problemnaia literatura," *KN* 3 (1929): 206–09; anon., rev. of *Pervaia devushka*, *Rost* 2 (1930): 27; Al. Berezin, rev. of *Pervaia devushka*, *Zemlia sovetskaia* 4 (1929): 63–64; M. Sh., "Massovaia biblioteka. 'Molodoi gvardii,'" *Zemlia sovetskaia* 12 (1929): 58–59.

23. See also A. Dubovikov, rev. of *Pervaia devushka*, *MG* 2 (1929): 92–94.

24. V. Zlobin, "Pisatel' komsomolii Mark Kolosov," *Rezets* 2 (1932): 15.

25. Mashbits-Verov, rev. of *Komsol'skie rasskazy*, 313.

26. M. Kolosov and V. Gerasimova, *Proba [The Test]* (M: Moskovskii rabochii, 1930); first publ. in *MG* 1 [1929]: 26–61.

27. G. Brovman, "Kak zakaliaiutsia kadry," *MG* 3 (1932): 144.

28. See, for example, V. Kuzmin, rev. of *Proba, NLP* 10 (1932): 28–31.

29. Ibid., 30–31; N.N., "Po zhurnalam," *NLP* 3 (1929): 70; anon., rev. of *Proba, NLP* 1 (1931): 47.

30. See P. Bogdanov, "Komsomol'skii chitatel' v smotre," *MG* 3 (1932): 147–50.

31. M. Rafail, *Za novogo cheloveka* (L: Priboi, 1928).

32. Brovman, 146.

33. Rafail, 41.

34. Kolosov and Gerasimova, 19.

35. M. Kolosov, "O moem tvorchestve," *Rost* 17–18 (1932): 9–10.

36. Yury Libedinsky, *Rozhdenie geroia* [Birth of a Hero], 2nd ed. (L: Goslitizdat, 1931).

37. I. Vinogradov, "Iu. Libedinskii i napostovstvo," *Literaturnaia ucheba* 5 (1933): 73.

38. N. Svirin, "Shag vpered, dva shaga nazad," in *Bor'ba za metod: sbornik diskussionykh statei* (M.L: Gosizdat, 1931), 155.

39. Anon., "Chitateli o 'Rozhdenii geroia,'" *Na pod"eme* 2–3 (1931): 259–60.

40. T. Kostrov, "Rozhdenie . . . geroia?," in *Bor'ba za metod*: 83–90.

41. V. Nalivakhin, "Opiat' i eshche o 'Rozhdenii geroia,'" *LG,* June 9, 1930, p. 2.

42. A. Tarasov-Rodionov, "Mertvorozhdennyi geroi," *LG,* Apr. 21, 1930, pp. 1, 3.

43. Anat. Gorelov, "Literaturnaia robinzonada," *MG* 12 (1930): 94–97.

44. M. Gelfand and A. Zonin, "K diskussii o tvorcheskom metode," *Pechat' i revoliutsiia* 4 (1930): 8.

45. A. Kurella, "Protiv psikhologizma," *NLP* 5 (1928): 29.

46. Ibid., 30; see also Boris Kushner, "Prichiny otstavaniia," *KN* 11 (1930): 139.

47. Kurella, 28.

48. Gelfand and Zonin, 11; Kostrov, 89.

49. Gelfand and Zonin, 10; Vinogradov, 73; G. Lebedev, "Otzvuki men'shevist-stvuiushchego idealizma v khudozhestvennom tvorchestve," *P,* Jan. 10, 1932, p. 3.

50. A. Borisov, "Tret'e rozhdenie geroia," *Krasnaia gazeta,* Aug. 20, 1930, p. 4. On the novel's republication see also anon., "V rabochem redsovete GIZ," *LG,* Aug. 10, 1930, p. 3.

51. Pantelemion Romanov, *Tovarishch Kisliakov* [Comrade Kisliakov] (M: Nedra, 1930).

52. Romanov, "Novaia skrizhal'," *NM* 1–5 (1928).

53. Quoted in "'Tverdolobye druz'ia' Panteleimona Romanova," *LG,* June 15, 1931, p. 3.

54. S. Blokh, rev. of *Tovarishch Kisliakov, Zemlia sovetskaia* 9 (1930): 190–91.

55. Ak. Rykachev, "Panteleimon Romanov: intelligentsiia i revoliutsiia," *LG,* July 5, 1930, p. 2; I. Ermakov, "Intelligentsiia v zerkale Panteleimona Romanova," *LG,* Sept. 24, 1930, p. 3.

56. Iu. Krasovsky, "'Tovarishch Kisliakov' i Panteleimon Romanov," *NLP* 19–20 (1930): 90; V. Kirshon, "Protiv besprintsipnosti i politikanstva," *NLP* 11 (1930): 4.

57. Ermakov, 3; see also A. Bek, "Roman, napravlennyi protiv sovetskoi intelligentsii," *Rost* 5 (1930): 30–32; E. Blium, rev. of *Nedra,* bks. 18–19, *MG* 15–16 (1930): 142–46; and P. Fedotov, "Novyi roman Panteleimona Romanova," *Krasnaia gazeta (vech. vyp.),* Apr. 24, 1930, p. 4.

58. Krasovsky, 92.

59. Rykachev, 2.

60. "'Tverdolobye druz'ia,'" 3.

61. Eugene Lyons, "Sovetskaia literatura v Amerike," *LG,* Dec. 5, 1933, p. 4.

62. Rykachev, 2.

63. Ermakov, 3.

64. Panteleimon Romanov, letters to the editor, *LG* Apr. 14, 1930, p. 4; July 15, 1930, p. 4.

65. Kirshon, "Protiv besprintsipnosti," 4–14.

66. Bek, 31.

67. The tension in RAPP between political orthodoxy and literary creativity has been treated most extensively by Edward J. Brown, *The Proletarian Episode in Russian Literature, 1928–1932* (New York: Columbia UP), 1953.

68. I. Bespalov, "V zaschitu deistvitel'nosti," *KN* 9–10 (1930): 192–202.

69. A. Vysotsky, "V storone ot stolbovoi dorogi," *Sibirskie ogni* 7 (1930): 96.

70. V. Ermilov, "'Rozhdenie geroia Iu. Libedinskogo," in *Bor'ba za metod,* 117–40.

71. Kruzhok kritiki "Rost," "Protiv idealizma, protiv skhmetizma," *LG,* June 2, 1930, p. 3.

72. Aleksandr Bezymensky, "Rech' tov. Bezymenskogo," *XVI S"ezd vsesoiznoi kommunis-ticheskoi partii (b). Stenograficheskii otchet* (M-L: Gosizdat, 1930), 393–96.

73. "Strana dolzhna znat' svoikh geroev," *P,* May 18, 1931, p. 3.

74. "Sotsialisticheskaia stroika i ee geroi," *P,* May 18, 1931, p. 1; on the role of *Pravda* and

other major print organs in orchestrating the "performance"—the shaping of official reality that was so central to early Soviet and later Stalinist culture, see Jeffrey Brooks, *Thank You, Comrade Stalin! Soviet Public Culture from Revolution to Cold War* (Princeton: Princeton UP, 2000).

75. Iu. Libedinsky, "O pokaze geroia i prizyve udarnikov," *NLP* 28 (1931): 1–4; see also Z. Grigoreva, "Za luchshii pokaz geroev piatiletki," *NLP* 18 (1931): 45–46; and I. Makarev, "Pokaz geroev—general'naia tema proletarskoi literatury," *NLP* 31–32 (1931): 27–36; 33 (1931): 10–15; 35–36 (1931): 57–60.

76. M. Rabinovich, "Kak ne nado pisat' o sotsstroitel'stve," *NLP* 22 (1931): 35; and anon., "Vse, chto nuzhno znat' khalturshchiku dlia pokaza geroia," *NLP* 30 (1931): 32–3.

77. On how this manifests itself in socialist realism, see Clark, *The Soviet Novel*, chap. 6.

78. E. S. Dobin, "Georika mass i optimizm bor'by," in *V sporakh o metode*, 54–55.

79. D. Tamarchenko and N. Tanin, "Napostovstvo ili voronshchina," *Pechat' i revoliutsiia* 5–6 (1930): 40–47; G. Lebedev, "Otzvuki men'shevistvuiushchego idealizma v khudozhestvennom tvorchestve," *P,* Jan. 10, 1932.

80. Yury Libedinsky, "Petya Gordiushenko," *P,* June 23, 1931, p. 3.

81. *Sovetskaia literatura na novom etape: stenogramma pervogo plenuma orgkomiteta soiuza sovetskikh pisatelei* (M: Sovetskaia literatura, 1933), 183. The plenum was held Oct. 29–Nov. 3, 1932.

82. Ibid., 134–35.

83. Fedor Gladkov, *Energiia [Energy]*, *NM* 5 (1932): 65.

84. N. Slepnev, "Roman o sotsialisticheskom stroitel'stve," *Oktiabr* 10 (1933): 223–26; see also "Literatura i stroitel'stvo sotsializma," *P,* July 11, 1933, p. 2; "Rabochie o khudozhestvennoi literature: 'Energiia' F. Gladkova," *Oktiabr* 5 (1935): 201–08. On the distinction between love plots typical of the 1920s and 1930s, see Irina Gutkin, *The Cultural Origins of the Socialist Realist Aesthetic, 1890–1934* (Evanston: Northwestern UP, 1999), 143ff.

85. Nikolai Ostrovsky, *Kak zakalialas' stal'* [How the Steel Was Tempered] (M: Molodaia gvardiia, 1934).

86. Stites, *The Women's Liberation Movement*, defines this shift as a "sexual Thermidor" (390); Leon Trotsky, *The Revolution Betrayed*, 5th ed. (New York: Pathfinder, 1972; first English edition, 1937), described this change as "Thermidor in the family" but did not speak specifically of sex.

87. Friedrich Engels, "Kniga otkryveniia," in Karl Marx and Friedrich Engels, *Sochineniia*, vol. 21, 2nd ed. (M: Gosudarstvennoe izdatel'stvo politicheskoi literatury, 1961): 8.

88. Regarding this change in official Soviet policy toward the family, that is, its "embourgeoisement," Clements argues that it reflected in fact the collective opinion of average Soviet citizens; Goldman also acknowledges the pressures of reality and inclination of people not to favor the revolutionary tendency as influences on changed policy but credits the driving force behind it to Stalin and his vision of the family, which she identifies as a "tragedy"; see Goldman, *Women, the State and Revolution*, 337ff. Siegelbaum, in *Soviet State and Society Between Revolutions* (155), focuses more on material conditions instead of ideological causes as the primary source.

9. Conclusion

1. Ilya Ilf and Evgeny Petrov, "Savanarylo," *Sobranie sochinenii,* vol. 3 (M: Gosizdat, 1961): 281. See Kon, 69.

2. Harriet Borland, *Soviet Literary Theory and Practice during the First Five-Year Plan, 1928–1932* (New York: King's Crown Press, 1950),1; Ermolaev, 45.

3. A. Blium, *Za kulisami 'Ministerstva pravdy': tainaia istoriia sovetskoi tsenzury, 1917–1929* (St. Petersburg: Akademicheskii proekt, 1994); for a more nuanced analysis of censorship in this period, see Michael S. Fox, "Glavlit, Censorship and Party Policy," *Soviet Studies* 6 (1992): 1045–68.

4. See, for example, Stephen Kotkin, *Magnetic Mountain: Stalinism as a Civilization* (Berkeley: U of California P, 1995); Véronique Garros, Natalia Koreneveskaya, and Thomas Lahusen, *Intimacy and Terror: Soviet Diaries of the 1930s* (New York: New Press, 1995); Sarah Davies, *Popular Opinion in Stalin's Russia: Terror, Propaganda and Dissent, 1934–1941* (New York: Cambridge UP, 1997); Sheila Fitzpatrick, *Everyday Stalinism: Ordinary Life in Extraordinary Times: Soviet Russia in the 1930s* (New York: Oxford UP, 1999).

5. Katerina Clark, *Petersburg: Crucible of Cultural Revolution* (Cambridge: Harvard UP, 1995); Thomas Lahusen, *How Life Writes the Book: Real Socialism and Socialist Realism in Stalin's Russia* (Ithaca: Cornell UP, 1997); Evgeny Dobrenko, *Formovka sovetskogo pisatelia: sotsial'nye i esteticheskie istoki sovetskoi literaturnoi kul'tury* (St. Petersburg: Akademicheskii proekt, 1999).

6. Michel Foucault, *The History of Sexuality*, vol. 1, trans. Robert Hurley (New York: Vintage, 1978), 83–84.

7. Edward Said, *The World, the Text, and the Critic* (Cambridge: Harvard UP, 1983), 246.

8. Carolyn Porter, "Are We Being Historical Yet?" *South Atlantic Quarterly* 87 (1988): 765.

9. Dobrenko, 69.

10. Naiman, "Za krasnoi dver'iu: vvedenie v gotiku nepa," *Novoe literaturnoe obozrenie* 20 (1996): 67.

11. Christopher Read, *Culture and Power in Revolutionary Russia: The Intelligentsia and the Transition from Tsarism to Communism* (New York: St. Martin's, 1990), 187.

12. Read, 168.

13. Engelstein, "Combined Underdevelopment," *op. cit.* Her views are elaborated in an exchange with, among others, Naiman, in "Symposium," *Slavic Review* 53 (1994): 193–224.

14. Regarding Stalinism and subjectivity, Naiman has recently made clear that his postmodernist approach does not go so far as to eliminate the human subject and that allowance should be made in the Stalinist period for "divergent narratives." In this he distinguishes himself from others whose study of subjectivity in the Stalinist period targest the assumption of the individual as an agent or actor in history, preferring to focus on how language acts through the person. See Naiman, "On Soviet Subjects and the Scholars Who Make Them," *Russian Review* 60 (July 2001): 307–15; Igal Halfin and Jochen Hellbeck, "Rethinking the Stalinist Subject: Stephen Kotkin's 'Magnetic Mountain' and the State of Soviet Historical Studies," *Jahrbücher für Geschichte Osteuropas* 44 (1996) H.3: 456–63; Halfin, *From Darkness to Light*; and Jochen Hellbeck, "Working, Struggling, Becoming: Stalin-Era Autobiographical Texts," *Russian Review* 60 (2001): 340–59.

15. Aron Zalkind, "Kakova zhe nasha molodezh'?" *Izvestiia,* Mar. 8, 1928, p. 6, complained that with regard to studying youth, there was no "united, general plan," which led to the profusion of contrary images of youth both in sociological studies and literature.

16. Katherine Binhammer, "The Sex Panic of the 1790s," *Journal of the History of Sexuality* 6 (1990): 409–34.

17. Karl Aimermakher, *Politika i kul'tura pri Lenine i Staline, 1917–1932* (M: AIRO-XX, 1998).

18. On the continuation of the top-down model, see Catriona Kelly, Hilary Pilkington, David Shepherd, and Vadim Volkov, "Introduction: Why Cultural Studies," *Russian Cultural Studies: An Introduction*, ed. Catriona Kelly and David Shepherd (Oxford: Oxford UP, 1998), 1–20.

19. David-Fox, *Revolution of the Mind.*

20. Siegelbaum also avoids a single, simple answer for understanding this period; "What is so striking about this 'interval' [NEP] between revolutions, what sets it apart from subsequent decades of Soviet history . . . was its tremendous indeterminacy. it makes sense, therefore, to treat the period in social historical terms, that is, to regard the constituent groups of Soviet society not merely as objects of official policy but as collective subjects" (226).

21. Gary Saul Morson and Caryl Emerson, *Mikhail Bakhtin: Creation of a Prosaics* (Stanford: Stanford UP, 1990), 30ff.

22. David Halperin, "Historicizing the Sexual Body: Sexual Preferences and Erotic Identities in the Pseudo-Lucianic Erôtes," *Discourses of Sexuality: From Aristotle to Aids*, ed. Donna C. Stanton (Ann Arbor: U of Michigan P, 1992), 261.

23. See Rudolf Schlesinger, *The Family in the U.S.S.R.* (London: Routledge, 1949), 81–153; see also Goldman, 214ff.; and Beatrice Farnsworth, "Bolshevik Alternatives and the Soviet Family: The 1926 Marriage Law Debate," in *Women in Russia,* ed. D. Atkinson, A. Dallin, and G. Lapidus (Stanford: Stanford UP, 1977).

24. Healy, 127.

25. Alan Sinfield, *Faultlines: Cultural Materialism and the Politics of Dissident Reading* (Berkeley: U of California P, 1992), 44.

26. Evgenii Gromov, *Stalin: vlast' i iskusstvo* (M: Respublika, 1998), 423.

Index